THE DEVELOPMENTAL PSYCHOLOGY OF PERSONAL RELATIONSHIPS

Edited by

ROSEMARY S. L. MILLS AND STEVE DUCK

JOHN WILEY & SONS, LTD

Chichester · New York · Weinheim · Brisbane · Singapore · Toronto

Other Wiley Editorial Offices

John Wiley & Sons, Inc., 605 Third Avenue,
New York, NY 10158-0012, USA

WILEY-VCH Verlag GmbH, Pappelallee 3,
D-69469 Weinheim, Germany

Jacaranda Wiley Ltd, 33 Park Road, Milton,
Queensland 4064, Australia

John Wiley & Sons (Asia) Pte Ltd, 2 Clementi Loop #02-01,
Jin Xing Distripark, Singapore 129809

John Wiley & Sons (Canada) Ltd, 22 Worcester Road,
Rexdale, Ontario M9W 1L1, Canada

Library of Congress Cataloging-in-Publication Data

Mills, Rosemary S. L.
    The developmental psychology of personal relationships / edited by
Rosemary S. L. Mills and Steve Duck.
        p.   cm.
    Includes bibliographical references and index.
    ISBN 0-471-99880-X (pbk.)
    1. Interpersonal relations in children.   I. Duck, Steve.
    II. Title.
BF723.I646M55   1999
155.4'18—dc21
                                                     99–40991
                                                        CIP

British Library Cataloguing in Publication Data

A catalogue record for this book is available from the British Library

ISBN 0-471-99880-X

Typeset in 10/12pt Times by Dorwyn Ltd, Rowlands Castle, Hants
Printed and bound in Great Britain by Bookcraft (Bath) Ltd, Midsomer Norton, Somerset
This book is printed on acid-free paper responsibly manufactured from sustainable forestry, in
which at least two trees are planted for each one used for paper production.

THE DEVELOPMENTAL PSYCHOLOGY OF PERSONAL RELATIONSHIPS

Series Information

This book forms one of a series of paperbacks which are dedicated to the study and application of processes by which individuals relate to each other in social and family settings. Each book provides an *expanded* and *up-to-date* version of a section in the original *Handbook of Personal Relationships* (second edition) edited by Steve Duck.

The series is aimed at students on courses studying personal relationships and related subject areas, researchers and scholars in the relationships field, community/health psychologists, counsellors, therapists and social workers.

The Social Psychology of Personal Relationships
Edited by William Ickes and Steve Duck
ISBN: 0-471-99881-8

The Developmental Psychology of Personal Relationships
Edited by Rosemary S.L. Mills and Steve Duck
ISBN: 0-471-99880-X

Communication and Personal Relationships
Edited by Kathryn Dindia and Steve Duck
ISBN: 0-471-49133-0

Families as Relationships
Edited by Robert Milardo and Steve Duck
ISBN: 0-471-49152-7

Clinical and Community Psychology
Edited by Barbara Sarason and Steve Duck
ISBN: 0-471-49161-6

CONTENTS

ABOUT THE EDITORS

Rosemary S. L. Mills received her Ph.D in Psychology from the University of Toronto and is Associate Professor of Family Studies at the University of Manitoba. Her research has been concerned with socioemotional development in the context of the parent–child relationship, with particular emphasis on factors contributing to the development of internalizing problems. Her current research projects focus on the links between hurtful communication in the family, the development of shame-proneness, and maladjustment in childhood.

Steve Duck is the Daniel and Amy Starch Distinguished Research Professor at the University of Iowa and has been a keen promotor of the field of personal relationships research since it was formed. He co-founded the first International Conference on Personal Relationships in 1982, and was founder and first editor of the *Journal of Social and Personal Relationships*, first President of the International Network on Personal Relationships, the professional organization for the research field, and editor of the first edition of the *Handbook of Personal Relationships*. The Steve Duck New Scholar Award was endowed and named in his honor by a group of independent scholars to recognize his promotion of the work of younger professionals and his dedication to developing the field.

ABOUT THE AUTHORS

Linda K. Acitelli is an Associate Professor in the Department of Psychology at the University of Houston. Her research on relationships has been funded by the National Institute of Mental Health. Her major research interests are cognition and communication in relationships, specifically thinking and talking about relationships and the factors that determine their impact on individual and relationship well-being. In 1995, the International Network on Personal Relationships awarded her the Gerald R. Miller Award for her early career achievements.

Karen Caplovitz Barrett, who received her Bachelor's in Human Development and Family Studies from Cornell University, and her Master's and Ph.D. in Developmental Psychology from the University of Denver, is currently Associate Professor of Human Development and Family Studies at Colorado State University. She is the editor of a recent issue of *New Directions for Child Development* (Number 77, The communication of emotion: Current research from diverse perspectives), and is author of a number of articles on her functionalist approach to emotional development, including a chapter in the recent volume, *What develops in emotional development?* (1998, Plenum) and a recent article on the development of non-verbal communication of emotion in volume 17 of the *Journal of Nonverbal Behavior*. Her empirical work concerns emotional development in the context of the parent–child relationship, with particular focus on the development of "social" emotions such as shame, pride, and guilt.

Patricia M. Crittenden has a multidisciplinary background in developmental and clinical psychology and special education. She received her Ph.D. from the University of Virginia, under the guidance of Mary D. S. Ainsworth, and has been a member of the faculty of the University of Miami and a visiting faculty member of the University of Virginia, San Diego State University, New South Wales Institute of Psychiatry, and the University of Helsinki. She has published numerous empirical articles and chapters on maltreatment and attachment as well as a book on cross-cultural aspects of parent–child adaptation. Her most recent work consists of a series of theoretical papers and empirical studies on a Dynamic-Maturational approach to the development of psychopathology across the life-span. These papers address issues of multidimensional risk, the non-linear process of development and the implications of theory for prevention and treatment. Currently she teaches at universities and institutes for training psychotherapists in North and South America, Europe and Australia and is engaged in cross-cultural research in a number of countries.

Archie Kwan is a graduate student at the Ontario Institute for Studies in Education, University of Toronto.

Beth Manke is an Assistant Professor of Developmental Psychology at the University of Houston. She earned her Ph.D. in Human Development and Family Studies in 1995 from the Pennysylvania State University. Dr Manke is the Director of the Texas Multi-Ethnic Sibling Study, a university–community collaborative project designed to pinpoint specific sources of environmental influence related to individual differences in children's social development, and to address within- and between-family differences in an ethnically diverse sample.

Claire Monks is currently working toward her Ph.D. at Goldsmiths College, University of London under the supervision of Professor Peter Smith and Dr John Swettenham, funded by a grant from the Economic and Social Research Council. She gained a Master's Degree in Research Methods in Psychology from the University of Reading in 1996. Her research interests lie in the investigation of school bullying during the formative years, including links with social cognition and the family.

Robin O'Neil is currently a Research Analyst for Orange County Social Services Agency in Santa Ana, CA, and adjunct lecturer in the Department of Psychology and Social Behavior at the University of California, Irvine. She received her Ph.D. in Social Ecology at UC Irvine and held a postdoctoral position at UCLA, where she studied children with ADD. From 1993–1998, O'Neil was Research Associate and co-Director of the Social Development Project at the University of California, Riverside. She has interests in family–work relationships as well as family–peer linkages.

Ross D. Parke is a Distinguished Professor of Psychology and Director of the Center for Family Studies at the University of California, Riverside. He is past president of the Division 7 (Developmental Psychology) of APA, and in 1995 received the G. Stanley Hall Award from this APA division. He is currently editor of the *Journal of Family Psychology* and past editor of *Developmental Psychology*. Parke is author of *Fatherhood* (1996) and co-author of *Throwaway Dads* (1999) (with Armin Brott). His research interests include the father's role in infancy and early childhood, family–peer linkages, and the impact of economic stress on families of different ethnic backgrounds.

Michal Perlman is a Social Sciences and Humanities Research Council of Canada postdoctoral fellow in the psychology department at the University of California, Los Angeles. She received her Ph.D. from the University of Waterloo in 1997. Her research focuses on patterns in the conflict interactions of families with young children. Most recently she has begun studying the role of marital conflict in children's development of their own behavioral patterns during conflict. She is also interested in the presence of behavioral contingencies in the non-conflict interactions of parents and children.

Caroline C. Piotrowski, Ph.D., is Associate Professor of Family Studies at the University of Manitoba. She is the principal investigator of a project funded by the Social Sciences and Humanities Research Council of Canada investigating the effects of exposure to violence on the quality of children's conflict management, their sibling relationships, and their individual adjustment. Her research interests include the development and maintenance of children's conflict styles in the context of mutual influences between parent and child, sibling, and marital relationships, and the role of constructive conflict management in the prevention of family violence.

Samantha Poisson is a former graduate student at the Ontario Institute for Studies in Education, University of Toronto.

Avigail Ram received her B.A. in Psychology from Carleton University and is now a Ph.D. student in Developmental Psychology at the University of Waterloo. Her research is concerned with processes of family conflict with specific concentration in the area of sibling conflict. Her current research is focused on the application of information about conflict processes from the literature on adults' negotiation of disputes to that of sibling conflict.

Hildy S. Ross is a Professor of Psychology at the University of Waterloo. She received her Ph.D. from the University of North Carolina at Chapel Hill in 1971. Her research has focused on the study of the peer and sibling relationships of young children, with recent emphasis on processes of sibling conflict. The roles of parents as third parties to the disputes of their children and the narrative representations of family conflict processes are two related directions of her current research.

Alan Russell is Associate Professor in Human Development and Dean of Education at The Flinders University of South Australia, where he has taught for more than 20 years. His research over that time has focused on parent–child relationships, with particular emphasis on sex differences (both sex-of-parent and sex-of-child). Most recently, his research and writing have been directed to issues of differences in parenting styles and their possible consequences for children's social development. His current research projects examine links between parent–toddler play and preschool children's social development, and cross-national differences in parenting and child development.

Barry H. Schneider is Professor of Psychology at the University of Ottawa, Canada. His major research interests are cultural differences in children's friendships and the friendships of children who are aggressive and socially withdrawn.

Afshan Siddiqui is a Ph.D. student in Developmental Psychology at the University of Waterloo. She received her B.Sc. in Psychology from the University of Alberta and M.A. from the University of Waterloo. Her research primarily deals with the nature of sibling conflict resolution. In particular, she is currently examining the effects of parental intervention on the resolution of sibling conflicts. As well, her research will examine the related issue of the use and effectiveness of mediation as a parental intervention technique.

Andrea Smith is a doctoral student in the Department of Human Development and Applied Psychology, OISE, University of Toronto. She is collaborating with Barry Schneider and Martin Ruck on a study of the peer networks of Canadian adolescents of African origin.

Peter K. Smith is Professor of Psychology at Goldsmiths College, University of London. He has been researching the topic of school bullying for about 10 years, and is editor of *School Bullying: Insights and Perspectives*, and *Tackling Bullying in your School: a Practical Handbook for Teachers* (both with S. Sharp) (1994), and *The Nature of School Bullying: A Cross-National Perspective* (with Y. Morita and others) (1999), all published by Routledge. He is a Fellow of the British Psychological Society and sits on several journal editorial boards. He has additional research interests in attachment, play, and grandparenting.

Maria von Salisch studied psychology in New York, Hamburg, San Francisco and Berlin, taking her Ph.D. from the Freie Universität Berlin in 1989 where she is now an Assistant Professor. She published a book on children's friendship in German and is co-editor with Ann Elisabeth Auhagen of *The Diversity of Human Relationships* (Cambridge University Press, 1996). Her research interests are peer relationships and emotional development in the context of close personal relationships, especially negotiation of anger and shame.

Lee West is a doctoral candidate in the Communication Studies Department at the University of Iowa. Her research interests include how social expectations organize and are reinstantiated through naturally occurring conversations, specifically, in the (re)production of class, gender and race in both everyday talk and the discourse of academe. She is a co-author of a chapter on cross-sex friendship.

INTRODUCTION

The chapters in this volume are concerned not with the way specific relationships develop but rather with the way individuals learn to relate to other people. A basic premise guiding theory and research in this area is that the most formative learning experiences are relationship experiences. Our ways of relating to other people are largely determined by the relationships in which we have participated. Attempts to understand the nature of the learning processes have gradually been moving beyond separate accounts of specific types of relationships (parent–child, peer, sibling) to include the identification of linkages across different relationships. This has stimulated new ideas and new research on the processes of relationship learning. The chapters in this volume review these recent advancements and point to challenging directions for the future.

In "Sewing Relational Seeds: Contexts for Relating in Childhood," Steve Duck, Linda Acitelli, Beth Manke, and Lee West begin with a call for developmental psychologists to focus more on the dynamic processes of moment-by-moment relating rather than the static description of relationships in freeze frame. They go on to discuss the implications that such a focus has for both theoretical and methodological choices. Researchers are confronted with choices about the aspect on which to focus, the level at which to analyze it (individual? dyad? family system? culture?), and the perspective to take in measuring it (relationship partners themselves? other people?). The decisions made by researchers reflect their implicit theories of relating, shape their methods of inquiry, and channel them in one direction to the exclusion of others. For example, the decision that is often made to strip away the situational and temporal contexts that influence relating is itself a decision about the nature of relating, and tends to stack the empirical deck to come out in its support. More attention to the contexts of relating would help guard against this occupational hazard.

In their contribution, "The Influence of Significant Others on Learning About Relationships: From Family to Friends," Ross Parke and Robin O'Neil review recent research on each of the major subsystems in the family (parent–child, marital, sib–sib), showing how research has begun to move beyond description to the explanation of processes. They distinguish between an initial phase focusing on description of the influences on children's relationship learning, and a second, more explanatory phase involving an effort to identify the processes through which learning occurs. Research in the first phase has raised awareness of the range of different ways in which family subsystems influence relationship learning. For example, we are now more cognizant of the important indirect role that parents play in their children's social development by arranging opportunities for social interaction, the possible direct impact that marital discord may have on children, and the indirect influence that parent–sibling interactions may have on children's relationships with their siblings. Research in the second phase reveals a good deal of convergence on two basic sets of mediating processes: affect management skills (encoding and decoding of emotion, emotional understanding, emotion regulation) and cognitive representational processes (representations, attributions, and beliefs). Parke and O'Neil conclude by outlining a comprehensive model specifying the linkages among the major family subsystems and setting out a research agenda to guide the study of these linkages and the way they combine to influence children's relationship learning.

Maria von Salisch takes up the theme of mediating processes in her chapter, "The Emotional Side of Sharing, Social Support, and Conflict Negotiation between Siblings and between Friends." There has been a relative neglect of emotional processes until recently. It is difficult to overstate their importance, however, given the highly emotional nature of social relationships. It is by experiencing the emotions elicited by interaction with others that children acquire the affect management skills and difficulties that shape their styles of relating to others. Conflicts seem to provide a prime medium in which such learning occurs. But as von Salisch points out, any interaction that involves the sharing of emotions ("emotion talk," i.e., the communication of internal states), whether or not it is a conflict situation and whether the emotion is positive or negative, is an important regulatory process and an opportunity for learning. In her review, therefore, she discusses the significance of three types of emotion processes in sibling and friend relationships—the sharing of positive emotions, the sharing of negative emotions about third parties or the self, and the negotiation of anger-provoking disagreements—and describes developmental changes in these processes from early to late childhood.

Emotional communication is also the focus of the chapter contributed by Rosemary Mills and Caroline Piotrowski. In "Emotional Communication and Children's Learning about Conflict," they argue that the quality of emotional communication in the family plays an important role in children's relationship learning in general and the ability to handle conflict in particular. The more family conflicts are characterized by open communication, in which difficult emotions are mutually acknowledged and responded to, and the less they are characterized by distressing and hurtful communication, the more likely children are to develop the emotional competencies required to handle conflict situations constructively. They speculate about the way in which the quality of emotional communication influences the development of emotional competencies, and suggest that more information about the constellation of emotions activated by hurtful messages would help to illuminate the learning processes that occur. Self processes, such as self-evaluation and self-attribution, are undoubtedly of prime importance in mediating the effects of emotional communication on relationship learning.

In "The Development of the Self-in-Relationships," Karen Caplovitz Barrett addresses the role of the self in relationship learning. She argues that the notion of the self in opposition to others is something of a false dichotomy, reviews evidence indicating that the self is relational from its earliest beginnings, and points out that the self-conscious emotions (pride, embarrassment, shame, guilt) are as other-oriented as they are self-oriented. These "social/self-conscious" emotions contribute to the development of the "self-in-relationships," which guides interaction with others. These emotions are concerned with meeting or failing to meet social standards, and hence serve to help children interact appropriately and develop and maintain positive relationships with others. Without a sense of guilt and the self-evaluation it entails, for example, children would not take responsibility for their actions or try to repair harm done to others. At the same time, these emotions are themselves socially constructed, in the sense that socialization experiences (particularly relationship experiences) have a significant impact on their formation. For example, discipline strategies that highlight standards without impairing the parent–child relationship may be the ones most likely to arouse optimal levels of guilt and shame—levels high enough to motivate socially appropriate behavior but not so high as to interfere with it.

Whether relationship learning contexts differ for girls and boys, and lead to sex differences in relationship styles, is an issue that is moving to center stage. In his chapter, "Sex Differences in Children's Relationship Learning," Alan Russell focuses on sex differences in peer relationship styles and qualities that seem to parallel those proposed in the gender literature on adults (e.g., relational independence vs. interdependence), and entertains the notion that they originate from different experiences in parent–child relationships and are carried over to subsequent close relationships through a process of relationship replication. Certain stylistic features of parent–child relationships do indeed seem to differ on the basis of the parent's and the child's sex. To examine how relationship experiences with parents may be carried over to peer relationships, Russell makes use of research based on two theoretical approaches: (1) *social learning theory*, in which it is assumed that children acquire relationship styles and qualities (behavior, thoughts, feelings) and generalize them to interactions in subsequent close relationships, and (2) *attachment theory*, in which it is assumed that children form internal working models and relationship expectations, which influence behaviors, thoughts, and feelings in subsequent close relationships.

Claire Monks and Peter Smith also focus on relationship styles in their chapter, "Relationships of Children Involved in Bully/Victim Problems at School." They review what is known about bully/victim relationships, their structural features, and their developmental pathways, and discuss the implications for intervention. Evidence indicates that boys and girls differ in their styles of bullying, with male bullies displaying more physical aggression and female bullies engaging in more indirect and relational aggression, in which the goal is to damage the victim's peer relationships (e.g., spreading rumors, shunning). Research on the developmental pathways that lead to bully/victim problems suggests that family relationships play an important role along with social factors in school peer group networks. As might be expected, research reviewed by Monks and Smith indicates that the family relationships of children involved in bully/victim problems differ for boys and girls.

Children's family and peer relationships provide different contexts for learning to relate to others partly because they involve different experiences of power. In "An Analysis of Sources of Power in Children's Conflict Interactions," Michal Perlman and her colleagues Afshan Siddiqui, Avigail Ram, and Hildy Ross analyze the sources of power in children's relationships and consider their implications for learning about conflict. Drawing upon French and Raven's (1959) typology of social power and research in the social psychological literature on conflict resolution in the "formal" relationships of adults, they identify differences across children's relationships (parent–child, sibling, friend/peer) in the sources and the exercise of power within conflict interactions. These differences suggest new ways of thinking about power and its impact on children's conflict interactions. The contexts in which children learn about power and conflict are much more complex and varied than researchers have appreciated, and are bidirectional. It might be quite fruitful if researchers were to characterize these power relations less in terms of balance of power and more in terms of the sources of power available and how they are used.

Barry Schneider, Andrea Smith, Samantha Poisson, and Archie Kwan focus on the cultural context of relationship learning in "Cultural Dimensions of Children's Peer Relations." The identification of cultural differences, by revealing what is universal across cultures and what is sensitive to cultural influences, provides clues about the determinants of relationship processes. In a review of studies of peer relations in different cultures and subcultures, the authors describe evidence for both similarities and differences in such social behaviors as cooperation, aggression, assertiveness, and shyness. They show how the findings mirror the social, economic, and spiritual characteristics of the cultures, and suggest that the dimension of individualism vs. collectivism is useful in describing the sorts of differences that exist. But they also point out that conceptual and methodological advances are needed in order to move beyond the level of global description. They suggest that more elaborate conceptions of individualism and collectivism, along with improved methods and measures, are needed so that more fine-grained research on cultural differences can be done.

Finally, Patricia Crittenden considers the question of the long-term impact of early relationship learning, in "The Effect of Early Relationship Experiences on Relationships in Adulthood." She presents a dynamic-maturational model of relationship patterning and discusses its fit with several major models of adult relationships. Crittenden's model is an account of the mental processing of information about relationship concerns and the organization of interpersonal strategies for managing these concerns. The model begins with two basic assumptions: that relationships serve important functions, and that the brain has evolved to promote the processing of information relevant to these functions. In a synthesis of social learning, cognitive-developmental, and information-processing theories, Crittenden proposes that relationship experiences lead to the development of internal representational models of relationships that vary along two dimensions: the source of information considered most predictive (cognitive or affective) and the degree of information integration. These representations are viewed as dynamic processes whose aim is to maintain a balance among sources of information and response strategies. Because of the way the brain has evolved, early conditions are disproportionately important to the interpretation of present conditions. As a result, despite the repeated modification of mental models by maturation and experience, residues of very early experiences can still be found in the functional organization of behavior in adulthood.

The contributions to this volume show that the study of relationship learning has moved well beyond the investigation of dyads to the examination of systems of influence ranging all the way from the level of the family system to that of the culture. They also describe advances in the study of relationship learning processes. Emotion and self-construal processes are firmly at centerstage, more emphasis is being placed on the bidirectional nature of relationship learning processes, and the contextual nature of these learning processes is receiving more attention. In reviewing these advances, the contributors to this volume provide a critical analysis that will help set the agenda for the next phase of research on relationship learning.

ROSEMARY S. L. MILLS AND STEVE DUCK

Chapter 1

Sewing Relational Seeds: Contexts for Relating in Childhood

Steve Duck

University of Iowa

Linda K. Acitelli, Beth Manke

University of Houston

and

Lee West

University of Iowa

The question "What is a personal relationship?" was offered over 10 years ago as a central theoretical and methodological issue facing researchers into personal relationships in general (Duck, 1990; Kelley, 1984). An additional question is whether relationships are best represented as attitudes (Berscheid & Walster, 1978), communicated emotions (Teti & Teti, 1996), patterns of reciprocity in behaviors (Russell & Searcy, 1997), patterns and qualities of interaction (Hinde, 1981), forms and processes of communication (Duck & Pond, 1989), the product of tensions between opposing dialectical forces

The Developmental Psychology of Personal Relationships.
Edited by Rosemary S. L. Mills and Steve Duck. © 2000 John Wiley & Sons Ltd.

(Baxter & Montgomery, 1996), or all or some blend of (some of) the above and much else besides (Fincham, 1995).

These issues arise no less significantly for the study of children's relationships. We encourage developmental psychologists interested in personal relationships to focus more on relat*ing* than on relation*ships*. In order to address this theme in the chapter, five main issues particularly salient to the study of children's relationships will be considered. The five issues are: 1) *Adopting an approach to studying relationships*. This entails implementing one's theoretical and measurement tools of choice. These choices have implications for what one sees (and thus ignores), and how one interprets data. A related issue in many respects is: 2) *Choosing a topic of interest: substance and focus.* This process includes recognizing that in choosing a topic, most developmental researchers typically adopt a structural versus functional perspective (i.e., using categories and static variables instead of focusing on dynamic processes). Also, the bulk of research has examined a limited range of substantive constructs: warmth, conflict, control and self-disclosure. 3) *Choosing the (best?) informant* (i.e., insider versus outsider perspective). 4) *Recognizing the importance of context*; 5) *Children's experiences of multiple relationships* in the course of the routine happenings of their everyday lives. These themes are, of course, interrelated and frequently overlap both conceptually and practically, and some do not allow us to partition their discussion quite that exactly in the chapter.

WHAT IS A RELATIONSHIP?

Given the interconnection of the above themes, relational partners themselves as well as researchers can be unclear whether (and what sort of) a relationship really exists between two people. The opening questions thus take on a particular significance in terms of various ontological, epistemological, and methodological research orientations, practices, and operationalizations. If relationships "are" attitudes, then we need only ask the attitude-holder some questions in order to establish the existence of a relationship. On this model, we would learn by assessing attitudes about intimacy and using them as the basis for nomination of peers as friends, and for assessment of beliefs about sociality and their influence on relating (Miller, 1993). If relationships "are" primarily the product of a mixture of an individual's emotional experience, internal working models, styles of attachment, and communication of feelings (Teti & Teti, 1996; von Salisch, 1997; Parke & O'Neil, 1997), then one would do research focused on the discovery of individual internal states relevant to relating. If relationships "are" patterns of interaction, from which an observer might deduce a pattern of emotions, etc., then one might focus somewhere else, for example on the nature of competence in peer relationships (Pettit & Clawson, 1996). If relationships "are" in existence only when both partners agree that they are, then one must assess both partners as part of the research process, but would then miss the social and psychological significance of one-sided nominations (Bigelow, Tesson & Lewko, 1996). If relationships "are" characterized by dialectical tensions and their management (Baxter & Montgomery, 1996), then one should not necessarily expect consistency of behavior in relational partners or in individuals across relationships. Particularly if given relationships "are" interdependent with other relationships (Parke & O'Neil, 1997), such that even the personal is truly the social (Milardo & Wellman, 1992), then we face the positively Clintonian problem of defining whether in fact they can ever "be" anything—or can be measured—in isolation from the influence of the other relationships with which they co-exist (Dunn, 1988a; Furman & Buhrmester, 1985b; Parke & O'Neil, 1997). Finally, if relationships "are" essentially bi-directional in their influences (Pettit & Lollis, 1997), then one must stop seeing them as the possessions of individual participants and instead focus on the ways in which they are enacted moment by moment.

These considerations might prompt the recognition that the use of the term "relationship" is actually a summary statement that freezes processes at a particular moment and also masks a variety of activities, motivations, experiences, and directions of influence—a convenient summary term but a summary term all the same. As such, use of the term confronts researchers with important choices about the summarized aspects on which to focus attention. As Manke and Plomin (1997) advise, for example, one choice for relationship researchers is the level of analysis at which to explain relationship activity, whether the level be the individual, the dyad, or the larger family system (or, one might also add, the cultural environment that defines the acceptable natures of relationships; Duck, 1998). This choice is a prerequisite for researchers even identifying or differentiating relationships and their gradations.

There is a second choice facing researchers also, and identified by Duck and Sants (1983), that even once the unit of analysis is decided, one is then faced with the choice of the perspective to take upon it: any two individuals in "the same relationships" may have different views of it. When one of the observers is a relational partner and one is a researcher, what is one to do if the two perspectives are different and irreconcilable? Who is "right"? The matter is more than vacuous, especially when some researchers rate children's friendships by asking peers and teachers who are a target's friends and then compare those ratings with the target's self-ratings not of the friendship but of something else (social behavior), as Menesini (1997) did. The implicit depiction here is that peers and teachers *know*, and hence that friendships are objectifiable and determinable from the observations made by other people. (Obviously those who accept such definitions could not count as "relationships" any form of secret extramarital affair.)

In the case of children, the choices are further complicated by the fact that children and adults have different cognitive abilities and so also a different grasp of social concepts. Thus even once one identifies a relationship and classifies it (as in a parent–child relationship, for example), one needs to recognize that the two partners are, in a subtle psychological sense, NOT in the same relationship (Duck, 1994a). Nor are the relative influences of their bidirectional effects equivalent (Dunn, 1997), whether or not one compounds the observation by consideration of power issues in relationships. Also to lesser extents, the same is true of siblings or peers where one partner might, by reason of more advanced cognitive development, understand the relationship in ways different from the other (Dunn, 1996), such that the strength of bidirectional effects could differ between partners in the same relationship, as well as in different relationships of the same target child (Lollis & Kuczynski, 1997). Hence the matters of deciding what is a relationship, how one recognizes it, how it may be measured, what happens in it, and who should legitimately tell us about it become relevant sites of reflection. But not necessarily in that order or that separately.

CHOICES OF TOPIC AND STYLE OF RESEARCH AS IMPLICIT THEORIES OF RELATING

Following several previous commentators (Dunn, 1997; Montgomery & Duck, 1991), we note that an investigator's attempts to remove context in order to focus on a notionally key variable, like the intention to reach for a particular methodological tool or to exclude certain phenomena from the study, is itself a decision about the *nature* of the problem to be researched. Built into our methods of inquiry and our strategies of empirical study are outlooks, presumptions, and perspectives that mold the way we pursue the investigation of a problem. This is as true in the developmental psychology of personal relationships as elsewhere: to look for a stable, reliable measure of children's sociometric choices, for example, is to presume that children's sociometric choices are stable (Sants, 1984); to assume that relationships have bidirectional influences is to make an assumption about the nature, distribution, and operators of power in a relationship (Dunn, 1997); to treat relationships as enduring beyond the observable patterns of interaction is to locate a mechanism of endurance within the person (Manke & Plomin, 1997).

Such issues are important when researchers set out to focus on particular relationships and aspects of relationships. In a sense everyone obviously knows what parent–child relationships are and what a peer relationship is: they are, respectively, relationships that involve at least one parent and at least one child or at least two children close in age. However, that is a simple structural or categorical definition rather than a functional psychological one or one defined in terms of qualities of experience. Neither all parent–child relations nor all peer relationships are like all other instances of the class. We also know that a child's network of relationships involves a set of other people, sociometrically interconnected in some way (Moreno, 1934), and we can deduce from that pattern of connection whether or not a child is popular, rejected, or neglected (Asher & Coie, 1990). But again that is primarily a structural concept, and a network cannot be said meaningfully to exist at all without interaction and communication or, indeed, choices of how to spend time within the structure (Bronfenbrenner, 1979). Can a network truly exist without some communication actually taking place between members or choices being not only expressed but also *enacted*? As soon as one focuses on that issue, then one is forced to recognize that the nature of the relationship is itself strongly influenced by the nature of communication and interaction as well as by the presumed existence of structure, and indeed some of the most interesting work on children's networks looks at exactly these issues (Bronfenbrenner, 1979). Therefore, one must consider the role of actual communication in the psychological processes that we readily assume to underlie the structural and behavioral interactive aspects of children's relationships (O'Connor, Hetherington, & Clingempeel, 1997).

The emphasis on structure rather than on process conceals the fact that, from the point of view of the subjects of our studies living their complex lives, those lives are characteristically uncertain and dynamic. Part of the reason why human beings (both research participants and research conductors) prefer prediction and control is to reduce the sensation of complexity that is otherwise ubiquitous—and holding on to a sense of enduring structure is one way to do it. One pervasive human characteristic is to develop categories and labels that imply stasis and fixity (Bowlby, 1980; Bruner, 1990; Duck, 1994a). The fluid and uncertain quality of relationships is absent from much theory and research that seeks "reliability" as a criterion of successful measurement. However, the creation of such order is a psychological process of construction, not simply the uncovering of an existing state of affairs (Bruner, 1990). All the same, children are surely as aware as are adults that relationships can break up or become stormy as well as endure in tranquillity. At that point of disturbance, structure is nothing and process is everything.

This is particularly important when one acknowledges that relationships are depicted in research and in subjective reports at the moment of observation, even where researchers develop techniques to assess such things as "synchronicity" with others (Pettit & Mize, 1993). Such summary measurement risks depicting relationship processes themselves in a form generalized from that moment, or all synchronicities as typified by the one observed, so that relationships are then discussed as entities characterized totally by that one measurement or report. Yet in treating relationships as cross-sections, unities, states, plateaux, or turning points on a graph, researchers or speakers may overlook the *simultaneous* presence and intersection of a number of features and options or the pressures of real alternative options to the path actually taken. For example, behavioral choices are always made between real alternative options (Kelly, 1955): to understand the choice, one has also to understand the psychological and social context of alternatives in which it was made (Dixson & Duck, 1993). Any descriptions of events represent the observer's choices about what to notice and how to describe it to a given or presumed audience, whether that audience be another child, an adult, a parent, or a researcher. It is also necessary to portray—even for children—the rhetorical context by which the choice was circumscribed and the audience to whom it was reported, and to depict not only the outcome but the processes and dynamics surrounding it.

As an example, the difficulty of adding precise order to a set of unseemly varieties has been one of the traditional difficulties of stage theories (Selman, 1980) or strict categories for internal working models (Bowlby, 1988), where there is rarely 100% conformity of observation to the stages or categories that "explain" the majority of observables. Interestingly, researchers invariably explain such imperfect correspondence in terms of measurement error rather than by reference to the inherent variability of experience (Bigelow, 1977). Yet life, even for a child, is messy and complex in important respects. This may be inferred from the fact that, for example, bidirectional effects may differ for different domains of a given relationship (Dunn, 1997; Lollis & Kuczynski, 1997), or other relationships within the family may influence patterns of bidirectional effects (O'Connor, Hetherington, & Clingempeel, 1997). However, other acknowledged aspects of children's relational life point toward the same fluctuation or variegation of experience (for example, instabilities of sociometric status, management of peer pressures, re-occurrence of bullying, and other matters discussed below and elsewhere in this volume).

We believe that the problems of incorrectly-implied uniformity of experience are exemplified in the attachment and parent–child literature. A particularly good example of the problems associated with the use of categories can be seen in the use of Baumrind's (1971) typology of parenting. Although one parent in a family may be characterized as authoritative (high on demandingness and warmth), another parent in the same family may not be authoritative. Likewise, parents may use one type of parenting style (e.g., authoritative) with one child in a family, but an entirely different parenting style (e.g., permissive) with another child. Furthermore, the disadvantages of using typologies to categorize relationships are to be found in the exclusion of the variability that occurs not just across parent but within daily life. A parent could vary in parenting style with the same child depending on the issue in question (e.g., homework versus recreational issues), or the kind of day the parent had, or as a function of human changes in mood and circumstance. These three types of within-family variability are typically ignored when researchers employ this parenting typology, thereby masking the complex dynamic nature of relationships. Of course, readers will readily appreciate that we use this one example when other examples of such typologies likewise exist in developmental psychology and are subject to the same critique.

THE UNCERTAINTIES OF DAILY LIFE

All of the substantive choices made by researchers in conceptualizing relationships involve similar stripping away of some of its normal variabilities, accompaniments, and contexts so that researchers can choose to focus their study more effectively. One might look to the broader field of personal relationships, for example, and note that a relatively large volume of research on adults has focused on self-disclosure as a source of relational growth, even though recent analyses (Dindia, 1997) indicate that it actually occurs naturally no more than 2% of the time. The literature on developmental psychology shows us that researchers there usually focus on warmth, conflict, control, and self-disclosure, and less often explore respect, expectations, power, guilt, or humor. This supplementary list still leaves out such common aspects of everyday life as inconsistency, unpredictability, fear, anxiety, worry, impatience, sense of progress, and achievement, and a host of other things that might be relevant to the way a person, specifically a child, might experience life in relationships.

Developmental research also tends to focus on particular relationships, such as parent–child relationships, but has until recently had less to say about such relationships as siblings (Dunn, 1996) or, within that, greater subtleties such as the way in which siblings gang up against parents (Nicholson, 1998). Although there is a growing awareness that single relationships do occur in a nexus of other relationships (Burks & Parke, 1996), the interactions of those relationships are a rich ground for continued diligence if researchers wish to understand fully the child's experience of relational life. As part of our argument, we propose, then, that whenever messy parts of real life and social context are stripped away by a researcher's need to provide realism in studies or conceptual clarity in theory, they must later be consciously and explicitly reconnected to the explanation of the stripped-down processes (Acitelli, 1995).

We do not deny the value of focused research certainties or styles of explanation, but instead we see many of them as preferences of explanatory style chosen by scholars from the range of possible explanations. From the phenomenal pool of uncertainty, observations are retrospectively made into predictable patterns from the many different sequences possible from a given starting point—whether by relaters or by researchers (Duck, 1994a). The kinds of predictabilities and certainties chosen by everyday relaters on the one hand and researchers on the other are partly determined by the different projects, needs, and audiences for whom each set of persons creates those explanations at a given moment. In the case of social scientists, our methods encourage researchers to isolate particular aspects of relationships from others in order that we may study them more effectively. The consequence is that certain occurrences in relationships are given priority by such methods. The nature of everyday relationships—despite all their tedium, repetitious boredom, or occasional unpredictable flourishes—tends to be represented by *interesting phenomena* that evince researchers' local and focused enthusiasms for theoretical topics, like attachment or conservation, rather than the mundane conduct and experience of everyday life. Researchers' enthusiasms essentially lead to the endorsement of the proposition that relationships are composed of all (and only) those notable things to which researchers have so far given their attention—as if everyday life were experienced as the news headlines. Equally, models of relating tend to address the positive and rational sides of relationships (Duck, West, & Acitelli, 1997) and there are only rare and very recent efforts devoted to the apparently irrational (Spitzberg & Cupach, 1998), or to dark aspects such as shame and anger (Retzinger, 1995), daily hassles (Bolger & Kelleher, 1993), or enemyship (Wiseman & Duck, 1995).

In the case of a child struggling to become one of those people who has acquired the culturally-transmitted sense of the order of things and the culturally accepted ways of doing them, the order is in fact won through hard battle with incoming inconsistencies and ambiguities. Children, too, presumably experience a dark side of life that must be "managed into" the good, as it is for adults (Wood & Duck, 1995). Children's lives are not the unalloyed joys that are represented both directly in many cultural stories and implicitly in some research. Contained amongst a pleasant insouciance are also rejection, doubt, bullying, constraints by grown-ups, and lack of power or self-determination that make childhood more than a simple haven of peace, tranquillity, dedicated learning, and uniformly rewarding personal growth.

We believe, therefore, that the chapter's opening questions come most sharply into focus if one attends to communication and "contexts" in modifying and influencing the ways in which relating is carried out (Duck, 1993; 1994a). Scholars such as Hinde and Stevenson-Hinde (1988) have taken a bottom-up approach and looked for consistencies—such as in personality or traits—across such contexts as school and home. Others such as Hartup (1989) take a top-down approach and explore the ways in which contexts like parent–child interaction ultimately constitute resources for the child in different relationships. It is important to note that "context" is differently theorized in these cases. A weak view of context is that it is the momentary backdrop against which otherwise consistent actions are carried out (such as place, environment, or situation; Argyle, Furnham, & Graham, 1981)—rather like a scenic backdrop in a stage play. A stronger view is that place, time, school environment, ritual, family life, ceremony, celebration, and other temporal contexts such as life-developmental stage, render different the experiences of relaters on those occasions or in those places (Werner, Altman, Brown & Ginat, 1993; Pettit & Clawson, 1996). The strongest view is that context is like the water in which fishes swim, and which is inextricably part of everything that is done there, such that relationships are steeped in developmental, cultural, educational, attitudinal, societal, normative, conversational, and dialectical or pedagogical contexts (Allan, 1993; French & Underwood, 1996; Putallaz, Costanzo, & Klein, 1993). For example, Mills and Rubin (1993) considered links between parents' internal working models and the behavioral skills of children within the context of socio-ecological resources and setting conditions for relating.

Certainly those who note the effects of culture on relationships and vice versa (Fitch, 1998) are making a different version of the same point as those who argue that relational partners exert influence on each other. Just as family is a context and parental beliefs are also (Mills & Rubin, 1993), and siblings, family styles, school, and friendships exert influences on the individual, so also does cultural milieu. The upshot of this latter view is essentially that one describes occasions and practices that are meaningfully described as "relational" but that "relationships" do not exist objectively as entities independent of such occasions and practices. The practices and behaviors of particular relationships may well differ from those observable in other relationships and thus it is not in any *simple* sense that children replicate in other relationships the things they learn from interaction with parents. Such things as power are perhaps enacted in parent–child relationships differently from the way they are with peers (see Perlman et al., this volume).

Such contexts offer theoretical and methodological choices that "bind in" particular ways of comprehending the items that count as phenomena to be explained. Usually such choices also rely on the unseen forces of metaphors or other favored terminology that both assist and ultimately frame the viewing of those phenomena (Duck, 1994a). Implicit understandings of relationships, like any theory, contain a number of important assumptions, some explicated and some held implicit because they are assumed and shared within the researchers' discourse community. In the discourse of relationship researchers, an important unspoken assumption, for example, concerns the nature of personhood or agency, and so models of relating implicitly contain representations of varying degrees of human agency. As a powerful example, familiar to researchers and everyday thought alike, consider the model of attraction that is widely accepted. The early research on attraction (e.g., Berscheid & Walster, 1969) used the metaphor of magnetism, which actually implicitly denies active human agency. Instead it focuses empirical efforts on the location of inherent individual characteristics that propel people towards one another *willy nilly* (Berscheid & Walster, 1978). Implicit in this powerful metaphor is the notion that the pre-existing *characteristics* of a person, rather than behaviors or social contexts, result in liking. The metaphor therefore draws attention away from agents' behavior expressed or performed in a dynamic social context at a particular moment (McCall, 1988), or from the use of economic resources available to the partners for the conduct of their relationship (Allan, 1995; Wellman, 1985) or from sets of cultural beliefs and norms that influence individual cognitions and practice (Allan, 1993). The magnetic metaphor thus entails an implicit notion that the agency of a person is subordinate to uncontrollable forces (magnetism, attraction). Equally powerful and important in the child development literature on relationships is the implicit depiction of a child's agency in the social world. Most developmental theories take an explicit or implicit position on whether the child is an active agent in the environment or a passive but organizing recipient of the imprints of others. One's view concerning the child's ability to act upon his or her environment has real ramifications for how one views the child's contribution to the construction or enactment of relationships. Do children "make" relationships or do they "take" relationships given to them?

As a further example of subtle effects of chosen research style, studies of child development focus on internal and individual qualitative change and take relationships as essentially determinate (Bigelow & La Gaipa, 1980; Miller, 1993; Pettit & Mize, 1993). By contrast, many studies of adult relationship development are more likely to focus on incremental (i.e., quantitative) change in the relationships and to take the persons as determinate, noting that it is *relationships* that reach greater levels of intimacy, or more closeness, or exhibit more disclosure (for example, Honeycutt, 1993). By contrast with research on adults, studies of the development of intimacy in children's relationships are, in these authors' experience, extraordinarily rare.

A CONSEQUENCE OF THE EXPERIENCE OF MEMBERSHIP IN MULTIPLE RELATIONSHIPS

Russell (this volume) notes that children's lives are played out primarily through relationships with others. In the context of our other remarks, we note a hidden and, so far as we know, unrecognized implication of this fact which follows on from the above observations. The child faces a number of challenges and types of relational stress that appear to extend beyond those experienced by adults where subtle differences of age and grade are less relevant forms of complexity. Where researchers have recognized the varieties of relationships that children experience, such as siblings, family, parents, peers, and teachers, there is less attention to the fact that these are all kinds of relationships that children must handle. Especially for children, resolution of contradictions of demands by different powerful adults may be a source of both learning and tension (for example, where teachers and parents set different standards for behavior). Moving between these psychological, behavioral, and relational contexts and managing their tensions and contradictions are features of childhood that merit at least as much attention as that presently given to the carry-over between home and work in adults (Crouter & Helms-Erickson, 1997).

Furthermore, in everyday life, particular parts of relationships and relationship roles are variably foregrounded from time to time both in the larger historical sense (cf. Elder's, 1999, work on children's relationships in the Great Depression) and in the sense of life-stage changes (e.g., Steinberg, Darling & Fletcher's, 1995, work on relational change between parents and children during the child's pubertal development). Not only do the forms of relationships change as a function of historical context (see Fisher, 1996 on the historical differences in family form) but no relationship offers one uniform or consistent experience all the time, as measures defining *the* closeness of a relationship would imply (Duck, West, & Acitelli, 1997). In daily life people are forced to choose particular roles or aspects of the relationship as foci on different occasions. For example, central to the understanding of personal relationships in development is the issue of how particular circumstances *warrant* different psychological reconstructions of the relationship between children, just as for adults (Duck, West, & Acitelli, 1997). Where adults experience tensions of competing loyalties between relationships, needing occasionally to make a choice to give time to one equally deserving relationship over another (Baxter et al, 1997), so too one can imagine that children must make similar choices, not only between people but equally between play and work, school and family responsibilities, self-directed efforts and other-directed efforts, or group and individual issues. Thus, the everyday conduct of children's relationships likely involves momentary choices between relationships (especially if the parents become divorced, Coleman & Ganong, 1995), between different distributions of time with different partners, and even strains on loyalties to different persons who may make simultaneous, competing demands on their relational resources or provisions. These could be requests to form sibling alliances against parents (Nicholson, 1998) or requirements to balance out the demands of friends and family (von Salisch, 1997) or needs to negotiate amounts of time spent with extended kin (Fisher, 1996; Stephens & Clark, 1996). A child or adolescent may be faced with conflicts between or among different relationships—to spend time with playmates or alone, with siblings or school pals, to stay longer at an enjoyable school social event or return home at an hour appointed by parents, fulfilling obligations to parents or to other adolescents, or, in the particular case of adolescent girls, spending time with self-preferred partners or with those approved by the peer group (Senchea, 1998). In real life everyday relationships, a person's commitments to a particular relationship can be assessed as much by the relative distribution of time *between* relationships as by the balance between internal reward and cost systems *within* relationships. This problem is not duly assessed for children in research that explores relationships as if a relationship were a decontextualized entity *in* which the person simply exists (Baxter & Montgomery, 1996).

Children must negotiate membership in multiple relationships, and recent literature attempts to establish the links between children's multiple relationships (e.g., Dunn, 1988). Recent scholarship focuses on the ways in which experience in one relationship may be translated to other relationships. Little of this research, however, focuses on the ways in which children combine competing and complementary relationships to form a coherent social network. This is a very important point for developmental psychology researchers, who have only recently begun to look at the discrepancies among children's relationships (e.g., how children's sibling relationships differ from peer relations). We need to go even one step further to examine how children combine all of these relationships, despite the discrepancies, into a functional social network. The efforts and paradoxes involved in this task of combining relationship perhaps differ for children who may be more or less constrained in relationship opportunities (e.g., children without a father figure, children with four sets of grandparents, only children with no siblings, home-schooled children without peers to interact with, children in single-sex schools, etc.).

THE PARADOXES OF SCIENTIFIC OBSERVATION

Whereas some researchers have noted that there are "insider" and "outsider" ways to look at relationships (Olson, 1977; Duck & Sants, 1983; Surra &

Ridley, 1991; Wood & Cox, 1993), less often is it noted that the outsider position is not simply outside the experience of the insiders, but that it typically imports other consequential elements into its depiction of those inside phenomena. For example, the outsider position presents only one cross-section in time, whereas the insider position is enriched by many cross-sections in time because partners can rely on memory as well as any present observations (Dixson & Duck, 1993). This compounds our earlier observation that the outsider position necessarily "stabilizes" the interior dynamics of the participants by recording their momentary position rather than their fluctuations.

While the limits of the outsider perspective are clear, though under-reported in scientific articles, the insider's view is also imperfect. For example, insiders can become enmeshed in their experience and thus do not see a full picture of what is happening in their relating. Outsiders, particularly researchers with complex understandings of particular stratified processes, may have theoretical and critical lenses that allow them to notice and comprehend things that insiders do not even see. A position that claims outsiders are objective and detached can go too far, but one can also go too far in honoring the native's perspective. Natives have information to give, insights to offer, experiences to report in depth, but they may also experience a reality that is partial, flawed, complex, overbearing, or incomplete in ways that are different from *but no less than the realities experienced by researchers.*

Readers will recognize the foregoing point as a restatement of an earlier point, now raised in a more complex set of concepts. The issue of "reliability" now resurfaces as the issue of how to get inside (as well as outside) a relationship and reassemble the model of the interior as we describe the exterior. The cross-sectional outsider position adopted by most social scientific research on relationships will necessarily represent relationships processes as mono-chromatic objects, and our goal in the future must be to color them in. The main way to do this is for researchers to look within individual relationships on several occasions in order to depict the variety of patterns, rather than presume a fixed pattern of experience in the relationship on the basis of one point of measurement, as is presently implicit in many of our methods. Statistical methods are premised on locating probabilities, bounded by variances that constitute "error". Present research designs often allow only for one-shot data collection, with research findings then used to generalize beyond that moment, and represent the relationship (e.g., its intimacy) in toto. Where Hinde (1981) called for more description of relationships (using an ethological analogy), we call for more work on the variabilities perceived by relationship partners such as the contradictions and uncertainties with which partners must cope (Duck, 1994b; Duck & Wood, 1995), variations in expectations about the relationship (Miell, 1987), and the changing or varied patterns of talk in and about relationships (Acitelli, 1988, 1993; Duck, Rutt, Hurst, & Strejc, 1991). Here we place less emphasis (but still place some emphasis) on external, behaviorally-based description alone. By analogy, if a researcher adopts metaphors that focus on monolithic stasis, it is like assuming that the

ue Receipt
niversity of Plymouth (1)
ate: Thursday, February 09, 2012
me: 3:10 PM
ard number: 0021090446

em ID: 9005411756
itle: Cisco network security : little blac
ue date: 01-03-2012   23:59

em ID: 9007248339
Title: Mastering Cisco routers.
Due date: 01-03-2012   23:59

tem ID: 900184996X
Title: Cognitive psychology / John B. E
Due date: 16-02-2012   23:59

Item ID: 9008700611
Title: Conservation psychology : under
Due date: 16-02-2012   23:59

Item ID: 9004138839
Title: Developmental psychology of pe
Due date: 01-03-2012   23:59

Total items: 5
Please keep your receipt until you
have checked your Voyager account

ue Receipt

iversity of Plymouth (1)

ate: Thursday, February 09, 2012

me: 3:10 PM

ard number: 002109044.

em ID: 9005411756

itle: Cisco network security : little blac

ue date: 01-03-2012 23:59

em ID: 9007246339.

Title: Mastering Cisco routers

Due date: 01-03-2012 23:59

Item ID: 6001845564X

Title: Cognitive psychology : Jerry B. E

Due date: 16-02-2012 23:59

Item ID: 9008700541

Title: Conservation psychology : under

Due date: 16-02-2012 23:59

Item ID: 9004138839

Title: Developmental psychology of po

Due date: 01-03-2012 23:59

Total items: 5

Please keep your receipt until you

have checked your Voyager account

real point about boiling water is the particular mark it reaches on the thermometer, not the interior ebullience and structural change that takes place in the fluid mechanics of its constitution, or that "good sex" is a check mark in a diary rather than something energetic, diachronic, and composed of complex actions.

The more complex overlay of the preceding point is that even if data collection occurred more than once, force-fit answers to questionnaires could still limit participants' ability to explain the nuances of giving the same answer at two different points of data collection (for example a "2" on a Likert scale of intimacy may not mean exactly the same to all children on all occasions with the constancy that the number 2 implies) or from the simultaneous perspective of the Insider and Outsider measured separately. What occurs is a "glossing of difference": participants summarize the variety of their experience and so speak to their general feeling of the relationship rather than describing only the specific moment (yet in real-life break-up of relationships, for example, individuals may be guided by the fear that to give voice to specific dissatisfaction can make it real; Duck, 1982). Researchers must compare not only the variegated range of experiences of the Insider and Outsider perspectives but must go further and connect the Insider and Outsider perspectives: gathering of questionnaire data should be supplemented by dialogue between researcher and participants about those data.

We suggest, therefore, in keeping with our arguments about representations that have integrity, that "external" observation must in the future be more consistently combined with "internal" observations gathered over a long enough time period to display internal variabilities. Researchers must also replace the simple emphasis on "reliability" (which deliberately seeks to strip out variability) and instead recall what it is that reliability leaves out of our understanding of the fluctuations of relationships.

CONCLUSIONS

To recognize continuous tensions and variability in relational emphases is to require a representation of relationships that sees them as multiplex, variable, subject to recharacterization, describable in many ways simultaneously, open-ended, to some extent contentious, and certainly the kind of conceptual entity that can be the subject of legitimate disputes about their "true nature" on occasion. Such tensions and choices may be viewed as descriptive or rhetorical (as may their management). One observation in the study of communication and personal relationships is that partners make choices about the language in which to characterize a relational act at a given point in time (Duck & Pond, 1989), a choice that carries rhetorical, moral, and social behavioral implications (Shotter, 1992). A person obviously also has a choice to describe a particular relational act in a way that decontextualises it from the processes that swarmed around it at the time. Any person's selection of a description of features of a relationship at a particular time is a rhetorical act not a simple descriptive one; that is to say, people (including children) describe relationships—or anything else—in a way that is consistent with a particular world-view and purpose, on a particular occasion, for a particular audience, or in a particular context (Duck, Pond, & Leatham, 1994).

Equally, researchers have similar kinds of descriptive and rhetorical choices available to them and the choice of "mechanisms to emphasize will depend on the theoretical perspective and methods chosen by a particular investigator" (Dunn, 1997, p. 569). The selection of items to describe or explain within the mix of available phenomena is itself not dictated only by the phenomena but also partly by the conventions of science, partly by the preferences of the researcher, and partly by the impulse of a theory to direct attention towards particular things. It is therefore important if we are to describe relationships usefully—let alone explain them—that researchers keep reminding themselves to return that which they took away in order to create a better experiment or a more focused study for a particular purpose on a particular occasion. Having, for good reasons, focused on a single process or the interaction of just two processes by momentarily removing them from their active sites and contexts of operation, any explanation of those processes has to remember to reinsert the previously removed parts of the picture. Dunn (1997, p. 569) warns that researchers must be aware of the extent to which "choices of level of description and analysis constrain the kinds of conclusions we can draw."

We believe that in making such claims, relationship researchers should ask ourselves what our research designs would look like if we were to investigate *relating* rather than *relationships*? A shift from focusing on the noun to the verb could be profitable in our quest to see how behaviors construct (over and over again) the loose definition of partners, friends, and family.

ACKNOWLEDGEMENTS

We are grateful to Rosemary Mills for her helpful comments on previous drafts of this chapter.

Chapter 2

The Influence of Significant Others on Learning about Relationships: from Family to Friends

Ross D. Parke and Robin O'Neil

Department of Psychology and Center for Family Studies, University of California, Riverside

INTRODUCTION AND ASSUMPTIONS

A major issue that has intrigued theorists over the past century concerns the ways children develop the knowledge and skills necessary to manage relationships with others. Freud viewed relationships among family members, especially the mother–child relationship, as critical for later social and personality development. In the modern era Bowlby, in his classic fusion of psychoanalytic and ethological theories, has continued the focus on early family relationships as the foundation for later relationships both inside and outside the family. Our goal in this chapter is to review briefly the major issues that guide current research in this domain and to set an agenda for future research in this area. Two phases of research activity can be distinguished. In the first phase, research focused on description of the impact that patterns of family interaction have on children's developing relationships. In the more recent phase, the focus is on the processes and pathways that account for the linkages noted in Phase I research.

The Developmental Psychology of Personal Relationships.
Edited by Rosemary S. L. Mills and Steve Duck. © 2000 John Wiley & Sons Ltd.

Certain assumptions guide our review. First, we build upon and extend the conceptualization of links among family relationships set out in Dunn (1988b) by conceptualizing the family as a social system (Hinde & Stevenson-Hinde, 1988; Parke & Buriel, 1998). According to this viewpoint, multiple subsystems of family members need to be considered, including parent–child relationships, the marital relationship, and sibling relationships. It is assumed that these sub-systems are interdependent and one goal of research is to explore the mutual influences among these subsystems. Implicit in the notion of family subsystems is the notion that different levels of organization within the family need to be recognized, including dyadic, triadic, and family levels of analysis. Second, it is important to distinguish between various ways in which family members influence each other. Research has traditionally focused on face-to-face interaction, such as parent–child, husband–wife, or sib–sib exchanges (Maccoby & Martin, 1983). More recently, the impact of witnessing the interaction between other individuals (e.g., parents or siblings) on children's developing relationships has received attention (Cummings & Davies, 1994; Fincham, 1998). Third, family management of opportunities to learn and experience social relationships is emerging as a new way in which families influence children's learning about social relationships (Ladd, LeSieur, & Profilet, 1993; Parke & Bhavnagri, 1989). Fourth, we recognize that families are embedded in a variety of external social systems including neighborhoods and communities which, in turn, influence the functioning of the family unit (Bronfenbrenner & Morris, 1998). Fifth, relationship learning changes across time as well as context. As Elder and other life-course theorists have noted, historical contexts need to be considered in light of rapid shifts in family organization and structure, the changing nature of family–work relationships and the reliance on outside agencies for child care (Elder, 1998; Elder, Modell, & Parke, 1993). Sixth, developmental shifts in the way that significant others influence learning about relationships need to be recognized. Although the traditional focus of research has been on infancy and childhood, recent research on adolescence is providing a corrective to the developmental profile. Finally, adults' development as well as children's development is recognized as important in understanding the emergence of relationships within and beyond the family. The timing of adult entry into various roles, and the impact of normative and non-normative transitions are recognized as playing an influential part in both adults' and children's relationships (Elder, 1998; Parke, 1988).

PARENT–CHILD RELATIONSHIPS

Consistent with a family systems viewpoint, recent research has focused on a variety of subsystems, including parent–child, marital, and sib–sib systems. In this section we consider the parent–child subsystem and the relation between parent-child interaction patterns and children's social relationships.

In the first set of studies we consider, the question that is being addressed is whether the style of parent–child interaction is related to children's peer relationships. Two research traditions can be distinguished. First, in the attachment tradition, the focus has been on the impact of early infant–parent attachment on social adaptation in the peer group. This literature suggests that a secure early attachment is associated with better peer relationships in preschool, childhood, and adolescence (Elicker, Egeland, & Sroufe, 1992). (For review of this work, see Sroufe, Carlson, & Shulman, 1993.) Since research in the attachment tradition is reviewed elsewhere in this volume (see Crittenden, this volume), our focus will be limited to research in the second tradition. The second tradition is illustrated by studies of the relations between particular styles of childrearing or parent–child interaction and children's social competence with peers. This research has progressed through several phases over the past decade. In the first phase, studies were designed to demonstrate that variations in patterns of parent–child interaction were, in fact, related to peer outcomes. The aim of these studies was a careful description of the specific types of parent–child interaction that, in turn, would be most predictive of variations in peer outcomes. More recently a second phase of research has begun, namely the search for mediating processes that, in turn, can account for the observed relations between the two systems.

PHASE I: PARENT–CHILD INTERACTION AND PEER COMPETENCE

The first phase of this research is based on the assumption that face-to-face interaction may provide the opportunity to learn, rehearse, and refine social skills that are common to successful social interaction with peers. Research in this tradition has yielded several conclusions, which will be briefly reviewed (for fuller discussion of this phase, see Parke & O'Neil, 1997). First, the nature of the style of the interaction between parent and child is linked to peer outcomes. Consistent with Baumrind's (1973) early classic studies which found that authoritative parenting was related to positive peer outcomes, more recent studies have confirmed that parents who are responsive, warm, engaging, and synchronous are more likely to have children who are more accepted by their peers (Harrist, Pettit, Dodge, & Bates, 1994; Putallaz, 1987). In contrast, parents who are hostile, over-controlling, and express negative affect have children who experience more difficulty with age-mates (Barth & Parke, 1993; Boyum & Parke, 1995; Carson & Parke, 1996; Harrist et al., 1994; MacDonald & Parke, 1984). Recent work (Ladd & Kochenderfer-Ladd, 1998) suggests that parenting style affects not just social acceptance but peer victimization as well (see also Monks & Smith, in this volume). In this study, high intrusive demandingness and low responsiveness were associated with peer victimization for both boys and girls, and parent–child relationships characterized by intense closeness were associated with higher levels of victimization in boys. In this case, extreme closeness which may be akin to overprotection may inhibit the development of independence and hence increase boys' vulnerability to victimization. This work suggests that more attention needs to be given to the links between specific parenting practices and specific aspects of children's behavior with peers.

Family interaction patterns not only relate to concurrent peer relationships, but cross-time relationships as well (Barth & Parke,1993). For example, Isley, O'Neil, & Parke (1996) found that parental negative affect assessed in kindergarten predicted children's social acceptance one year later.

Although there is overlap between mothers and fathers, evidence is emerging that fathers make a unique and independent contribution to their children's social development. Recent studies (Isley et al., 1996) have shown that fathers continue to contribute to children's social behavior with peers after accounting for mothers' contributions. Although father involvement is quantitatively less than mother involvement, fathers have an important impact on their offspring's development. Quality rather than quantity of parent–child interaction is the important predictor of cognitive and social development.

In summary, both the style of parent–child interaction as well as the affective quality of the relationship, especially fathers' emotional displays, are important correlates of children's success in developing relationships with others.

Parental Instruction, Advice-giving, and Consultation

Learning about relationships through interaction with parents can be viewed as an indirect pathway since the goal is often not explicitly to influence children's social relationships with extra-familial partners such as peers. In contrast, parents may influence children's relationships directly in their role as a direct instructor, educator, or advisor. In this role, parents may explicitly set out to educate their children concerning appropriate ways of initiating and maintaining social relationships. (For a fuller discussion of this literature, see Parke & O'Neil, 1997.)

Russell and Finnie (1990) found that the quality of advice that mothers provided their children prior to entry into an ongoing play dyad varied as a function of children's sociometric status. Mothers of well-accepted children were more specific and helpful in the quality of advice that they provided. In contrast, mothers of poorly-accepted children provided relatively ineffective kinds of verbal guidance, such as "have fun", or "stay out of trouble."

Similarly, Mize and Pettit (1997) found that when mothers suggested more positive strategies and framed social dilemmas in nonhostile, optimistic terms, children were rated as better liked, less aggressive, and more socially skilled. Their findings also indicated that a synchronous, warm style of imparting parental advice remains a unique predictor of social acceptance even after controlling for the content of social coaching, particularly among boys. To date, however, these studies have continued to focus on relatively young children, typically preschoolers. Little is known about the role that parental advice-giving or coaching plays in facilitating older children's relationships with peers. In addition, previous studies have focused almost exclusively on mothers, leaving relatively unexplored the role that fathers' advice-giving plays in the development of competent peer interaction styles.

Recent findings suggest the importance of both mothers' and fathers' advice-giving to the development of children's social acceptance and competence with peers (O'Neil, Garcia, Zavala, & Wang, 1995). Parents were asked to read to their third-grade child short stories that described common social themes (e.g., group entry, ambiguous provocation, relational aggression) and to advise the child about the best way to handle each situation. High quality was considered to be advice that promoted a positive, outgoing, social orientation on the part of the child rather than avoidance or aggressive responses. The findings varied as a function of parent and child gender. Among father–son dyads and mother–daughter dyads, parental advice that was more appropriate and more structured was associated with less loneliness and greater social competence among children. However, in contrast to the gender-specific findings for the content of parental advice, the quality of parent–child interactions during the advice-giving session was positively related to a number of indicators of children's social competence, to less loneliness in mother–son and mother–daughter dyads, and to lower levels of depressed mood in father–son dyads. These findings suggest that parental interaction style may make important contributions to children's social adjustment, irrespective of parent or child gender. In contrast, the impact of the "message" that parental advice conveys to children may be more strongly influenced by parent and child gender. Similarly, other results from a study based on a triadic advice-giving session in which mothers, fathers, and their third-grader discussed how to handle problems that their child had when interacting with peers, indicated that parental style of interaction appeared to be a better predictor of children's social competence than the actual solution quality generated in the advice-giving session (Wang & McDowell, 1996). Specifically, the controlling nature of fathers' style and the warmth and support expressed by mothers during the advice-giving task were significant predictors of both teacher and peer ratings of children's social competence. When fathers were more controlling during the advice-giving sessions, children were described by teachers and peers as more disliked.

The direction of effects in each of these studies is difficult to determine and future models that explain links between parental management strategies and children's social development need to incorporate bidirectional processes. Under some circumstances, parents may be making proactive efforts to provide assistance to their children's social efforts, whereas under other circumstances, parents may be providing advice in response to children's social difficulties (see also Ladd & Golter, 1988; Mize, Pettit, & Brown, 1995). Overly involved or highly directive parents, for example, may be attempting to remediate their children's poor social abilities. Alternatively, high levels of control may inhibit children's efforts to develop their own strategies for dealing with peer relations. Comparison of data from kindergarten, third grade, and fifth grade suggests gender-based shifts in parental advising and consulting. In early childhood, both mothers and fathers appear to use advice-giving as a mode of social skill training. However, by middle childhood, mothers appear to do more remediation of poor social skills, whereas fathers appear to be involved in advising and consulting with their child about social relationships when children have already acquired good social skills (Wang, 1998).

These studies suggest that direct parental influence in the form of supervision and advice-giving can significantly increase the interactive competence of young children and illustrate the utility of examining direct parental strategies as a way of teaching children about social relationships.

PHASE II RESEARCH: PROCESSES MEDIATING THE RELATIONS BETWEEN PARENT–CHILD INTERACTION AND PEER OUTCOMES

A variety of processes have been hypothesized as mediators between parent–child interaction and peer outcomes. These include emotion encoding and decoding skills, emotion regulatory skills, cognitive representations, attributions and beliefs, and problem-solving skills (Ladd, 1992; Parke, Burks, Carson, Neville, & Boyum, 1994). It is assumed that these abilities or beliefs are acquired in the course of parent-child interchanges over the course of development and, in turn, guide the nature of children's behavior with their peers. It is also assumed that these styles of interacting with peers may, in turn, determine children's level of acceptance by their peers. In this chapter we focus on two sets of processes that seem particularly promising candidates for mediator status: affect management skills and cognitive representational processes.

Affect Management Skills

Children learn more than specific affective expressions, such as anger or sadness or joy, in the family. They learn a cluster of processes associated with the understanding and regulation of affective displays which we term "affect management skills" (Parke, Burks, Carson, & Cassidy, 1992). It is assumed that these skills are acquired during the course of parent–child interaction, and are available to the child for use in other relationships. Moreover, it is assumed that these skills play a mediating role between family and peer relationships. Three aspects of this issue are examined, namely (1) encoding and decoding of emotion, (2) cognitive understanding of causes and consequences of emotion and (3) emotion regulation.

The Relation between Emotional Encoding and Decoding Abilities and Sociometric Status

One set of skills that are of relevance to successful peer interaction and may, in part, be acquired in the context of parent–child play, especially arousing physical play, is the ability to clearly encode emotional signals and to decode others' emotional states. Through physically playful interaction with their parents, especially fathers, children may be learning how to use emotional signals to regulate the social behavior of others. In addition, they may learn to accurately decode the social and emotional signals of other social partners.

Several studies (Beitel & Parke, 1985; Field & Walden, 1982; see Hubbard & Coie, 1994, for a review) have found positive relationships between emotional decoding ability and children's peer status. Emotional encoding is linked with children's social status as well. Others (Buck, 1975) have found positive relationships between children's ability to encode emotional expressions and children's popularity with peers. Carson and Parke (1998) extended earlier work by examining how sociometric status is related to emotional production and recognition skills within the family. Some families may utilize idiosyncratic affect cues that are not recognizable in interactions outside of the family. Their communications may reflect a "familycentric" bias. In support of this possibility, Carson and Parke found that undergraduates were better able to recognize the facial expressions of popular children than those of rejected children. This suggests that the emotional production skills of popular children are different from those of rejected children, because rejected children's facial expressions are not as well recognized outside the family. These studies provide support for the links between children's emotional encoding and decoding skills and their sociometric status.

The Relation of Emotional Understanding to Peer Competence

In order to develop a more comprehensive model of the role of affect in the emergence of peer competence, we recently examined other aspects of this issue. Successful peer interaction requires not only the ability to recognize and produce emotions, but also requires a social understanding of emotion-related experiences, of the meaning of emotions, of the cause of emotions, and of the responses appropriate to others' emotions. Cassidy, Parke, Butkovsky, and Braungart (1992) evaluated this hypothesized role of emotional understanding in a study of 5- and 6-year-old children. Based on interviews with the children about their understanding of emotions, they found that a higher level of peer acceptance was associated with greater: (1) ability to identify emotions, (2) acknowledgement of experiencing emotion, (3) ability to describe appropriate causes of emotions, and (4) expectations that they and their parents would respond appropriately to the display of emotions. Similarly, Denham, McKinley, Couchoud, and Holt (1990) found that children's understanding of the type of emotion that would be elicited by different situations was positively related to peer likeability. These findings confirm the findings of other research that suggests connections between other components of social understanding and peer relations (Dodge, Pettit, McClaskey, & Brown, 1986). The next step, of course, is to determine how variations in family interaction may, in fact, contribute to individual differences in children's cognitive understanding of emotions (see Cassidy et al., 1992; Denham, 1998).

Emotion Regulation

An interesting body of research is emerging which suggests that parental support and acceptance of children's emotions are related to children's ability to manage emotions in a constructive fashion. Several recent theorists have suggested that these emotional competence skills are, in turn, linked to social competence with peers (Denham, 1998; Eisenberg & Fabes, 1992a; Parke, 1994). Parental comforting of children when they experience negative emotion has been linked with constructive anger reactions (Eisenberg & Fabes, 1992a). Several studies have suggested that parental willingness to discuss emotions with their children is related to children's awareness and understanding of others' emotions (Denham, 1998; Dunn & Brown, 1994).

This pattern of findings is consistent with recent work by Gottman, Katz, and Hooven (1997) on parents' emotion philosophy or meta-emotion. By "meta-emotion" these researchers refer to parents' emotions about their own and their children's emotions; "meta-emotion structure" refers to an organized set of thoughts, a philosophy, and an approach to one's own emotions and to one's children's emotions. In a longitudinal analysis, Gottman, Katz, & Hoover (1997) found that fathers' acceptance and assistance with their children's sadness and anger at 5 years of age was related to their children's social competence with peers at 8 years of age. Moreover, fathers' assistance with anger predicted academic achievement. Gender of child influenced these relationships. When fathers help daughters with sadness the daughters were rated as more competent by their teachers. When fathers help their daughters regulate anger, girls were rated as more socially competent by their teachers, showed higher academic achievement, and their dyadic interaction with a best friend was less negative. Fathers who are more accepting of their sons' anger and assist their boys in regulating anger have sons who were less aggressive.

Other findings suggest that the strategies parents employ to manage children's negative emotion are associated with children's emotional reactivity, coping, and social competence (O'Neil, Parke, Isley, & Sosa, 1997). When mothers reported that they encouraged the expression of negative affect when their child was upset, children indicated that they would be less likely to use social withdrawal as a strategy to deal with emotional upset. Similarly, mothers who reported that they would help the child find solutions to deal with emotional distress had children who reported that they would be more likely to use reasoning to cope with emotional upset. Mothers who expressed more awareness and sensitivity to their child's emotional state in a family problem-solving task had children who expressed less positive affect and more negative affect in the problem-solving task. When mothers modeled problem-solving approaches to handling disagreement and upset, children were less likely to report becoming angry when faced with an upsetting event, less likely to express negative affect during the parent–child discussion task, were clearer in their emotional expressions, and were more likely to adopt problem-solving strategies in the discussion task.

Fathers' regulation of children's emotions was also related to social competence. Fathers who reported being more distressed by their child's expressions of negative affect had children who were more likely to report using anger and other negative emotions to cope with distressing events. When fathers reported using strategies to minimize distressing circumstances, children were more likely to report using reasoning to cope with a distressing situation. Fathers who reported emotion- and problem-focused reactions to the expression of negative emotions had children who were described by teachers as less aggressive/disruptive. This work highlights the role of fathers in learning about relationships, especially in learning the emotion regulatory aspects of relationships. Fathers provide a unique opportunity to teach children about emotion in the context of relationships due to the wide range of intensity of affect that fathers display and the unpredictable character of their playful exchanges with their children (Parke, 1995, 1996).

Display Rules for Emotional Expression

During early and middle childhood, children acquire and begin to use rules for the socially-appropriate expression of emotion. Most work in this area has focused either on the developmental course of display rule knowledge within the preschool and elementary school years (Garner, 1996). A few studies have examined links between display rule knowledge and social competence. Underwood, Coie, and Herbsman (1992), for example, found that aggressive children have more difficulty understanding display rules.

Recently, we have explored the relations between children's use of socially-appropriate rules for displaying negative emotions and social competence with peers (McDowell & Parke, submitted for publication). We employed Saarni's (1984) "disappointing gift paradigm", which enabled us to assess children's ability to mask negative emotions in the face of disappointment. Our data indicate that, among fourth graders, children, especially girls, who display positive affect/behavior following the presentation of a disappointing gift (thus, using display rules) are rated more socially competent by teachers and peers. Recent evidence (Hubbard & Coie, 1994; Underwood, Coie, & Hebsman, 1992) also suggests that display rule utilization may vary across social contexts (e.g., peers vs. adults). Underwood and colleagues, for example, found that the likelihood of masking anger toward teachers increased with age. However, among girls, the likelihood of expressing anger toward peers increased as they became adolescents. Only recently have researchers begun to examine links between children's experiences with parents and their ability to use display rules. Garner and Power (1996), studying a preschool sample, found that children's negative emotional displays in a disappointment situation were inversely related to observed maternal positive emotion. More recently, McDowell and Parke, in press, found that parents who were highly controlling of their children's emotional expressiveness, especially boys, demonstrated less knowledge about appropriate display rule use. Finally, Jones, Abbey, and Cumberland (1998) reported a further link between family emotional climate and display rule knowledge. These investigators found that maternal reports of negative emotional family expressiveness were related to self-protective display rules and negatively to prosocial display rules. However, much remains to be understood regarding the intergenerational continuity between parents' and children's display rule use.

Together, these studies suggest that various aspects of emotional development—encoding, decoding, cognitive understanding, and emotion regulation—play an important role in accounting for variations in peer competence. Our argument is that these aspects of emotion may be learned in the context of family interaction and serve as mediators between the parents and peers. Accumulating support for this view suggests that this is an important direction for future research.

COGNITIVE REPRESENTATIONAL MODELS: ANOTHER POSSIBLE MEDIATOR BETWEEN PARENTS AND PEERS

One of the major problems facing the area of family–peer relationships is how children transfer the strategies that they acquire in the family context to their peer relationships. A variety of theories assume that individuals process internal mental representations that guide their social behavior. Attachment theorists offer working model notions (Bowlby, 1969), whereas social and cognitive psychologists have provided an account involving scripts or cognitive maps that could serve as a guide for social action (Bugental & Goodnow, 1998). Researchers within the attachment tradition have examined attachment-related representations and found support for Bowlby's argument that representations vary as a function of child–parent attachment history (Main, Kaplan, & Cassidy, 1985). For example, children who had been securely-attached infants were more likely to represent their family in their drawings in a coherent manner, with a balance between individuality and connection, than were children who had been insecurely attached.

Research in a social interactional tradition reveals links between parent and child cognitive representations of social relationships. For example, Burks and Parke (1996) found some evidence for similarities between children and mothers in their goals, attributions, and anticipated consequences when they responded to a series of hypothetical social dilemmas. These studies suggest that children may learn cognitive representational schemes through their family relationships, although the precise mechanisms through which these schemas are acquired are not yet specified.

Next, we turn to an examination of the evidence in support of the general hypothesis that parents of children of different sociometric status differ in their cognitive models of social relationships. Several aspects of cognitive models including attributions, perceptions, values, goals, and strategies have been explored (see Bugental & Goodnow, 1998; Mills & Rubin, 1993). Several studies will illustrate this line of research. Pettit, Dodge, and Brown (1988) found that mothers' attributional biases concerning their children's behavior (e.g., the extent to which they view an ambiguous provocation as hostile or benign) and the endorsement of aggression as a solution to interpersonal problems were related to children's interpersonal problem-solving skills that, in turn, were related to their social competence. Other evidence suggests that parents hold different patterns of beliefs about problematic social behaviors such as aggression and withdrawal and that these patterns are associated with their children's membership in various sociometric status groups (Rubin & Mills, 1990). In this study, parents were concerned about both types of problematic behavior, but expressed more negative emotions, such as anger and disappointment, in the case of aggression. Few mothers or fathers made trait attributions to explain aggressive or withdrawn behavior, but instead attributed these behaviors to temporary or changeable conditions, such as "age or age-related factors." Strategies for dealing with these two types of behavior differed as well; the modal strategies were moderate power for dealing with aggression and low power for social withdrawal. This work is important because it suggests that parents do, in fact, have sets of beliefs concerning children's social behavior that may, in part, govern their behavior (Goodnow & Collins, 1991).

MacKinnon-Lewis, Volling, Lamb, Dechman, Robiner, & Curtner (1994) found that mothers' and sons' hostile attributions were significantly related to the coerciveness of their interactions. Moreover, mothers' attributions were related to reports of their children's aggression in their classrooms. Similarly, Rubin, Mills, and Rose-Krasnor (1989) found a link between mothers' beliefs and their preschoolers' social problem-solving behavior in the classroom. Mothers who placed a higher value on such skills as making friends, sharing with others, and leading or influencing other children had children who were more assertive, prosocial, and competent social problem-solvers. Additionally, the degree to which mothers viewed social behavior as externally caused or controllable was associated with higher levels of social competence among their children. In related work, Spitzer, Estock, Cupp, Isley-Paradise, and Parke (1992) assessed perceptions of *parental influence* (e.g., how much influence parents feel they have regarding their children's social behavior) as well as perceptions of *parental efficacy* (e.g., how easy or hard they found it to help their children's social behavior). Parents, especially mothers, who were high in both perceptions of influence and efficacy had children who were higher in their levels of social acceptance as rated by peers and teachers. Few effects were evident for father perceptions.

We have also explored the links between parent and child cognitive representations of social relationships (Spitzer & Parke, 1994). In this study, parents and their children responded to a series of vignettes reflecting interpersonal dilemmas by indicating how they might react in each situation.

Open-ended responses were coded for goals, causes, strategies, and advice. The cognitive representations of social behavior of both fathers and mothers were related to their children's representations. Moreover, both mothers' and fathers' cognitive models of relationships were linked to children's social acceptance. Mothers who are low in their use of relational and prosocial strategies have children with high levels of peer-nominated aggression. Similarly, mothers who provided specific and socially-skilled advice have more popular children. Fathers' strategies that are rated high on confrontation and instrumental qualities are associated with low teacher ratings of children's prosocial behavior and high teacher ratings of physical and verbal aggression, avoidance, and being disliked. Fathers with relational goals have children who are less often nominated as aggressive by their peers and rated by teachers as more liked and less disliked.

Research in the attachment tradition of cognitive working models provides additional support for the role of cognitive representational processes in exploring the link between family and peer systems. Cassidy, Kirsh, Scolton, and Parke (1996) found that children of varying attachment relationships responded differently to hypothetical scenarios involving ambiguous negative events. Securely-attached children had more positive representations about peer intent in ambiguous situations than did insecurely-attached children. Moreover, Cassidy et al. (1996) found that the link between attachment and relationships with close friends is mediated partly by peer-related representations. This finding is supportive of our general argument and of Sroufe and Fleeson's proposition "that relationships are not constructed afresh, nor are new relationships based on the simple transfer of particular responses from old relationships. Rather it is assumed that previous relationships exert their influence through the attitudes, expectations and understanding of roles which they leave with the individual" (1986, p. 59). Together, this set of studies suggests that cognitive models of relationships may be transmitted across generations and these models, in turn, may serve as mediators between family contexts and children's relationships with others outside of the family.

Attentional Regulation as a Third Potential Mediating Mechanism

In concert with emotion regulation and social cognitive representations, attentional regulatory processes have come to be viewed as an additional mechanism through which familial socialization experiences might influence the development of children's social competence. These processes include the ability to attend to relevant cues, to sustain attention, to refocus attention through such processes as cognitive distraction and cognitive restructuring, and other efforts to purposefully reduce the level of emotional arousal in a situation that is appraised as stressful (Lazarus & Folkman, 1984). Attentional processes are thought to organize experience and to play a central role in cognitive and social development beginning early in infancy (Rothbart &

Bates, 1998). Thus, Wilson (1998) aptly considers attention regulatory processes as a "shuttle" linking emotion regulation and social cognitive processes because attentional processes organize both cognitions and emotional responses, and thus, influence the socialization of relationship competence. In support of direct influences, Eisenberg, Fabes, Bernzweig, Karbon, Poulin, and Hanish (1993) found that children who were low in attentional regulation were also low in social competence. Other recent work suggests that attentional control and emotional negativity may interact when predicting social competence. Attention regulatory skills appear to be more critical among children who experience higher levels of emotional negativity. Eisenberg argues that when children are not prone to experience intense negative emotions, attention regulatory processes may be less essential to positive social functioning. In contrast, the social functioning of children who experience anger and other negative emotions may only be undermined when these children do not have the ability to use attention regulatory processes, such as cognitive restructuring and other forms of emotion-focused coping.

Work emanating from our laboratory (O'Neil & Parke, in press) suggests, in addition, that attentional processes may work in tandem with emotion regulatory abilities to enhance social functioning. Parenting style may be an important antecedent of children's ability to refocus attention away from emotionally distressing events. Data from fifth graders in our study indicated that when mothers adopted a negative, controlling parenting style in a problem-solving discussion, children were less likely to use cognitive decision-making as a coping strategy. In addition, children were more likely to report greater difficulty in controlling negative affect when distressed. Lower levels of cognitive decision-making and higher levels of negative affect, in turn, were associated with more problem behaviors and higher levels of negative interactions with classmates (as reported by teachers). Similarly, when fathers adopted a negative, controlling style, children were more likely to use avoidance as a mechanism for managing negative affect. In addition, fathers who reported expressing more negative dominant emotions such as anger and criticism in everyday interactions, had children who reported greater difficulty controlling negative emotions. Avoidant coping and negative emotionality, in turn, were related to higher levels of parent-reported problem behaviors.

BEYOND PARENT–CHILD INTERACTION: PARENTS AS MANAGERS OF CHILDREN'S SOCIAL RELATIONSHIPS

Parents influence their children's social relationships not only through their direct interactions with their children. They also function as managers of their children's social lives (Hartup, 1979; Parke, 1978) and serve as regulators of opportunities for social contact with extra-familial social partners.

Parental Monitoring

One way in which parents can affect their children's social relationships is through monitoring of their children's social activities. This form of management is particularly evident as children move into pre-adolescence and adolescence and is associated with the relative shift in importance of family and peers as sources of influence on social relationships. Monitoring refers to a range of activities, including the supervision of children's choice of social settings, activities, and friends. Parents of delinquent and antisocial children engaged in less monitoring and supervision of their children's activities, especially with regard to children's use of evening time, and were less in control of their sons' choice of friends, than parents of non-delinquent children (Patterson & Stouthamer-Loeber, 1984). It is unlikely that parental discipline, interaction, and monitoring are independent. In support of this view, Steinberg (1986) found that children in Grades 6 to 9, especially girls who are on their own after school, are more susceptible to peer pressure to engage in antisocial activity (e.g., vandalism, cheating, stealing) than are their adult-supervised peers. In addition, Steinberg found that children of parents who were high in their use of authoritative parenting practices were less susceptible to peer pressure in the absence of monitoring, whereas children of parents who were low in authoritative childrearing were more susceptible to peer pressure in nonsupervised contexts. Isolating other conditions or variables that alter the impact of monitoring would be worthwhile. Developmental shifts may be important, because younger children are less likely to be left unsupervised than older children; moreover, it is likely that direct supervision is more common among younger children, whereas distal supervision is more evident among adolescents. Finally, recent work (O'Neil & Parke, submitted for publication; Parke & O'Neil, 1999) suggests that monitoring and limitation of children's activities are, in part, determined by parental perceptions of neighborhood quality. When parents perceive the neighborhood to be of poor quality, they increase their level of supervision and limit their children's activities which, in turn, leads to higher social competence. This suggests a new direction for future research, namely the determinants of different levels of parental monitoring and supervision.

Parental Participation in Children's Organized Activities

In addition to choosing a neighborhood as a way of increasing access to children, parents influence their children's social behavior by functioning as an interface between children and institutional settings, such as child-oriented clubs and organizations (e.g., Brownies, Cub Scouts, etc.). These mediational activities are important because they permit the child access to a wider range of social activities and opportunities to practice developing social skills that may, in turn, contribute to their social development.

There are clear sex-of-parent and social-class differences in these activities. Mothers are more involved in the interface between the family and social institutions, and view these settings as being more important for the development of social relationships than do fathers (Bhavnagri, 1987). O'Donnell and Stueve (1983) found social-class differences both in children's utilization of community organizations and in the level of maternal participation. Working-class children were only half as likely to participate in activities as were their middle-class peers, and working-class children were more likely to use facilities on an occasional rather than a regular basis. Middle-class mothers were more likely to sign their children up for specific programs, whereas working-class mothers were less likely to involve their children in planned activities. The level of maternal participation varied by social class, with better-educated and economically-advantaged mothers participating more heavily than working-class mothers.

Unfortunately, we know relatively little about how these opportunities for participation relate to children's social behavior with their peers. One exception is Bryant (1985), who found that participation in formally-sponsored organizations with unstructured activities was associated with greater social perspective-taking skill among 10-year-old children, but had little effect on 7-year-olds. In light of the importance of this skill for successful peer interaction (Rubin, Bukowski, & Parker, 1998), this finding assumes particular significance. Moreover, it suggests that activities that "allow the child to experience autonomy, control and mastery of the content of the activity are related to expressions of enhanced social-emotional functioning on the part of the child" (Bryant, 1985, p.65). In support of this argument, Ladd and Price (1986) found that children who were exposed to a higher number of unstructured peer activities (e.g., church, school, going to the swimming pool or library) were less anxious and had fewer absences at the beginning of kindergarten.

We have limited understanding of how these activities differ as a function of children's age, but it appears that there is an increase with age in participation in sponsored organizations with structured activities (e.g., clubs, Brownies, organized sports), with preadolescent children participating the most (Bryant, 1985; O'Donnell & Stueve, 1983). Finally, more attention to the ways in which fathers participate in these types of activities is needed, especially in light of their shifting roles (Parke, 1996).

Parent as Social Initiator and Arranger

Parents play an important role in the facilitation of their children's peer relationships by initiating contact between their own children and potential play partners, especially among younger children (Ladd & LeSieur, 1995). Ladd and Golter (1988) found that children of parents who tended to arrange peer contacts had a larger range of playmates and more frequent play companions outside of school than children of parents who were less active in initiating peer contacts. When children entered kindergarten, boys but not girls with parents who initiated peer contacts were better liked and less rejected by their classmates than were boys with noninitiating parents. Other evidence (Ladd, Hart, Wadsworth, & Golter, 1988) suggests that parents' peer management (initiating peer contacts; purchasing toys for social applications) of younger preschool children prior to enrollment in preschool was, in turn, linked to the time that children spent in peers' homes. Ladd and Hart (1991) found that parents who arranged a larger number of peer informal play contacts tended to have children with a larger range of playmates. In addition, these investigators found a positive relationship between the number of child initiations and the size of the playmate network. Finally, parents who frequently initiated informal peer play opportunities tended to have children who were more prosocial toward peers and spent less time in onlooking and unoccupied behaviors.

Children's own initiation activity has also been linked with measures of social competence. Children who initiated a larger number of peer contacts outside of school tended to be better liked by their peers in preschool settings. The Ladd and Hart (1991) study serves as a corrective to the view that initiation activity is only a parental activity and reminds us that variations in the level of activity played by children in organizing their own social contacts is an important correlate of their social competence.

Future research should detail how parental and child initiating activities shift over the course of development. It is clear that parental initiating is important, but over time it decreases and the factors that govern this decrease are important issues to explore. Moreover, it is critical to understand when parental initiation activity can, in fact, be beneficial and when it is detrimental to children's emerging social competence. Younger children may learn through observation of their parents how to initiate social contacts. On the other hand, as the child grows older, social competence may, in fact, be negatively affected if insufficient independence in organizing their social contacts is permitted. At the least, a child may regard it as inappropriate for a parent to continue to initiate on their behalf beyond a certain age, and parental micromanagement may be viewed as interfering rather than helpful and a potential source of embarrassment for the child.

Together, these studies provide evidence of the possible facilitory role of parents in the development of social competence with peers. Little is known, however, about the possible determinants of parental utilization of neighborhood social resources, including other children as playmates, or of parental initiating and arranging activities.

Adult Social Networks as a Source of Potential Peer Contacts for Children

In addition to the role played by parents in arranging children's access to other children, parents' own social networks of other adults, as well as the child members of parental social networks, provide a source of possible play partners for children. Cochran and Niego (1995) suggested several ways in which these two sets of relationships may be related. First, the child is exposed to a wider or narrower band of possible social interactive partners by exposure to the members of the parent's social network. Second, the extent to which the child has access to the social interactions of his or her parents and members of their social network may determine how well the child acquires a particular style of social interaction. Third, in view of the social support function of social networks, parents in supportive social networks may be more likely to have positive relationships with their children which, in turn, may positively affect the child's social adjustment both within and outside the family.

Cochran and Niego (1995) have provided support for the first suggestion, namely, that there is overlap between parent and child social networks. Specifically, these investigators found that 30–44% of 6-year-old children's social networks were also included in the mothers' networks. In other words, children often listed other children as play partners who were children of their mother's friends. Finally, the overlap was higher in the case of relatives than nonrelatives but both kin and nonkin adult networks provided sources of peer play partners for young children. Other evidence from Sweden (Tietjen, 1985) suggests that there is overlap in the social networks of parents and children. However, in this case, there was overlap only between mothers and their 8- to 9-year-old daughters; no relations were evident in the case of mothers and sons. In light of the failure to find gender differences in network overlap across generations in other studies (e.g., Cochran, Larner, Riley, Gunnarsson, & Henderson, 1990), this issue merits further examination, especially the potential role of culture in accounting for these findings.

Another way these two networks may be linked was proposed by Coleman (1988), who argued that when both parents and their children are acquainted with other parents and their children, they form network closure. According to Coleman, when network closure exists, there are likely to be more shared values and more social control over their offspring, which, in turn, would be related to better social outcomes. In support of this view, Darling, Steinberg, Gringlas, and Dornbusch (1995) found that social integration (as indexed by network closure) and value consensus were related to adolescent social and academic outcomes. Specifically, adolescents who reported high degrees of contact among their parents, friends, and their friends' parents, as well as high levels of interaction with nonfamily adults, were less deviant and higher in academic achievement than their peers who were less socially integrated. However, neighborhood effects were evident, with positive effects present only when the neighborhoods were "positive". In poor neighborhoods, integration produced negative effects. Moreover, the quality of parenting received by other children in the network influences children's own social outcomes. When the majority of parents in the network were authoritative in their child-rearing, adolescents had lower levels of deviant behavior (e.g., substance abuse), especially when adolescents perceived their own parents as authoritative as well (Fletcher, Darling, Steinberg, & Dornbusch, 1995). While more detailed and precise measures of network closure are needed, this focus on the overlap of networks and its link with children's social outcome is a promising one.

Several other studies suggest that the quality of adult social networks do, in fact, relate to children's social behavior. In an Australian study, Homel, Burns, and Goodnow (1987) found positive relations between the number of "dependable" friends that parents report and 11-year-old children's self-rated happiness, the number of regular playmates, and maternal ratings of children's social skills. Second, parents' affiliation with various types of formal community organizations was related to children's happiness, school adjustment, and social skills. Unfortunately, the reliance on self-reports limits the value of these findings, but they do support the importance of parental, or at least maternal, social networks as a factor in potentially affecting children's social relationships. Recently, O'Neil, Lee, Parke, and Wang (submitted for publication) extended this work by showing a relation between parents' enjoyment of friends in their network and peer ratings of social competence. The more parents enjoyed their friends, the less the child was disliked and perceived as aggressive by peers. Moreover, the more contact that parents had with relatives, the less disliked children were by their peers. Finally, these investigators found that maternal and paternal social networks have distinctive links to children's social relationships. Fathers who rated their networks as less enjoyable had children who were more aggressive and more disliked by peers, whereas the less contact that mothers had with their friends, the higher teachers rated their children on avoidance of interaction with other children.

The role that parents' own social network plays as a source of opportunities for children to develop relationships and practice social skills with peers is likely to diminish over the course of children's development as youngsters become more active arrangers of their own social lives. Older children, however, may continue to learn styles of interaction with peers by observing their parents' attitudes toward and behavioral styles with network members. Thus, we would continue to anticipate some positive associations between the indices of relationship quality between parents' and youngsters' social networks.

Finally, the quality of the relationship that adults develop with friends in their social network is an important correlate of their children's friendship quality. Doyle and Markiewicz (1996) found that mothers who reported having supportive friends had children who experienced more closeness with their best friend. Or, if mothers felt less secure about their best friendship or rated their friends as interesting, their own children were more likely to have a best friend. The findings concerning the links between lack of mothers' security about their friendships is consistent with earlier work on maternal recollections of their childhood peer experiences. In this work, Putallaz, Costanzo, and Smith (1991) found that mothers who had anxious peer relations as children had children who were more socially competent, which supports a compensatory model of parenting. More recently, Simpkins and Parke (submitted for publication) found that the quality of both maternal and paternal friendships was related to children's friendship quality. However, the quality of the parents' best friendship was a better predictor of daughters' friendships, while both the quality of the parents' best friendship and the breadth of their social network were predictive of sons' friendships. As these studies illustrate, the quality and scope of adult friendships and social networks are important correlates not just of children's peer competence but of their friendship qualities as well.

CONTRIBUTIONS OF THE MARITAL DYAD TO CHILDREN'S UNDERSTANDING OF CLOSE RELATIONSHIPS

In the preceding section, parents were conceptualized as active influences, both directly and indirectly, on the development of children's social competence and understanding of relationships. Considerable evidence emerged in support of the parent–child relationship as a primary socializing influence on children's social development, in general, and on the development of specific relationship skills. However, children's experiences in families extend beyond their interactions with parents. As outlined in Dunn (1988a), evidence suggests that children's understanding of relationships also is shaped through their active participation in other family subsystems (e.g., child–sibling) as well as through exposure to the interactions of other dyadic subsystems (e.g., parent–parent) or participation in triadic relationships (e.g., child–sib–parent, child–parent–parent).

Influence of Marital Satisfaction and Discord on Child Outcomes: Phase I Research

Several decades of investigation have amassed considerable evidence indicating that dimensions of marital functioning are related to aspects of children's long-term overall adjustment and immediate coping responses in the face of interparental conflict. Although the size of the associations is not always large, a range of studies link marital discord and conflict to outcomes in children that are likely to impair the quality of interpersonal relationships, including antisocial behavior, internalizing and externalizing behavior problems, and changes in cognitions, emotions, and physiology in response to exposure to marital conflict (Erel & Burman, 1995). Although less empirical work has been directed specifically toward examination of the "carry-over" of exposure to marital conflict to the quality of children's relationships with significant others such as peers and siblings, a body of literature is beginning to emerge which indicates that exposure to marital discord is associated with poor social competence and problematic peer relationships (Katz & Gottman, 1991; Kerig, 1996).

Mechanisms Linking Marital Discord to Children's Adjustment: Phase II Research

Until recently, theoretical frameworks typically conceptualized marital discord as an indirect influence on children's adjustment that operated through its effect on family functioning and the quality of parenting (Fauber & Long, 1991). Factors that include affective changes in the quality of the parent–child relationship, lack of emotional availability, and adoption of less optimal parenting styles each have been implicated as potential mechanisms through which marital discord disrupts parenting processes. In one investigation, for example, Katz and Kahen (1993) found that when parents used a mutually hostile pattern of conflict resolution, fathers were more likely to be intrusive and children were more likely to express anger during a parent–child interaction task. In addition, fathers' intrusiveness predicted more negative peer play and more aggressive play with a best friend. Interestingly, this study also suggests that an individual parent's style of handling conflict may be related to the quality of their *partner*'s relationships with children in the family. When fathers were angry and withdrawn in a conflict resolution task, mothers were more critical and intrusive during interactions with their child. Maternal criticism and intrusiveness, in turn, was associated with unresponsiveness or "tuning out" by the child during mother–child interactions and higher levels of teacher-rated internalizing symptoms. Similarly, Cowan, Cowan, Schulz, and Hemming (1994) examined the influence of marital quality on children's social adaptation to kindergarten with results suggesting evidence of both direct and indirect links to children's social adjustment. Interestingly, internalizing difficulties (e.g., shy/withdrawn qualities) were predicted by the influences of marital functioning on parenting quality, whereas externalizing difficulties (e.g., aggressive/antisocial qualities) were predicted directly by qualities of marital interaction.

Family systems theory suggests that not only does marital discord interfere with dimensions of the mother–child or father–child relationship, it also may impair qualities of the mother–father–child triadic relationship by interfering with the effectiveness of how the mother and father work together with the child. In a study that examined the contribution of marital adjustment to the effectiveness of joint mother–father supportiveness, Westerman and Schonholtz (1993) found that fathers', but not mothers', reports of marital disharmony and disaffection were significantly related to the effectiveness of joint parental support toward their children's problem-solving efforts. Joint parental support was, in turn, related to fathers' and teachers' reports of children's behavior problems. Men's lack of involvement in the triadic family process could account for these findings. As Gottman (1994) has shown, women tend to engage and confront, while men tend to withdraw, in the face of marital disharmony.

Despite considerable progress in elucidating specific parenting processes that are impaired by interparental conflict, a number of systematic investigations suggest that parental conflict also is associated with behavior problems independent of its influence on the parent–child relationship (Jenkins & Smith, 1991). Recently, models that view the influence of marital discord on children's adjustment as being primarily *indirect* have been challenged on a number of conceptual and methodological grounds (Davies & Cummings, 1994; Fincham, 1998), stimulating considerable empirical interest in the examination of the *direct effects* of exposure to marital distress on children's adjustment. Accordingly, in the past five years, the focus of attention has turned to elucidating specific processes by which the marital relationship itself directly influences children's immediate functioning and long-term adjustment. As Fincham (1998) notes, "recent studies that simultaneously estimate indirect and direct effects show that both occur (e.g., Harold, Fincham, Osborne, & Conger, 1997) and shift the question to one of determining how indirect and direct effects interact" (1998, p. 545). A parallel research trajectory over the past several years has been movement away from studies that focus on global measures of marital satisfaction or adjustment to studies that focus on more specific aspects of marital interaction, particularly aspects of marital conflict, in order to identify the dimensions of the marital relationship that are most likely to influence children's immediate cognitive, emotional, and physiological functioning. These immediate responses or "microprocesses", in turn, have been hypothesized to be critical links to children's long-term social adjustment in the face of interparental conflict (Fincham, 1998).

Although the investigation of these questions is considered by Fincham (1998) to be underdeveloped at this point, a number of promising directions appear destined to shed considerable light on processes by which exposure to marital conflict may influence children's interpersonal competence, social adjustment, and interpersonal understanding. Analog studies, for example, have become a useful experimental methodology for systematically varying dimensions of interadult conflict in order to assess their influence on the immediate cognitive and emotional functioning of children. Such studies have begun to show that the form of expression of marital conflict plays a critical role in how children react. A recent review of the literature (Davies & Cummings, 1994) indicated that several aspects of parental conflict appear to be relatively consistently associated with poor outcomes for children. More frequent interparental conflict and more intense or violent forms of conflict have been found to be particularly disturbing to children and likely to be associated with externalizing and internalizing difficulties. Grych, Seid, and Fincham (1992), for example, found that children who were exposed to an audiotaped analog of marital interaction responded with distress, shame, and self-blame to intensely angry adult exchanges. Davies and Cummings's review also indicated that conflict which was child-related in content was more likely than conflict involving other content to be associated with behavior problems in children. Indeed, in an analog study conducted by Grych and Fincham (1993), when the content of the conflict was child-related, children reported greater shame, responsibility, self-blame, and fear of being drawn into the conflict.

Other studies suggest that resolution of conflict, even when it was not viewed by the child, reduces children's negative reactions to exposure to interadult anger and conflict. Exposure to unresolved conflict, for example, has been found to be associated with negative affect and poor coping responses in children (Cummings, Ballard, El-Sheikh, & Lake, 1991). In addition, the manner in which conflict is resolved may also influence children's adjustment. Katz and Gottman (1993), for example, found that couples who exhibited a hostile style of resolving conflict had children who tended to be described by teachers as exhibiting antisocial characteristics. When husbands were angry and emotionally distant while resolving marital conflict, children were described by teachers as anxious and socially withdrawn.

Conflict is inevitable in most parental relationships and is not detrimental to family relationships and children's functioning under all circumstances. In particular, as recent work suggests, disagreements that are extremely intense and involve threat to the child are likely to be more disturbing to the child. In contrast, when conflict is expressed constructively, is moderate in degree, is expressed in the context of a warm and supportive family environment, and shows evidence of resolution, children may learn valuable lessons regarding how to negotiate conflict and resolve disagreements (Davies & Cummings, 1994).

Less well understood at this point in time are the specific emotion regulatory and cognitive- processing mechanisms through which exposure to interparental conflict is "carried over" into children's understanding of close relationships and social competence with others (see Mills & Piotrowski, in this volume). Two recent conceptual frameworks have emerged, however, that reflect promising new paradigms from which to examine these "carry over" questions. Using a cognitive-conceptual model derived from the stress and coping field, Grych and Fincham (1990) focus on the cognitive and affective meaning that exposure to conflict has for the child. They suggest that certain dimensions of interparental conflict (e.g., intensity and content of conflict) and contextual factors (e.g., family emotional climate, past history) are used by the child to appraise or interpret the personal relevance of interadult conflict. In this model, three appraisals influence the child's coping responses to interparental conflict, comprising the level of perceived threat to the child, the child's perceived coping efficacy, and causal attributions and ascription of blame made by the child. Over time, a family environment that is characterized by high interparental conflict may play a role in the development of children's cognitive models of familial and extrafamilial relationships by exposing children to hostile and negative interpretations of interpersonal experiences and social situations (Cummings & Davies, 1994) and by undermining the child's sense of efficacy in regard to how to cope in social situations with peers and significant others. Further, children who are exposed to chronic levels of intense, unresolved conflict also may feel the threat of imminent separation which may influence children's responses in the face of conflict. Katz and Gottman (1993) and others have suggested that in extremely conflict-ridden marriages, children's externalizing behaviors may be an attempt to divert attention onto themselves and away from marital problems in order to circumvent divorce or separation.

Although little empirical work has examined these links, some evidence exists to suggest that the quality of the marital relationship may shape the cognitive dimensions of the family climate. Parents who report more satisfaction with their marriages have been found to speak in longer utterances to their children and to encourage more cognitive participation by the child in family conversations (Pratt, Kerig, Cowan, & Cowan, 1992). A number of studies suggest that spouses in discordant marriages are more likely than those in happy marriages to focus on negative aspects of interactions with their partners, to overlook positive behaviors, and to attribute their partners' behaviors to hostile intentions (Bradbury & Fincham, 1989). Children who are exposed to marital discord may develop similar attribution processes in response to interactions with significant others. A number of researchers also have suggested that modeling of negative behavior patterns that children observe when exposed to marital conflict may be an important mechanism through which nonadaptive interaction styles are transmitted to children (Easterbrooks & Emde, 1988; Katz & Gottman, 1993).

In a model that builds on the cognitive-contextual framework, Davies and Cummings (1994) downplay cognitive factors and emphasize the primacy of emotions as organizers of interpersonal experience. In an extension of the literature linking attachment security in the parent–child relationship and quality of emotional functioning (see prior section), they propose that emotional security also derives from the quality of the marital relationship. They posit that the emotion-laden quality of marital conflict contributes to emotionality playing a primary role relative to cognitive processes in determining how children react to interparent conflict. They hypothesize that some forms of conflict are more likely than others to threaten the emotional security of the child and interfere with the ability to cope effectively with ongoing stresses and challenges. More specifically, they propose that several interrelated processes account for the impact of emotional security on children's functioning. First, emotional security affects the ability of the child to regulate his or her own emotions. Second, emotional security influences the child's motivation to intervene to regulate the behavior of their parents. Third, they postulate that emotional security affects the cognitive appraisals and internal representations of family relationships that are made by children. In a direct test of the model, Davies and Cummings (1998) assessed the links among children's emotional security, level of destructive and constructive marital functioning, and children's internalizing and externalizing behaviors. As predicted by the emotional security model, the links between marital discord and children's internalizing symptoms were mediated by measures of emotional security. In this study, emotional security/insecurity was indexed by the level of emotional reactivity in response to simulated conflict involving the mother and a stranger and the positive/negative internal representation of the marital relationship. Only partial support was found for the mediational role of emotional security between marital discord and children's externalizing symptoms. In this case, only the emotional reactivity measure of emotional security served as a mediator. In spite of the support found for this model, emotional security accounted for only half of the variance in the links between conflict-ridden marital functioning and children's symptoms. Moreover, direct paths from marital conflict to children's outcomes, especially internalizing symptoms, were still evident.

Other evidence supports the role that chronic, intense marital conflict plays in undermining children's emotion regulatory abilities. Gottman and Katz (1989) hypothesized that chronic marital tension might influence children by activating physiological processes and generating in the child a "flooding" of sadness and anger in response to the conflict. Activation of the autonomic system and chronic emotional flooding, in turn, were hypothesized to interfere with the development of emotion regulation skills and promote avoidance of high-level interaction styles with others. They found that maritally-distressed couples employed a parenting style that was cold, unresponsive, angry, and low in limit-setting and structuring. Children who were exposed to this style of parenting exhibited high levels of stress hormones and displayed more anger and noncompliance. In addition, these children tended to play at low levels with peers and displayed more negative peer interactions. Not all problematic marriages are similar, however. Some problematic marriages are likely to be characterized by lower levels of openly-expressed anger and hostility and higher levels of active withdrawal from interaction. The findings from other recent work suggest that children in marriages characterized by withdrawal, rather than interaction accompanied by anger, react differently (Katz & Gottman, 1993). These authors argue that withdrawal may be even more stressful for children than an angry but engaged marital relationship.

Although more work is clearly needed before conclusions can be drawn regarding the mechanisms through which interparental conflict influences children's understanding of relationships, a number of potential mechanisms have been suggested and the challenge for future work lies in applying these models to empirical investigations of the links between children's exposure to interparental interaction and the development of their own relationship skills.

CONTRIBUTION OF SIBLINGS TO CHILDREN'S UNDERSTANDING OF CLOSE RELATIONSHIPS

Rich and extensive descriptions of the normative patterns that characterize sibling relationships over the course of development (Buhrmester & Furman, 1990; Dunn, 1988a, b) suggest that, in addition to parents, siblings may play a critical role in the development of children's understanding of interpersonal relationships. A number of studies indicate that most children are likely to spend more time in direct interaction with siblings than with parents and significant others and that interactions with siblings provide a context for the expression of a range of positive social behaviors including friendly, cooperative exchanges, joint fantasy play, shared humor, and discussions about feelings as well as numerous conflictual encounters and experiences with conflict resolution (Dunn, 1988a, b). Further, this rich array of interactions between siblings has been found to be typified by greater emotional intensity than the behavioral exchanges that characterize other relationships (Katz, Kramer, & Gottman, 1992).

Sibling relationships have been hypothesized to contribute to children's understanding of relationships in a number of significant ways. A social learning framework analogous to the one posited to explain parental contributions to the development of children's social competence (Parke, MacDonald, Burks, Carson, Bhavnagri, Barth, & Beitel, 1989), predicts that through their interactions with siblings, children develop specific interaction patterns and social understanding skills that generalize to relationships with other children (McCoy, Brody, & Stoneman, 1994). In addition, relationships with siblings also may provide a context in which children can practice the skills and interaction styles that have been learned from parents or others (McCoy et al., 1994). Older siblings function as tutors, managers, or supervisors of their younger brother or sister's behavior during social interactions and may function as gatekeepers who extend or limit opportunities to interact with other children outside of the family (Edwards & Whiting, 1993). Also paralleling the indirect influence that the observation of parent–parent interaction has on what children learn about relationships, a second important avenue of influence on children's developing understanding of relationships is children's observation of parents interacting with siblings.

Siblings as Socializing Influences: Phase I Research

Children's experiences with siblings provide a context in which interaction patterns and social understanding skills may generalize to relationships with other children (McCoy, Brody, & Stoneman, 1994). According to Stocker and Dunn (1990), interactions with siblings provide a setting in which children "develop social understanding skills which may enable them to form particularly close relationships with a child of their choice, a close friend." We begin, again, with an examination of descriptive studies that address the question of whether systematic links exist between sib–sib relationships and other relationships that children develop. In general, there appears to be a mixed body of evidence in support of links between sib–sib patterns of interaction and interaction styles that develop in the context of friendships and more general peer relationships. The pattern of findings from the small, but growing, number of studies provide a modest and somewhat inconsistent picture of the connections between children's patterns of interacting with siblings and patterns of interacting with peers (see Parke & O'Neil, 1997, for a fuller review of this work). Some studies report modest evidence of a straightforward "carry-over" of interaction styles between children's relationships with siblings and peers. For example, Hetherington (1988) found that when children's relationships with their siblings were described as hostile and alienated as opposed to warm and companionate, they evidenced poorer peer relationships and other behavior problems. Others report little evidence of a carryover effect between siblings and peers. Abramovitch, Corter, Pepler, and Stanhope (1986), for example, found little evidence that patterns of sibling interaction were related to the interaction styles of children with a friend. Older siblings are more likely to assume dominant roles such as managers of activities and teachers during the course of their interactions with siblings, whereas the same children were more likely to adopt an equalitarian style during interactions with friends. Putallaz and Sheppard (1992) have posited that children with adequate social skills exhibit cross-situational specificity by adapting to the specific demands of each social relationship—behaving in a more reciprocal equalitarian manner with classmates and in a more asymmetric, hierarchical fashion with siblings. In contrast, among children who lack social competence, deficits in social skills such as heightened aggressiveness and inability to initiate interaction will generalize across sibling and peer contexts.

Finally, the sibling relationship may play a role in compensating for other problematic relationships by providing an alternative context for experiencing satisfying social relationships and protecting children from the development of adjustment difficulties. East and Rook (1992) found that children who were socially isolated in their peer relationships were buffered from adjustment problems when they reported positive relationships with a favorite sibling. Similarly, Stocker (1994) reported support for the compensatory role of at least one positive relationship (either sibling, friend, or mother) as protection from the development of behavioral conduct difficulties.

Because a system of multiple family relationships typically antedates children's significant relationships outside the family, frameworks for studying the links between children's significant relationships have tended to emphasize the carry-over from parental and sibling relationships to relationships with friends and peers. Kramer and Gottman (1992) examined the role that positive relationships with peers play in children's adaptation to the birth of a new sibling. The findings from this study indicated that children who displayed a more positive interaction style with a best friend and who were better able to manage conflict and negative affect, behaved more positively toward their new sibling at both 6 months and 14 months. Further, the results of path analyses led Kramer and Gottman to speculate that management of conflict, a skill that is particularly useful when interacting with siblings, may be more likely to be learned in interactions with peers than in direct interactions with parents.

Mechanisms that Explain Links between Sibling Relationships and Children's Relationships outside the Family: Moving Toward Phase II Research

Although these studies present only a modest pattern of evidence in support of the generalization concerning links between sibling subsystems and children's styles of interacting in other significant relationships, this work sets the scene for important future work that will shed light on the contexts under which strong, weak, or compensatory connections might be expected between relationship systems as well as the processes through which children's experiences with siblings are translated into relationship skills that are used in other relationships. The findings from existing studies suggest, for example, that greater generalization of hostile, aggressive interaction styles in both sibling and peer systems may emerge when children lack adequate relationship skills (Putallaz & Sheppard, 1992) or when children are experiencing stressful, negative family relationships (Dunn, 1993). In contrast, under other circumstances, the associations between sibling relationships and relationships outside the family may be moderated by a number of features that uniquely characterize each relationship. Dunn (1993) has pointed out, for example, that friendship involves a mutual and reciprocated relationship with another individual, whereas siblings do not necessarily feel this way about one another. She also notes that in contrast to sib–sib relationships, friend and peer relationships represent a more unique combination of backgrounds, experiences, and temperaments that may generate interaction styles that are the result of two unique individuals' approach to relationships. Further, there appear to be different role expectations for sib and friend relationships that may differentially influence interaction styles. For example, reason and negotiation appear to be more common in peer interactions than sibling interactions (Dunn, 1993). Finally, a number of factors such as birth order and birth spacing appear to play an important role in determining the relative level of competency and the balance between leader/follower roles in sibling relationships, which may influence the extent of correspondence expected between sibling and peer relationship styles. The challenge of future work will be to more systematically examine the moderating and mediating influences of these factors in order to better unravel normative patterns of associations between sibling and peer relationships.

Siblings as Managers of Children's Social Lives

Just as parents function as managers of children's social lives, siblings in many cultures perform similar management functions in relation to their younger siblings. Cross-cultural work indicates that in both African and Polynesian cultures children, especially girls, become involved in sibling caretaking activities at a relatively early age (Edwards & Whiting, 1993). Relatively little is known, however, about the caregiving role of siblings in contemporary Euro-American families. Whiting and Whiting's (1975) study of patterns of sibling interaction in New England families suggests that formal caregiving responsibilities may not be as common in American culture as in other cultures. However, Bryant (1989) suggests that although parents may not formally assign caretaking duties to children, children frequently voluntarily assume the roles of caretaker, tutor, and teacher of younger siblings and make unique contributions to the socialization of young children. Most work examining these roles has focused on the influence that instruction from older siblings may have on children's cognitive development (e.g., Rogoff, 1990), and has only infrequently focused on children's social development. Although some work exists which suggests that children actively request advice from their older siblings and that siblings are viewed as sources of counsel and support (see Dunn, 1993), relatively little is known about the role that siblings play as supervisors, managers, or advisors of children's social lives and the influence that this may have on the development of children's knowledge of relationships. Given the amount of time that most children spend in the company of siblings, this is an area that clearly is ripe for future empirical investigation.

Beyond the Sibling Dyad—Children's Observations of Parental Interactions with Siblings

Not only are children active participants in relationships, but they also spend time observing the interactions of other family subsystems, and these experiences appear to provide an important indirect avenue for learning about relationships. Just as children have been found to be particularly attentive to affectively-charged interactions between parents, a number of studies indicate that children attend to the interactions that occur between parents and siblings (Dunn, 1993). Again, parallel to the findings that focus on children's responses to parent–parent interaction, children appear to be particularly attentive to parent–sibling interactions that involve the expression of affect (e.g., disputes or games) and actively attempt to intervene in these interactions in order to draw attention to themselves (Dunn, 1993). Further, as family systems theory predicts, the birth of a sibling has been linked to changes in the relationship between mother (or father) and the firstborn child, with changes being moderated by the quality of the parent–child relationship and gender of the firstborn child (Howe & Ross, 1990). In families with firstborn girls, if the mother–daughter relationship was particularly positive before the birth of the sibling, a more hostile relationship was likely to develop between the firstborn daughter and her sibling. In contrast, when mother and daughter had a more conflictual relationship, siblings were more likely to have a close, friendly relationship with one another one year later (Dunn & Kendrick, 1982). Interestingly, just as the negative impact of marital conflict appears to be ameliorated when parents have conversations with the child regarding the conflict (Fincham, 1998), parental management strategies are likely to moderate the child's reaction to a new sibling, perhaps by actively influencing the child's attribution processes. Dunn and Kendrick (1982) found that if the mother used conversation to help the child think of his/her infant sibling in more positive way (for example, by focusing on the infant as an individual with needs and feelings), the child reacted in a more positive way. These findings suggest that close monitoring and sensitivity to relative differences in relationships begin to emerge early in children's significant relationships, and social comparison and cognitive-attributional processes may play an important role in how information about relationships is processed. These findings suggest, once again, that "carry-over" or generalization of positive dimensions of one relationship to other significant relationships may be too simple a mechanism to explain links between relationships. Several other principles seem relevant. First, social comparison processes appear to be operating that foster in children an understanding of the uniqueness of relationships and that may give children opportunities to learn about complex emotions such as jealousy and rivalry. Second, from an early age, children appear to take an active role in the construction of their relationships and may actively seek out positive relationships as alternatives to problematic or negative relationships.

More fruitful investigation of the links between relationships as well as a better understanding of the processes through which children come to understand the uniqueness of specific social relationships may come with movement from a socialization framework to a relationships framework. Dunn (1993) points out that one disadvantage of a socialization approach is that it examines when and how social competence and social understanding are generalized from parent–child relationships to other relationships, but it does not adequately take into account the fact that even when a child acquires social competencies through interactions in one relationship, he/she may not be motivated to apply these skills in another relationship. In contrast, a relationships perspective takes into account the fact that each relationship reflects a unique set of demands and rewards as well as different challenges to a child's socio-cognitive abilities. This perspective may lead to the generation of questions concerning the unique aspects of the child (e.g., temperament, attachment security, self-confidence), the relationship partner, the dynamic of the relationship itself, and the broader social ecology (e.g., family stress, life transitions) and how they may contribute to a child being motivated or disinclined to behave in a socially competent manner. As Dunn points out, the goal is to specify "for *which* children, at *which* stages of development, *which* dimensions of particular relationships are likely to show associations with other relationships" (1993, p.121).

PUTTING THE PIECES TOGETHER: TOWARD A MULTIPLE SOURCES MODEL OF RELATIONSHIP LEARNING

Our family systems viewpoint argues for the construction of a comprehensive model in which the contribution of parent–child, parent–parent, and sibling relationships are all recognized. Figure 2.1 outlines a comprehensive model of how children learn about social relationships from significant family members. To date, few studies have simultaneously addressed how these subsystems combine to produce their impact on children's relationship learning (see Katz, Kramer, & Gottman, 1992 for recent exceptions). Little is known about the

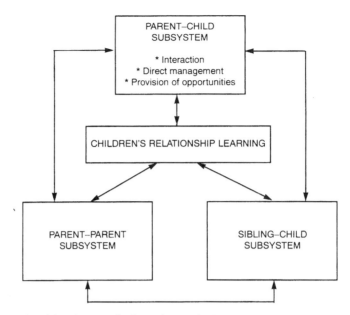

Figure 2.1   Model indicating the hypothesized relations among family subsystems and children's relationship learning

relative weighting of parent–child relationships versus other family relationships. Nor do we understand how the impact of these different relationships changes as the child develops. The most crucial issue remains, namely, the specification of the pathways through which these different relationships exert their influence. It is evident from our model that multiple pathways are possible and there is support for both direct and mediated effects. As noted earlier, marital relationships exert both direct (e.g., witnessed effects) and indirect (e.g., marital relationships influence parent-child patterns) effects. Similarly, parent–child relationships could influence marital relationships. For example, a disciplinary encounter with a difficult-to-control child could, in turn, trigger a marital conflict due to disagreement about the child's misbehavior or management of the child, the carry-over of negative mood or the alignment of parent and child against a third party. Less is known about the impact of parent–child relationships on marital interactions than the reverse effects.

Moreover, recent research has begun to identify individual differences across families or family typologies (Bell & Bell, 1989; Dickstein, Siefer, Hayden, Schiller, Sameroff, Keitner, Miller, Rasmussen, Matzko, & Magee, 1998) as well as at the level of family subsystems, such as marital dyads (Gottman, 1994). As a next step, can we characterize families usefully in terms of the relative importance of various subsystems? Some families may invest heavily in directly parenting their children, but tend to protect their children from their marital problems. Earlier evidence suggests that exposure to marital conflict is higher for boys than girls (Cummings & Davies, 1994;

Hetherington, Hagan, & Anderson, 1989). Similarly, some families may encourage close sib–sib relationships, while others tend to encourage sibs to
form separate social spheres. In turn, this kind of social arrangement will
result in different types of relationship learning.

Do all combinations produce equally socially competent children or are
some ingredients in this mix more important than others? Do different combinations produce different, but equally well-adjusted children in terms of
their social relationships? Can children in a family with a poor marriage
compensate by investing "relationship energy" into another subsystem such
as the sib–sib or parent–child systems? Studies of divorce (Hetherington,
Hagan, & Anderson, 1989) suggest that a close sib–sib relationship can help
buffer children during a stressful divorce.

CONCLUSIONS AND UNRESOLVED ISSUES

This chapter reflects considerable progress in our understanding of how children learn about social relationships. However, progress is clearly uneven
across the significant family subsystems that we have examined. Much more is
known about the impact of the parent–child relationship than of other relationships, such as the marital and sibling relationships, on children's relationship learning. Similarly, our understanding of the ways in which the
subsystems are linked and how they operate together to produce their effects
remain limited.

The multidirectionality of influence is often included in our models but less
often empirically evaluated. This concept of multidirectionality can take several forms. Within the family itself, the interplay among the subsystems needs
more attention. As noted above, the mutual influence of parenting and marriage or sibling relationships needs more attention, instead of assuming that
the direction of influence is usually singular (e.g., from marital interaction to
parenting). Even when these subsystem links are more clearly understood, the
assumption remains that the direction of influence flows from the family to
extra-familial relationships. Although there is considerable evidence that
extra-familial social friends and social networks have an impact on parent–
child relationships (Belsky, 1984), we rarely explore this issue with children.
What is the impact of children's extra-familial relationships with friends, peers
and relatives on their family relationships? As has been found in several
studies, for example, children's relationships with peers/friends can influence
their adjustment to a new sibling (Kramer & Gottman, 1992) and their relationships with their parents (Repetti, 1996).

Distinctions need to be made between short-term and long-term opportunities for learning about relationships. The vast majority of research has
focused on long-term models in which the effects of stable family influences
(e.g., interaction style, management style, disciplinary views, marital satisfaction) are addressed and their relationships to some relatively enduring aspect
of the child's relationship with other children are measured. In contrast, little

attention has been devoted to short-term effects of fluctuations in either family functioning on peer relationships or peer experiences on the child's relationships in the family. The Repetti (1996) study is a good example of the impact of short-term shifts in the quality of peer relationships on subsequent experiences with family members. On the family side, what is the impact of being involved in an argument with a sibling or parent prior to going to school on subsequent peer relationships? Events in which the target child is directly involved (e.g., argument with a friend, conflict with sibling) and events that are witnessed (e.g., watching a friend receive an injury or an insult at school, witnessing mother–father or parent–sibling conflict) are both worth examination.

It is also important to distinguish between micro and macro level changes. In the Repetti work, for example, short-term (micro) shifts were studied, but less is known about the long-term impact of these repeated micro events on changes in relationships. Do these repeated school-based negative events lead to a change in the nature of parent–child relationships? To take a further example, does a child who develops a close friendship relationship, but who has a poor relationship with their parents, over time develop a better parent–child relationship?

Another issue that needs attention is the specification of the conditions under which children learn similar rather than complementary lessons about relationships from significant others. The bulk of the evidence suggests that most children learn to adopt similar styles and models of relationships. However, there is other evidence from adults which suggests that they compensate for their earlier, often poor, relationships by developing a very different approach to relationships. Involved fathers, for example, often report that their own fathers were uninvolved and their current views of father–child relationships are in response to their own relationship history (Parke, 1996). The factors that promote similarity versus compensatory relationships are not well understood.

In addition, a variety of temporary stressors of moderate duration merit exploration as well. The impact of divorce, parental job loss, or residential relocation may affect the quality of children's peer relationships. For example, Hetherington, Cox, and Cox (1979) found a significant deleterious impact of divorce on the peer relationships of preschool-age children, especially boys. Similarly, Ladd et al. (1988) found that families with two incomes and relatively stable residences (fewer moves) tended to have larger peer networks. More work on the impact of different types of family stress is needed, and Patterson and her colleagues (Patterson, Griesler, Vaden, & Kupersmidt, 1992) as well as Conger and Elder (1994) have made substantial progress along these lines, especially concerning the impact of family socioeconomic circumstances on children's peer relationships.

A developmental analysis of these issues is clearly needed. As other research suggests (Collins & Russell, 1991), the direction of influence between parent and child is more balanced across development, as issues of autonomy become of more central importance to the child and adolescent. Even fundamental descriptive data concerning the ways in which different interactive strategies or managerial processes shift across development are lacking at this point. More importantly, the ways in which the family strategies (e.g., as interactive partner, manager, or direct tutor) relate to social relational competence at different points in the child's development merit investigation.

How do parents of different ages manage their children's social relationships? Recent data suggests that late-timed fathers, who began their childrearing in their mid-thirties, have different styles of interaction from early-timed fathers, and are less physical and more cognitively oriented in their interaction styles (Neville & Parke, 1997; Parke & Neville, 1995). How do these differences alter children's social relationships? Similarly, late-timed mothers are more likely to continue employment outside the home than early-timed mothers (Daniels & Weingarten, 1982). How is their greater use of day care likely to alter children's social relationships?

A major concern is our limited understanding of the generalizability of the processes that have been discussed. Little is known about how variations in ethnicity, race, and class influence how families teach their children about social relationships (see Parke & Buriel, 1998). Variations across ethnic lines represent important opportunities not only to explore the universality of processes and mechanisms, but also provide naturally occurring variations in the relative salience of certain key determinants such as interactive style or emotional expressiveness. As we become aware of our own cultural diversity, it becomes important that we begin to make a serious commitment to an exploration of this diversity—both theoretically and through systematic empirical inquiry. The search for a balance between processes that are universal and processes that are unique to a particular cultural, racial, or ethnic group represents an important challenge for the future (see also Schneider, Smith, Poisson & Kwan, this volume).

The range of influence agents that play a role in shaping children's social relationships needs to be expanded. Grandparents and other extended kin provide models and guidelines about social relationships and their contribution needs more attention in future research (Tinsley & Parke, 1984; Smith, 1995).

In sum, families play an important role in children's relationship learning, but only by focusing on the interplay among the subsystems are we going to advance our understanding of this issue.

ACKNOWLEDGEMENTS

Preparation of this chapter was supported in part by National Science Foundation Grant SBR 9308941 to Ross D. Parke and National Institute of Child Health and Human Development Grant R01 HD32391 to Ross D. Parke and Robin O'Neil. Thanks to Heather Guzman for her preparation of the manuscript.

Chapter 3

The Emotional Side of Sharing, Social Support, and Conflict Negotiation between Siblings and between Friends

Maria von Salisch

Freie Universität Berlin

Children's relationships with other children are often intensely emotional. Even a cursory glance at infants' delight when imitating their siblings' sounds, at preschoolers' serious faces when fighting over a toy, or at children's exuberant movements when engaged in high-spirited horseplay reveals how deeply emotional children's relationships with their companions can be. Other examples come easily to mind, such as primary school children gossiping over the "disgusting" characteristics of specific classmates, or preadolescent chums discussing incidents which caused embarrassment to themselves or others. Indeed, one could make the point that the intensity (intense vs. weak), the variability (restricted to few vs. ranging freely across the whole range of emotions), and the social desirability (little vs. much) of the emotions expressed as well as the ability to share, negotiate and resolve (conflicting) feelings are indicators of the quality of children's relationships

The Developmental Psychology of Personal Relationships.
Edited by Rosemary S. L. Mills and Steve Duck. © 2000 John Wiley & Sons Ltd.

with other children. Failure to study the emotional processes involved in these relationships would mean missing a good part of children's experience in their lives.

Studying children's emotional development without embedding it in their interpersonal relationships would be equally deficient, for the following reasons (von Salisch & Bänninger-Huber, 1994): (1) From the first day of life children are social beings who orient to other people. The emotions communicated through face, voice, gestures, and movements play an important role in the development of the infant's self (Stern, 1986) as well as in the establishment of attachment relationships. (2) Emotions can be defined as "processes of establishing, maintaining, or disrupting the relations between the person and the internal or external environment, when such relations are significant to the individual" (Campos, Campos, & Barrett, 1990). Since interpersonal relationships are important to most people, many emotions arise in the context of relationships (Scherer, Wallbott, & Summerfield, 1986), particularly in those with close associates. In his classic treatise on anger, Averill (1982) concluded that among adults anger was elicited in more than half of the cases by a "loved one" or by "someone you know well and like". (3) Emotion regulation takes place not only within the individual but also in interpersonal relationships. People influence each other in the perception and experience of their feelings. Processes such as emotion socialization or social support are unthinkable without (close) interpersonal relationships. (4) In face-to-face interactions people shape each other's behavior and attitudes, often without being aware that they are doing so. Simple reinforcement (Malatesta & Haviland, 1982) as well as more complex phenomena such as attunement (Stern, 1986), responsivity, or empathy can best be understood in the context of interactions with long-term relationship partners, such as family members and friends (Saarni, Mumme, & Campos, 1998).

Emotional processes in friendships and sibling relationships play a significant role in social and emotional development because siblings, peers, and friends seem to play a more important part in children's growing up than has been assumed so far (J.R. Harris, 1995). Many of the regulatory processes which have been described between parents and children are likely to take place between siblings as well: older siblings are likely to selectively reinforce their baby sibling's smiles and other signs of enjoyment (Malatesta & Haviland, 1982), are likely to be sources of social referencing (Sorce, Emde, Campos, & Klinnert, 1985) when parents are not available, and can comfort their younger siblings when they are sad or upset over their mother's absence (Teti & Ablard, 1989). There is, however, an important difference between parent–child and child–child relationships: relationships between children, who are not too far apart in age, are characterized by symmetrical reciprocity (Youniss, 1980). Because of the reciprocal nature of these relationships, children will face unique challenges about the expression and regulation of emotion within these relationships (Brown & Dunn, 1992). No mother, for example, would seriously "dare" her child to jump from a wall in order to show that he is not afraid of heights, whereas a peer might do so. Other implications of reciprocal relationships for children's emotional development will be discussed below.

These and other considerations speak to the need for a systematic investigation of the emotional processes involved not only in children's relationships with their parents but also in those with other children. What such investigation requires is a change in perspective; that is, a reconceptualization of the emotional mechanisms underlying some of the phenomena in children's relationship research which have been described in the past. The following overview will focus on two child–child relationships, namely children's relationships with their siblings and with their friends. Siblings and friends are both peers insofar as they are members of the same generation (von Salisch, 1996), but they differ from "ordinary" peer relationships in that children spend much time in them, they are maintained over longer periods of time, and the children know each other well (Krappmann, 1996). Three kinds of emotional processes will be considered: children's sharing of positive emotions (e.g., enjoyment, humor, or amusement), their sharing of negative emotions (e.g., sadness, anxiety, shame, or anger) generated by third parties or the self and their negotiation of anger-provoking diagreements. Sharing of emotions can be explicit and verbal, as when children discuss emotionally-arousing incidents, or implicit and nonverbal, as when they giggle together. The sharing of emotions is important to study because it means expressing and often validating feelings, which implies a common evaluation of the circumstances which have elicited them. This may be significant not only for the adaptation of the individual child but also for the quality of the dyadic relationship. The final section will focus on the communication of anger occurring in the context of conflicts with siblings or friends. The objectives are to highlight the importance of studying these emotion processes and to describe their development over the course of childhood and preadolescence. Emphasis will be placed on the similarities between the processes of relating to siblings and to friends, leaving the differences between these relationships for exploration in future research.

SHARING POSITIVE EMOTIONS

Although conflict and negative emotions have been studied the most, there is no denying that children's relationships consistently include the sharing of happiness or enjoyment (Parke, 1994). In fact, Hartup (1983) considers the peer context as a unique opportunity for children to develop competencies in reciprocating positive emotions. Children's shared mirth can be as loud as toddlers' uproarious laughter or as quiet as the amused glances preadolescent friends exchange when a disliked classmate commits a faux pas. Smiling and laughing have probably developed from distinct phylogenetic origins; precursors of the relevant muscle movements can be identified in monkeys and apes (van Hooff, 1972).

Significance

One of the precursors of laughter in apes is the play face, and this is the context in which smiling and laughing can most often be observed in human infants. Malatesta and Haviland (1982) counted up to 12 smiles when they observed mothers and their infants of three and six months during six minutes of free play and a reunion. There is no reason to believe that it would be any fewer if the babies were playing with a friendly older sibling. Stern (1986) suggested that the exchange of emotions in repetitive play with caretakers and family members provides infants of about two to seven months with numerous opportunities to experience the patterned quality of their inner feelings. This helps the infants to distinguish between the self and the other person and contributes to the establishment of their core self. Between eight and 18 months the nonverbal sharing of enjoyment—for example over a new accomplishment of the child—is considered an indicator of attunement between two separate and mutually responsive selves. Attunement represents a new quality of closeness in the relationship, because it involves sharing not only one's focus of attention but also one's intentions and (underlying) affective states. At about one year of age children demonstrate social referencing; that is, watchful glances at mothers, fathers, or substitute caretakers in the face of potential danger (Sorce et al., 1985). Also in later years, younger siblings are known to cast an apprehensive eye on their older siblings when confronted with an ambiguous situation, such as an adult who comes to visit once a year. In each of these cases, a reassuring smile informs the child that there is no risk, that everything is okay.

As everybody knows, sharing a smile with a congenial companion is more rewarding than smiling to oneself, and there are numerous research findings which attest to the social facilitation of smiles and laughter (e.g., Chapman, 1976). The particularly cordial Duchenne smile (Ekman, Davidson, & Friesen, 1990), which produces crows' feet and wrinkles around the eyes, creates emotional resonance in the interaction partner; he or she is induced to join with the same cordial type of smile, especially if it is a close friend (von Salisch, 1989). The contagious nature of smiles and laughter implies that their exchange can escalate to spirals of ever deeper and almost unstoppable cathartic laughter which in the end is deeply relaxing (Ruch, 1993). When analyzed in more depth, sharing positive emotions involves the communication and mutual validation of an (implicit) evaluation of the self, the interaction partner, or other circumstances as delightful, amusing, or relieving. Experiencing and acknowledging commonality makes the people involved feel good and strengthens their emotional bond, especially when it has a positive overtone. Their motivation to maintain the relationship should be increased (Oatley, 1992).

Sharing their good feelings should also help children to cope with the frustrations they encounter while growing up. Be it rules and restrictions by parents, teachers, or institutions, be it other children making fun of them, or be it their own lack of skills—all this causes expected frustrations. The intensity of children's gleeful laughter when an adult behaves like a fool certainly speaks for children's many frustrations. Being able to appreciate the absurdity of situations one cannot change (Lefcourt & Martin, 1986) and having a companion who concurs with this evaluation should help children to master these normal frustrations of growing up (McGhee, 1979).

Development

Infancy and Preschool Period

The exchange of smiles starts very early in life. Social smiles at specific persons first appear around the second month and laughter can first be heard around the fourth month of life (Saarni, Mumme, & Campos, 1998). Toddlers who meet in playgroups greet each other with the exchange of obvious signs of enjoyment, such as smiles or laughter (Ross & Goldman, 1976). When language begins to develop in the second year of life, these exchanges become more verbal and sometimes take on a humorous quality. With the advance of symbol formation, object play, and pretend play children begin to enjoy incongruous situations. Later in the second year, most children make their first jokes about misnaming objects or persons. Distorting the reality in these fantasies can be an amusing game with siblings or friends, especially when the word play centers around forbidden topics, such as farts or stinky diapers (Dunn & Brown, 1991). Starting at about three years of age, children are able to come up with jokes about more complex concepts, such as ritual insults about gender or intelligence. In addition, repetitive rhymes, nonsense, and taboo words, as well as sexual innuendos, are all considered to be funny by preschoolers. Exciting activities and vigorous physical play can also bring out children's mirth. By about seven years of age, children start to appreciate puns, riddles, and jokes which involve double meanings. When confronted about their risqué content they can always pretend that the serious meaning was intended (McGhee, 1979). The ability to share humor and to amuse one another seems to be one of the components indicating a growing intimacy in children's relationships with one another (Dunn & Brown, 1991; Chapman, Smith, & Foot, 1980). Therefore, it is no surprise that previously unacquainted preschoolers who manage to establish positive reciprocity are more likely to become friends than their less congenial agemates (Gottman, 1983). Among peers and siblings there are marked differences in their ability to hit this lighthearted tone: Dunn (1993) reports that the amount of humor shared among preschool siblings varies between an average of zero to seven jokes per hour of home observation.

Middle Childhood

These differences between sibling pairs are to some extent preserved into the school years; correlations assessing the stability of positive sibling behaviors ranged between 0.42 and 0.60 in three studies spanning three and four years respectively (Dunn, 1993; Brody, Stoneman, and McCoy, 1994). When longer time-spans were assessed the results became more muddled, partly because of intervening life events and partly because different positive behaviors were aggregated into a compound variable indicating a positive relationship (e.g. Dunn, Slomkowski, & Beardsall, 1994). Sharing excitement or happiness in jokes or silliness plays an important role in the friendships of school-age children. In a recent survey in Germany, over 90% of the children reported that they "fooled around" with their friends; indeed, this ability seemed to be a central category in their evaluation of their friendships. In a confirmatory factor analysis, Oswald, Krappmann, Uhlendorff, and Weiss (1994) identified this component as the "fun factor" in children's friendships. Newcomb and Bagwell (1995) confirmed, in their meta-analysis of over 82 mostly North-American studies, that pairs of friends smiled and laughed more and generally had a better time when collaborating on a task than nonfriends.

Preadolescence and Adolescence

Field and her co-workers (Field, Greenwald, Morrow, Healy, Foster, Gutherz, & Frost, 1992) corroborate that the behavior of preadolescent best friends in a "free talk" situation in the laboratory seems to be more relaxed, more playful, and more positive in affect than the behavior of acquainted children. In a field study of adolescent humor, Sanford and Eder (1984) observed that adolescents in grades six to eight tended to share practical jokes, funny stories, or humorous behavior with their close friends, often with the intention of conveying peer norms or exploring sensitive issues, such as romantic relationships, bodily functions, or sexuality, which were usually not discussed directly. A self-report study indicates that fifth- and sixth-graders take advantage of numerous opportunities to exchange humor; preferred occasions are during meals or while shopping, conversing, or talking on the telephone (Zarbatany, Hartmann, & Rankin, 1990). An observation study of adolescents and their friends confirmed that those youngsters who reported having a harmonious friendship showed more positive affect and less jealousy and were better able to negotiate issues of power than less congenial friends (Gavin & Furman, 1996).

These studies provide a patchwork of findings which suggest that the sharing of positive emotions is an important feature of children's relationships with their siblings and their friends. Studies of the antecedents suggest that a positive sibling relationship is promoted by a mother's expressiveness of positive emotions (Stocker, Ahmed, & Stall, 1997), a facilitating father (Volling & Belsky, 1992b), a positive relationship between the parents (Brody, Stoneman, & McCoy, 1994), family cohesion and family expressiveness (MacKinnon, 1989), and a non-active temperament in the younger or in both siblings (Stoneman & Brody, 1993). What is missing are studies charting children's humorous exchanges at different stages of development in more detail. Including verbal and nonverbal components is important, because there are at least 18 different types of smiles, only two of which indicate felt enjoyment of the person showing it (Ekman, 1985). In order to gain a more complete understanding of the sharing of humor, amusement, and other positive emotions, self-report data must be validated by observations and vice versa. Exploring the implications that these joyful and enjoyable exchanges have for children's relationships, their adjustment, and their health may be just as worthwhile as the examination of the concomitants of negative peer interactions has proven to be in the past (e.g., Gottman & Katz, 1989).

SHARING NEGATIVE EMOTIONS ABOUT THIRD PARTIES OR THE SELF

Everybody, including children, at times feels sad or hurt, anxious or fearful, embarrassed or ashamed. Although there is every reason to believe that the structural features of the antecedents of children's emotions are about the same as those of adults, the development of these appraisals has not received much scientific attention. When and how infants and children acquire the dimensions relevant for the different emotion appraisals is in large part a white spot on the map of scientific research. Exceptions include the development of shame (Lewis, 1992) and some aspect of anger (Lewis, Alessandri, & Sullivan, 1990). By the preschool years most of the appraisals that are relevant for emotions seem to be acquired. For example, just like adults, children often report that sadness was elicited by loss of control over something important to them (e.g., Fabes, Eisenberg, McCormick, & Wilson, 1988). Even though the abstract features of the eliciting situations may be similar for children and adults, the concrete contents of the emotion elicitors are likely to vary. Only children, for example, report being worried about being attacked by monsters and other creatures of the dark (Silverman, La Greca, and Wasserstein, 1995). The specific contents of the situational elicitors of emotions among children and adolescents need to be described with respect to both their normative development and their interindividual variations.

Significance

Studies of adolescents and adults indicate that when they have feelings of anger, anxiety, and shame they communicate them between 64% and 78% of the time, often to more than one person (Rimé, Philippot, Boca, & Mesquita, 1992). Saarni (1995) reports that 20% to 42% of the children in middle childhood consider social support to be the best strategy for coping with aversive emotions, especially with sadness and fear. Sharing negative emotions with others provides the individual with an opportunity to clarify ambiguous emotional sensations, to cognitively articulate, label, and formulate often diffuse feelings, to redefine challenged concepts of self and others, to garner social support in coping with these often overwhelming emotions, and to tap into the culture's concepts for defining and managing their emotional experiences (Rimé et al., 1992). Sharing their fortunes and misfortunes with nonjudgmental and trustworthy confidants helps children to develop a rich and realistic understanding of themselves and their peers, and contributes to their interpersonal sensitivity (Youniss, 1980). In addition, sharing should keep their relationships intense and lively, because emotions are usually elicited by something that is important to them (Campos, Campos, & Barrett, 1990).

Having a same-sex friend with whom they can share their embarrassment, their distress, their anxieties, and their disappointments in a satisfying way assists preadolescents and adolescents in their concurrent adjustment (Buhrmester, 1990) and in their coping with the tasks of social development, such as gaining acceptance in their peer group or dealing with the complexities of sexual and romantic relationships. All in all, having a close reciprocal friendship seems to help preadolescents in developing a more positive self-esteem which is still evident more than ten years later in young adulthood (Bagwell, Newcomb, & Bukowski, 1998). In addition, exploring negative, ambivalent, or conflicting feelings in the face of life transitions and life events may contribute to children's adjustment to these disruptions in their lives (Dubow, Tisak, Causey, Hryshko, & Reid, 1991). Maltreated children who had at least one reciprocated or "high-quality" friendship, for example, showed stronger increases in their self-esteem over a period of four years than their maltreated agemates without such good fortune (Bolger, Patterson, & Kupersmidt, 1998). Older siblings and friends may also provide advice or help in the practical implementation of plans designed to overcome the current difficulties (Berndt, 1989; Kramer & Gottman, 1992). On a more general level, when negative emotions are acknowledged and validated by the friend or sibling, it implies a similar view of the events which instigated them. The experience of shared meaning is likely to relieve the individual (he or she feels "understood") and to deepen their relationship (Duck, 1994a).

Compared to parents, children are at a particular advantage when it comes to understanding the emotions of a fellow child, even in their early years. Because children are on a similar developmental level of understanding themselves and "the world", the meanings which one child attaches to events may be immediately "accessible" to the other. Or as Judy Dunn put it: "Since what distresses, pains or excites a sibling is very close to what distresses, pains or excites the child, the child is likely to be far better placed to understand and find remedies for a sibling's distress than for the distress of an adult" (1983, p. 793). This argument can easily be extended to close friends, who seek each other out, spend much time together, and tend to know each other quite well. In addition, children often have a better understanding of the peer context which elicited the emotion than adults. From this perspective, sharing negative emotions becomes akin to the relationship provisions of intimacy and nurturance (Furman & Robbins, 1985). Breadth and depth of shared emotions as well as the ability to "work them through" should be a hallmark of warm and intimate relationships. Not being able to share most of these feelings may in the long run contribute to psychological maladjustment. Experiencing criticism or rejection when trying to share their negative emotions should "add insult to injury"; that is, it should maintain or intensify not only the existing aversive emotions, but should add the feeling of being misunderstood and rebuffed (see Mills & Piotrowski, this volume). The implications for the quality of children's and adolescents' friendships and their self-esteem are obvious, but need to be confirmed in further empirical studies.

Caution is warranted, however, in this research, because reciprocal effects are likely. Friends may not only help by providing social support in the face of problems, but the problems may also affect the quality of the friendship. Among adolescents, for example, depressive symptoms predicted covert hostility in their best friendship some time later (Windle, 1994). Friendships, in which one or both parties lie, spread rumors, or show other types of covert hostility should therefore be less suited to provide the support needed to overcome the depression. Similarly, physically-abused children were observed to show somewhat fewer signs of global intimacy and to engage in more conflict behavior with a friend than their nonabused agemates (Parker & Herrera, 1996).

Development

The Preschool Period

At 18 to 24 months most children utter their first emotion words and begin to talk about feelings and other inner states. Starting at about three years of age, children increasingly talk with their older siblings about feelings, mostly in the context of play or humor. While mothers tend to discuss the child's feelings in the context of controlling the child, older siblings prefer to talk about their own feelings, which tend to arise from their own immediate needs. The reciprocal sibling relationship makes fewer allowances than parents and challenges the child to decenter and attend to the feelings of the other child. The results are not always peaceful: more negative *and* more positive emotional expressions can be observed between siblings than between mothers and children (Brown & Dunn, 1992; Dunn, Creps, & Brown, 1996). In addition, there are marked differences between sibling pairs in how often they discuss their feelings: in one sample the number of turns ranged from none to as many as 32 conversational turns of emotion talk per hour of home observation (Dunn, 1993). The more the children referred to emotions and other mental states while talking with their friends and their siblings, the better they were able to cooperate with them (Brown, Donelan-McCall, & Dunn, 1996). Some preschoolers indicated that they would share their bad dreams, fights, or worries with their siblings and sought contact with them when they were sad or unhappy, especially when their parents were unavailable (Zelkowitz, 1989).

Another perhaps more circumstantial way in which feelings are communicated is through enactment in joint pretend play (Howes, Unger, &

Matheson, 1992). After a little "framing", both children slip into a shared fantasy world. Children as young as 18 months were able to participate in these delightful and challenging plays—provided that they had a friendly older sibling who created an opening scene and steered them through the rough spots. Between 24 and 30 months, younger siblings made increasingly active contributions to the shared pretend play and became less compliant in following their older siblings' directions. For one-quarter to one-third of the preschool sibling pairs, joint pretend play was a riveting activity sometimes extending over more than 140 conversational turns (Dunn, 1993). References to emotional states occurred more often during sophisticated negotiations of the play scripts between the siblings (Howe, Petrakos, & Rinaldi, 1998).

Children enter shared fantasy worlds not only with their siblings but also with some of their friends. For Gottman (1986), coordinating fantasy play, self-exploration, and managing conflicts are the most important social processes among preschool friends. Gottman (1986) describes how preschool boys use fantasy play in order to master their fears. He details how the two boys start off by discussing poison, then move on to the danger of rattlesnakes and finally explore the power of sharks, realizing that they are up against no small foe. After considering climbing a tree, shooting the creature, or transforming it into metal, they finally conclude that it can only be contained by an even more powerful metaphor—concrete. In another study, Kramer and Gottman (1992) suggest that fantasy play with their "best friends" can help young children cope with their real-life fears and worries, in this case the birth of a younger brother or sister. Preschoolers who were better able to "manage" their conflicts with their friends, who were able to achieve a higher quality of play and sustain longer episodes of fantasy play—often about the new baby—had a more positive and affectionate relationship with their younger sibling, when he or she was six and fourteen months old.

Middle Childhood and Preadolescence

Gottman and Mettetal (1986) make the point that the most salient social process in middle childhood is gossip that evaluates the qualities of other children in a negative way. Friends can be overheard to share their anger and contempt at some classmate's characteristic or behavior. Agreeing about the evaluations implied in these emotions not only builds solidarity among the friends but also helps the children in their efforts at managing emotions which do not adhere to the rather strict standards of the peer society. Under the disguise of discussing a peer's "disgusting" behavior they can also explore their own unacceptable emotions. Being accepted by friends and peers may thus stimulate children in middle childhood to regulate the display of disruptive emotions, such as anger (von Salisch, 2000), anxiety (P. Harris, 1989) or fear (Altshuler & Ruble, 1989). Social support among friends in the primary school years has clear limitations, however: even though having many friends reduces children's feelings of loneliness and increases their academic readiness at the beginning of formal schooling, the same effects are obtained by peer acceptance (Ladd, Kochenderfer, & Coleman, 1997). In addition, perceived social support from a friend cannot compensate for insecure attachment to the mother in the preschool period (Booth, Rubin, & Rose-Krasnor, 1998).

Around the age of ten, friendships among children often attain a new quality of sharing and intimacy (Sullivan, 1953; Buhrmester & Furman, 1987). In Selman's (1980) stage model, children around this age start to conceptualize friendship as a framework for reciprocal intimate disclosure which is to be preserved for mutual and long-term benefits. Sharing secrets, which includes disclosing feelings that are not socially desirable, presupposes that the friend is trustworthy, and will not tell the damaging information to other people. As many authors have noted, preadolescent close friendships thrive on the discussion of problems and preoccupations, many of which involve the sharing of embarrassment, anxiety, and other negative emotions (e.g., Hirsch & Dubois, 1989). In Gottman and Mettetal's (1986) model, the accompanying processes of self-exploration and help in sorting out these feelings are the most salient processes in the friendships of preadolescents and adolescents. Preadolescents tend to provide a good deal of social support to their friends by distracting them. This disruption has the effect of livening up the friends' feelings and preventing them from engaging in ever new cycles of negative affect generated by self-attributions of responsibility (Denton & Zarbatany, 1996).

Siblings may not be on the forefront of emotional support, but in 60% to 95% of families with a school-age child they figure among the top ten providers of social support (Bryant, 1985; Reid, Landesman, Treder, & Jaccard, 1989), especially when assistance is needed in regard to parents or finances. In Buhrmester and Furman's (1987) study, the ratings of self-disclosure towards the "best" friend soon surpass those toward the "favorite" sibling, which stay about the same over the whole time. Indeed, between grades three and twelve the degree of intimacy, affection, and companionship in the sibling relationship actually decreases on average (Buhrmester & Furman, 1990). There are, of course, large individual differences in the warmth and closeness of the sibling relationship, larger perhaps than in voluntary friendships. Over the seven years between preschool and preadolescence the stability of warmth and closeness in the sibling relationship was about $r = 0.35$. Affectionate and intimate attitudes and behaviors were reported more frequently when the siblings were two sisters, when the family belonged to the middle class, and—perhaps surprisingly—when mothers indicated that the family had experienced some adversity, such as accidents, illnesses, or peer problems (Dunn, Slomkowski, & Beardsall, 1994). In this sample, very few parents experienced serious marital problems, but other studies report contradictory findings. Whereas Hetherington (1988) observed increased levels of sibling conflict in families with marital disharmony or difficult stepparent relationships, Jenkins (1992) reported that siblings may provide considerable support for each other. Since low support from parents is often not compensated by high support from siblings (van Aken & Asendorpf, 1997), it becomes important to specify the circumstances under which siblings (and perhaps friends) can help children and adolescents in coming to terms with the ever more frequent experience of marital conflict, separation, and divorce.

Not all friendships are equally intimate. About one-third of the male adolescents interviewed by Youniss and Smollar (1985) reported no "best friendship" involving trust, intimacy, and conflict resolution by "talking it over". Children who were low-accepted by their peers were more lonely and tended to engage less often in intimate exchanges about problems, secrets, or "things that make one friend sad or mad" with the friend (Parker & Asher, 1993). Having a sibling may help some of these rejected or neglected children, particularly those who are isolated from their peers. High levels of support from a sibling helped to lower the high levels of anxiety and immaturity in these children (East & Rook, 1992). Among aggressive grade-schoolers, sibling relationships characterized by some support and no more than moderate amounts of conflicts were correlated with lower aggressiveness and better emotional control in the eyes of teachers, and with less severe peer rejection (Stormshak, Bellanti, Bierman, and the CPPRG, 1996). Whether siblings' assistance provides a unique contribution to higher levels of adaptation and peer acceptance should be explored in longitudinal studies.

ANGER IN CONFLICTS BETWEEN CHILDREN

Anger, anxiety, shame, and contempt are not only aroused by the self or people outside the dyad but also by the relationship partners, that is, by the friends and siblings themselves. This can lead to disagreements between them. Since the 1970s, conflicts between unrelated peers have received much scientific attention, for the most part in research on social and cognitive development in the tradition of Piaget (1932/1986). Reviews of this literature can be found in Shantz (1987), Shantz and Hobart (1989) and in various chapters in the Shantz and Hartup volume (1992). In recent years the literature on conflicts between siblings has burgeoned. Interest in disagreements between siblings is not only motivated by social cognitive concerns (Dunn, 1988b), but also comes from the clinical side, because sibling discord is one of the most common and most persistent child-related problems parents complain about. A number of recent studies have found that amount and intensity of sibling conflict are influenced by child characteristics such as temperament, or rather by the temperamental match between the siblings (e.g., Munn & Dunn, 1989; Stoneman & Brody, 1993), relationship variables, such as mother–child attachment (Volling & Belsky, 1992b) as well as by family variables such as the mother's negative emotional expressiveness (Stocker, Ahmed, & Stall, 1997), the quality of the parents' marital relationship (MacKinnon, 1989; Hetherington, 1988), family harmony and family cohesiveness (Brody, Stoneman, McCoy, & Forehand, 1992), and differential or unresponsive treatment by one or both of the parents (e.g., Volling & Belsky, 1992b; Bryant &

Crockenberg, 1980). Vandell and Bailey (1992) provide an excellent review of these and other studies of family influences on sibling conflict.

In very few studies has there been an attempt to determine what emotions are associated with children's disagreements. As Shantz noted over ten years ago, which emotions precede and co-occur with claims and counterclaims is an almost uncharted territory, a proverbial blank spot on the map of scientific research (Shantz, 1987). Whether an assertion is made in a whiny or in a firm voice, whether the opposition to an initial claim is accompanied by surprise, fear, or anger, whether in the course of the negotiation excitement prevails, or whether the end is marked by one party withdrawing in a huff or by the exchange of smiles—all this throws light on the nature of disagreements and their resolutions. "Everyday" quarrels and bickering may be differentiated from "all-out" confrontations, and hostile jibes from "friendly" provocations, because the emotions expressed through face, voice, words, and gestures contextualize the conflict and elucidate its meaning.

In the following paragraphs, I will examine the expression and regulation of anger in disagreements between siblings and friends in three phases of their conflicts; that is, at the outset, during the course of the negotiation, and at the outcome. This requires bringing together the literature on anger regulation, which focuses on individuals, with the "dyadic" research on conflict. Anger is likely to be present at the beginning of the disagreement, because if no one is angry or upset at the other there would be no reason to oppose the other. However, not every experience of anger leads to overt confrontations (Fabes & Eisenberg, 1992); in a recent diary study 40% of the school-age children indicated that at least once over a one-week period they had felt intense anger but had not communicated this feeling to the person who had instigated it (von Salisch, 2000). It is also conceivable to have disagreements in which conflicting goals are pursued in "cold blood"; that is, without overt or covert emotions. Expressing anger has an effect on the negotiation of the divergent viewpoints. Vandell and Bailey (1992) argue among other things that high amounts of affect are a hallmark of destructive conflicts. Although extreme expressions of anger or distress are likely to make the negotiation more difficult, if not impossible, in the short run, and may increase the risk of escalation, their long-term effects are less clear. In some relationships (and cultures) conflicts have to be brought to a head before they can be resolved, even if this involves a shouting match. Tolerance for intense expression of anger varies, of course, between individuals, dyads, and relationships. Among Italian and Canadian children, the frequency of their conflicts was not predict-ive of the termination of the friendship six months later (Schneider, Fonzi, Tana, & Tomada, 1997). The other extreme, that is not feeling or not express-ing anger when unjustly attacked, is also not conducive to relationships (Eisenberg, Fabes, Nyman, Bernzweig, & Pinuelas, 1994) because it implies withdrawal in the face of opposition or a tendency to give in to the demands of the other child. (Children are rather hard on peers who do not stand up for their own rights; they call them "wimps".) Optimal for conflict resolution in the short run seems to be a "medium" level of anger, that is, enough to bring forward arguments (Dunn & Brown, 1994), to emphasize assertions, and to resist illegitimate requests, but not to the extent that it prevents negotiation. Being "a little" angry can, in addition, help children put forward their complaint when their friend or sibling is physically stronger or otherwise more powerful. Finally, one can ask what effect the expression and regulation of anger have on the immediate and the long-term outcome of the conflict. This question becomes very relevant for children's relationships with their siblings and friends when put in the following way: under what conditions do children feel that a conflict was constructive in the sense that they have "learned a lesson" from it (Shantz, 1993)?

Significance

Anger at another person is usually aroused when expectancies are violated (Oatley, 1992), when a goal-directed activity is frustrated and the other person is held responsible for it, or when the self is threatened (Lazarus, 1991). The experience of anger gives the child an opportunity to learn about wishes and preferences, expectancies, and vulnerabilities. The confrontation of divergent viewpoints is—in the best and theoretical case—followed by an exchange about the ideas and motives underlying the child's anger. Negotiating the child's anger helps a friend or sibling to gain a better understanding of the child's preferences and expectancies, attitudes and limitations, sensitive spots and strong points; in short, to develop sensitivity toward the angry child (Youniss, 1980; Rizzo, 1989). On a more general plane, talking about the "cause" of the angry feelings offers children a chance to change their construction of meaning, not only about the angry child, but also about the self and perhaps about the relationship. Conflict discussions may transform the participants' social roles vis à vis one another and may deepen their friendships (Whitesell & Harter, 1996; Selman, 1980, stage 3).

In the families of preschool children, discussion of emotions seems to promote children's cognitive-emotional development. Children who talked more often about (conflicting) feelings with family members and who used arguments in conflicts with their siblings tended to score higher on measures of affective perspective-taking (Dunn, Brown, Slomkowski, Tesla, & Youngblade, 1991; Slomkowski & Dunn, 1992; Howe, 1991). These children were better able to understand what a puppet would feel in an emotion-eliciting situation, such as going to the dentist, even when these feelings did not match their own feelings in the same situation. Emotion knowledge of this type seems to be a strong predictor of acceptance in the preschool peer group (Denham, McKinley, Couchoud, & Holt, 1990), of connected communication while playing with a friend (Slomkowski & Dunn, 1996) and of moral sensitivity in primary school (Dunn, Brown, & Maguire, 1995). How conflicts between preschool friends are resolved is, however, not predicted longitudinally by a child's early emotional perspective-taking but rather by the fact that mother and sibling tended to use child-centered arguments when negotiating a disputed point (Herrera & Dunn, 1997). In middle childhood, the negotiation of conflicts among peers is believed to stimulate moral development (Piaget, 1932/1986) and eventually result in the development of shared norms and values that apply to both children equally (Youniss, 1980; Keller, 1987). An empirical study confirmed that the way in which the friends resolved the dispute, not the amount of conflict at the beginning of the study, was important for the termination of a friendship about six months later (Schneider et al., 1997). The more sensitive the friends were when discussing how to distribute one chocolate egg among the two, the more likely they were to be friends half a year later (Fonzi, Schneider, Tani, & Tomada, 1997).

These are, of course, ideal outcomes. That it may be difficult to discuss a friend's or a sibling's angry feelings, and that anxiety or defensiveness may prevail when one is the target of these sentiments, is evident. Negotiations between children may go awry; that is, they may end in physical harm or escalate into cycles of mutual retaliation and coercion (Herzberger & Hall, 1993). Another possibility is "premature" submission, in which one child yields to force or gives in against his or her own wishes. A third possible "derailment" involves the use of hostility or denigration when presenting one's case or when opposing the argument of the other. Denigrating the other child time and again causes psychological harm to the "victim", because it is likely to engender not only a model of the relationship partner as hostile, but also a model of the self as vulnerable, inadequate, and ultimately worthless. Denigration in closed-field situations seems to go along with more openly aggressive behavior in less constrained situations, which ultimately predicts peer rejection (von Salisch & Uhlendorff, 1998).

When one child devalues the other over and over again, most friends will end their friendship (Selman, 1980), but in a sibling relationship there is no "escape". When older sisters of about ten years of age displayed anger or disparagement at their later-born sisters in a teaching situation, the later-borns tended to reciprocate with anger, disparagement, competitive statements, and the refusal to help or share with the older sister, leading to a vicious cycle of mutual competition and devaluation (Bryant & Crockenberg, 1980; Stoneman & Brody, 1993). A consequence of a multitude of such interactions may be a tendency to depreciate the self, which was found primarily among younger siblings (Minnett, Vandell, & Santrock, 1983). Perhaps this is because in early and middle childhood older siblings have more power to define the situation and the relationship than do younger ones (Furman & Buhrmester, 1985b). A study showing significant correlations between an older sibling's hostile comments and the younger sibling's tendency to internalize problems two years later (Dunn, Slomkowski, Beardsall, & Rende, 1994) fits this picture. It should be noted, however, that these findings are correlational and need to be replicated with a larger and more representative sample in which younger siblings' internalizing tendencies at the outset of the study are controlled. What is also needed is a study tracing the development of the cognitive, expressive, and interactive aspects of contempt and denigration in the context of children's relationships with parents and peers.

Development

The preschool years

On the basis of mothers' diaries, Goodenough (1931) reports that children of two and three years of age start to become angry when they encounter difficulties in their play with other children. Anger tantrums were more likely when the children were in bad health, when they had gone without a meal for some time, when they were tired, or when they had a larger number of older siblings. Dunn and Munn (1986) corroborate from family observations that an average of eight conflicts per hour take place between preschool siblings. About half of these sibling conflicts revolve around rights, possessions, and property; about every tenth disagreement is marked by intense anger and distress (Dunn & Munn, 1987). Similar findings emerge from the obervations of Fabes and his co-workers (1988) in a nursery school serving children between 3½ to 5½ years of age. These authors concluded that anger is almost always elicited in social situations, most of which involve other children. In about half of the cases, anger was aroused in the context of disagreements over material goods or possessions, and a further 28% were associated with physical confrontations, such as being pushed by another child. When friends had shown ambiguous behavior, preschoolers were less likely to react with anger than when nonfriends had behaved in an ambiguous way. Friends, so it seems, tend to receive the benefit of the doubt (Fabes, Eisenberg, Smith, & Murphy, 1996). That anger and conflict behaviors are embedded in specific relationships is also supported by Dunn and Munn's (1986) observation of siblings: the more anger and distress the toddler-aged younger siblings showed during conflicts with their older brothers or sisters, the less likely they were to share, help, comfort, or cooperate with this sibling in other situations, or to engage in pretend play with him or her, when they were 33 months old.

There are two studies which detail what happens when preschoolers show facial expressions of anger, disgust, or contempt (or threat) in the course of conflict negotiations in laboratory or closed-field situations. Matsumoto, Haan, Yarbrove, Theodorou, and Carney (1986) report that preschoolers' expression of these negative emotions (as well as the expression of unfelt smiles or no emotions) made it more likely that their friends and partners would stalemate, betray, or default in their next move during a simplified Prisoner's Dilemma game. Only the expression of felt (Duchenne) smiles raised the probability of a moral solution, and if this was reached, both children seemed to be so relieved or so satisfied that the display of anger or disgust was less likely in the next move. Even if the expression of these negative emotions does not facilitate moral solutions, it may nevertheless help children in getting (or keeping) what they want. This is the finding of Camras' (1977) experiment, in which two unacquainted preschoolers had a single gerbil to play with. When players showed one of those facial expressions which ethologists call "threat faces", their partners were likely to wait longer before renewing their request for the animal. Lowering their brows, wrinkling their noses, or making a pouting mouth thus helped the children to keep the cuddly beast.

In a study of preschoolers in an open-field situation, i.e., during free-play in a nursery school, Fabes, Eisenberg and their co-workers observed that children had quite different ways of dealing with their anger. Whereas boys tended to vent their anger (Fabes & Eisenberg, 1992), to show more intense irritation or to retaliate with physical means (Eisenberg et al., 1994), girls tended to put up more active resistance (Fabes & Eisenberg, 1992) or to object verbally to the other child's offensive behavior (Eisenberg et al., 1994) or to reject the provocateur (Fabes et al., 1996). Children's ways of regulating their anger during the peer provocation were further associated with their ways of coping with other problems, their temperament, their social competence (as judged by their teachers) and last but not least their sociometric status among their peers (Fabes & Eisenberg, 1992; Eisenberg et al., 1994). For example, verbal objections, i.e., negotiating the incident, were positively correlated with constructive coping and not very intense emotional reactions in other situations, as judged by mothers and school personnel alike. When the anger was instigated by a well-liked peer, children generally became less aroused, even though the provocation was judged to be equally intensive. When provoked by a friend, boys responded less often with physical retaliation and more often by venting their feelings or putting forward an active defense (Fabes et al., 1996). Hartup, Laursen, Stewart, and Eastenson (1988), who also observed preschoolers' conflicts during free play, corroborate the lower affective intensity of mutual friends' quarrels, although these authors do not specify *which* emotions they coded. Whereas nonfriends tended to break up their play at the end of the confrontations, mutual friends were likely to remain in physical proximity or even to continue their play. Although children were not observed or asked about their emotions at this point in time, common sense suggests that the friends were probably no longer angry at each other.

Middle Childhood and Preadolescence

From observation in a first-grade classroom, Rizzo (1989) concludes that two-thirds of the conflicts between friends are caused by "normal" disagreements over the course of play and one-third by the violation of friendship expectations. When schoolchildren report what makes them angry, teasing and name calling, provocations, and ostracism are each mentioned by over one-fifth of the girls, whereas the boys' list is topped by scuffles and physical assaults (Shantz, 1993). Conflicts between siblings in middle childhood are motivated by some of the same topics, such as teasing and getting even, but also by control over resources, which is of course highly relevant in the family context, where there is much to share (Prochanska & Prochanska, 1985). Psychotherapists Bank and Kahn (1982) suggest that beyond the sometimes rather trivial issues on the surface there may be at least two further layers of sibling conflict, one the never-ending struggle for status in the family and the other an undercurrent of resentment which may have built up over some years of mutual "warfare". What a sibling's behavior "means" is more likely to have become set and hence to resist change, when siblings have adopted opposing social roles towards each other. It may therefore come as no surprise that quarreling, antagonism, and competition seem to be more pervasive between siblings than between friends, especially when siblings are close in age (Furman & Buhrmester, 1985a, b).

During the primary school years, children acquire an increasingly sophistic-ated understanding of other children's motives, even when something as pro-vocative as the destruction of their own property is involved: whereas first-graders only considered the perpetrator's (malevolent) intentions, third- and fifth-graders were also able to take prosocial motives and unavoidable acci-dents into account (Olthof, Ferguson, & Luiten, 1989). Friendship seems to play a minor role in these attributions. When aggressive boys were the victim of a peer's ambiguous action, they were more likely to attribute hostile mo-tives to the provocateur than their non-aggressive agemates (see also Dodge, 1986). But neither aggressive nor nonaggressive boys were influenced by the presence or absence of friendship between themselves and the perpetrator (Sancilio, Plumert, & Hartup, 1989). The attribution of a peer's malevolent intentions seems to go along with the report of more intense feelings of anger and a greater risk for aggressive retaliation, at least among "normal" black boys (Graham, Hudley, & Williams, 1992). The studies described here all used hypothetical stories to elicit the children's attributions. In order to ad-vance our knowledge, it is necessary to place children's attributions in the context of their relationships to specific friends (e.g., Whitesell & Harter, 1996) or siblings (e.g., Herzberger & Hall, 1993), and to study the attribution processes during the provocations children encounter while living together with these children.

When observing conflicts between peers, Shantz and Shantz (1985) con-cluded that aggression was rather seldom used: only 5% of the disagreements involved physical attacks and only 4% were accompanied by verbal deroga-tions. Studies of the development of anger regulation likewise conclude that overt aggression decreases over the school years, particularly among girls, whereas indirect forms of retaliation increase (von Salisch, 2000). By the end of their primary school years, children have a much wider repertoire of strat-egies for dealing with disruptive emotions, such that they are now better able to distance themselves physically or psychologically from their fear, distress (P. Harris, 1989), or anger (von Salisch, 2000). Over the years, children are also believed to acquire a more elaborate understanding of the temporal, interpersonal, and management aspects of conflict and emotional disequi-librium (Selman & Demorest, 1987; Saarni, 1995). Whether they make use of these growing abilities depends, of course, on the concrete circumstances. The more the sibling relationship is characterized, for example, by conflict, the more likely children are to hit and yell at their siblings, to slam the door or to think denigrating thoughts about them (e.g., "she is so stupid, that it is not worth my while to be mad at her") (Callondann, 1995). In divorced families, older boys were much more likely to make negative or demeaning remarks or facial expressions, or to grab, hit or push their younger sibling during a board game, than any other group of older children coming from divorced or married families (MacKinnon, 1989).

Board games like Parchesi challenge children's anger regulation skills because of the many frustrations built into them. For the researcher, these games present an excellent opportunity to study children's negotiation of their angry feelings in a closed-field setting which is not too contrived. That angry feelings are aroused and lead to debate is likely when, for example, two "best friends" are taught different rules for a board game. When Hartup, French, Laursen, Johnston, and Ogawa (1993) did just this, they observed that nine- and ten-year-old pairs of friends tended to disagree more frequently and at greater length than pairs of nonfriends. Compared to nonfriends' disagreements, friends' conflicts were more intense during their peak periods; unfortunately, the authors did not specify which emotions the children displayed "in the heat of the battle". Hartup and his colleagues interpret these findings, which contradict the stereotype children hold that friendships are characterized by a particular harmony (Berndt & Perry, 1986), by pointing out that friends know each other better and are more secure in their relationship than nonfriends. This gives friends the freedom to challenge each other's point of view and to disagree with enthusiasm.

Physically-abused boys who played a series of competitive games together with a friend of their own gender showed more negative affect (including threats, orders, and derogations) than non-abused boys, suggesting that experiences or characteristics of the child also influence children's emotions during conflicts with their friends (Parker & Herrera, 1996). Dishion, Andrews, and Crosby (1995) likewise observed that the more "delinquent" or "antisocial" an adolescent boy was, the more bossiness and coercion he showed while discussing plans and (social or emotional) problems with a male friend. Furthermore, relationally aggressive children reported more often than other children that they would exclude their best friend when they were angry at him or her and this report was confirmed by the friend (Grotpeter & Crick, 1996).

That close (female) friends tend to be more outspoken in a conflict is corroborated by von Salisch (1991), who observed close and casual pairs of friends while cooperating on a computer game with a built-in defect. An analysis of the eleven-year-olds' facial expression revealed that close female friends showed significantly more of the cordial Duchenne smiles than did casual friends or close male friends. Close female friends also displayed Duchenne smiles more frequently in combination with reproaches, as if they wanted to signal to their girl-friend: "your move was not okay, but we are still friends". That girls tend to deal with the relationship aspect of the friendship was also found by Miller, Danaher, and Forbes (1986), who observed that girls tended to ameliorate conflicts by expressing their anger in indirect ways, such as suggesting compromises, changing the topic of conversation, or negotiating the point of contention. Hartup and co-workers (1993) found that girls, especially female friends, tended to bolster their assertions with rationales, whereas male friends tended to insist on their point of view without arguments. This result can be interpreted as evidence for a stronger relationship orientation among female than among male friends.

When Raffaelli (1990) asked 112 youngsters in grades five to eight about their conflicts with friends and siblings, 23% said they never argued with their friends and 6% said that they never argued with their siblings. Whereas disagreements with friends revolved most often around physical attacks and relationship themes, such as betrayal, neglect (girls only), or untrustworthiness (boys only) (see also Youniss & Smollar, 1985), sibling discord was most often elicited by questions of property rights or by perceptions of verbal abuse. Even though preadolescent siblings indicated that they quarrelled "habitually", 66% of them reported that they felt angry during these conflicts, while only 13% reacted with indifference (Raffaelli, 1990). Because preadolescent siblings have known each other for a long time and the actions of one are in many ways predictable for the other, one might expect habituation to have occurred. Nevertheless, their conflicts tend to arouse angry feelings. When living together, one sibling's actions often have immediate consequences for the other, and siblings who do not defend their rights will soon find themselves at a disadvantage. Siblings' angry reactions thus further children's awareness of their respective wishes, characteristics, and attitudes. This is true for the child who has become angry as well as for the target of his or her wrath. Shantz and Hobart (1989) link this process to the development of individuation.

Unfortunately, there are no studies of preadolescent siblings' anger-arousing attributions. About friends, there is only a study by Whitesell and Harter (1996), who investigated differences in the attribution of blame, the violation of expectancy, initial and subsequent feelings, as well as strategies for coping when an insult was received from a specific friend as opposed to a neutral classmate. Findings confirmed the prediction that children interpreted the insults received from a friend with more benevolence, highlighting their own contribution to it, or calling it a "misunderstanding", than they did insults received from a neutral classmate. When the friend had called them names, preadolescents (especially girls) reported not more intensive feelings of anger, but stronger feelings of sadness, distress, and hurt. The youngsters indicated that they would avoid the insulting classmate in the future, but opted for "talking it over" and "working things out" with the friend. These findings support the conclusion that attributions, ensuing emotions, and coping strategies are embedded in specific relationships. The same behavioral act of name-calling acquires a somewhat different meaning according to whether it takes place in the context of an established mutual friendship or in a more "normal" peer relationship.

Sibling conflicts tend to be brief: 42% of sibling arguments are settled within five minutes and a further 46% are resolved within an hour. This may be explained in part by the fact that parents intervened to stop the disagreement in 27% of the conflicts between siblings (compared to 9% of the conflicts between friends). In a further 34% of sibling arguments, the siblings disengaged and in an additional 30% one sibling gave in to the other. A compromise was reached in only 9% of the disagreements between the siblings (compared to 13% of those between friends). About half (54%) of the conflicts between friends ended with both parties going their own way, especially among the girls. Although 49% of the siblings and 34% of the friends did not report any reparative actions after the quarrel, there was a substantive minority of friends and siblings (about 25%) who indicated that one of them says "I am sorry" (Raffaelli, 1990). These self-reported differences between siblings and friends should be supplemented by observational data, especially on the emotional concomitants of these conflicts.

Self-report data by Buhrmester and Furman (1990) suggest that conflicts with older siblings become less frequent during the years of preadolescence and adolescence, when interaction rates between siblings generally decrease (Larson & Richards, 1991). Beyond these general age-trends (which are based on cross-sectional group means), differences between sibling pairs tend to disappear. Whereas some sibling pairs develop a more distant relationship, others may enjoy the increasingly egalitarian and supportive aspects of the relationship (Buhrmester & Furman, 1990). That the sibling relationship is nevertheless still full of potential pitfalls is evident from Goodnow and Warton (1992) whose data detailed the many ways adolescents know when they want to hurt their brother's or sister's feelings.

CONCLUSION

In this chapter I have reviewed research on three emotional processes in children's friendships and sibling relationships; namely, their sharing of enjoyment, amusement and humor, their sharing of negative emotions generated by third parties (or the self), and the negotiation of anger-provoking disagreements within these relationships. Communication of positive and negative emotions (directed at people or events outside the dyad) implies shared evaluations of persons or circumstances. Emotional sharing which is akin to social support may be a key process in children's social and emotional development as well as in the establishment and maintenance of their close relationships. The emotional processes occurring in children's conflicts start out not from a concordance but from a divergence of viewpoints. They have to do with the negotiation and ultimately with the outcome of the disagreement, also on an emotional plane. As many theorists have pointed out, the ability to engage in and to resolve interpersonal conflicts stimulates individual children's development and marks the quality of their relationships. All in all, sharing, social support, and conflict resolution are three aspects of "emotion talk"; that is, the communication of internal states which are highly relevant to the person who feels them but may not be obvious to the relationship partner. As the well known German feminist (and socialist) Rosa Luxemburg put it (in an admittedly different context): "Sometimes there is nothing so revolutionary as talking about what is".

Chapter 4

Emotional Communication and Children's Learning about Conflict

Rosemary S. L. Mills

and

Caroline C. Piotrowski

University of Manitoba, Canada

In interpersonal relationships, the goals and strivings of relationship partners often—perhaps more often than not—come into conflict. Conflicts are challenging and emotion-laden events with the potential to be either beneficial or harmful to individuals and relationships, depending upon the way they are handled. Optimal responses to conflict require skills such as open communication, rational argument, negotiation, compromise, and the use of strategies that are not threatening or harmful. Such skills require a high degree of emotional competence. Conflict experiences play a special role in the development of emotional competencies because they involve difficult and intense emotions that are challenging to deal with (e.g., Dunn & Brown, 1991). Emotional communication occurring in conflict experiences, particularly in the family (but in other close relationships as well; see von Salisch, in this volume), may be a prime medium in which these competencies develop. The

The Developmental Psychology of Personal Relationships.
Edited by Rosemary S. L. Mills and Steve Duck. © 2000 John Wiley & Sons Ltd.

purpose of this chapter is to describe recent work on its role in the development of children's emotional resources for dealing with conflict.

In keeping with a family systems perspective (e.g., Parke & Buriel, 1998; Parke & O'Neil, in this volume), we assume that children learn about conflict from all family relationships, and that the pathways of influence involved are both direct (e.g., observing parents' marital disputes) and indirect (e.g., through the effect of marital conflict on parent–child disputes). We will emphasize conflict experiences in these relationships, because of the special role conflict plays in the development of emotional competencies. The scope of this chapter will be limited, however, to parent–child and parent–parent conflict as sources of children's learning about conflict, as emotional communication during sibling conflicts is considered elsewhere in this volume (see von Salisch Chapter 3). Although the empirical work has not yet been done to establish links between emotional communication during conflicts and children's development of specific conflict management skills, there is emerging evidence to suggest that emotional communication plays an important role in children's development of the emotional competencies required to handle conflict situations constructively. That evidence is the focus of this review.

EMOTION AND EMOTIONAL COMMUNICATION

A functionalist perspective on emotion and emotional communication guides the present review. This perspective emphasizes the motivational, adaptive function of emotion. Emotion has been defined as ''the person's attempt or readiness to establish, maintain, or change the relation between the person and the environment on matters of significance to that person'' (Saarni, Mumme, & Campos, 1998, p. 238). There are several key components of this definition.

First, emotions arise in response to *events of significance* or concern to the individual. Events may be significant by virtue of their relation to biological survival, or they may become significant through learning. Learning may occur through direct experience of the implications that events have for one's goals, or through social communication, in which others' emotional reactions endow events with significance.

Second, emotions are *regulatory*, in the sense that they influence individuals' responses to their concerns. These regulatory effects include the interpretation of events, the accessing of potential responses, the selection of responses, the enactment of behavior, and the monitoring of consequences (Dodge, 1991). The effects occur both within and between individuals. Thus, the emotions experienced by an individual have self-regulatory effects on various aspects of the individual's response, and the emotions an individual communicates to another person have a regulatory effect on the other person.

Third, emotions themselves are *regulated*. According to Thompson (1994), ''emotion regulation consists of the extrinsic and intrinsic processes responsible for monitoring, evaluating, and modifying emotional reactions, especially their intensive and temporal features, to accomplish one's goals" (pp. 27–28). It includes external regulation by others, through their actions and communication signals, as well as self-regulation. What gets regulated includes neurophysiological arousal, the deployment of attention, the interpretation of external situations and internal cues of emotion, access to external support, exposure to emotional demands, and the choice of modes for expressing emotion (e.g., Thompson, 1994). Although this definition emphasizes the intensity and duration of emotional reactions, emotion regulation can also affect the particular emotion experienced, such as when an individual avoids being exposed to a certain emotion, chooses between emotions (by deciding how to interpret an event), or defensively substitutes one emotion for another.

Finally, emotions are *relational processes*, in that goals are achieved through transactions between relationship partners, i.e., interactions in which each adapts and changes in response to the other. Emotional communication itself is a transactional process of sending and receiving emotion signals, requiring adjustments and changes in each partner based on perceptions or interpretations of the signals. Through the sending and receiving of emotion signals, relationship partners respond to each other's states and concerns.

From this functionalist perspective, it is difficult to see how one can overestimate the importance of the role emotional communication plays in emotional development. It may be largely through emotional communication, between as well as with others, that children learn to appraise experiences and events, learn rules about emotions, and acquire strategies for regulating their emotions. It is also through emotional communication that children learn how, or if it is possible, to satisfy their needs and concerns. Emotional communication is "good" when it serves its functions, and such communication should promote the development of adaptive or competent emotional functioning.

EMOTIONAL COMMUNICATION IN THE PARENT–CHILD RELATIONSHIP

The parent–child relationship is fertile ground for learning about conflict, partly because it is a primary context for conflict (see Perlman, Siddiqui, Ram, & Ross, in this volume) and hence for the development of emotional competencies. Beginning in early infancy, children are highly sensitive to emotional communication. They observe emotional expressions and apparently "take on" others' emotional states through contagion. They are highly responsive to the modeling of emotional expressiveness, contingent responding to their emotions, and direct instruction about emotions (e.g., Halberstadt, 1991). A large body of research has accumulated showing that these emotion socialization processes help children acquire such skills as recognizing their own and others' emotions, feeling empathy for others' emotional states, expressing and communicating about emotions, and coping with aversive or distressing emotions (see Denham, 1998, for a review). However, the quality of the communication itself (e.g., clarity of signals, accuracy of reading signals) and its relation to the development of the child's emotional competencies, are only now becoming a focus of theory and research.

The Quality of Emotional Communication between Parent and Child

Attachment theorists assume that the dyadic pattern of emotional communication between parent and child functions as a form of mutual emotion regulation (e.g., Bretherton, 1990; Cassidy, 1994). Bretherton (1987, 1990) suggests that, in infancy and beyond, mutually satisfying parent–child communication, in which attachment signals are mutually comprehended and responded to, is required in order for the child to construct and maintain adequate working models or "schemas" of the self, the parent, and the attachment relationship.

In some dyads, emotional communication between parent and child (the sending and receiving of emotion signals, including the discussion of emotional issues at later ages) is open, fluent, and coherent. All expressions of emotion are mutually recognized, acknowledged, and understood, and none is ignored or misconstrued. In these dyads, partners can construct and maintain adequate internal working models, because error-correcting feedback is available. In other dyads, emotion signals are selectively ignored or misunderstood (especially signals of distress), and each partner's internal working models are inadequate because material is excluded and error-correcting feedback is not available. The "lack of open communication between attachment partners may be associated with restricted flow of information about attachment issues not only *between* partners, but *within* each partner's representational system" (Bretherton, 1990, p. 64).

The dyadic pattern of emotional communication between parent and child has been described as forming a "communicative package" (Cassidy, 1994, p. 240) in which partners signal to each other both their own wishes and their cooperation with the other's wishes. In "secure" parent-child dyads, the parent accepts the full range of emotions the child expresses, and responds sensitively most of the time. From this experience, the child learns that emotion signals are useful in alerting others to distress and eliciting comfort and help. Emotions can be expressed openly, directly, and clearly in the expectation of a satisfying response. In other dyads, some material is excluded from communication. In "dismissing-avoidant" dyads, the parent consistently rejects emotion signals (particularly those of distress), and the child learns to suppress or mask negative emotions (perhaps positive ones as well), i.e., not demand comfort or care, in order to cooperate with the parent's wishes and avoid rejection. In "preoccupied-ambivalent" dyads, the parent frequently neglects emotion signals, and the child learns to heighten or magnify negative emotions and distress signals in an attempt to gain the parent's attention and elicit care.

From the functionalist perspective on emotional communication that we described earlier, it is possible to see why open communication should promote emotional development. Such communication will tend to involve rich and extended exchanges, clear signals, and the acknowledgement and validation of the child's emotions, all of which should help the child to regulate emotions, acquire information about emotions, and develop a high level of emotional understanding. There is some indirect evidence to support this idea. Cassidy (1994) drew upon studies linking parent responses in the Adult Attachment Interview to infant behavior in the Strange Situation to argue for the proposed relation between communication patterns and children's styles of emotion regulation. Indirect evidence that open communication may also be associated with emotional understanding has been reported by Laible and Thompson (1998), who found that preschoolers who were securely attached to their mothers (and presumably, therefore, in a relationship characterized by open communication) were better at identifying negative emotions in others.

The dyadic communication patterns described by attachment theorists are believed to be a product of transactions between the parent and the child. Although the nature of these transactions is not well-understood (see Duck, Acitelli, Manke, & West, in this volume), the work of temperament researchers yields insight into the way in which the child's characteristics may contribute to the quality of emotional communication between parent and child. Kochanska (1998) has found that avoidant infants tend to be temperamentally relatively unperturbable, while ambivalent infants tend to be relatively prone to distress. Extrapolating to emotional communication, it is possible that low expressiveness becomes the emergent quality of dismissing-avoidant dyads in part because avoidant infants are temperamentally relatively unperturbable and consequently low in expressiveness, difficult to read, and tolerant of the parent's nonresponsiveness. Heightened negative expressiveness may become the emergent quality of preoccupied-ambivalent dyads partly because ambivalent infants are temperamentally prone to distress and hence difficult for the parent to respond to consistently.

How does inadequate communication interfere with the development of emotional skills and abilities? We now turn to research that permits some speculation about this.

The Effects of Inadequate Emotional Communication

Inadequate communication in which emotions are not acknowledged, validated, or understood, may be distressing to children. Research on ambiguous communication, in which the emotional meaning is masked or conflicting, provides some evidence to support this idea. Bugental and colleagues (e.g., Bugental, 1992; Bugental, Brown, & Reiss, 1996) have studied the effects of ambiguous communication by examining the differential reactions children have to the expressive behavior of adults with high versus low perceptions of power. Adults with low perceived power are more prone than other adults to an ambiguous communication style, presumably because of apprehension or uncertainty in challenging caregiving situations; they show speech nonfluencies (e.g., stutters, repeated words), speech pauses, and false smiles (e.g., lacking eye involvement) to a greater extent than adults with high perceived power (Bugental, 1992; Bugental, Brown, & Reiss, 1996). They are also inclined to give unclear evaluative feedback and to dissemble. Bugental and Happaney (in press) found that low-power (ambiguous) mothers, in a reverse pattern to that of high-power (unambiguous) mothers, evaluated children they perceived as difficult more positively than children they perceived as easy. The discrepancy between their private and public evaluations suggested both emotional dissemblance and ambiguity.

In a study of the effects of ambiguous communication on emotion regulation, Bugental, Lyon, Lin, McGrath, and Bimbela (in press) had 7- to 10-year-olds play a computer game in response to instructions provided by a videotaped adult "teacher" who had either an ambiguous or unambiguous communication style. Children responded to ambiguous communication with a decrease in attentional engagement (indexed by autonomic orienting). Attentional disengagement was interpreted as an emotion regulation activity aimed at protection from distress. As further evidence for this interpretation, children rated the ambiguous adults more negatively than the unambiguous adults, suggesting that they found ambiguous adults to be a source of distress.

Inadequate Communication and Hurt Feelings

Why would inadequate communication be distressing? One possible answer is suggested by the notion that inadequate communication involves the frequent failure to acknowledge and/or validate emotion signals. Disruptions in interpersonal relatedness are considered to be inherently painful (e.g., Baumeister & Leary, 1995; Kaufman, 1989; see also Barrett, in this volume). Emotional reactions to "breaks in the interpersonal bridge" (Kaufman, 1985, 1989) have become the subject of study, although so far the topic has been studied only in adults (Leary, Springer, Negel, Ansell, & Evans, 1998; Vangelisti, 1994; Vangelisti & Crumley, 1998). In the few studies that have been done to date, college students have been asked to describe a time when someone said or did something that hurt their feelings. The findings are quite consistent across studies. Events perceived as hurtful typically involved a sense of "relational devaluation" (Leary et al., 1998), i.e., a perception of not being as important, close, or valuable to another person as the individual desires; they include events such as criticism, betrayal, rejection, ostracism, abandonment, or being ignored or excluded. The closer the relationship, the more hurt the individual was by the event. The more the event made them feel rejected by the perpetrator the more hurt they felt, and the more hurt they felt the more negative their self-perceptions. Thus, feelings of hurt, rejection, and negative self-evaluation were strongly related. Although it is not clear to what extent these findings can be generalized to children exposed to inadequate communication, one hypothesis they suggest is that inadequate communication engenders feelings of rejection, hurt, and negative self-evaluation, and that these feelings, in turn, interfere with the development of emotional competencies.

Hurtful behaviors have been defined as psychologically or emotionally harmful (L'Abaté, 1997; Vangelisti, 1994; Vangelisti & Sprague, 1998). Although hurt feelings have been given scant attention, there is some consensus that hurt involves a complex constellation of discrete component emotions, but that it is not wholly constituted by these emotions and has in addition to them a painful quality all its own that makes it a distinct, unique emotional state in its own right (L'Abaté, 1997; Leary et al., 1998). The discrete components associated with it may unfold sequentially in the aftermath of a hurtful event (Leary et al., 1998), and may vary in type and intensity depending on the nature of the event and the defensive strategies the individual uses to regulate emotional reactions. According to some theorists, for example, shame is a prime consequence of breaks in interpersonal relatedness, and may lead to anger as a form of defensive substitution (e.g., Kaufman, 1989; Retzinger, 1995). More attention needs to be paid to the role these emotions may play in hurt feelings and the way in which hurt feelings may interfere with the development of emotional skills and abilities.

In summary, from an attachment theory perspective "good" communication is that which recognizes, acknowledges, and responds to the child's states and concerns. Inadequate communication is distressing to the child, and may occur as a result of transactions between parent and child that lead to the exclusion of certain emotions and possibly to hurt feelings in the child. The nature of these feelings, their effects on emotional development, and their implications for learning about conflict are not well-understood and need to be examined more closely.

The factors conducive to good communication also need to be studied. In the next section, we describe recent work on some of the factors that may be important.

Parent and Child Contributions to the Quality of Emotional Communication

Information is accumulating about factors that affect the quality of emotional communication between parent and child. We will focus on recent work exploring the parent's approach to emotions and examining the moderating effects of child characteristics such as temperament and gender.

Coaching versus Dismissing Emotions

In an exploratory study of parents' feelings and beliefs about emotions, both their own and their child's, Gottman and colleagues (Gottman, Katz, & Hooven, 1996, 1997) interviewed (separately) parents of 4- to 5-year-olds about their experiences of anger and sadness, their philosophy about the expression and control of these emotions, and their attitudes and beliefs about their child's anger and sadness. On the basis of the interviews, parents were classified as having a "meta-emotion philosophy" of either "coaching" or "dismissing" emotion. Parents with a coaching philosophy were aware of emotions in themselves and in their child; viewed their child's negative emotion as an opportunity for intimacy or teaching; validated their child's emotions; and helped their child label emotions and solve the problems that led to them. Parents with a dismissing philosophy viewed anger and sadness as potentially harmful; believed in dealing with these emotions by ignoring or denying them as much as possible so that they would go away; and were neither insightful about their child's emotions nor helpful in problem-solving.

Children whose parents had a coaching philosophy were, at age five, better able to soothe themselves physiologically by focusing attention (as indexed by suppression of vagal tone); good physiological regulators, in turn, were better at regulating emotionally-driven behavior at age eight; and good behavioral regulators were doing better at age eight in several domains (peer relations, achievement, health). Thus, a coaching philosophy appeared to influence emotional behavior regulation through effects on physiological self-regulation. What mediates this influence is open to speculation. Coaching parents were low in parental derogation (derisive humor, intrusiveness, criticism), but low derogation was not related either to physiological regulation or to behavioral regulation. It was suggested, instead, that by talking to their children about their negative emotions, coaching parents may help their children to lower their autonomic arousal (stress) and self-regulate their emotions (e.g., by focusing attention, self-soothing).

The relations found between parental coaching and physiological regulation were consistent with the predicted direction of effects (from coaching to physiological regulation) but also with the reverse direction or with bidirectional effects. It is quite possible, then, that whether a parent selects a coaching or a dismissing approach to emotions depends partly on certain temperamental characteristics of their child.

Research on "emotion talk," which begins at a very early age (e.g., Bretherton, Fritz, Zahn-Waxler, & Ridgeway, 1986; Dunn, Bretherton, & Munn, 1987), suggests that one of the important ways in which emotion coaching may contribute to the development of emotion regulation is by helping children to clarify their own and others' emotions (e.g., Bretherton et al., 1986; Dunn & Brown, 1991). Causal discussions with toddlers, in which mothers explicitly explained the causes and consequences of affective states, were predictively related to the children's ability to discern what others may be feeling (Dunn, Brown, & Beardsall, 1991).

Interestingly, discussions of emotion were especially likely to occur in the context of conflict (Dunn, Brown, & Beardsall, 1991), presumably because there is more motivation to discuss feelings when they are negative. However, in highly negative families, mothers and children were *less* likely to discuss feelings when the child was in a negative emotional state (Dunn & Brown,

1994); beyond a certain point, conflict and distress may interfere with rather than promote the discussion of emotions. This effect seems to be generally consistent with Bretherton's (1990) suggestion that insecure attachment relationships are associated with less open communication.

It has been reported that mothers talk more and use more socioemotional language than fathers (Leaper, Anderson, & Sanders, 1998), and do more coaching of emotions (Gottman, Katz, & Hooven, 1997). It may be, then, that mothers discuss emotions more than fathers (see Russell, in this volume). Research also indicates that mothers give explanations more in emotion talk with sons than with daughters, and are more inclined to simply label emotions with daughters than with sons (Cervantes & Callanan, 1998; Fivush, 1989). Fivush (1989) suggested that mothers may encourage boys to engage in problem-solving and emotional control and encourage girls to focus on emotional states and sensitivity. Perhaps boys and girls are encouraged to make different kinds of attributions about interpersonal conflicts.

It is also possible that parents approach certain emotions differently with girls and boys. There is evidence that parents have different feelings about certain emotions in girls and boys (e.g., Brody & Hall, 1993), which they may wittingly or unwittingly communicate. Birnbaum and Croll (1984) presented parents with hypothetical stories about emotional states in children, and found that parents showed more acceptance of anger in boys than in girls, and more acceptance of fear in girls than in boys. However, before firm conclusions can be drawn about the moderating effects of parent and child gender, more research will need to be done on gender differences in parental approaches to emotion.

Parents' feelings and beliefs about themselves may also influence their approach to emotions. Parental cognitions about the balance of power in adult–child relationships are thought to be an important factor moderating the way parents react to children who have characteristics that threaten their sense of control (e.g., Bugental, Blue, Cortez, Fleck, Kopeikin, Lewis, & Lyon, 1993). Adults who believe that they have less power than children feel threatened by challenging or demanding child characteristics and tend to respond defensively to restore a sense of control. They may respond by disengaging or acting aggressively, depending on the options available to them. In one study with implications for emotional communication, adults (nonparental women) heard samples of audiotaped conversations with children whose voices varied in pitch, and were asked to rate how successful they thought they would be in training each child to do a task, and how difficult they thought it would be to interact with each child. Compared to women who were high in perceived power, those with low perceived power had more negative expectations about training and interacting when the child's voice was higher-pitched (more "attention-grabbing"). On the basis of findings such as this, it might be expected that parents with low-power schemas of adult–child relationships would be highly apprehensive and reactive to emotionally-arousing interactions with their children. Not surprisingly, as we noted earlier, low-power parents are prone to ambiguous communication in these interactions (e.g., Bugental, Brown, & Reiss, 1996).

Use of Emotions in Discipline

Parents also take different approaches to the use of emotions in disciplinary interactions. Parents attempt to directly induce certain emotions in their children, in order to obtain certain goals (e.g., to foster or minimize particular emotions, to gain compliance or control). Specifically, we will consider the impact of different kinds of emotional messages on children's development of empathy and guilt. These emotions play an important role in the constructive management of interpersonal conflicts. They motivate prosocial behavior by blurring the boundary between self and others and making the other person's distress part of the individual's own concern (e.g., Zahn-Waxler & Kochanska, 1990). Without these emotions, no effort would be made to balance the needs of self and other, and conflicts would be dealt with egoistically. Disciplinary encounters are a primary context for parental messages that contribute to, or interfere with, the development of empathy and guilt.

In an early analysis of the effects of different discipline strategies, Hoffman (1970a, 1982) proposed that discipline emphasizing "other-oriented" induction (making children aware of the consequences of their behavior for others) is optimal for promoting prosocial development and moral internalization. Other-oriented inductions carry a note of mild disapproval, and a message about the other person's distress and the child's role in causing it. These inductions are emotionally arousing. They capture the child's attention, arouse empathy and guilt, motivate prosocial behavior, and heighten the child's sense of being internally motivated.

According to Hoffman's analysis, parental messages are important not only for their informational content but also for their emotional intensity. Their intensity affects the child's level of emotional arousal and motivation to process the informational content of the message. While other-oriented inductions are considered to be arousing, punitive or coercive messages are believed to be overarousing; they cause emotional distress, not just discomfort. Emotional distress interferes with processing any explanations that might be delivered along with them, directs the child's attention to the consequences for the self rather than the other person, and heightens extrinsic rather than intrinsic motives for behaving prosocially. This self-concern and extrinsic orientation is incompatible with empathy and guilt.

The accumulated evidence generally supports Hoffman's analysis. Other-oriented induction in combination with mild disapproval does seem to be associated with emotional arousal, empathy, and guilt. In an early study, for example, children whose mothers frequently talked to them about the effects of their behavior on other people and expressed their disapproval of the child (e.g., "That really hurt—and I don't want to be near you when you act like that") were more likely to make reparation for wrongdoing, a behavioral reflection of empathy-based guilt (Zahn-Waxler, Radke-Yarrow, & King, 1979). Other studies yield consistent findings indicating that other-oriented inductions are positively related to children's sympathetic and sad reactions to others in distress (Eisenberg, Fabes, Carlo, Troyer, Speer, Karbon, & Switzer, 1992; Miller, Eisenberg, Fabes, Shell, & Gular, 1989), and demonstrate that empathy and empathy-based guilt mediate the relation between other-oriented induction and prosocial behavior (Krevans & Gibbs, 1996).

Emotional distress, on the other hand, tends to be incompatible with feeling care and concern for others. In adults, for example, higher levels of shame (a form of self-focused distress) were associated with lower levels of empathy (Tangney, 1995). It seems reasonable to expect, then, that exposure to personally distressing messages will undermine the development of empathic concern for others. Indeed, Eisenberg, Fabes, and colleagues found that negative control practices and emotional restrictiveness in mothers were related to markers of anxiety and personal distress in children (heart rate acceleration) and indices of low sympathy and empathic sadness concerning others in distress (Eisenberg et al., 1992; Miller et al., 1989). Children's feelings of concern for others were positively related to prosocial behavior, whereas personal distress resulting from exposure to another's distress was negatively related to prosocial behavior (Eisenberg & Fabes, 1998). Personal distress reactions in preschoolers were related to *compliant* prosocial responding (Eisenberg, Fabes, Miller, Shell, Shea, & May-Plumlee, 1990; Eisenberg, McCreath, & Ahn, 1988), but this was interpreted as a coping strategy (compliance to avoid distress) rather than a reflection of prosocial motives (Eisenberg & Fabes, 1992a). Taken as a whole, research on the development of empathy and guilt suggests that other-oriented messages gently restrain the child's egocentrism and contribute to the development of empathy and guilt, whereas distressing messages heighten self-concern at the expense of concern for others.

There is evidence suggesting that the effects of parental emotion-induction techniques vary with individual differences in the temperamental characteristics of the child. For example, children who were temperamentally prone to anxiety or distress were more responsive to discipline emphasizing other-oriented reasoning than discipline emphasizing power assertion (Kochanska, 1995, 1997a). These children may also be more prone to distress in response to emotion-induction techniques.

Messages that Hurt

Leary and colleagues (1998) found a very strong correlation between feelings of hurt and distress in college students. This may be because the distressing messages that heighten self-concern the most are those that hurt. Given the complex mixture of discrete emotions believed to be associated with hurt feelings, as we noted earlier, a differentiated analysis is needed of the emotional reactions elicited by parental messages and behaviors that hurt. Some evidence is beginning to emerge to suggest, for example, that one of the emotions engendered by hurtful parental messages is shame. Shame was more pronounced in children (aged 5 to 12 years) whose parents perceived them as falling short of their ideals (especially concerning personal attributes and self-control) (Ferguson & Stegge, 1995). Even in early childhood, hurtful parental messages may evoke shame. Children aged 3 to 5 years whose parents made fewer positive and more negative evaluative statements to them during task performance showed shame in response to task failure (Alessandri & Lewis, 1993, 1996). Although these findings are suggestive, the extent to which hurtful parental messages tend to engender shame, what other emotions they tend to evoke, and what developmental changes may occur in children's emotional reactions to these messages, are questions that have yet to be addressed.

Research is also needed on the parental goals associated with hurtful communication. Vangelisti and Sprague (1998) suggest that hurtful messages may be used strategically to gain control, punish disagreeable behaviors, or vent feelings of distress. Some of these messages appear to be designed to gain control while avoiding confrontation, similar to the notion of relational aggression (see Monks & Smith, in this volume). Guilt-induction and "love withdrawal" (the expression of emotional rejection) are potent examples of such a strategy (e.g., Vangelisti, Daly, & Rudnick, 1991; Williams, Shore, & Grahe, 1998). In a study of undergraduate students, Vangelisti et al. found that self-reported use of guilt-induction was related to shyness and low social assertiveness. Similarly, parents with relational schemas of low power (Bugental, 1992) may be prone to the use of guilt-induction and love withdrawal with their children. An exploratory study of mothers and daughters yielded findings suggesting that mothers were more inclined to report using guilt-induction and love withdrawal with their daughters when they perceived themselves as low in power (providing their daughters were temperamentally relatively anxious—and hence acquiescent) (Mills, in press).

The effects of hurt feelings on the development of emotional competencies in children also need to be examined. Vangelisti and Crumley (1998) found that the reactions of college students who felt hurt commonly included both assertive or externalizing responses (e.g., lashing out, defending the self) and acquiescent or internalizing responses (e.g., crying, apologizing). The more hurtful a message was, the more likely the person was to respond by acquiescing. Researchers have yet to study individual differences in responses to hurt and their relation to early patterns of exposure to hurtful parental behavior. Children who are frequently hurt may gradually acquire strategies for defending themselves against hurt that involve excessively aggressive or submissive patterns of behavior (see Monks & Smith, in this volume).

In summary, the content of parental emotional messages appears to play an important role in shaping the discrete emotions children experience and the way in which they regulate them. Emotional messages that are distressing or hurtful seem to interfere with the development of prosocial emotions and may contribute to the development of maladaptive strategies for defending the self against hurt. Further exploration of hurtful messages and their effects on defensive strategies would help to extend models of the development of children's relationship difficulties outside the family, such as peer aggression and social withdrawal (e.g., Rubin, Stewart, & Chen, 1995). Such problems may derive in part from excessive exposure to hurtful messages in the context of parent–child conflicts.

EXPOSURE TO EMOTIONAL COMMUNICATION BETWEEN PARENTS

In addition to emotional communication with their parents, children also learn from emotional exchanges *between* their parents. While family emotional climate can be influenced by interactions between any and all family members, interactions between parents can be seen as the bedrock of family expressiveness and the primary influence on the emotional undertone of the household (Gottman, Katz, & Hoover, 1997). A large body of recent research has focused upon a genre of parent-parent interactions that are often highly emotional and are therefore particularly salient for children: marital conflict. Because of the potentially profound significance interparental conflicts can hold, such as being the first indicators of parental unhappiness, impending violence, separation or divorce, they are of deep consequence to children. Whether "witnessed" directly or through some other means (e.g., changes in emotional climate), children's exposure to and awareness of interparental conflicts have been shown to significantly influence their emotional well-being (Davies & Cummings, 1994) as well as their own subsequent management of conflict (Cummings, Iannotti, & Zahn-Waxler, 1985; Cummings & Smith, 1993).

It must first be emphasized that exposure to emotional expression in marital conflict is not exclusively or consistently distressing for children. These conflicts can be positive learning opportunities, especially if they are managed constructively or resolved positively (Cummings, Ballard, El-Sheikh, & Lake, 1991; Easterbrooks, Cummings, & Emde, 1994). In a longitudinal study of how toddlers reacted during constructive conflict episodes between their parents, Easterbrooks and her colleagues found that young children were equally likely to either play independently or try to gain their parents' attention amidst marital problem-solving discussions. Toddlers judged by their parents to have a difficult temperament were likely to exhibit fewer positive behaviors during parental exchanges; however, given the young ages of the children involved (12–36 months), these behaviors were more variable than stable (Easterbrooks, Cummings, & Emde, 1994).

In cross-sectional work focusing on school-aged children's and adolescents' responses to interadult conflicts, those resolved by compromise or apology were compared to those partially resolved by submission or change of topic and those left unresolved by continued fighting or "silent treatment" (withdrawal) (Cummings et al., 1991). Resolved anger elicited the least negative responses across ages. Although this particular study focused solely on how conflicts ended rather than what they were about or how they were managed, it does provide evidence that children as young as 5 years of age are sensitive to the nature of resolution and report feeling less distressed, scared, and angry when exposed to conflicts resolved constructively.

Hostile Conflict: Forum for Distressing Messages

Because of the wide range of variability in conflict styles and degree of emotional intensity during marital disputes (Gottman, 1994), most children are exposed to distressing messages between their parents to some degree. According to Gottman's (1994) impressive body of work, disputes involving hostile personal criticism, contempt, defensiveness, and avoidance or "stonewalling" are most indicative of a hostile and degenerating relationship.

Hostile marital conflict has been clearly identified in the literature as a risk indicator for children's adjustment; however, not all children react in the same way. The specific mechanisms of influence on children's well-being are still under intense investigation (Rutter, 1994). In this section, we will review evidence pertaining to two main questions. First, what is it about exposure to hostile conflict that is most distressing for children? Second, how do children's responses to these distressing events vary systematically according to their own individual characteristics?

Emotions and Hostile Conflict

While it has long been known that marital dissatisfaction and children's maladjustment are linked, the many and varied processes through which dissatisfaction is expressed to children are still under scrutiny. Recent work has shown that more frequent and severe marital conflicts are linked to greater maladjustment difficulties (Jenkins & Smith, 1991), while encapsulated or concealed conflict has no clear adverse effects (Hetherington, 1989). So the frequency and severity of the conflict between others appears to play a role in children's responses—but what exactly are they responding to?

Cummings and Cummings (1988) have suggested that the level of anger expressed during conflict determines the effect of marital discord on child psychopathology. That is, the fact that one or both parents express anger at the other represents a seriously distressing event for children. Therefore, two conflicts initiated and carried out in the same fashion, and resolved in the same manner, can have profoundly different consequences for children based upon the nature and intensity of the emotions expressed. In support of this view, Grych and colleagues (Grych, 1998; Grych & Fincham, 1993; Grych, Seid, & Fincham, 1992) found that exposure to more intensely angry marital interactions in an analogue situation was related to self-reports of greater distress, anger, sadness, shame, and self-blame in children (7- to 12-year-olds). Based on these findings, it can be concluded that children find angry parental exchanges distressing and painful—even shame-inducing.

Much like the case of constructive conflict, it must be remembered that exposure to the expression of anger per se may not necessarily be detrimental for children. If parents provide models of appropriate anger management, exposure to anger may in fact enhance children's own emotional expression and control. We argue, therefore, that while exposure to the expression of anger may be tied to children's short-term discomfort, it is *unresolved* anger between parents that is most distressing to children and carries the greatest risk for lasting adjustment difficulties. Work that has addressed children's response to conflict resolution supports this view. Using an analogue methodology, Cummings and colleagues (1991) found that exposure to unresolved conflict was associated with negative affect and poor coping responses in children.

However, it is possible that parents may successfully solve a problem but leave a conflict *emotionally unresolved*. If this is the case, the resolution of the concrete issue may be less important than the resolution of emotions, as children may be sensitive to continuing angry feelings between their parents. In keeping with our argument, Shifflet-Simpson and Cummings (1996) found that children responded to such emotional cues. Specifically, children aged 5 to 7 years of age clearly distinguished between an angry apology and one delivered with sincerity. Older children (aged 9–12 years) reported feeling more distressed when conflicts ended with the expression of negative emotion than with positive emotion. Given these findings, previous work concerning children's preferences for differing types of resolution between adults needs to be interpreted in a different light. It is possible that children's reactions to differing resolutions of issues have been confounded with their reactions to the quality of *emotional* resolution.

Unresolved feelings of anger between partners may also influence children indirectly through the parent–child relationship. Some researchers argue that marital conflict primarily affects children through disruption in parenting practices (Fauber & Long, 1991). Several of these potential mechanisms were outlined earlier in this chapter. The point here is that marital conflict is likely to *both* directly and indirectly influence children through different mechanisms. The emotional tone of marital conflicts and the potential for "spillover" of unresolved negative emotions from one relationship into another appear to be of marked importance for children's well-being.

These encouraging sources of evidence concerning the effects of exposure to emotional resolution between parents complement previous work on open communication styles in parent–child relationships. As discussed earlier in this chapter, some researchers propose that more open lines of communication concerning emotions between parents and children, and presumably therefore more emotional resolution, promote children's sense of security and well-being (Bretherton, 1990; Cassidy, 1994). Clearly, these two avenues of research need to be brought together; more work specifically targeting links between emotional communication styles between parents and children and emotional resolution in marital relationships needs to be done.

While the effects of children's exposure to anger have received much attention, a plethora of other emotions are also part of the marital conflict landscape. Gottman (1994) identified the expression of contempt, or active humiliation of the other person, as an important marker of hostile conflict. The source of such hostility is believed to be feelings of shame (Retzinger, 1995; Scheff, 1995; Tangney, 1995), which we suggest may be a key component of hurt feelings. While both the induction and expression of shame in interpersonal conflict may be subtle, their influence is pervasive and distressing and may be the root of continuing unresolved hostile conflict. For example, Scheff (1995) proposed that interminable or continuing family conflicts are most often caused by feelings of shame. Specifically, "if shame is evoked but goes unacknowledged, the result may be a repetitive cycle of insult and revenge" (Scheff, 1995, p. 393). From this perspective, feelings of shame and rage may be *felt* only as anger, but are conjoined in a self-perpetuating positive feedback loop. The effect of exposure to this cycle of shame and rage in marital conflicts on children is currently an open question.

It seems likely that much of the current confusion in the literature surrounding the identification of meaningful patterns in children's responses to hostile marital conflict may be alleviated by closer inspection of key emotional characteristics of these interactions. The study of shame appears to be one promising avenue for future research.

As noted, there is a wide range of variation in how children respond to marital conflicts. Thus far, several factors have been identified as potentially important for understanding these individual differences, including age, temperament, gender, and perhaps most importantly, children's understanding of these events.

Individual Differences in Children's Responses

Models of coping in children and adolescents distinguish between approach coping, seen as strategies designed to address the problem directly, and avoidant coping, seen as strategies designed to avoid the problem or minimize the impact of the stressor (Ebata & Moos, 1991). Use of active problem-solving strategies when a stressor is not controllable may be maladaptive (Forsythe & Compas, 1987), and marital conflict certainly can be considered an uncontrollable stressor in children's lives. When faced with these instances of little or no control, some children may effect active coping strategies, such as directly intervening in parental disputes, despite the fact that it makes them a potential target for parental anger and places them at risk for triangulation in the marital relationship (Minuchin, 1992).

However, approach coping *following* interparental conflicts, such as seeking out one or both parents after conflicts have subsided, may be an adaptive strategy. As seen in Cummings's work, when children were debriefed following a conflict and simply told it was resolved amicably (they did not actually see the resolution), they were less likely to report distress (Cummings & Davies, 1994). Thus, children who approach parents following conflict may obtain reassurance or other relevant information that may help them to cope. Some research suggests that preschool-aged children are more likely to seek out the company of a sibling rather than a parent following marital disputes

(Berthelson, Smith, & O'Connor, 1996). However, current research has not yet systematically addressed the nature or influence of children's self-comforting strategies following hostile parental disputes.

Two main patterns of maladjustment in response to chronic exposure to hostile conflict have been identified. As often denoted in the literature, some children tend to demonstrate externalizing or under-controlled behaviors, including physical and verbal aggression and noncompliant behaviors, while others tend to demonstrate more internalizing or over-controlled behaviors, such as depression, anxiety, and somatic symptoms (e.g., Katz & Gottman, 1993). Recent research has suggested that children's *appraisals* of hostile marital conflict may be an important mediator influencing differing patterns of maladjustment (Grych & Fincham, 1990). In particular, their *emotions* in reaction to exposure to conflict appear to be crucial elements that influence later adjustment (Crockenberg & Forgays, 1996).

Feeling threatened, powerless, and at fault appear to be especially important mediators of children's patterns of maladjustment. The sex of the child may be an important moderating factor (Snyder, 1998). For example, the more destructive school-aged children appraised marital conflict to be, the more boys felt threatened by it and the more girls were prone to self-blame. Feeling threatened and unable to cope effectively was related to overall maladjustment (internalizing and externalizing problems) in boys, while self-blame was linked to internalizing problems in girls (Cummings, Davies, & Simpson, 1994). Kerig and colleagues (Kerig, Fedorowicz, Brown, Patenaude, & Warren, 1998) demonstrated that when girls believed they had direct control over parental hostility and aggression, they endorsed more active coping responses. For boys, perceived control was related to venting, a coping strategy involving rumination as well as both verbal and physical release of emotion (e.g., physical aggression). In this study, more frequent and verbally aggressive marital conflicts were positively linked to self-blame in girls. Girls' self-blame was also linked to greater exposure to and involvement in marital conflicts. Finally, self-blame was associated with maladaptive coping strategies for both boys and girls.

Taken together, these findings suggest that the combination of feeling threatened, powerless, and at fault creates a risk factor for maladjustment greater than any single factor alone; reports of self-blame and powerlessness suggest that children may also be experiencing feelings of guilt and shame, although the possible mediating roles of these emotional reactions has not been directly assessed in previous work. Determining whether some children develop a cognitive appraisal style of self-blame and helplessness accompanied by an emotional appraisal style of guilt and shame appears to be an important direction for future research.

Persistence over Time

The question of why some children's maladjustment patterns are short-lived, while for others these patterns persist, remains unanswered. Several different ideas about why this might be the case have been broached in the literature. For example, Cummings and Davies's (1994) sensitivity hypothesis proposes that, rather than becoming habituated to hostile interparental disputes, children instead become *more* sensitized over time due to their heightened anticipation of and apprehension about the stressful event. These authors attribute children's increasing sensitivity to a growing fear that basic emotional security within the family is threatened by hostile interparental conflict; that is, the more frequent and severe children perceive these events to be, the more likely they are to feel concerned and distressed that the relationship between their parents and between parents and themselves is fragile and deteriorating.

The question of timing, or when exposure to hostile interparental conflict begins in a child's life, is integral to the sensitivity hypothesis, as there are marked developmental differences in children's coping strategies at different ages. For example, younger children are more likely to respond to others' negative emotion in a contagion fashion or with distress on their own part (Saarni, Mumme, & Campos, 1998). Recent work by Bugental demonstrated that 5- to 6-year-olds react to another child's expression of negative emotion in a potentially fear-provoking situation (medical examination) with higher autonomic arousal (increase in heart rate and skin conductance) than 9- to 10-year-olds do (Bugental, Blue, Cortez, Fleck, & Rodriguez, 1992); the younger children were also less likely to accurately recall events that occurred in this situation, indicating a narrow focus of information processing associated with distress. Therefore, early exposure to hostile interparental conflicts during the toddler or preschool years may contribute to chronic high arousal and distress. If it persists, the child may fail to develop an expanding repertoire of adaptive coping strategies, contributing to longer term adjustment difficulties.

The sensitivity hypothesis is supported by work finding that children's prior exposure to conflict and resolution is related to their responses to current conflict episodes (El-Sheikh, Cummings, & Reiter, 1996). Preschoolers responded differently to interadult conflict as a function of whether they had just witnessed a live argument that was resolved or unresolved. Those children who had just seen a resolved dispute between adult actors exhibited lower behavioral distress, and were more likely to predict a lower likelihood of a conflictual outcome in the future (El-Sheikh et al., 1996). In other work examining cognitive styles in children with different symptomatologies, children clinically identified as anxious or oppositional were compared to nonclinical children (Barrett, Rapee, Dadds, & Ryan, 1996). Anxious children showed greater sensitivity to threat (i.e., interpreted ambiguous situations as threatening) than nonclinical children, and tended to choose avoidant solutions. Oppositional children also were more prone to feel threatened than nonclinical children; however, they tended to endorse aggressive rather than avoidant solutions. These findings support the notion that once a pattern of hyper-sensitivity is in place, it may become ingrained over time through the development of cognitive representations or schemas; how it is dealt with may depend on the child's general regulatory style. If we extrapolate to children's sensitivity to hostile marital conflict, exposure early in a child's life and for an extended period may contribute to schemas of conflict in which children begin to see conflict as leading to contempt, defensiveness, mutual hostility, and unresolved anger, and incorporate this expectation and the emotional reactions it elicits (e.g., feeling threatened) into their own interpersonal conflict management styles.

Children's schemas or representations of conflict, together with their emotional reactions, may mediate their ongoing long-term sensitivity to interpersonal conflict and their general psychological adjustment. In recent work providing support for this view, Davies and Cummings (1998) found that children's representation of marital relations, as well as their emotional reactions to conflict (distress, vigilance, hostility), mediated their adjustment problems (particularly internalizing problems).

This view is quite compatible with the notion that conflict "scripts" develop over time. Children as young as preschool-age have been shown to have well-developed, culturally-shared scripts for commonly occurring events such as a visit to a restaurant or a doctor (Nelson & Gruendel, 1986). We suggest that children may also develop such scripts for conflicts in close interpersonal relationships based upon their history of prior exposure to and involvement in these events. And while children are certainly more than capable of distinguishing the appropriateness of certain behaviors in differing relationships (e.g., a dispute with a friend is handled differently from a dispute with a mother or a sibling), a more general conflict script may also be expressed (differently within different relationships) in which the child is disposed to feel threatened, at fault, or helpless. The development of a negative attributional bias in peer relationships has been well-documented (e.g., Crick & Dodge, 1994). We suggest that some children with such a bias may have acquired it through exposure to distressing messages and unresolved negative emotion between their parents.

SUMMARY

We have suggested that the more children experience emotional communication that is open to the expression and resolution of difficult emotions in conflict situations, the more likely they are to develop skills and abilities in emotional communication, emotional understanding, and emotion regulation, all of which facilitate constructive responses to conflict. The more inadequate emotional communication is, the more likely children are to experience emotional distress and acquire patterns of maladjustment. Shame, anger, and other hurt feelings appear to be important components of children's distress, particularly in families that manage conflict through the use of hurtful communication. A closer examination is needed of the role hurt feelings play in children's distress and their effects on the development of emotional competencies. Empirical work is also needed to determine whether specific links do, in fact, exist between exposure to hurtful communication in the family and children's strategies for dealing with interpersonal conflicts.

ACKNOWLEDGMENTS

The author would like to thank Steve Duck for his helpful comments on an earlier draft of this chapter.

Chapter 5

The Development of the Self-in-Relationships

Karen Caplovitz Barrett

Colorado State University, USA

PROLOGUE

This chapter regards the development of self in relation to others. In order to cover this topic thoroughly, one would need an entire, very large book. I have elected to discuss general issues regarding the self and social relationships that should apply to most age groups, but then to focus the review of empirical literature primarily on toddlerhood, the first period of development during which the development of self is widely believed to be a prominent influence on other domains of development. The other major time period during which self development is seen as a major influence is adolescence. Some of what is discussed in this chapter should pertain to that period as well; however, the "self" of toddlerhood is very different from the "self" of adolescence, so some ideas may not apply.

Attachment is an important topic that is extremely relevant to this chapter, in that it is believed to involve the development of working models of self and relationships. However, that large topic is covered extensively elsewhere (Zeifman & Hazan, 1997), so it will receive only cursory attention herein.

Finally, this chapter will emphasize *affective* aspects of the self, given that whenever the self is involved in significant relationships with the animate and/ or inanimate environment, emotion processes result (e.g., see Barrett, 1995;

The Developmental Psychology of Personal Relationships.
Edited by Rosemary S. L. Mills and Steve Duck. © 2000 John Wiley & Sons Ltd.

Barrett & Campos, 1987; Higgins, 1989). In particular, the relevance of the "social" or "self-conscious" emotions for the development of self and relationships will be emphasized, including the issue of how Erikson's "developmental crises" might relate to cultural differences in individualism vs. interdependence.

Many chapters on "self" would begin by defining "the self." Like many other current writers, however, I do not believe that "the self" is a single entity (e.g., see Fogel, 1995; Hermans, Kempen, & van Loon, 1992; Kagan, 1991; Lewis, 1991b; Neisser, 1991) that is amenable to a unitary definition.

Some define the "selves" as differing primarily in level—with "level" defined primarily in terms of changes in self-understanding that are permitted by changes in cognitive abilities with development (e.g., Case, 1991; Lewis, 1991b). Few would question the assumption that changes in cognitive abilities allow for more complexity in conceptions of self. However, in this chapter, I will focus on interesting new developments that suggest the need for a concept of "self in relationships"—that suggest that the traditional dichotomization into self *versus* other may be misleading.

The chapter will begin by noting that self *in opposition to* other is more of a Western than an Eastern phenomenon, and is overstated even in Western societies. Then, I will provide some evidence that self and relationships with others develop in tandem, as a function of one another, and that a crucial aspect of the self is the self-in-relationship. Third, I will suggest that "self-conscious" or "social" emotions, such as shame and pride, play an important role in the development of self-in-relationship. Then, finally, I will briefly outline an approach that incorporates these ideas.

INDIVIDUALISM VERSUS COLLECTIVISM AND INDEPENDENCE VERSUS INTERDEPENDENCE

The growth of cross-cultural research; the increased "cross-talk" among the disciplines of psychology, anthropology, and sociology; and the growth of a new discipline of "cultural psychology" all have contributed to increased awareness by Americans that many assumptions about self and other that we take for granted are not shared by certain other cultures. Examination of views of self and other in cultures characterized by differences in "collectivism" versus "individualism" has suggested that the isolated, autonomous, independent self is not universally constructed (e.g., Raeff, 1997; Sampson, 1988; Triandis, 1995). On the contrary; in some cultures (and to some degree in our own, especially for females), at the heart of the "true self" is an interdependent or relational self. In fact, "standing out" as different from others is considered damaging to the self in such cultures (see also Markus & Kitayama, 1994).

The basic idea behind the distinction between individualism and collectivism is that "self" is defined differently in different cultures. In some cultures, such as the United States and Canada and much of Europe, the person is defined as an individual entity who chooses and controls his/her interactions and relationships with others, and who has (and conceptualizes) a set of definable attributes that distinguish him/her from others. The self is this distinctive set of characteristics and/or the person's concept of them. The goal of the person is to distinguish him/herself from others as a unique, special individual, to achieve as much as he/she can as an individual, and to be autonomous relative to others.

Interpersonal relationships are valued; however, they are seen as "healthy" only to the extent that each individual's needs are met, each person is free to pursue personal interests, each person freely commits to the relationship, and each person is valued for his/her "true inner self," rather than for the self that the other would like him/her to be. One should help others, but one is justified in expecting reciprocity (Miller, 1995); it is "against human nature" to be happy in a "one-sided" relationship in which one gives more to a relationship than does one's partner. Moreover, it is important, in relating to others, to "maintain appropriate boundaries." One feels pride (which is a positive experience) when one excels, especially in comparison to esteemed others, and anger when others do not allow one to pursue one's own goals.

In contrast, in other cultures such as Japan, China, India, and much of Africa and Latin America, the person is more likely to be viewed in relation to his/her duties, roles, and responsibilities toward others. The self is defined, in a central way, by these roles and relationships; the self is not wholly separate from them. A person typically feels joy when fulfilling responsibilities/ duties and negative emotion when "standing out" as different (Markus & Kitayama, 1994). "Amae," an emotion that one experiences in Japan when one is in a dependent relationship with another (such as a parent) and one wants that person's indulgence, is considered reasonable and expectable, even in older children and adults. An Indian emotion, "lajya," whose closest translation into English is "shame," is viewed as positive, and is purposefully displayed as a show of civility and commitment to maintaining harmony. In short, it feels good to be connected with and/or in harmony with one's group and to fulfill one's duties and obligations to those group members. The bounded, insular, "self-actualizing" person is an enigma or even an immoral person; the happy, well-adjusted person is interdependent with a group and makes group members happy through his/her behavior (see Markus & Kitayama, 1994; Sampson, 1988).

The majority of writers seem to consider independence to be a central, defining characteristic of individualism and interdependence to be a central, defining characteristic of collectivism, although they acknowledge that individuals within each culture vary in their degree of individualistic versus collectivistic tendencies. Recently, however, Raeff (1997) proposed that individualistic and collectivistic societies vary in the *forms* of independence and interdependence that are fostered, but both types of cultures actively socialize children to display both types of tendencies. Consistent with this assertion is the acknowledgment above that individualistic cultures value interpersonal relationships, but just have different expectations about what relationships entail.

In this chapter, it will be suggested that independence and interdependence are fostered in all cultures and that independence is not antithetical to interdependence. Nevertheless, the concept of individualism versus collectivism is viewed as valuable in uncovering some implicit biases that exist in our Western literature on the development of self and other, and in highlighting ways in which our individualistic culture leads us to downplay the importance of the interdependent self. If a child is socialized to be interdependent in a collectivistic way, for example, what happens to Erikson's (1963) "normative" developmental crisis of autonomy versus shame and doubt? Relatedly, the developmental task of distinguishing self *versus* other seems predicated on an *independent* self; to an interdependent self, the self is defined in relationship to others. Given that most of our literature is written by Western authors, it may be that an undue emphasis has been placed on the independent self and therefore on the development of self as the development of the ability to distinguish self from others. I will now discuss evidence that more attention to the self-in-relationships is needed, even in research regarding Western cultures.

SELF VERSUS OTHER

Most treatments of the development of the self during infancy and toddlerhood propose that this development involves distinguishing self from other. This is a proposal upon which quite disparate theoretical approaches are in agreement (although specifics vary), including Mahler's theory (Mahler, 1958; 1968), Piaget's theory (e.g., Piaget, 1952), and Martin Hoffman's theory (Hoffman, 1976), among many others. The basic idea is that newborn infants act upon a world without distinguishing their actions and/or needs and desires from that world.

For most psychoanalytic theories, the social world is emphasized; the baby and caregiver are at first fused, only later to be distinguished. For Piaget, the inanimate world is emphasized, with the baby unaware that the object world is separate from its own actions; however, the social world should be unknown as well. Another basic assumption of all of these approaches is that in order to "develop a self," one must distinguish it from other people and things.

In recent years, however, several separate lines of work have independently suggested that this view of development of self *versus* other should be reevaluated. First, a burgeoning literature on the capabilities of young babies has suggested that even the earliest self is a *relational* self; young babies are receptive *and responsive* to social stimulation, and are capable of modifying their own behavior so as to change social stimulation (e.g., DeCasper & Fifer, 1980).

Second, research on self development during infancy and toddlerhood has suggested that the tendency to engage in other-oriented responses such as empathy, altruism, and coordinated action are related to the development of self-recognition/self-consciousness (e.g., Asendorpf & Baudonniere, 1993; Johnson, 1982). Although some would interpret this as support for the idea that what is developing is a sense of self versus other (e.g., Johnson, 1982; Lewis, 1991b), these other-oriented responses, especially empathy, would seem to involve a feeling of connectedness with and similarity to others. Perhaps these other-oriented responses involve differentiation of other from self, followed by higher level integration, but if so, the higher level integration seems to develop remarkably quickly. Alternatively, perhaps a self that is developing during infancy and toddlerhood is, at its very core, an interpersonal self (see also Neisser, 1991).

And, third, research on self-regulation has suggested that others' regulation of the baby's state is by no means antithetical to the development of self-regulation (Kopp, 1982), compliance with parental demands is not necessarily antithetical to "internalized" self-regulation (Kochanska & Aksan, 1995), and self-assertion in toddlers is associated with child-rearing approaches that should promote close relationships (Crockenberg & Litman, 1990).

I will first briefly discuss the literature regarding each of these three topics in turn. Then, I will discuss how "social" emotions contribute to the development of the self-in-relationships, followed by a brief discussion of what I believe "self" and "relationship" entail during the first three or so years of life.

Young Babies' Responsiveness to Social Stimuli

Over the past two decades, a wealth of information on the young baby has been obtained. Research has laid to rest the depiction of the young infant as an disorganized and inept being who is insulated from the world by an "absolute stimulus barrier" (e.g., Mahler, 1958; Sroufe, 1979). Current evidence suggests that the newborn is an active organism who is "built" to interact with others. Days or even hours after birth, the baby will suck with a particular rhythm in order to hear its mother's voice (DeCasper & Fifer, 1980), can discriminate its mother's personal odors from those of other lactating women (MacFarlane, 1975), and will cry when other neonates cry (Sagi & Hoffman, 1976). Infants' visual responses to other people are limited by the poor acuity of the neonate. However, by about 7 weeks of age, when acuity has made some improvement, infants look at the facial features of people, and make eye contact with a person who is talking to them (Haith, Bergman, & Moore, 1977).

By 3 months of age, babies interact smoothly when face-to-face with a parent, but show gaze aversion, increased heart rate, and decreased smiling when that same parent becomes unresponsive (e.g., Cohn & Elmore, 1988; Field, Vega-Lahr, Scafidi, & Goldstein, 1986; Fogel, Diamond, Langhorst, &

Demos, 1982; Mayes & Carter, 1990; Murray & Trevarthen, 1985; Stack & Muir, 1990). But infants are not only perceptive about their parents; by 3 months, babies smile less at an unfamiliar person who does not make eye contact with them, even when that person continues to smile and vocalize contingently toward them (Hains & Muir, 1996). Moreover, by 4 months, infants look more at a male when hearing a male voice and at a female when hearing a female voice even when those persons are unfamiliar.

Further, soon babies become responsive to the meaning of others' emotions. By about 7 months, babies match emotion information across perceptual modalities (Walker, 1982), and by 10 months, use another's emotion communication to guide their reactions toward ambiguous events (e.g., Sorce, Emde, Campos, & Klinnert, 1985). From 8 to 10 months of age, infants increasingly "share" their smiles with their mothers, smiling and then turning to their mothers, and doing so much more frequently if their mothers are responsive. Moreover, there is evidence that such affect sharing is purposeful (Jones & Hong, 1995). In short, throughout infancy, babies are responsive to other people. Moreover, infants seem to quickly develop expectations that others will be responsive to them, that others can provide information to them about the affective significance of events around them, and that their own emotions are of interest to others. Many of these findings call into question theoretical notions of a "normal autistic phase" during early infancy, during which time the baby lacks awareness of others (Mahler, 1958), and these findings and others suggest that the baby begins with a propensity for interacting with others and never loses that inclination.

Nor is the self *merged* with others; the young baby can tell when the parent is unresponsive and can tell males from females; the older baby can relate others' reactions to its own responses to novel events, and seems to understand when the caregiver is receptive to its affect sharing. The baby develops in a social world, and its senses of self, other, and relationships grow together.

Self Development and Other-oriented Attributes during Toddlerhood

Not only does the infant relate to others and regulate its own behavior in response to the behavior of others; the ability to respond appropriately to others and the self develop together. A consistent pattern is emerging from studies relating toddlers' level of self development and their ability to relate to others. Twelve- to 36-month-olds who have been classified as having secure attachment relationships with their parents are more advanced in their level of agency (acting on self, mother, and dolls), than are those classified as insecurely attached (Pipp, Easterbrooks, & Harmon, 1992). Moreover, securely attached 18- to 36-month-olds show more advanced featural self-recognition than do those classified as insecurely attached (Pipp, Easterbrooks, & Harmon, 1992). Thus, toddlers who are more advanced in their senses of self and agency seem to have better relationships with their parents.

Similarly, toddlers who have more advanced knowledge of their appearance and/or agency seem to relate better to peers. Toddlers who recognize themselves in a mirror and/or in pictures are more likely to help others who appear to be hurt (Johnson, 1982), to show empathy for others (Bischof-Kohler, 1988, cited in Asendorpf & Baudonniere, 1993; Bischof-Kohler, 1991; Zahn-Waxler, Radke-Yarrow, Wagner, & Chapman, 1992), and to show coordinated imitation of peers (Asendorpf & Baudonniere, 1993). Finally, toddlers who show a higher level of agent use in pretend play are better able to engage in cooperative problem-solving with peers (Brownell & Carriger, 1990). In several of these studies, the effects of age were controlled, and age did not account for the relation of self development measures to other-oriented measures (although, in the Zahn-Waxler et al. study, effects were found at 24 months but not at 18 months).

All of these findings suggest that, at least during toddlerhood, self development and other-orientation go hand-in-hand. Does this mean that, given our individualistic society, the way to relate well to others is to see self and other as distinctly different and separate entities (and to relate to others as such)? Or, is it possible that rather than or in addition to developing individualistic selves, toddlers, even in American culture, establish interdependent or interpersonal selves? These findings suggest an important direction for future research—delving into whether an interdependent self is an important aspect of self during early development in American cultures, and, if so, just what the development of an interdependent self is like in our country. Research also is needed regarding how our culture's socialization patterns affect the development of an interdependent self as well as children's social relationships.

Other-regulation, Self-regulation, Internalization, and Socialization

It has long been assumed that children must learn to regulate their behavior according to societal and parental standards, and that until such "self-regulation" is possible, parents and other socializing agents must regulate children's behavior. According to traditional Western theories, children "internalize" the standards that socializing agents convey. According to Freudian theory, the child introjects the parent and parental "shoulds and shouldn'ts" to form a superego, in connection with the resolution of the Oedipus conflict, when the child is 5 or 6 years of age. Until the Oedipus complex is resolved and the superego established, the child is dependent on others in order to determine how to behave; only after the superego is established can the child be truly moral, because only then does the child regulate his/her own behavior (Freud, 1923/1961).

Traditional Social Learning Theory, although of course not proposing a superego, suggested also that the child must internalize the parents' rules and behavior in order to demonstrate self-regulation (e.g., see Aronfreed, 1968).

Both Freudian and traditional Social Learning Theory approaches seem to suggest that a) the child is more moral once the regulation comes from within, and b) that once rules are internalized, the child does not rely on others to determine how to act. Freudian theory very explicitly indicates an age at which the standards are introjected, as though after that age, others are rather irrelevant; children govern their own behavior.

Even some current views seem to adhere to the belief that self-regulated behavior is a desired end-state that children achieve with development (although, as we shall see, they operationalize "self-regulation" in ways that do not preclude others' involvement). For example, in a recent review article on "conscience" development, Kochanska (1993) states:

> The gradual developmental shift from external to internal regulation that results in a child's ability to conform to societal standards of conduct and to restrain antisocial or destructive impulses, even in the absence of surveillance, is the essence and hallmark of successful socialization (Kochanska, 1993; pp. 325–326).

This approach implies that a well-socialized child need not heed the directives, or specific, current needs and desires of other people, in determining how to behave unless those directives, needs, or desires directly bear on a known rule. It suggests that Gilligan's (1977) "morality of care" is irrelevant to socially appropriate behavior. It also implies that once one has internalized societal standards, one no longer looks to others for guidance. And, it implies that the child who is "high in self-monitoring" or who cares deeply about others' reactions and opinions is less self-regulated than one who is such a principled person that s/he must act in accordance with those principles even if many people will suffer because of the principled action.

In majority-culture American society, many of these beliefs may seem reasonable; the self independently acting in a principled way may seem the epitome of the self-regulated, moral person. However, this may not be at all true for many subcultures in the United States, and many other cultures.

Moreover, as any parent or developmentalist knows, even "good" children do not stop requiring others' directives once they have internalized societal rules. In fact, adults need others' guidance as well.

Current researchers interested in self-regulation or "conscience" are now attempting to distinguish the type of compliance that seems to involve self-regulation (or internalization) from the type of compliance that seems guided only by others' behavior (e.g., see Kochanska & Aksan, 1995; Kopp & Wyer, 1991). It seems clear to such researchers that there is a great deal of difference between complying because situational demands require compliance, versus doing so because one *wants* to behave appropriately ("committed compliance": Kochanska & Aksan, 1995). Moreover, a growing body of research connects such desire to behave appropriately with a positive interaction pattern between parents and children.

Baumrind's (1971) seminal study on childrearing styles that predict later "instrumental competence" was one of the first to highlight the importance of a positive emotional climate in the family for the fostering of socially-desirable behavior. The primary characteristics that distinguished her "authoritarian" parents from her "authoritative" parents was the mutually loving and respectful interaction pattern between parent and child. And, as is well-known, authoritative parenting was associated with the most socially desirable child behavior.

Since that study, a consistent pattern has been found for the parenting style associated with long-term compliance, "early internalization," self-regulation, or "impulse control". In short, research suggests that a warm, reciprocal relationship, in which children and parents seem to "meet minds" and interact harmoniously, is associated with self-regulated/compliant behavior. One of the first studies that directly addressed the importance of relationship quality to children's likelihood of complying with socializing agents was Londerville and Main's (1981), which indicated that securely-attached children were more willing to comply (and less defiant).

More specific information about the *interaction* patterns associated with children's willingness to comply was provided by subsequent studies. Maccoby (see Maccoby & Martin, 1983; Parpal & Maccoby, 1985), for example, found that children were more willing to comply with their mothers' requests after those mothers were (by instruction) responsive to their children's interests, and Rocissano, Slade, & Lynch (1987) found that toddlers who engaged in "synchronous" interactions with their mothers were more compliant to those mothers. Moreover, mothers who were less directive during compliance tasks, and who reported themselves as encouraging independence in their children had 2-year olds who were more compliant in still another study (Silverman & Ragusa, 1990). Children whose parents are more responsive to them are not only more compliant, however; they also show more self-assertion (Crockenberg & Litman, 1990; Kuczynski, Kochanska, Radke-Yarrow, & Girnius-Brown, 1987; Matas, Arend, & Sroufe, 1978), but not more defiance (Crockenberg & Litman, 1990).

Moreover, there is evidence (in addition to the work on attachment) that the reason that children willingly comply with responsive parents is that they have a more positive relationship with those parents. Kochanska & Aksan (1995) found that concurrent, zero-order correlations revealed positive relations between "committed compliance" and gentle control and guidance, social exchange (as a maternal control strategy), and mother–child mutually positive affect as well as between a measure of internalization and both social exchange and mutually positive affect. Zero-order correlations also revealed *negative* relations between negative control and both committed compliance and internalization. However, examination of the relation between affect and maternal control strategies at home and the child's committed compliance 1 to 3 weeks later in the laboratory revealed that only mutually positive affect positively predicted later committed compliance. Maternal negative control, on the other hand, was negatively associated with later committed compliance. Moreover, mutually positive affect during one laboratory situation also was positively correlated with the child's committed compliance in the other laboratory situation; whereas, none of the maternal control variables was significantly correlated with committed compliance in the other situation.

Finally, in follow-up analyses, a *parent–child mutual* responsiveness measure was developed, which predicted children's concurrent and later unsupervised compliance (construed as internalization) (Kochanska, 1997b). These findings suggest that the positive relationship between parent and child may be the most important factor in ensuring that the child will willingly commit to parental rules, and a negative relationship in ensuring that s/he will not. Thus, positive relationships with others are crucial in fostering *self*-regulation. Again, relationship development and self development are positively related.

THE "SOCIAL/SELF-CONSCIOUS" EMOTIONS DURING TODDLERHOOD AND THE DEVELOPMENT OF SELF-IN-RELATIONSHIPS

Self-regulation does not just involve "cold" awareness of how to behave and ability to control behavior. It also involves *caring* about behaving appropriately. In recent years, this emotional side of self-regulation has once again become the target of investigation. Although the connection between guilt and internalization was discussed by Freud (1923/1961) and others many decades ago, until remarkably recently, shame received virtually no attention, and empirical research on the early development of guilt, shame, and related emotions was almost nonexistent.

Now, a growing empirical literature suggests that shame, pride, embarrassment, and guilt have their origins in toddlerhood (see Barrett, Zahn-Waxler, & Cole, 1993; Lewis, Alessandri, & Sullivan, 1992; Lewis, Sullivan, Stanger, & Weiss, 1989; Stipek, Recchia, & McClintic, 1992), and are particularly relevant to a discussion of self, other, and relationships for at least three, interrelated reasons: a) they are frequently referred to as "social emotions," and yet also frequently are referred to as "self-conscious" emotions, b) they both affect and are affected by the development of self, and c) they affect and are affected by relationships with others. Also of interest in the present context is that the cultures that Benedict (1946) considered "shame" cultures are interdependent or collectivistic cultures, and those that she considered "guilt" cultures are characterized predominantly by independence, suggesting that the relative emphasis of a culture on the "self side" of self-in-relationship may promote more of one type of social emotion (guilt) and emphasis on the "relationship side" of self-in-relationship may promote more of another social emotion (shame). Regardless of which social emotion is emphasized, however, what emerges is a view of the baby as developing more and more complex views of self *in relationships* with the animate and inanimate environment because of the development of these emotions, and developing more complex versions of these emotions because of the development of the self-in-relationship.

Social and/or Self-conscious Emotions?

Pride, embarrassment, shame, and guilt often are referred to as "social" or "interpersonal" emotions (see Barrett, 1995; Baumeister, Stillwell, & Heatherton, 1995; Jones, Kugler, & Adams, 1995), and also often are referred to as "self-conscious" emotions (e.g., see Lewis et al., 1989; Tangney & Fischer, 1995). Although if self is opposed to other, it would seem perplexing that both descriptors could apply, careful examination of these emotions suggests that both descriptors are apt.

It is beyond the scope of this chapter to review all of the major theoretical approaches to these emotions. However, most theories and self-report data suggest that in all of these emotions, the self is implicated. In embarrassment, the person/self (or presentation of self) seems to be on display (see Buss, 1980; Edelmann, 1987; M. Lewis, 1995; Miller, 1995); in shame, more central self-attributes or the entire self seem exposed, scrutinized, or negatively evaluated (see Barrett & Campos, 1987; Buss, 1980; Edelmann, 1987; H. Lewis, 1971; M. Lewis, 1991a). In guilt, the person feels responsible for something s/he did that was inconsistent with his/her own standards (Barrett & Campos, 1987; H. Lewis, 1971; Tangney, 1995). In pride, the person feels that s/he has accomplished something significant or met social standards (e.g., M. Lewis et al., 1989; Stipek, Recchia, & McClintic, 1992).

Moreover, there is evidence that the development of self-recognition in a mirror is related to the development of embarrassment (M. Lewis et al., 1989; Pipp, Robinson, Bridges, & Bartholomew, 1997; but see also Schneider-Rosen & Cicchetti, 1991, for contrary findings with lower SES children). Many theorists postulate that self-recognition is a prerequisite to "true" shame and/or pride and/or guilt as well (e.g., Buss, 1980; M. Lewis, 1991; Mascolo & Fischer, 1995; Stipek, 1995), although an empirical basis for this claim is lacking. Given that virtually all characterizations of these emotions include self-evaluation as a component, and most developmental theories assume that ability to evaluate the self or at least see the self as an object is therefore required for these emotions, it seems reasonable to consider these emotions to involve self-consciousness.

Yet, these emotions also are intrinsically social. First, these emotions are almost invariably connected with (real or imagined) interaction with a person. Guilt is aroused when someone perceives him/herself to have harmed a person—usually another, but potentially the self taken as an object (see Barrett, 1995; Baumeister, Stillwell, & Heatherton, 1995). Moreover, there is some evidence that more guilt is experienced when a loved and/or esteemed other is harmed than when a stranger is harmed, and that one is more likely to purposefully try to make *loved ones, rather than strangers* feel guilty (Baumeister, Stillwell, & Heatherton, 1995).

Shame typically involves the perception that *someone* finds one wanting or deficient (Barrett & Campos, 1987; H. Lewis, 1971; Stipek, Reccia, and McClintic, 1992); an observing other is perceived, even if only in one's mind. The traditional approach to shame claims that, unlike guilt, which involves internalized moral standards, shame is experienced *when one is caught* by someone while committing (or with evidence that one has committed) a wrongdoing (e.g., Benedict, 1946; Erikson, 1963). In fact, this public/private distinction still is evident in some current theories (e.g., see Buss, 1980; Hogan & Cheek, 1983). Most current theorists, however, would argue that shame may be experienced even when no one else is present physically (e.g., Barrett & Campos, 1987; Creighton, 1990; H. Lewis, 1971; Stipek, 1983; Wurmser, 1987). Still, the *sense* of being observed seems to be present during the experience of shame (see H. Lewis, 1971; Ferguson, Stegge, & Damhuis, 1991). Embarrassment, too, seems to involve exposure in the face of real or perceived others and/or evaluation by real or perceived others (see Buss, 1980; Edelmann, 1987; M. Lewis, 1995; Miller, 1994).

Another way in which these emotions are social is that socialization centrally influences the development of these emotions. In fact, it seems accurate to characterize social emotions as social *constructions*. If humans did not live in social groups, there would be no need for the social emotions. The central concern of the person experiencing social emotions is meeting or failing to meet standards of society and/or socializing agents; these emotions serve to highlight and enforce such standards (e.g., see Ausubel, 1955; Barrett & Campos, 1987; Baumeister, Stillwell, & Heatherton, 1995; Lindsay-Hartz, De Rivera, & Mascolo, 1995). Moreover, social emotions also highlight the importance of and/or repair social relationships (Barrett & Campos; 1987; Baumeister, Stillwell, & Heatherton, 1995; Lindsay-Hartz, De Rivera, & Mascolo, 1995).

The behavior-regulatory functions of shame and guilt are social as well. Shame serves to distance the experiencing individual from important others, especially others who can evaluate or are evaluating one. In particular, in shame, activated behaviors are aimed at removing the *face* from exposure to others' evaluation. The shameful person avoids looking at others, hides his face, slumps his body, lowers his head, and/or removes himself from contact with others (e.g., see Barrett, 1995; H. Lewis, 1971; M. Lewis, 1991b; Tangney, 1995). These same behaviors serve social regulatory/social communication functions. The gaze aversion, slumping, hiding, and social withdrawal behaviors communicate deference and submission to others, and indicate that one feels "small," "low," or unworthy, in comparison to those others.

Guilt serves different functions that also are quite social. Guilt-relevant behaviors are aimed at repairing the damage caused by the person's wrongdoing and/or at confessing, both of which also help repair the person's relationship with the person who was harmed (e.g., see Barrett, 1995; Baumeister, Stillwell, & Heatherton, 1995; Ferguson, Stegge, & Darnhuis, 1991). Finally, like shame, guilt highlights the importance of social standards.

Shame, Guilt, and the Development of Self

One type of adaptive function of social emotions that has been virtually unstudied is the role of these emotions in the development of the self. As has been mentioned, many theorists believe that shame and guilt become possible only *after* the child has objective awareness of self. It is my position that shame and guilt also are highly important influences on the *development* of such awareness (see also Barrett, 1995).

The shame experience *highlights* the self as others see one (or as one must appear to others). It causes one to step back from the self as agent and to evaluate that self and, thus, helps one elaborate and/or modify one's view of self. Moreover, as an affective experience, it draws the person's attention to the *significance* of the experience.

It seems likely that most of a child's earliest experiences of shame occur in the presence of a caregiver with whom the child has a history of interactions. I find Bowlby's (1980) notion of a "working model" of self and other quite useful in conceptualizing the sense of self during infancy and toddlerhood and how shame might impact its development. According to Bowlby (1980), a child's interactions with a caregiver help shape "working models" of self and other. To the extent that the parent is responsive to the baby, the baby develops a view of that parent as responsive *and* a reciprocal view of self as worthy of being responded to. To the extent that caregivers show that they love the baby, the baby develops a notion of the caregivers as loving and the self as lovable. Such working models need not be cognitively elaborate and may at first involve "procedural" knowledge, such as expectancies that the child's actions will bring desired outcomes via the parent and that the parent will provide what is needed. Later, as the child's cognitive sophistication and interaction history become richer, the working models should become more elaborate and sophisticated, including both procedural and declarative knowledge (see Schachter & Tulving, 1994).

To the extent that the child views himself/herself as competent in obtaining satisfaction from the caregiver, and, in the shame-inducing situation, finds herself incompetent to obtain satisfaction (the caregiver actually may attempt to *prevent* the child from obtaining a desired end such as a china figurine), modification of the model is needed. Moreover, the painful nature of the shame experience motivates such modification by bringing the discrepancy into vivid awareness.

The child's initial revision may be to indicate that the caregiver is not so wonderful after all, or the child is not so wonderful after all, or both. To the extent that shame is infrequent, however, and the caregiver–child relationship is good in general, the shame may serve to highlight the contexts in which child or mom is "not wonderful," underscoring the standards being conveyed and/or the child's specific deficits. Moreover, the pain of shame should help discourage future violations of those standards, which should help the child form a working model of herself as a "good child." On the other hand, to the extent that shame experiences are very frequent, the child may come to view herself as incompetent and/or bad, and to become a shame-prone (and potentially, a depression-prone) individual. As further development of a sense of self occurs, the shame experience may induce the child to compare the other's beliefs about her to her own beliefs. This may further elaborate the child's beliefs and feelings about herself.

Guilt is most likely to influence the development of self as agent. To the extent that *guilt* rather than shame is more frequently experienced in the context of standard violations, the focus should be on the harmful *act* (and the child's responsibility for that act), rather than on a globally bad self (see H. Lewis, 1971; M. Lewis, 1991). Thus, the child's power to harm others should be highlighted, and, to the extent that reparation occurs and leads to positive outcomes, the power of the child to help others should be highlighted as well. Therefore, whereas frequent shame experiences should cause the child to view himself as bad, frequent guilt experiences should help the child see that he has the power to control his behavior—and that he can derive pleasure from helping others and discomfort from hurting others. In fact, there is some evidence that more frequent experience, according to maternal report, with engaging in destructive behavior (breaking toys) or behavior that is discrepant from parents' "ought expectancies" is associated with display of more guilt-relevant behavior (Barrett, Zahn-Waxler, & Cole, 1993; Ferguson & Stegge, 1995). This would also explain why many studies have revealed *positive* correlations between aggression and prosocial behavior (see D. Barrett & Yarrow, 1977; Friedrich & Stein, 1973; Murphy, 1937; Muste & Sharpe, 1947; Yarrow & Waxler, 1976; but for opposite findings see D. Barrett, 1979; Harris & Siebel, 1975; Rutherford & Mussen, 1968).

Relationships and the Development of Self-consciousness and Self-regulation

It was mentioned earlier that shame, guilt, and pride can be viewed as social emotions because they are centrally concerned with social standards, they help to enforce such standards, they impact social behavior, and they help to repair relationships that have been damaged by infractions of standards. To the extent that parents and other socializing agents share the values of their larger society, moreover, they help children interact "appropriately" with others, increasing the likelihood that positive relationships will be built with others. Not only do these emotions help children in forming and maintaining relationships, however; the formation of relationships may affect the development of these emotions.

If the person is a self-contained individual, who is primarily concerned with actualizing his/her own goals and self, then why should that person adhere to social standards? In many cases, such standards are *contrary* to purely selfish interests. The child wants the toy that the other child has, for example; why shouldn't s/he just take it? An important question is just how social goals become significant goals for the individual. Significance is the crucial feature distinguishing emotion-inducing "appreciations" or "appraisals" from ordinary cognitive processes. A person can be aware that the light is red and she is not supposed to walk across the street, for example, but unless abiding by that law is a significant goal for her, she should not experience guilt (nor shame) when she crosses anyway.

Cultures differ greatly from one another with respect to whether or not *a number of* particular behaviors are *pre*scribed or *pro*scribed, as well as which standards are held to be crucially important (Shweder, Mahapatra, & Miller, 1987), which suggests that most standards are largely arbitrary, specific to particular cultures, and socialized by the socializing agents in that culture. How do such standards gain significance for the individual—how does the individual come to see them as important to him/herself and his/her well-being? I have suggested that both the establishment of standards as goals and the endowment of such goals with significance, begin in conjunction with the baby's interactions with parents and other loved ones (Barrett, 1995).

The infant's close, extended contact with the parent enables that parent to be the first, and arguably the most important, socializing agent for the infant, and all of the many types of interactions of a parent with a baby are relevant to the development of guilt and shame. The most basic way in which parent–infant interactions help establish societal standards as goals and endow those goals with significance is through the effect of such interactions on the nature of the important parent–infant relationship. The nature of the relationship that forms should affect the child's desire to accept and heed the parents' standards—the child's belief that if the parent deems them significant, they probably are significant. In addition, the parent–child relationship should affect the child's tendency to care about hurting others, both because he has learned to care about someone (the parent) and because a nurturant parent, with whom the baby would be most likely to form a positive relationship, would model caring behavior. Consistent with these ideas are the data, reviewed earlier, suggesting that toddlers who have positive interactions and relationships with their parents are more likely to show long-term compliance with their parents' requests and internalization. Also consistent with this idea are data indicating that children of more nurturant parents show greater empathy (e.g., Barnett, 1987).

In most discussions of socialization influences on the development of guilt, reparation, or self-regulation, emphasis is not placed on the overall relationship between parent and child, but rather on discipline strategies (e.g., Hoffman, 1984; Power & Chapieski, 1986; Schneider & Larzelere, 1988; Zahn-Waxler, Radke-Yarrow, & King, 1979). The assumption in much of this literature seems to be that discipline is important because it teaches a child to obey standards, even in the face of other desires, by teaching socially valued behavior and/or punishing socially undesirable behavior (e.g., see Hoffman, 1984).

Interestingly, however, those discipline strategies that are associated with long-term manifestation of appropriate behavior tend to be those which *highlight the significance* of appropriate behavior, and do so in a way *that does not impair the parent–child relationship*. Research with infants and toddlers has suggested that usage, at high levels, of techniques that threaten the parent–child relationship are ineffective in promoting self-regulation on a long-term basis. High usage of physical punishment is associated with lower "impulse control" and shorter latency to recurrence of misbehavior (Power & Chapieski, 1986; Schneider & Larzelere, 1988), and high usage of unexplained prohibitions is associated with lower levels of reparation for misdeeds (Zahn-Waxler, Rodke-Yarrow, & King, 1979). Moreover, although high usage of love withdrawal is associated with greater immediate reparation, it is not associated with later reparation (Zahn-Waxler, Rodke-Yarrow, & King, 1979) and is associated with *shorter* latency to recurrence of misbehavior (Schneider & Larzelere, 1988).

On the other hand, when some of the same techniques are used at lower levels, and in a manner that is less threatening to the parent–child relationship, they may be more effective. Use of corporal punishment at low (but nonzero) levels is not associated with poorer impulse control, and actually is associated with *longer* delay in recurrence of misbehavior when combined with inductive explanations (Power & Chapieski, 1986; Schneider & Larzelere, 1988; see also Hoffman, 1970b re: older children). It seems quite possible that when such punishment does not occur sufficiently frequently and/or intensely that it impairs the parent–child bond, and it is accompanied by clear indication of which behaviors were unacceptable, it serves to highlight the significance of those particular acts.

The technique that has been associated with the greatest tendency for toddlers to make reparation for wrongdoings, both concurrently and on a long-term basis, is high usage of emotion-laden explanations—particularly those that include statements about general standards for behavior (Zahn-Waxler, Radke-Yarrow, & King, 1979). This set of techniques highlights the significance of the misbehavior and/or the standards, while also making clear just what the standard is. Moreover, it does so in a way that is not likely to threaten the parent–child relationship—that is not excessively harsh and authoritarian. A particular version of this technique, induction (noting the consequences of misbehavior for others), has been associated with internalization and "guilt" in older children (however, the latter was not clearly distinguished from shame: see Hoffman, 1970). This type of discipline also has been studied as part of a general style of parenting (authoritative/reciprocal) in which the child is listened to, valued and reasoned with, and yet standards that parents believe in are highlighted and adhered to. This style, in turn, has been associated with long-term manifestation of socially valued behaviors in older children (see Baumrind, 1967, 1971; Maccoby & Martin, 1983). Thus, evidence suggests that a positive, mutual relationship with parents or caregivers forms the foundation for the development of self-regulation and reparation (which, as mentioned earlier, is a guilt-relevant behavior). It seems likely that children care about the rules and standards because they care about the persons imposing those standards; the rules and standards thus become significant to the child, and emotions like guilt and shame are aroused when these rules are violated. Obviously, this proposal is quite speculative at present; much more research is needed on the connection between the parent–child relationship and the development of the social/self-conscious emotions.

THE SELF IN RELATIONSHIPS

All of the information presented thus far suggests that the early development of the self is intimately intertwined with the development of relationships. Although we cannot, at present, rule out the possibility that the self *versus* other dichotomy is appropriate in individualistic societies, there seems to be enough reason to question this idea to warrant careful investigation of an interpersonal self or self-in-relationships.

An interpersonal self (or interpersonal selves) would seem important to the functioning of all societies; without a sense of connectedness with others, there would seem to be no real motivation to follow societal rules whose main benefit is to others (unless others are constantly monitoring and punishing "inappropriate" behavior). It seems plausible that, even in our predominantly individualistic culture, interdependent, interpersonal selves develop. Mainstream American culture allows one to experience pride as a positive emotion, yet even it negatively sanctions boastfulness and tactlessness following one's accomplishments. Even in mainstream American culture, toddlers show apparent embarrassment when simply asked to dance in front of others; according to Lewis (1995) and Darwin (1872/1965), this suggests that simple exposure to the gaze of others seems sufficient to trigger embarrassment.

The person we are constantly changes as we relate to the world around us, and our relationships with others and with the world change as our sense of self does. We do learn about ourselves through our relationships with others, and, in fact, *are* different people when interacting with different others (see Duck, West, & Acitelli, 1997; Fogel, 1995; Hermans, Kempen, & van Loon, 1992). Some would propose that we do not even have an identity that is separate from our relationships with others (Fogel, 1995).

Perhaps the extent to which people have views of themselves that can be separated from their relationships changes with development. Perhaps the need for autonomy shown by toddlers in our culture is a result of socialization to create a sense of agency and autonomy in the context of an interdependent self. The toddler may already feel connected with others, but may have a new ability to be sufficiently autonomous to truly help or challenge those others. Moreover, as the toddler grows older and comes in contact with an increasing assortment of socializing agents, who may not always agree, the many "selves-in-relationship" may conflict with one another. Much more research is needed regarding the origins of the interpersonal self in our society. Study of cultures and subcultures in which the interpersonal self is emphasized may give us a basis for studying the development of this self in our own society. Does the development of self foster the development of relationships? Does the development of relationships foster the development of self? Perhaps these are two sides of the same question. This is certainly an issue worth studying more in the future.

ACKNOWLEDGMENT

I would like to thank Rosemary Mills, as well as David MacPhee and the other members of the "Development of the Self in the Social Context" research cognate, for their comments on a previous version of this chapter.

Chapter 6

Sex Differences in Children's Relationship Learning

Alan Russell

School of Education, The Flinders University of South Australia, Australia

Children's lives, like those of adults, are played out primarily through relationships with others, especially close relationships. Sex or gender, the focus
of the present chapter, is a factor in these relationships, at least insofar as each
individual in a relationship is of a particular sex. The terms "sex" and "gender" have been used at times both imprecisely and inconsistently. To assist
the present discussion, a distinction is made between sex and gender as proposed by a number of writers (e.g., Canary & Emmers-Sommer, 1997; Ruble
& Martin, 1998; Wood, 1996b). Comparisons of mothers and fathers, or boys
and girls, relate to biologically-based categories and concern sex differences.
In undertaking these comparisons, it is usually assumed that "gender" constructions, and roles associated with males and females, are critical in the
differences. While sex and gender are closely related, there is not a one-to-
one correspondence (Deaux, 1984; Sanfilipo, 1994). For example, girls and
boys can display both masculine and feminine characteristics. Sex-based comparisons are relevant for gender and relationship learning to the extent that
males and females differ on gender. However, more than sex comparisons are
needed for a full understanding of the role of gender. At this stage, though,
sex comparisons provide the best basis for a discussion of gender and relationship learning.

The Developmental Psychology of Personal Relationships.
Edited by Rosemary S. L. Mills and Steve Duck. © 2000 John Wiley & Sons Ltd.

SCOPE AND PLAN OF THE CHAPTER

The chapter begins with a contrast   nstream treatment of
children's peer relationships and the lit   socialization and sex
differences. The purpose is to show th   gender literature has
much to say about sex differences ir   tionship styles and
qualities, the peer relationship literature   ed limited attention
to these differences. The discussion then   -girl differences in
relationship styles and qualities. Issues a   e origins of these
differences are taken up in the next section.   nphasis will be on
learning in the context of parent–child rela   rke & O'Neil, in
this volume). Brief attention is given to the   ent/personality.
Matters of research design and data analysis   addressed briefly, and
directions for future research suggested.

A thorough discussion of gender and relationship learning would require attention to biological factors, socialization (including the family, media, peers, and school), and cognitive processes. By focusing the present discussion on selected aspects of family socialization, effects on relationship learning arising from gender stereotypes, role requirements, normative expectations, and social-structural influences, as well as school and peer experiences, are put to one side. In a full discussion in the cognitive area, recognition would be given to the role of gender schemas, including social identity theory (Maccoby, 1988; Ruble & Martin, 1998), self-construals (Cross & Madson, 1997), and internal working models (Kerns, 1996). Again, however, these factors are mentioned only briefly in the present chapter.

The Central Theme

Although mention will be made of other theoretical approaches to children's relationship learning, the emphasis will be on the idea that the behaviors, attitudes, roles, and strategies experienced in parent–child relationships tend to be replicated in subsequent close relationships (Sroufe & Fleeson, 1986). The notion of replication links closely with the claim that children learn about relationships from the relationship style that they experience with their parents (Mize & Pettit, 1997; Russell, Pettit, & Mize, 1998). For example, if parents' relationship style involves reasoning and collaboration, children can be expected to learn skills of reasoning and collaboration that are used in other relationships. In this sense, the parent–child relationship is replicated in other relationships.

If relationship replication occurs, then the specific qualities of the relationship that children experience with parents are critical. For this reason a major part of this chapter is devoted to the examination of whether and how there might be distinctness in relationship qualities and styles based on parent sex and child sex. As a caution, it is acknowledged that if qualities in the peer relationships of girls, for instance, are also present in girls' relationships with their mothers, this is consistent with a proposition that aspects of parent–child relationships are replicated in children's peer relationships, but not proof that the direction of causation is from parent–child to child–peer relationships (Lamb & Nash, 1989).

The idea of relationship replication contains a number of problematic components. These include issues about the meaning and nature of relationships, both between parents and children, and among children themselves. Relationships evolve and change (see Duck, Acitelli Manke & West, in this volume). Change is a feature of children's relationships for no other reason than that development occurs. Relationship change makes the idea of relationship replication somewhat problematic (what is replicated?). Nevertheless, there are continuities as well as discontinuities in relationships. Stylistic features of relationships appear to be the most likely to display continuities across both time and context, a reason the present emphasis is on qualities and styles. Qualities and styles pertain to aspects of relationships such as a tendency to be warm and accepting, or to use negotiation when conflict occurs, or a preference for intimacy in smaller groups over a looser but larger network of friends.

CONTRASTING LITERATURES: MAINSTREAM PEER RELATIONSHIPS VERSUS GENDER SOCIALIZATION AND SEX DIFFERENCES

There appears to be a separation between the mainstream literature on children's peer relationships and the literature devoted more specifically to sex/gender issues. Rubin, Bukowski, and Parker's (1998) authoritative review is within the mainstream literature on children's peer relationships. They devote only a short section to sex differences, in which it is noted that despite the long-standing view of qualitative differences in the relationships formed and maintained by males and females, sex differences in children's peer relationships have been neglected in the research. A relative absence of attention to sex differences is also suggested from an examination of the second edition of Duck's (1997) *Handbook of Personal Relationships*. For the Developmental Psychology section of the Handbook, there were no index entries for either "sex differences" or "gender differences". The one entry under "gender" referred to a single paragraph discussing cross-sex and cross-race friendships.

The mainstream literature on children's peer relationships can be contrasted with what is a relatively separate literature on sex/gender and relationships (e.g., Canary & Dindia, 1998; Wood, 1996a). Although seen as limited and stereotypical by some (Canary & Emmers-Sommer, 1997), the gender literature presents a supposed distinction between a "feminine" relationship style and a "masculine" style, based on the instrumental orientations of males and the expressive orientations of females (Parsons & Bales, 1955). Aries

(1987) captured this distinction in saying "the interactions of men can be characterized as more task-oriented, dominant, directive, hierarchical and women's as more social-emotional, expressive, supportive, facilitative, cooperative, personal, and egalitarian" (p. 170). In a similar way, Wood (1995) argued that male friendships involve shared experiences as the route to closeness, whereas female friendships emphasize personal communication and the nurturance of relationships. Further extending the distinction, Eagly (1987) noted the communal, expressive, and interpersonally-oriented aspects of female roles, and agentic and self-expressive aspects of male roles. With respect to the agentic, Canary and Emmers-Sommer (1997) concluded "men's activities more likely involved initiating relationships" (p. 138). These descriptions overlap with Cross and Madson's (1997) proposal that men tend to independent self-construals, where representations of others are separate from the self. In contrast, women were considered to develop and maintain interdependent self-construals, with others considered part of the self.

SEX DIFFERENCES IN CHILDREN'S RELATIONSHIP STYLES AND QUALITIES

A core issue for the present discussion is whether differences in relationships proposed in some of the gender literature on adults are discernible in children's peer relationships. Although patterns of sex differences are complex, and one-to-one correspondence between the adult and child literature could not be expected, parallel types of sex differences appear to be evident in children's relationship qualities and styles. Some of the differences emerge at quite young ages (certainly during the preschool years). In considering the child literature, it will be apparent that operationalizations of relationship qualities and styles differ. Some work focuses on interactions, other at the broader level of relationships (Hinde, 1987). Also, there are variations in terms of attention to behaviors, versus cognitions, or speech styles.

A clear finding from research on boys and girls is a preference for interacting in same-sex groups (Leaper, 1994; Maccoby, 1988, 1990). Maccoby (1988, 1990) argued that this sex segregation is based on the following types of differences in the relationship and interaction styles of boys and girls within same-sex groups. Girls form closer and more intimate relationships in smaller networks than boys do (Bryant, 1985). When interacting with a friend, girls' interactions are more interconnected, synchronous, and contain more joint displays of positive affect (Youngblade & Belsky, 1992). In contrast, boys' interactions occur in larger groups. Boys have more extensive networks (Bryant, 1985), where mutual interests and activities, and issues of dominance and status are more prominent, and where there is a greater use of directive styles (Benenson, 1990; Leaper, 1994; Maccoby, 1990).

In a recent review, Leaper (1994) also pointed to differences in the relationship and interaction styles of boys and girls. Leaper concluded that boys favor assertion (independence and instrumentality) over affiliation (interpersonal closeness and expressiveness), whereas the reverse applies to girls. He proposed that there is an emphasis on self-assertion in boys' play and on affiliation in girls' play, with a social orientation and an emphasis on interpersonal closeness in girls' relationships. Boys focus on self-reliance, he suggested, with a greater emphasis on competition and dominance, whereas social sensitivity, nurturance, and affection are more important for girls.

A selection of findings from early childhood to adolescence will be used to show sex differences in children's relationship styles and qualities from infancy to adolescence. In infancy, Biringen, Robinson, and Emde (1994) reported that daughters of sensitive mothers in their second year, but not sons, were likely to respond to maternal affect by matching the mother's affect during play. In contrast, sons of the same age were more active than daughters in initiating, directing, and elaborating the flow of the social interaction. Sachs (1987) examined the pretend play of boys and girls between 24 and 64 months of age. Boys were more likely to use simple imperatives such as "lie down", or to give directions. Boys used prohibitions five times more than girls did. Girls more than boys used tag questions that mitigate or provide an opportunity for the listener to concur or disagree. Similarly, girls used joint utterances five times more than boys did. Joint utterances imply cooperation between the listener and hearer, and talk about joint activities and roles.

Much evidence relevant to the present discussion has come from studying children in early or middle childhood. For example, Benenson, Apostoleris, and Parnass (1997) used their results from 4- and 6-year-olds' interactions in playgroups to conclude "that the organization of relationships in male and female peer cultures differs even in early childhood" (p. 542). Power, McGrath, Hughes, and Manire (1994) observed that girls more than boys (aged 2, 4, and 6 years) stated their desires and preferences, and used logical argument in response to parent control attempts. In Black's (1989) study of 3- and 4-year-olds, boys and girls displayed different styles in pretend play encounters. Girls more than boys used linked turn-taking in their conversation, so that turns were related to each other interactionally and topically. Black discussed her results in terms of girls valuing the interaction, with boys' play being related to efforts to have their chosen theme accepted. Also with 4-year-olds, Eisenberg (1996) found that in conflicts with parents, girls more than boys used explanations and reasons.

The results of Harrist, Zaia, Bates, Dodge, and Pettit (1997) indicated that boys and girls might exhibit different forms of relationship difficulties within the category of social withdrawal. Proportionally, there were more girls in the withdrawal subtype labeled unsociable and more boys in the subtypes labeled passive-anxious and active-isolate. Further, within a given subtype, some social information-processing differences were found between boys and girls. The findings point to differences between boys and girls not only in relationship qualities, but also in factors associated with these qualities, e.g., boys and girls high on immaturity, a quality of withdrawn children, might display different social information-processing abilities. An implication could be that the mechanisms associated with the acquisition of the quality (e.g., relationship immaturity) differs for boys and girls.

Several studies have examined the relationship styles of boys and girls in middle childhood and adolescence (e.g., Leaper, 1991; Maccoby, 1990). Leaper (1991) found that girls in middle childhood exhibited more collaborative speech acts and cooperative exchanges than boys, whereas boys displayed more controlling speech acts. Maccoby (1990) emphasized differences in the influence strategies of boys and girls, providing evidence that boys of this age use a style involving direct commands, with girls more likely to use polite suggestions and accommodating behavior.

In middle childhood and adolescence, differences in the social networks for boys and girls have been found. Cairns, Cairns, Neckerman, Gest, and Gariepy (1988), for example, reported greater definition and clarity of the social networks of girls in comparison with boys in a sample of fourth and seventh grade children. Girls were less likely to be identified in more than one cluster of peers, and there was greater agreement among peer reports about which girls were in the peer clusters than about which boys comprised the clusters. These data suggest that girls participate in closer or more coherent and identifiable peer networks than boys do.

Parker and Herrera (1996) observed 9- to 14-year-olds in interactions with a best friend. Girl friends were more positive in interactions, had a greater global intimacy, and showed higher levels of peak intimacy than boys did. Intimacy involved disclosure of personal information, e.g., about thoughts, feelings, personal experiences, and close relationships. The results of Kerns, Klepac, and Cole (1996) also were in the direction of girls showing more intimacy in interactions with a same-sex friend. With a different emphasis, Rydell, Hagekull, and Bohlin (1997) measured prosocial orientation in 7- to 10-year-olds. Prosocial orientation pertained to qualities such as being generous, helping, sharing, and preventing conflict. Rydell (personal communication, May, 1998) reported that sex-of-child tests have consistently shown girls to be higher on prosocial orientation.

Chung and Asher (1996) examined children's goals and strategies in conflict situations, and compared boys and girls in fourth through sixth grade. Boys' goals were more control-oriented in the sense of having control over one's activities, possessions, and personal space. For boys, control goals were significantly more sought than relationship goals (concerned with maintaining a good relationship with the other person), whereas this was not the case for girls' goals. Girls more than boys chose conflict resolution strategies that were prosocial (accommodating the needs of the other; e.g., both playing with the toy in dispute). Boys more than girls chose hostile/coercive strategies (e.g., counteracting the other's actions by grabbing back the toy).

Although a selective review, the evidence outlined here suggests there are sex differences in children's relationship qualities and styles that parallel or link to differences noted in the literature on gender and relationships of the kind outlined by Aries (1987), Canary and Emmers-Sommer (1997), Cross and Madson (1997), Eagly (1987), and Wood (1995).

SIMILARITIES VERSUS DIFFERENCES

Rather than highlighting differences, a number of researchers note that there are considerable similarities in the relationship styles and qualities of boys and girls, or of males and females (Black & Hazen, 1990; Leaper, 1991; Wentzel & Caldwell, 1997). For example, Leaper (1991) pointed to similarities in the communication patterns of boys and girls, before discussing differences. At times, limited statistical power in the analyses undertaken could be a factor in the failure to obtain significant sex differences (e.g., Black & Hazen, 1990), a frequently occurring problem in work on sex differences (Russell & Saebel, 1997). It would be unreasonable to dismiss all failures to find sex differences as due to lack of power, however. Accordingly, it must be accepted that differences between boys and girls occur at the same time as considerable sex similarity. In the sex/gender literature, there is a comparable debate about the extent and importance of similarities versus differences (Canary & Dindia, 1998; Canary & Emmers-Sommer, 1997; Duck & Wright, 1993).

SEX AND RELATIONSHIP LEARNING IN THE FAMILY CONTEXT

Although there are a number of ways in which sex differences in children's relationship styles and qualities could be acquired, the main emphasis here is on the possibility of relationship learning arising from children's relationships with parents. Before turning to the family, however, there will be a short discussion of temperament/personality in order to balance the emphasis on socialization processes.

Temperament/Personality and Sex Differences in Relationship Styles and Qualities

Temperament and personality appear to be closely linked, with temperament argued to be a biologically-based aspect of personality (Buss, 1989), and having a substantial effect on personality (Hagekull & Bohlin, 1998). Child temperament/personality could contribute to the development of relationship qualities and styles either as a main effect or in interaction with socialization (Graziano, Jensen-Campbell, & Sullivan-Logan, 1998; Kochanska, 1997a). With respect to the latter, Kochanska (1997a) showed that socialization had a different effect depending on the child's temperament. Parental efforts at developing social skills, for instance, might have different effects depending on the child's level on a temperament quality such as sociability. If boys and girls differ on sociability, this could have an impact on parental efforts at socializing relationship knowledge and skills.

Social behavior and relationship style appear to arise to some degree directly from personality and/or temperament (Kagan, 1998; Lippa, 1995; Newman, Caspi, Silva, & Moffitt, 1997; Park, Belsky, Putnam, & Crnic, 1997;

Pulkkinen, 1996), suggesting that biological factors contribute to relationship qualities and styles (Kagan, 1998). For example, Park et al. (1997) showed that early temperament contributed to later social inhibition. Newman et al. (1997) concluded from their research that individual differences identified in early childhood temperament could be linked with adult interpersonal styles.

Research on the Big Five personality factors shows that personality contributes to sex differences in relationship qualities and styles. For example, Lippa (1995) found that two of the factors, agreeableness and conscientiousness, were higher for women, and masculinity was linked to extraversion and femininity to agreeableness. Rowe's (1994) conclusions and Feingold's (1994) meta-analysis are consistent with Lippa's results. In addition to linking sex or gender and personality, recent claims have focused on genetic contributions to personality. Caspi (1998) used Loehlin (1992) to support a conclusion that about 40% of the variance of agreeableness is genetic. Rowe (1994) argued that sex-linked personality traits are similar to other personality traits in the substantial role of heredity. This argument is supported by Scarr's (1992) conclusion that about half of sociability is explained by temperament.

If genetic factors are implicated in sex differences in personality and temperament, temperamental differences between boys and girls at quite young ages would be predicted. The consensus seems to be that there are some, but relatively minor, sex differences in temperament early in life (Buss, 1989; Prior, Sanson, & Oberklaid, 1989; Rothbart, 1989). A possible conclusion has been suggested by Buss (1989). He argued that because the differences emerge more with age, socialization is likely to be implicated (see also Goldsmith, Buss, & Lemery, 1997), but because there are some differences early in life, biological factors also might be involved.

In addition to temperament, other biologically-based differences between boys and girls could contribute to differences in relationship qualities and styles. Language develops earlier in females than in males, with males more vulnerable to insults affecting language development and retention (Gleason, 1987). Gleason noted from Maccoby and Jacklin (1974) that males are more physically aggressive, arguing that differences in relationship styles between boys and girls could be partly in response to differences in neurological and behavioral dispositions. Girls' more rapid biological, cognitive, language, and socio-emotional development (Keenan & Shaw, 1997) could be a factor in sex differences in relationship qualities and styles. It can be seen that girls' more rapid development than boys in a number of areas, in addition to some temperament differences, could affect early relationship learning.

THEORETICAL APPROACHES TO THE STUDY OF RELATIONSHIP REPLICATION

Much recent research has focused on the family as the source of children's learning about peer relationship skills (Parke, Burks, Carson, Neville, & Boyum, 1994; Parke & Ladd, 1992; Rubin, Bukowski, & Parker, 1998; Russell,

Pettit & Mize, 1998). There is now a body of research relevant to a discussion of sex differences in relationship learning. Selections from that research will be examined here, with the theme of relationship replication discussed using literature based on the theoretical tradition of social learning theory, and the literature based on attachment theory. This helpful distinction between two theoretical traditions was made clear by Fagot (1997).

The latter two theoretical approaches have common core features with respect to relationship replication. Although most identified with attachment theory (e.g., Sroufe & Fleeson, 1986), at the center of both approaches is the notion that behaviors, thoughts, and feelings experienced in relationships with parents are replicated in children's subsequent close relationships. In attachment theory, the replication is assumed to occur through the development of internal working models and relationship expectations. In contrast, the present emphasis is more behavioral, where it is argued that children develop relationship qualities or styles through their relationship experiences with parents that are carried over to interactions with peers. Foremost, this means that children's relationships with parents and with peers will have common features, with the assumption being that the common features arise from learning in the parent–child context that is carried over to the peer context.

If relationship replication occurs, and the separate parent–child sex combinations display different relationship characteristics, then the learning associated with each of these relationships will differ. For example, if one parent–child relationship involves extended turn-taking interactions (e.g., mother–daughter relationships), and another involves power assertive control (e.g., father–son relationships), the learning associated with each will differ accordingly. Using this reasoning, a central issue is whether the different parent–child sex combinations contain different relationship qualities and styles.

In the following discussion, the type of outcome measure must be kept in mind. There have been four categories of outcomes: measures of children's friendships (e.g., whether they are in close friendships), social status (e.g., popular, rejected), social competence/skillfulness, and finally, measures of specific social skills or behaviors. Although each outcome category contributes something to the discussion, measures of specific social skills and behaviors are the most helpful. This is because they can show a link between a particular relationship characteristic experienced in the family and the *same* characteristic in children's peer relationships. Specific social skills and behaviors deal with children's actual behavior, whereas measures such as social status pertain to products of social functioning (Cavell, 1990).

SOCIAL INTERACTION RESEARCH: MOTHER–FATHER DIFFERENCES IN RELATIONSHIP QUALITIES AND STYLES

Research on mother–father differences within what Fagot (1997) described as "social interaction theory" has often, but not exclusively, observed parent–

child interactions. Selections from the research will be used to illustrate mother–father differences in relationship styles. Our own research on differences in the parenting styles of Australian mothers and fathers of pre-school children (Russell, Aloa, Feder, Glover, Miller, & Palmer, 1998) provides an example. Mothers were higher than fathers on the use of three individual styles composing the authoritative pattern: reasoning/induction, warmth and involvement, and democratic participation. In contrast, fathers were higher than mothers on the overall authoritarian pattern, with fathers especially more likely than mothers to use a style called "non-explanations" (the parent demands behavior without giving an explanation). Fathers more than mothers, it was concluded, used power assertive styles with their children, with mothers more than fathers using verbal strategies involving cooperation and reasoning. These results for parents show parallels with the styles and qualities of male/boys' and female/girls' relationships noted earlier.

A number of other studies have found differences in mother–child and father–child relationships, including the behavior of parents toward children and of children toward parents (Lindsey, Mize, & Pettit, 1997; Power et al., 1994; Russell, Mize, & Saebel, in press; Stevenson, Leavitt, Thompson, & Roach, 1988). Stevenson et al. (1988), who focused on infants and preschool children, found mother–child dyads engaged in more instructive play than father–child dyads. Instructive play contains a substantial verbal component in terms of naming objects, colors, etc. Consequently, mother–child play could be said to be more verbal. The verbal engagement and communication so occurring (from both mother and child) are consistent with the sex difference in relationship qualities and styles already identified. It is also in line with the meta-analysis of Leaper, Anderson, and Sanders (1998), where it was found that mothers were more talkative with their children than fathers were.

In observations of parent–toddler play (Russell, Mize, & Saebel, in press) differences in the styles of mothers and fathers also paralleled sex differences in relationships outlined earlier. Fathers were more likely than mothers to use a directive-type play style, where they are "in charge" of the play agenda, and influence the form and direction of play more than the child. In contrast, mothers were more likely than fathers to use a child-centered or facilitative style, where the parent is oriented to the child's agenda, and encourages and assists according to the child's preferences. Mothers, therefore, were more oriented than fathers to the "other", and less oriented to being "in charge". This is consistent with women more than men focusing on relationship-centered goals in parent–child disagreements (Hastings & Grusec, 1998).

Lindsey, Mize, & Pettit (1997) observed mother–child and father–child play in a sample of preschool children. Mothers more than fathers complied with children's play suggestions. The greater responsiveness of mothers to children's suggestions appears consistent with styles in girls' relationships. The compliance of mothers implies a greater emphasis on the child's agenda. Fathers were more likely to use play directives (commands/directions). The father–child data suggest qualities that are consistent with features of boys' relationships noted earlier.

Power et al.'s (1994) findings support our own and those of Lindsey, Mize, & Pettit (1997). Parent–child control interactions were observed in the home with children aged 2, 4, and 6 years. Fathers were more likely to use a directive form of control (e.g., imperatives), whereas mothers were more likely to use less direct forms, such as question directives (e.g., "do you want more milk?") and embedded imperatives (e.g., "can you give it to me"?). Similarly, Gleason (1987) found fathers used twice as many directives and commands as mothers with their children aged 2 to 5 years during dinner (38% of fathers' utterances were imperatives, i.e., giving orders). Mothers used less directive forms such as questions and suggestions. Leaper, Anderson, & Sanders' (1998) meta-analysis also showed fathers more than mothers use directive language with their children. Leaper, Anderson, and Sanders (1998) concluded that differences in the talk of mothers and fathers suggest that parents provide gender-typed role models for their children.

SOCIAL INTERACTION THEORY: DIFFERENCES IN RELATIONSHIPS WITH SONS VERSUS DAUGHTERS

Sex differences in relationship learning in the family might arise from differences in parental relationships with sons and daughters as well as from differences in relationships with mothers and fathers. In addition to relationships per se, questions of whether boys and girls are treated differently also need to be considered. For example, relationship-enhancing behaviors might be encouraged more in boys than in girls, as suggested by Block (1983). In discussing research on sons versus daughters, the sex of the parent is sometimes important, as the differential relationship or treatment could be specific to one parent.

Opinions vary about differential treatment and relationships with boys and girls. Maccoby and Jacklin's (1974) conclusion of little differential treatment and Block's (1983) that differential socialization had been underestimated are well-documented. The meta-analysis by Lytton and Romney (1991) also pointed to restricted differential treatment. Limitations of the Lytton and Romney (1991) meta-analysis have been noted (Leaper, Anderson, & Sanders, 1998; Ruble & Martin, 1998), e.g., the broadly-defined categories of parental behavior used by Lytton and Romney could mask potential differences. Further, the Lytton and Romney analysis, with its focus on treatment, had less to say about differences in relationships (Russell & Saebel, 1997).

Leaper, Anderson, and Sanders's (1998) meta-analysis of mothers' speech to boys and girls showed differences in parental treatment and relationships. These differences were for mothers, but differences also could be expected with fathers, who are more likely to differentiate on the basis of child sex (Lytton & Romney, 1991; Siegal, 1987). Leaper, Anderson, and Sanders (1998) found that mothers are more talkative and use more supportive language strategies with daughters than with sons. As the authors noted, these findings are consistent with a greater emphasis on verbal interaction and affiliation with daughters than with sons. Leaper, Anderson, and Sanders (1998) concluded that boys and girls are exposed to different styles of verbal interaction.

Some specific findings will be used to illustrate differences in parental relationships with sons and daughters. Leaper, Leve, Strasser, and Schwartz (1995) found mothers more likely to reciprocate supportive speech acts from daughters, although this result was restricted to a feminine sex-typed play activity. Lindsey, Mize, and Pettit (1997) found parents of preschool girls more likely to engage in pretense play than parents of boys. Girls, in turn, were more likely to engage in pretense play with their parents. This suggests a relationship system in which both girls and parents engage in pretense play, with the attendant imaginary and verbal components that are a feature of this type of play. We (Russell et al., 1998) reported that girls received more reasoning/induction than boys, and boys received more power assertive behaviors such as commands without explanations or reasons, as well as more responses from parents that involved angry outbursts. Finally, mothers have been found more likely to combine control with autonomy-granting (e.g., encouraging children to pursue their own goals) with boys than with girls (Pomerantz & Ruble, 1998). These specific results parallel findings for relationship qualities and styles of boys versus girls noted earlier, and are consistent with a view that boy–girl differences in relationship experiences with parents could be associated with differences in the relationship learning of boys and girls.

SOCIAL INTERACTION THEORY: STUDIES LINKING PARENT–CHILD RELATIONSHIPS TO CHILDREN'S PEER RELATIONSHIP STYLES AND QUALITIES

Studies linking parent–child relationships to children's peer relationship styles and qualities will be examined to determine whether there is evidence consistent with boys and girls learning from the relationship styles experienced with parents. A selection of studies will be discussed to explore the main issues and to suggest directions for future research.

Mize and Pettit (1997) investigated relations between mothers' behavior and preschool children's social competence. Mothers were observed interacting with their children in a nonsocial teaching task, where the child was helped to complete a block pattern. One code was for mothers' encouragement of problem-solving. At one end of the scale was the correct completion of the task and wanting the child to appear smart (a more "masculine" emphasis, with a focus on successful achievement). At the other end of the scale, the child's thinking and effort were encouraged (a more "feminine" emphasis, with a focus on indirect and supportive strategies). Girls, but not boys, whose mothers encouraged thinking received lower teacher ratings for aggression.

Another measure examined the use of hints, with a high score for nonspecific hints, and a low score for directives. There was a suggestion that this scale was related to teacher ratings of the child's social skills for girls, but not for boys. Their results point to mothers' styles containing indirect and supportive elements having a positive impact on the social behavior and skills of girls but not of boys. This possibility is also supported by Mize and Pettit's (1997) second study.

In the second study (Mize & Pettit, 1997), mother and child watched videotaped vignettes of children's peer interaction and social problem-solving (e.g., a dispute over objects, or rejection of group entry attempts). Mothers were asked to help their child understand why the things in the story happened and the best way to handle the situation. The more mothers emphasized prosocial (friendly, outgoing) strategies, and helped children attend to relevant social cues and consider alternative sources of action, the higher girls (but not boys) scored on measures of social competence. Mothers' use of these strategies appears be more effective with daughters than with sons. Mothers' use of relationship-oriented strategies and content with girls could be especially helpful for girls' social competence. The prosocial emphasis and reasoning involved, as well as the verbal nature of coaching strategies could produce a closer match between the mothers' behavior in this context and girls' rather than boys' characteristics. That is, verbal coaching (and in particular from mothers) could have greater influences on girls' than on boys' social skills.

In addition to social coaching, Mize and Pettit (1997) also observed mother–child play, with a focus on mothers' "responsive" style (measured by such things as synchrony of interaction, positive affect, and mutual gratification). They concluded that mothers' responsive style was a comparatively robust predictor of social competence in boys. Overall, Mize and Pettit's (1997) results prompt speculations about mechanisms in the relationship learning of boys and girls in the family. For example, boys could learn more from experience in actual interaction through the practice of skills, whereas the learning of girls might be more from supportive verbal guidance and coaching. However, it is unclear whether it is the style of interaction in coaching that is important for girls' learning about relationships or the content of the coaching.

Mize and Pettit's (1997) relatively small sample size and the fact that mothers but not fathers were examined limit conclusions. Furthermore, the outcome measures were teacher ratings of social skills, and sociometric assessments. There is a need, in addition to these types of measures, to examine links between *specific* aspects of parenting styles and behaviors, and *specific* styles and qualities in children's peer relationships. For example, might the measures of maternal coaching used here predict children's use of reasoning and suggestions in disagreements with peers? Some of these matters were taken up in a subsequent publication by Pettit, Brown, Mize, and Lindsey (1998).

Pettit et al. (1998) argued that children might acquire certain skills and competencies from interactions with fathers and others from mothers. They also suggested that the activity-oriented nature of father–child, especially father–son, relationships could mean that learning from fathers arises more from activity-type contexts. On the other hand, for mothers, and especially in the mother–daughter dyad, with an emphasis on verbal aspects of the relationship, lessons might be learned in social teaching and coaching contexts. Gottman, Katz, and Hooven (1997) made a comparable point, suggesting that mothers might contribute to children's learning about emotion regulation via instruction whereas fathers might contribute through play activities.

Pettit et al.'s (1998) results showed girls' social competence was predicted most strongly by mothers' social coaching, with boys' social competence predicted most strongly by fathers' dyadic play involvement. Further, mothers and fathers made independent (and sometimes contrasting) contributions to children's social competence. Mothers' active involvement in child play was associated with *lower* levels of peer acceptance, with the reverse for fathers. The authors suggested that dyadic play involvement and social coaching may represent somewhat unique socializing contexts with different social-development implications for boys and girls, and in which mothers and fathers may play roles of differing importance.

A number of studies show links between the specific qualities experienced in parent–child relationships and children's use of these qualities in peer interactions. Black and Logan (1995), for example, concluded from their study of parent–child and child–peer communication with children aged 24 to 60 months that "patterns children use in conversation with their parents are, for the most part, similar to those they use with their peers" (p. 267), e.g., parents of rejected children were more likely to respond noncontingently or not at all to their children's requests and their children did the same in peer interactions. Similarly, responsive communication in parent–child interactions was related to children's more responsive communication with peers. The small sample size (23 boys and 20 girls) restricted the possibility of analyses involving sex-of-child. To examine sex and relationship-learning issues, this type of study needs to be replicated with a larger sample and with a focus on sex-of-parent and sex-of-child differences.

Herrera and Dunn (1997) examined mother–child interaction at 33 months and child interactions with a close friend three years later. Mothers' behavioral style in conflict at 33 months paralleled the child's behavior with a friend three years later. If mothers defended their own interest at 33 months, for instance, children were more likely to threat, tease and insist on their own point of view with a friend three years later. Similarly, if mothers looked at the child's side and compromised at 33 months, the child tended to do these things with a friend. Again, the small sample size (total of 37 children) restricted the potential to examine sex differences. This type of research needs to be undertaken with a focus on sex differences.

Sex differences in children's relationship learning could arise because the *same* relationship with, or treatment of, the sexes leads to different outcomes for boys and girls (Jacklin, 1989; Lytton & Romney, 1991; Russell & Russell, 1992). This could happen through gender schemas (Bem, 1985), with boys and girls selecting from and learning different lessons from apparently the same experiences. Differences in parental behavior might not be as critical as how boys and girls process information related to parental behavior and their relationship experiences (Jacklin, 1989). For example, how do boys and girls process and react to fathers' use of a directive style and mothers' reasoning with the child? The results of Bryant (1985) show the relevance of this issue. He found that higher levels of extensive, casual involvement with adults in their neighborhood were associated with increased social perspective-taking skill in boys, but with decreased perspective-taking skill in girls. The same relationship experience appeared to have had different effects on boys and girls.

ATTACHMENT RESEARCH: SEX DIFFERENCES IN PARENT–CHILD RELATIONSHIPS AND IMPLICATIONS FOR CHILDREN'S RELATIONSHIP LEARNING

The literature on attachment provides several avenues for investigating sex and relationship learning, although mainstream attachment theory and research have paid little attention to sex/gender questions. Sroufe, Carlson, and Shulman (1993), for example, do not mention sex in their chapter about relationship learning using attachment theory. Attachment writers (e.g., Waters, Vaughn, Posada, & Kondo-Ikemura, 1995) tend to treat the model as universal and give little or no space to sex differences. When sex has been of interest, it has mainly been whether children form attachment relationships with fathers as well as with mothers (Fox, Kimmerly, & Schafer, 1991). Nevertheless, attachment theory gives prominence to differences in parent–child relationships (e.g., based on secure or insecure attachments) and assumes that these differences contribute to differences in children's relationship learning. It follows that if relationships with mothers and fathers and/or with sons and daughters differ, there will be differences in relationship learning.

A number of studies relevant to sex differences in relationships are available in the attachment literature. For example, Bridges, Connell, and Belsky (1988) reported differences in mother–infant and father–infant relationships in the Strange Situation. They commented on the "unique signatures" (p. 99) of mother–infant and father–infant relationships, with these differences organizing infant social interactions in the Strange Situation. Similarly, Steele, Steele, and Fonagy (1996) emphasized the specificity of mother–infant and father–infant relationships associated with patterns of attachment. They argued that "infants are able to discern and represent significant differences in their parents' states of mind concerning attachment in ways that influence their behavior with each parent . . ." (p. 553). Kerns (1996) discussed differences in mother–child and father–child attachments and suggested that they might have different external correlates.

Research on antecedents to secure attachment a   ings about
differences in relationships with mothers and fa   nd Belsky
(1992a) examined the antecedents of father–infant   found no
evidence of father responsiveness being related to   urity, suggesting differences between mothers and fathers in the relationship qualities
associated with secure attachment. van IJzendoorn, Kranenburg, Zwart-
Woudstra, van Busschbach, and Lambermon (1991) found mothers of
securely-attached girls were more sensitive than mothers of insecurely-
attached girls, but that this relation was reversed for boys, suggesting that the
relationship qualities associated with secure attachment differ for boys and
girls. Maternal sensitivity could underlie secure attachment only for girls. An
implication is that secure attachment could involve different relationship experiences and learning for boys and girls.

Research on links between attachment classification and child social outcomes also yields evidence of sex-based differences. Suess, Grossman, and
Sroufe (1992) related infant attachment classifications to children's observed
behavior in preschools. Play competence, conflict resolution, and behavior
problems were related to infant–mother attachment for girls, but not for boys.
This suggests that mother-child relationships associated with secure attachment might lead to different relationship learning for boys and for girls. To
speculate on processes yielding their findings, if sensitivity in mother–child
dyads is a factor in secure attachment for girls more than for boys, the results
of Suess, Grossman, & Sroufe (1992) could arise from the impact this sensitivity has on girls' social competence. Girls could acquire relationship styles
containing sensitive and responsive behaviors, for instance.

To understand relationship learning associated with secure attachment requires that features of parent–child relationships linked to attachment security (in addition to presumed sensitivity of mothers) be identified. This is
because the relationship learning will arise from the particular relationship
experiences of the child. Kerns, Cole, and Andrews (1998) found that attachment security scores for girls were associated negatively with the proportion
of peer contacts initiated by parents and positively with the proportion of peer
contacts initiated by girls. In other words, attachment security in girls could be
associated with a relationship in which parents place more emphasis on girls
themselves initiating peer contacts. There were no significant correlations
between the initiation of peer contacts for boys and their security of
attachment.

Kerns and Barth's (1995) results are also relevant here. With children 41 to
51 months of age, security of attachment to mother was related to mother–
child dyads maintaining play for longer. In contrast, security of attachment to
fathers was associated with fathers issuing more directives during play, and
with children making more suggestions and responding more positively to
fathers' initiations. In turn, mother–child attachment, and not father–child
attachment, was found to be related to peer popularity, but for boys only.
Father–child attachment, and not mother–child attachment, was related to
children's friendly-cooperative behavior at preschool. Finally, teacher reports

of friendly-cooperative behavior and popularity were more strongly related to mother–child than to father–child play measures.

Kerns and Barth (1995) suggested that children could learn an interaction style through play with their parents that carries over to play with peers. They argued that mothers' directive style with daughters could foster leadership skills in daughters that transfer to peer settings. The same result did not emerge for the mother–son dyad, raising questions about the effects of maternal directiveness on sons, and about ways in which sons might acquire leadership skills. Kerns and Barth (1995) noted that friendly-cooperative girls had less contentious and smoother relationships with their fathers, suggesting a possible transfer to the peer context of some aspects of fathers' interaction style with girls. The sex differences obtained by Kerns and Barth (1995) warrant further investigation in efforts to understand sex and relationship learning.

Youngblade and Belsky (1992) included mothers and fathers and examined attachment security at 1 year, parent–child interaction at 3 years, and positive and negative aspects of the child's observed styles and behavior in interaction with friends at 5 years of age. Security of attachment with fathers, but not with mothers, was related to positive qualities in the child's friendship interactions. Also, these positive qualities were related to mother–child interaction at age 3, but not to father–child interactions. Negative qualities in children's friendship interactions were positively related to negative aspects of father–child interactions at age 3, but negatively related to the same qualities in mother–child interactions. These results are difficult to explain, but add weight to the suggestion that children's relationship experience and learning could differ according to whether it is with mothers or with fathers.

A challenging finding of Youngblade and Belsky (1992) was that infants securely attached to their fathers were in friendships at age 5 that were less positive (less connected, less synchronous, and with less cognitively sophisticated play). This apparent anomaly might be explained when more is known about qualities of the father–child relationship associated with secure attachment. If fathers of securely-attached children are more directive (Kerns & Barth, 1995), this might be implicated in the finding. This suggestion is consistent with fathers' directiveness being negatively associated with child popularity (MacDonald & Parke, 1984).

LaFreniere and Sroufe (1985) measured preschool children's peer competence during a school year, and related it to attachment scores at 12 to 18 months of age. The peer measures included teacher ratings of social competence, sociometric status, and rates of social participation. An interaction between child sex and attachment was found for many outcome measures. The authors concluded that attachment was a powerful predictor of rated social competence and sociometric status, as well as of observed positive and negative affect, affiliation, and assertiveness in peer interactions, but only for girls, not for boys. Securely-attached girls, for example, were positive in interactions with peers and outgoing. The authors noted that maternal responsiveness might have different consequences for boys and girls. This study again suggests that the relationship underlying attachment security for boys and girls could be different, and/or that boys and girls select from and process relationship experiences differently.

Sex-of-child differences in relationship learning are also implied by Turner's (1991) results. Turner reported differences in the peer behavior of insecurely-attached preschool boys and girls. Insecurely-attached girls showed more dependent behavior, and more positive expressive behavior and compliance with peers than secure children. In contrast, insecurely-attached boys were more aggressive, disruptive, assertive, and controlling with peers than secure children. These findings could arise because (1) the relationship underlying insecure attachment in boys and girls is different, or (2) boys and girls process relationship experiences differently.

The results of Kerns, Klepac, & Cole (1996) also raise the prospect of different learning associated with the same attachment classification for boys and girls. Fifth and Sixth graders' friendship pairs comprising a securely- and an insecurely-attached girl displayed the highest level of intimacy during interactions, whereas pairs containing a securely- and an insecurely-attached boy displayed the lowest level of intimacy. This result could arise from insecure boys and girls experiencing different relationship learning with their mother, or processing their relationship experiences with mother differently. For example, insecure girls might respond to a lack of maternal sensitivity and responsiveness by attempts to gain closeness with others, with insecure boys reducing their orientation to intimacy.

Cassidy, Kirsh, Scolton, and Parke (1996) found several links between attachment status and children's representations of themselves and others in relationships. Their study opens up an important area for research on relationship learning, namely children's representations of relationships. If children develop representations of the parent and of the relationship as suggested by Cassidy et al. (1996), and if relationships with parents are somewhat sex-based, it follows that children's representations in these areas will be sex-related.

Cassidy et al. (1996) raised another significant issue for relationship learning. They argued that the child's "representation of the parent generalizes to representations of peers" (p. 901). Generalization is a significant issue for relationship learning insofar as generalization from one relationship (the parent–child) to another (the child–peer) is a necessary process in relationship learning. Interpretative processes at least must be implicated, with the relevance of features of both parent–child relationships and peer relationships taken into account by the child, possibly through such things as gender schemas. For example, if parental rejection is a central attachment-related measure, as argued by Cassidy et al. (1996), then the role of rejection could differ according to the sex of the child and/or the parent. If daughters seek closer relationships with mothers, and boys seek to separate from mothers, as argued in psychoanalytic theory (Chodorow, 1978; Washburn, 1994), then acceptance/rejection by mothers might be construed differently by boys and by girls, and thereby have different consequences for their relationship learning.

In summary, although sex has not been a central concern of attachment research and theory, findings from a number of studies point to the relevance of sex for relationship learning. There appear to be differences in the organization of attachment relationships as a function of both parent sex and child sex. Further, behaviors and relationship qualities associated with attachment security also appear to differ according to sex. There is evidence suggesting that the attachment context and associated behavior could lead to differences in relationship learning for boys and for girls. When relationship representations are taken into account, differences in children's processing and understanding of parent–child relationships as a function of sex gain prominence for the understanding of sex and relationship learning.

SUMMARY, CONCLUSIONS, AND RECOMMENDATIONS

There is a limited understanding at present of the acquisition of different relationship qualities and styles in boys and girls. The emphasis in this chapter was on the possibility that children's relationships with parents could be replicated in some form in relationships with peers. The notion is that through processes such as modeling and practice, and the acquisition of self-construals and social knowledge about relationships and relationship expectations, children acquire some of the relationship qualities and styles that they experience with parents. If children's relationship experiences with parents differ on the basis of sex (parent and/or child), this could provide a basis for the acquisition of different relationship qualities and styles for boys and for girls.

The basic proposition as expressed in the previous paragraph is relatively simplistic. Nevertheless, it sets out fundamental research needs, namely to identify differences in children's relationship qualities and styles in the family based on sex, and then to determine how these are linked to differences in children's relationship qualities and styles with peers. The linkage might take the form of a direct transfer from the family to the peer context. But it is also likely to have indirect components, involving cognitive processes such as children's interpretation and transformation of their experiences with parents, as well as processes associated with children's adaptation of relationship learning in the family for the peer context. Closeness with parents might be linked to closeness with peers, for example, but the form of closeness will differ, and therefore require some adaptation by the child.

Questions of indirect linkages would need to consider mediational processes. Candidates for mediation have been set out by Mize, Pettit, and Meece (in press). They include social-cognitive and social information processing skills, emotion understanding and regulation, and internal working models. The main emphasis in the present chapter has been on a relatively direct transfer from family to peer systems (such as "closeness" or "collaboration" being a feature of the two types of relationships), rather than via mediation.

The matter of direct transfer appears to be the first step for research within a "relationship replication" framework.

The understanding of sex and relationship learning will be enhanced by increased attention to *specific* peer relationship qualities and styles in children, rather than to categorical variables such as "social competence", "peer acceptance", or "having a close friend". The need for emphasis at the level of specific qualities was also highlighted by Kahen, Katz, and Gottman (1994). Categorical variables are likely to hide sex differences, as they are the products of social functioning rather than social functioning per se. From the present review, included among the specific qualities and styles that could receive research attention are: tendencies for girls to form closer and more intimate relationships in smaller networks, higher levels of positive affect and synchrony (e.g., linked turn-taking) in girls' relationships with each other, a focus on mutual interests and status in boys' relationships with each other, boys' greater tendency to use control strategies in relationships, girls' greater use of explanation and reasoning in response to conflicts, and girls' greater tendency to use collaboration and cooperation.

Two limitations have restricted the productivity of research on sex/gender and relationship learning. One is reduced power to detect sex differences due to relatively small sample sizes (Russell & Saebel, 1997). Unless sample sizes are increased substantially, research on sex and relationship learning will have only a moderate capacity to detect effects. The second limitation of current research has been the lack of theoretical development. This has meant that most of the emphasis here has been on sex, rather than gender, differences. To assist research on gender and relationship learning, there needs to be more attention to the measurement of gender per se. There are several theoretical frameworks in the gender literature that are helpful for the understanding of gender differences in relationship qualities and styles that could provide support for future research.

Among the helpful theoretical positions in the gender literature are "gender theory" (e.g., Ferree, 1990; Thompson & Walker, 1989; West & Zimmerman, 1987), gender schema theory (Bem, 1985), Maccoby's analyses of gender as a social category (Maccoby, 1988), analyses of gender and relationships, including communication (Canary & Dindia, 1998; Maccoby, 1990; Wood, 1996a), psychoanalytic theory (Chodorow, 1978; Washburn, 1994), and analyses of gender based on social roles (Eagly, 1987), activities (Canary & Emmers-Sommer, 1997), and social contexts (Deaux & Major, 1987). Many of these theoretical frameworks have implications for an understanding of links between children's family experiences and their peer relationship qualities and styles. For example, gender roles could be a factor in sex differences in relationships displayed both inside and outside the home, and facilitate children's learning of gendered relationship styles. There is a need for ideas of relationship replication to be extended to incorporate more from theoretical treatments of gender, in order to develop an account of differences in the relationship learning of boys and girls.

Although the present emphasis has been on relationship replication, it is clear that research in other directions is also needed to advance the understanding of gender and relationship learning. This could include work on the role of temperament and personality, family processes such as direct teaching or coaching of relationship qualities, and parents providing children with opportunities to learn particular relationship qualities and styles. With respect to opportunities, for example, parents of girls might encourage inter-action with other girls and within contexts that facilitate gender appropriate relationship qualities. Associated with the latter point is the importance of also understanding the peer group per se as a context in which sex/gender differences in relationship qualities and styles are acquired or developed.

Chapter 7

The Social Relationships of Children Involved in Bully/ Victim Problems at School

Claire P. Monks

and

Peter K. Smith

Department of Psychology, Goldsmiths College, University of London

Although the term "bullying" has long resonated in the English language, research on the topic only spans some 20 years, the first significant research program being that of Olweus (1978). However, the past 10 years especially have seen an upsurge in the study of bullying on an international basis (Smith, Morita, Junger-Tas, Olweus, Catalano, & Slee, 1999). Although closely related to (in fact, a subset of) aggression, bullying is essentially an issue of relationships—between "bully" and "victim"—as much as it is one of school and institutional environments. In this chapter, we review what has been found out about bully/victim relationships.

We first discuss the definition of the term "bullying", and describe the various types and forms of bullying which fall within this. Then, we briefly survey the general findings about the structural features of bullying in schools: its effects; and attitudes to bullying amongst pupils, parents and teachers. In the main body of the chapter we look at the developmental pathways of such

The Developmental Psychology of Personal Relationships.
Edited by Rosemary S. L. Mills and Steve Duck. © 2000 John Wiley & Sons Ltd.

relationships, starting with family background characteristics and moving to the social factors in school peer group networks. We discuss age and sex differences in relation to these pathways, and end by sketching out some implications for interventions to help reduce bullying in schools.

DEFINITIONS OF BULLYING

As with any interesting psychological concept, there is no universal agreement on definitional issues; however, there is now some degree of consensus amongst many researchers in this area that bullying is a form of aggressive behavior in which there is a power imbalance involved. Specifically, bullying is:

- behavior which hurts or harms another person
- with intent to do so
- the hurt or harm may be physical or psychological
- it is repeated
- there is a power imbalance such that it is difficult for the victim to defend him- or herself.

(Farrington, 1993; Olweus, 1993a; Smith & Sharp, 1994)

The first three of these criteria specify aggressive behavior. The fourth and fifth specify the subset of aggressive behavior which is bullying; that it is behavior which happens more than once and is done by a stronger person against a weaker. That is, it is a relationship characterized by continued aggression and with a power asymmetry—a "picking on" or "harassment" which can appear unfair to onlookers and which can have serious effects for those who are victims.

A succinct definition is the "systematic abuse of power" (Smith & Sharp, 1994). This captures the typical criteria just referred to. It is a broad definition, and could include family abuse and workplace bullying, as well as school bullying. In this chapter we will focus on school bullying, on which there is a clear body of research evidence.

TYPES OF BULLYING

Studies from the aggression literature have identified three main categories of aggressive behavior: physical aggression, verbal aggression and indirect (relational, social) aggression (Björkqvist, Lagerspetz, & Kaukiainen, 1992; Crick & Grotpeter, 1995). Similar categories can be applied to bullying (Rivers & Smith, 1994).

Of these, physical and verbal aggression have long been recognised. For example, the earlier definition of Olweus (1991) defined bullying in terms of "being hit, kicked, threatened, locked inside a room and things like that . . . it is also bullying when a child is teased repeatedly". In fact, physical bullying—the larger child hitting and beating up a smaller one—is probably the prototypical example of the term. However, verbal bullying is usually the most frequent. Teasing is a more ambiguous term, as some teasing can be in fun; much depends on how the teasing was intended and how it was taken by the recipient. More recent versions of the Olweus questionnaire, therefore, specify that the teasing should be "in a nasty way", or "not in a friendly and playful way".

Although the early version of the Olweus questionnaire did not explicitly include indirect bullying and social exclusion, these came to be recognized as important during the 1990s. Writing about aggression generally, Björkqvist, Lagerspetz, & Kaukiainen (1992) described indirect aggression as "some kind of social manipulation, that is, using others as a means of attack instead of attacking oneself, or otherwise manipulating the social network of the class, in order to exclude one target person from friendship groups". This includes behaviors such as gossiping, suggesting shunning of the other, spreading rumors or breaking contact with the person in question as indirect aggression.

Crick and Grotpeter (1995) introduced the concept of relational aggression, defined as "inflicting harm on peers in ways that damage peer relationships." This includes excluding someone from a game, telling the victim that they will not be friends with them unless they do what they say, and spreading rumors. Galen and Underwood (1997) have described a slightly broader term, social aggression, as "directed toward damaging another's self-esteem, social status, or both, and may take direct forms such as verbal rejection, negative facial expressions or body movements, or more indirect forms such as slanderous rumors or social exclusion".

There is overlap between the concepts of relational, indirect, and social aggression, but they are not identical. The concept of indirect aggression stresses that the aggression is not done face-to-face, but by a third party. The notion of relational aggression stresses the objective of the aggression—damaging peer relationships. Thus direct social exclusion—"you can't play with us, go away!"—would be relational and social, but not indirect. Spreading nasty rumors, however, would be relational, social, and indirect. Later versions of the Olweus questionnaire include "sent nasty notes" and "no one ever talks to them" to incorporate these types of bullying (Whitney & Smith, 1993).

These types of aggression and bullying are important in relation to age and sex differences. Björkqvist and colleagues have examined the types of aggressive behavior described in Finnish pupils between 8 and 18 years of age (Lagerspetz, Björkqvist, & Peltonen, 1988; Björkqvist, Lagerspetz, & Kaukiainen, 1992; Lagerspetz & Björkqvist, 1994). Although girls and boys did not differ in the amount of verbal aggression exhibited, boys tended to be rated as displaying more physical aggression and girls more indirect aggression; this sex difference did not hold for younger children, but became more pronounced in later childhood, together with some overall progression from physical through verbal to indirect forms of aggression, which was more marked (or occurred earlier) for girls than boys. Crick, Casas, and Mosher (1997) suggest that, when attempting to hurt others, children use methods which they expect to be the most hurtful to their victims. Boys tend to use physical aggression as this attacks the goals which are characteristic of boys, whereas girls use indirect and relational aggression, which attacks the friendship and intimacy goals held by girls.

Foster, DeLawyer, and Guevremont (1986) have also found sex differences in the way in which children viewed the various styles of aggression. They found that when asking children to describe behaviors which made them dislike peers, boys cited physical aggression whereas girls cited social exclusion. Similarly, Galen and Underwood (1997) report that only boys saw physical aggression as more hurtful than social aggression. Girls also viewed social aggression as more hurtful than boys did.

We have seen that traditional definitions of aggression and bullying tended to focus on the physical aspects, which have been found to be more characteristic of boys; probably because of the partial neglect of indirect and relational aggression until recently, bullying behavior has been studied rather more in groups of boys than girls (e.g., Olweus, 1980). The elaboration of indirect/relational/social forms of aggression and bullying has clearly been valuable both in redressing this and pointing toward age trends and different styles of bullying which may have different consequences (Crick, 1996, 1997). However, it is worth pointing out that individuals high in physical/verbal/direct aggression also tend to be high in indirect/relational aggression (for example, correlations between overt and relational aggression from 0.58 to 0.87, Tomada & Schneider, 1997; and 0.63, Crick, 1997). Thus we are talking about styles rather than types, so far as most individual pupils are concerned.

MAIN FEATURES OF BULLYING

The Extent of Bully/Victim Problems

The Olweus questionnaire (Olweus, 1993a) has been used extensively for large-scale survey work on the extent of bully/victim problems. It is a self-report instrument, including a definition of bullying (see above). It was first used in Norway, where Olweus reported some 16% of pupils being involved in bully/victim relationships: 7% as bullies, 9% as victims. In England, Whitney and Smith (1993) reported rather larger figures: in primary schools, 10% bullies and 27% victims; in secondary schools, 4% bullies and 12% victims. Roughly comparable figures are now available from many countries, including Australia, Canada, Spain, Italy, Portugal, Germany, Ireland, and Japan (Smith et al., 1999).

Main Structural Features of Bully/Victim Relationships

The survey results from different countries, although revealing varying inci-
dences and some culturally specific features, draw a generally similar picture
of some important features of bully/victim relationships (Smith et al., 1999):

- There are characteristic age differences. Self-reports of being bullied decline rather steadily over the 8- to 16-year period; self-reports of bullying
  others do not show this decline. There also tends to be some shift with age
  away from physical bullying and toward indirect and relational bullying.
- There are characteristic sex differences. Boys are more numerous in the
  bully category, but the sexes are more equal in the victim category. Boys
  practice/experience more physical bullying, girls more indirect and relational bullying.
- Although a majority of bullying relationships involve several bullies, a
  significant minority involves one-to-one relationships. Boys tend to be bullied by other boys (rarely by girls), but girls experience bullying from both
  sexes.
- A substantial proportion of self-reported victims say that they have not told
  a teacher, or someone at home, about the bullying. This proportion who
  have not told increases with age; this may reflect the more serious nature of
  victimization at older age groups mentioned above.
- The experience of being bullied correlates with health problems such as anxiety and depression (Salmon, James, & Smith, 1998). It also relates to low self-
  esteem (Slee & Rigby, 1993; Boulton & Smith, 1994). However, most findings
  are that bullies are not low in self-esteem, or are low only in measures (such as
  "behavioral self-worth") directly related to antisocial behavior.
- Although most pupils say they do not like bullying, a significant minority do
  say they could join in bullying. Also, these "pro-bullying" or "anti-victim"
  attitudes tend to increase with age, at least up to ages 14 or 15 years (after
  which they may start to decline).
- School is the place where the majority of bullying takes place; and in school
  mainly in public places such as the playground, the classroom, or corridors.
  Although there are large school variations in the incidence of bullying,
  factors such as the size of school, class size or rural versus big city setting
  are usually not related to this; the attitudes of teachers in bullying situations
  and the degree of supervision of free activities appear to be of major
  significance for the extent of bully/victim problems, as is also the existence
  of an effective school policy.

Types of Bully/Victim Relationship

Until recently most research into bullying has tended to focus on the dyadic
interaction between the bully and victim. Types of bully or victim have been

distinguished in terms of personality and behavior, as assessed by teacher reports, peer nominations or self-report. However, the emphasis has recently shifted toward a more holistic approach encompassing the larger social group, with types corresponding to roles in the group.

So far as bullying children are concerned, several researchers distinguished a small group of bullies who are less confident and popular than other bullies, sometimes called "passive bullies" (Olweus, 1994; Stephenson & Smith, 1989). However Salmivalli, Lagerspetz, Björkqvist, Österman, & Kaukiainen (1996) extended the categorization of bullies by examining bullying as a group process, involving not only bullies and victims, but also assistants to the bully, reinforcers, outsiders, and defenders of the victim. They administered the Participant Roles Questionnaire (50 items describing bullying-situation behavior) to 12–13-year-old Finnish students. Based on the peer evaluations of behavior, most children could be assigned to participant roles:

- Bullies (8.2%): ringleaders who start the harassment and encourage others to join in.
- Assistants (6.8%): more passive followers of the bully, who aid the bully in the harassment but do not start it.
- Reinforcers (19.5%): who laugh at the victim and cheer the bully on.
- Defenders (17.3%): who offer support to the victim by telling an adult, comforting the victim, or actively attempting to get the bullying to stop.
- Outsiders (23.7%): who keep their distance from the bullying situation and may pretend that nothing is going on.
- Victims (11.7%): who are targets of repeated aggression.
- No role (12.7%): who could not be assigned a clear participant role.

These roles showed moderate stability over 2 years (Salmivalli, Lappalainen, & Lagerspetz, 1998). The participant roles have also been identified in a group of younger English children aged 7–10 years (Sutton & Smith, 1999). They found that the roles Bully, Reinforcer, and Assistant are closely correlated with each other; those who start the bullying may at other times reinforce or assist. However, those who start the bullying (Bully and Assistant) are rarely victims, while Reinforcers (those who yell and laugh) are more likely to also be victims at times.

Amongst victims, the most common distinction has been between passive victims and provocative victims. Olweus (1994) describes passive victims as anxious, insecure pupils who do not appear to provoke the harassment they receive and fail to defend themselves adequately. By contrast, provocative victims could be seen as acting in a way to cause the bullying—for example, by barging into games inappropriately or taking things without asking. Pikas (1989) has made this distinction strongly and uses it as a basis for different types of intervention. Olweus (1994) describes provocative victims as hot-tempered and likely to answer back when insulted, although not usually very effectively. They may also try to bully other students themselves and are generally hyperactive and restless, unconcentrated and generally offensive and tension-creating and may annoy and provoke other children (Olweus, 1994). Olweus (1978) also described another subcategory of colluding victims, those who play the victim in order to gain acceptance.

A sizeable group of children cannot be classified simply as bullies or as victims, but appear to both bully other children and to be victimized. These children (up to one-half of all victims) have been labelled bully/victims (Stephenson & Smith, 1989; Boulton & Smith, 1994; Bowers, Smith, & Binney, 1994; Wölke & Schulz, 1997). Salmivalli (1998) notes that there probably is overlap between bully/victims and children described as provocative victims (Pikas, 1989; Olweus, 1978, 1984, 1994), aggressive victims (Schwartz, Dodge, Pettit, & Bates, 1997) or as reactive/proactive aggressors (Vitaro, Gendreau, Tremblay, & Oligny, 1998).

Graham and Juvonen (1998) identified three types of victims by examining peer and self-reports of victimization; "true" victims, "paranoids", and "deniers". "True" victims were those children who view themselves as being victimized and are viewed by their peers as victims. "Paranoids" are those who describe themselves as victims although their peers do not view them as such. "Deniers" have reputations of being victims, although they do not view themselves as such. These groups can be distinguished in terms of acceptance/rejection by the peer group and characterological self-blame for victimization, social anxiety, and self-worth. "Paranoids" who view themselves as victims (although the peer group does not view them as such) may be more vulnerable to psychological maladjustment, although they are not at risk for peer rejection. In contrast, "Deniers" are more likely to be rejected by the peer group, although they are not at risk for psychological maladjustment. "True" victims are at risk both for peer rejection and for psychological maladjustment.

DEVELOPMENTAL PATHWAYS AND FACTORS IN BULLY/VICTIM RELATIONSHIPS

Family Relationships

There is a considerable literature on parenting characteristics and family relationships which predict aggressive behavior in children. These include:

- Parenting characterized by negative emotional attitude, lack of warmth and involvement (Hinshaw, Zupan, Simmel, Nigg, & Melnick, 1997; Olweus, 1980)
- Parenting which is permissive and tolerant without setting clear limits on aggressive behavior towards siblings, peers, and other adults (Olweus, 1994; Loeber & Hay, 1994)
- Parents who use power-assertive methods such as harsh physical punishment and violent emotional outbursts and generally provide an aggressive role model (Olweus, 1980)

- Early insecure and disorganized attachment has been related to poorer peer relationships, lower social competence, and more aggressive relationships (Bost, Vaughn, Newell-Washington, Ciclinski, & Bradbard, 1998; Fagot & Kavanagh, 1990; Lyons-Ruth, 1996).

The findings specifically regarding family relationships of bullies and victims have been reviewed by Smith and Myron-Wilson (1998). The families of bully/victims have been found to be most dysfunctional and troubled with experiences of violence against the child or between adult family members, marital conflict, and often inconsistent discipline enforcement and poor monitoring of the children's activities by the parents (Bowers, Smith, & Binney, 1992, 1994; Schwartz et al., 1997). By contrast, bullies often experience harsh discipline but rarely violence against themselves. They perceive their family members as distant and disengaged and the relationship between siblings is often characterized by struggle for dominance and experiences of being dominated. Farrington (1993) found that the parents of bullies are much more likely to have been bullies themselves. Bullies and bully/victims describe little positive affect (warmth) and positive communication in their families (Batsche & Knoff, 1994). These families more often lack a father figure (Rigby, 1994; Bowers, Smith, & Binney, 1994). The families of (passive) victims are not particularly highly conflictual or troubled; however, the mothers are often overprotective, in particular towards children perceived as emotionally vulnerable in their temperament (Olweus, 1993b; Bowers, Smith, & Binney, 1992, 1994; Rigby, 1994). Olweus (1993b) suggested an additional pathway to victimization in boys when the father is highly critical and distant in his attitude towards his son and thus not providing a satisfactory role model.

Much of the research has focused on boys, and on physical bullying. The family relationships of girl bullies or victims may differ from those of boys (see Russell, in this volume). Rigby (1994) found that male bullies come predominately from families perceived as lacking positive affect and positive communication. In contrast, adolescent girls coming from similar families are as likely to be victimized at school as to become bullies. Rigby (1993) showed that family relationship difficulties are more serious for male bullies than female bullies (especially with fathers), but more serious for female victims than male victims (especially with mothers). Different maternal behavior toward boys and girls is related to victimization in both sexes. Finnegan, Hodges, and Perry (1997) found that maternal overprotectiveness, in particular when boys felt afraid and compelled to submit to their mothers during conflicts, was associated with victimization in boys. In contrast, victimization in girls was associated with maternal hostility, especially for girls seen as lacking physical strength. A common pathway towards victimization occurs when maternal behavior hinders a child's progress towards the relevant social and developmental goals according to gender. Smith and Myron-Wilson (1998) speculate that for girls, mothers' hostility may decrease their sense of connectedness in relationships (leading to anxiety), whilst for boys a mother's overprotectiveness may hinder their search for autonomy and independence.

Schwartz et al. (1997) reported on the early socialization of aggressive victims (bully/victims), passive victims (victims) or non-victimized aggressors (bullies). Children classified as aggressive victims at 10 years of age were significantly more likely to have had experiences with harsh, disorganized, and potentially abusive home environments 5 years earlier. Mother–child interactions at 5 years of age were characterized by hostility and restrictive or overly punitive parenting. In contrast, the non-victimized aggressors had a history of greater exposure to adult aggression and conflict, but not victimization by adults (see Mills & Piotrowski, in this volume).

The links between family background and bully/victim roles in school can be seen as the beginnings of possible developmental pathways, based on the child learning that certain kinds of behaviors are normative and/or developing working models of relationships as postulated by attachment theory. Troy and Sroufe (1987) linked insecure attachment to bully/victim characteristics in preschoolers, and Myron-Wilson (1998) found that bullies and victims were characterized by different subgroups within the insecure categories. It is also likely (but at present unsupported by data) that bully/victims might be over-represented in the disorganized attachment category, given the known links between disorganized attachment and abuse (Crittenden, 1988b).

Temperament and Personality

Family background factors may interact with temperament and personality in setting children on different developmental pathways. On the basis of path analysis, Olweus (1993b) found that weak temperament could lead to over-protectiveness in mothers and hence to victim status. Olweus (1980) also argues that an active, hot-headed temperament is more likely to lead to an aggressive, bullying child. Difficult temperament (early undercontrolled behavior as expressed by high reactivity to stress, excessive crying and irritability, poor consolability) early in infancy and toddlerhood has been found to be a significant precursor of aggressive behavior and poor social functioning in school in middle childhood (Sanson, Smart, Prior, & Oberklaid, 1993; Loeber & Hay, 1994; Eisenberg, Fabes, Bernzweig, Karbon, Poulin, & Hanish, 1997), and even into early adulthood (Moffitt, Caspi, Dickson, Silva, & Stanton, 1996; Newman, Caspi, Moffitt, & Silva, 1997). Kingston and Prior (1995) reported that children who had a history of aggression were differentiated from non-aggressive children on the basis of both difficult temperament and family interaction features. This included maternal ratings of the child as difficult, hostile interactions with siblings, and harsher parenting practices.

Several studies have examined the relationship of Eysenck's personality factors of extraversion, psychoticism and neuroticism (using the Junior Eysenck Personality Inventory) with the tendency to bully or be victimized. Slee and Rigby (1993) reported that Australian schoolboys' tendency to bully was significantly associated with psychoticism, whereas the tendency to be victimized was significantly associated with introversion. Byrne (1994) found a similar pattern of results with a sample of Irish children, with bullies being more hostile and victims more withdrawn; however, he also reports that both bullies and victims displayed high levels of neuroticism.

Mynard and Joseph (1997) extended these studies to include bully/victims. They replicated the previous findings, with bullying related to psychoticism and victimization related to introversion, and both bullying behavior and victimization were associated with neuroticism. Mynard and Joseph found that children who are both bullies and victims display high levels of neuroticism and high psychoticism.

External Characteristics or Deviations

"When children are asked why they are bullied they often refer to physical attributes, e.g. obesity, red hair, wearing glasses, or abnormalities of speech" (Dawkins, 1996). However, studies which have investigated physical differences between bullies, victims, and other children have not always found differences between the groups. In fact, with the exception of physique, Olweus (1978, 1993a) regards the issue of external characteristics as of little or no importance in bully/victim problems. However, he did use a quite broad definition of external deviations, and other studies have found a high risk for victimization in certain groups of children, for example, those with special educational needs.

So far as physique or physical strength is concerned, Lagerspetz, Björkqvist, Berts, & King (1982) found that victims were physically weaker than children rated as not involved in bullying. They were also more likely to be obese. Olweus (1978) also found, on the basis of teacher reports, that victims were physically weaker. Olweus (1993b) reports that physical weakness (together with the family and temperament factors reviewed earlier) does contribute significantly to the prediction of victim status.

Lagerspetz et al. (1982) reported that bullies are physically stronger than other children. However, based on teacher ratings, Byrne (1994) found that 14% of bullies were rated as being small in size. He questions the stereotypical view of the bully as big and strong and suggests that it is the positive attitude towards violence that really distinguishes the bullies.

Ethnicity

Ethnicity is usually obvious as an external feature; and, in addition, there is often some degree of societal prejudice against ethnic or racial minorities. Racial harassment or violence includes any act of bullying which appears to have a motivation which is racial in nature or where there is an allegation of racial motives. A number of findings suggest that racial teasing and harassment are significant, sometimes common, but that in other respects ethnicity does not interact strongly with bully or victim status.

The incidence of racial harassment may vary considerably in different localities. Tizard, Blatchford, Burke, Farquhar, and Plewis (1988) surveyed several inner city schools in London and report that being teased about one's color is a widespread problem, with approximately one-third of pupils reporting that this had happened to them, and more black than white children reporting this experience. However, Whitney and Smith (1993), in a survey of over 6000 children in the Sheffield area, found that of those children who reported being bullied, only 15% at junior/middle level and 9% at secondary level reported "being called nasty names about my color or race".

To make a more exact comparison, Moran, Smith, Thompson, and Whitney (1993) matched 33 Asian and 33 white children for age, gender, class/year, and school, and interviewed them about their experiences of being bullied or bullying others at school that term. There were no differences generally between the Asian and white students in terms of having friends, being bullied, or bullying others. However, there was a specific difference in the amount of racist name-calling experienced; none of the white pupils reported this, whereas 18% of the Asian pupils reported it as a way in which they were bullied that could be very hurtful to the recipient.

Boulton (1995a) also investigated the experiences of Asian and white pupils in English schools, and found no significant differences, in terms of ethnicity, in peer ratings of pupils as bullies or victims. However, significantly more Asian pupils reported experiencing racial name-calling by other-race children, with the opposite being found for non-racial types of teasing.

Junger (1990) reported similar findings in a sample of boys from the Netherlands who were interviewed about their experiences of bullying. The data showed no differences in the amounts of bullying experienced by ethnic minority and ethnic majority groups. However, the way in which they accounted for the harassment was different; when asked for the reason for the bullying, a large proportion (40–49%) of the boys from ethnic minority backgrounds cited racial motivations, whereas, in comparison, only 5–7% of the Dutch boys (who were in the ethnic majority) did so.

Siann, Callaghan, Glissov, Lockhart, and Rawson (1994) examined the effect of ethnic group on bullying in several English and Scottish schools. They found no significant differences between the ethnic groups in terms of levels of victimization or of bullying others. However, when asked "do you think pupils from ethnic minority backgrounds are more often bullied than white pupils?", 75.4% of ethnic minority pupils, but only 49.6% of ethnic majority pupils, answered "yes". Siann et al. suggest that at the subjective level individuals draw a distinction between bullying and racism. They may make this distinction because, although racist taunts are undeniably painful, they are not directed at the individual's sense of self. Thus, racial abuse directed at oneself may not be interpreted as bullying, whereas, when members of an ethnic minority reflect on the experience of their group or community as a whole with respect to racial abuse, they may interpret this as bullying.

Special Educational Needs

Children with some of the external deviations considered by Olweus (1978, 1993a), such as clumsiness, stuttering, and poor sight, would come within the category described (in the U.K.) as children with special educational needs. Several studies have indicated that such children are at high risk of being bullied. For example, Hugh-Jones and Smith (1999) interviewed stammerers in adulthood and found that 82% reported having experienced bullying at school. The likelihood of being bullied was related to the severity of the stammer and difficulties with friendships.

Dawkins (1996) compared the rates of bullying reported by two groups of children attending hospital clinics. One group of children attended the Child Development Clinic (CDC) with conditions which affected their appearance and/or gait, resulting in a visible abnormality. The other group attended a general pediatric clinic with conditions not associated with visible abnormalities. Significantly more of the CDC group reported being bullied (50% this term, with 30% being regular victims, compared with 21% and 14% of the non-CDC group respectively). The nature of the teasing for CDC children tended to focus on their disability. Logistic regression showed that victims were more likely to spend time alone at playtime, to be receiving extra help at school, and to be male, and less likely than non-victims to have at least two good friends. There was no indication that the children in the CDC group who had a visible disability were more likely to be victimized than the children with no visible disabilities once these four factors (time alone, extra help, being male, and number of friends) were taken into account.

Other studies have looked at experiences of children with learning difficulties. Martlew and Hodson (1991) compared bullying of children with and without MLD (moderate learning difficulty) in an integrated school. Mainstream children did not play with the children with MLD often, especially in older classes. The MLD children reported being teased significantly more and having fewer friends than their mainstream peers. There was no significant difference between younger mainstream and MLD children in terms of the amount of teasing experienced, but the older MLD children reported that they were teased significantly more than the non-MLD group. Similarly O'Moore and Hillery (1989) examined the experiences of victimization by remedial children (with learning difficulties) in several Dublin schools. Children in remedial classes reported that they were bullied significantly more often than children in mainstream classes did. In two English primary schools, Nabuzoka and Smith (1993) found significantly more children with special educational needs (SEN) (33%) were nominated by peers as victims, than children without (8%). Some of the victims did appear to be provocative victims (bully/victims).

Whitney, Smith, and Thompson (1994) matched children with SEN and children without SEN by age, gender, ethnicity, year group, and school. Children with SEN were much more likely to be bullied than the mainstream children with whom they were matched; nearly two-thirds of the children in the SEN group complained about being bullied, compared with a quarter of the mainstream children. Children with SEN tended to experience bullying which was related to their special needs. It was also found that the likelihood of a child with SEN being bullied was related to the nature of their special needs, as a smaller proportion of children with mild learning difficulties reported being bullied than those whose learning difficulties were moderate. Children with SEN reported having fewer friends than mainstream children, and teachers reported that children with SEN tended to choose other children with SEN as their friends.

Children with special needs may find it difficult to make friends within their peer group, sometimes due to the nature of their disability. Physical disabilities may make it difficult for children to join in activities such as running or physical games. Learning disabilities may make it difficult for children to form friendships, in part due to a lack of social skills, which may result in them responding inappropriately during interactions with peers. These characteristics may well be tied in to reduced acceptance and rejection within the peer group, in turn linked to victimization (see next section). Whitney, Nabuzoka and Smith (1992) postulated three factors which may increase the risk of a child with SEN being victimized.

- Characteristics (e.g., dyslexia, clumsiness, disability) may be used as a pretext for bullying.
- SEN children in a mainstream school may be less socially integrated because of their disability and therefore lack the protective factor of friends.
- Some children who have behavioral problems may act aggressively themselves in a manner consistent with provocative victims.

In general, the research findings on external factors, ethnicity, and special needs, suggest that while physical weakness may be a direct risk factor in being a victim, the situation is more complicated for other factors. In general, any increased risk associated with other factors may be largely explicable in terms of friends and the protection friends can provide against bullying. In addition, perceptions of bullying are important. Individual experiences of bullying may be ascribed by the victim to a specific disability. However, individual experiences of racial harassment may be discounted as bullying by the victim (although not by onlookers).

Sociometric Status and Friendship

Many researchers have examined the social status and networks of children and adolescents involved in bullying behavior. The research on special needs has indicated its importance, and more generally, Perry, Kusel, and Perry (1988) report results from a multiple regression which indicates that bully and victim status account for about half of the variance in peer rejection.

The literature is fairly consistent in its findings for victims of bullying. The general consensus is that victims tend to be lower in popularity than other children, low on peer acceptance, and high on rejection (Lindman & Sinclair, 1989; Rican, 1995; Olweus, 1978; Boulton & Smith, 1994; Perry, Kusel, & Perry, 1988; Salmivalli, Karhunen, & Lagerspetz, 1996; Lagerspetz et al., 1982). Slee and Rigby (1993) reported that the tendency to be victimized correlated negatively with self-appraisals of number of friends and popularity. Boulton and Underwood (1992) found that victims reported being unhappy and lonely at school and as having few friends.

Hodges, Malone, and Perry (1997) extended these findings, suggesting that the quality and not just the quantity of friends is an important moderator of the relationship between behavioral risk (internalizing/externalizing problems, and physical weakness) and victimization. They report that when friends possess qualities which leave them unable to protect the child (i.e., the friends are physically weak or are victimized themselves), the relation of behavioral risk to victimization was greater than when friends possessed qualities which would enable them to protect the child. The externalizing behaviors of friends also had an effect. It was found that when a child's friends exhibited externalizing problems, the child's own externalizing behaviors were less predictive of their victimization. This leads Hodges, Malone, and Perry to suggest that friends who are prone to externalizing behaviors may fight back on behalf of their friends and that this may serve a protective function.

The findings are not as clear-cut for bullies. Foster, DeLawyer, and Guevremont (1986) reported that aggression was associated with peer rejection, whereas sharing and providing help and support were associated with peer acceptance, results which would suggest that bullies would be rejected by the peer group. Lindman and Sinclair (1989) found that, in general, bullies were less popular than their peers. Lagerspetz et al. (1982) also found bullies were less popular than controls and only slightly more popular than victims. However, Olweus (1978) and Stephenson and Smith (1989) reported that bullies were average in popularity.

Dodge, Coie, Pettit, and Price (1990) found that the relation between bullying and peer status varied with age for boys. First graders who were popular engaged in more bullying than average first graders, whereas popular third graders did not differ from average in bullying. Rough play was not associated with rejection, although rejected boys displayed more reactive aggression and instrumental aggression than average boys. However, the laboratory setting of this study limits the generalizability of the findings.

Several studies report relevant sex differences here. Lindman and Sinclair (1989) found female bullies to be more popular than male bullies. Similarly, Rican (1995) reports that girl bullies are only slightly less popular than non-bullies, and are significantly more popular than girl victims; however, boy bullies are significantly less popular than their peers, and are less popular than boy victims.

Salmivalli et al. (1996) also reported male bullies being rejected by their classmates, whereas female bullies scored high on both social acceptance and social rejection (which is more consistent with the controversial profile described by Coie, Dodge, & Coppotelli, 1982). Female Reinforcers and Assistants were rejected, whereas male Reinforcers had a profile like popular children (low social rejection and high social acceptance) and male Assistants scored average on social rejection and acceptance. Outsiders scored below average on both variables. The children who were most highly accepted (and also scored low on rejection) were Defenders, making them the most popular children in the group.

Boulton and Smith (1994) reported that children who are rejected are more likely to receive bully nominations and victim nominations than children in the other sociometric groups (neglected, average, popular, controversial). Bullies and victims were also less likely to be classified as popular and more likely to be classified as rejected by their peers. However, as all of their bullies were boys, these findings only extend to male bullies. They also found that bullies were more likely to be classified as controversial, which suggests that they may be liked and disliked by similar numbers of peers. They suggest that this may account for teachers' ratings of bullies as being more popular than other children. They also speculate that being popular with some peers could account for why bullies continue with their aggressive behavior. The fact that some classmates dislike the bully may not matter to him if he has a group of friends in which he is popular. From this comes the suggestion that bullies may be members of groups which provide support and reinforcement for bullying behavior. Cairns, Cairns, Neckerman, Gest, and Gariepy (1988) found that aggressive adolescents may well be less popular within the class than their peers, but tend to be nuclear members of a small social group. Unlike victims, bullies tend not to be isolated. Although they are also often rejected by the peer group as a whole, they have been found to belong to a social subgroup in which they are popular. Cairns et al. (1988) found that aggressive children (not necessarily bullies) aged between 10 and 13 form "social clusters", and although these children were not well-liked by most of the other children, many expressed a high level of liking for each other. Poulin, Cillessen, Hubbard, Cole, Dodge, & Schwartz (1997) report similarity among friends, especially with respect to aggressive behavior. When they examined this further, they found that it applied only to proactive aggression (of which bullying is a form) and not to reactive aggression.

Salmivalli, Huttunen, and Lagerspetz (1997) examined the social networks of children involved in bullying. Children involved in harassing others, including bullies, assistants, and reinforcers, belonged to larger social networks than defenders, outsiders, and victims, suggesting that although they may be rejected by most of their peers they may be well-liked by their social group. Children tended to form networks with others who had similar or complementary participant roles in bullying to themselves. Children who bully others tend to associate with children who do the same, or assistants or reinforcers. Defenders and outsiders tend to form social networks together, sometimes including victims. Children who were harassed were least likely to belong to a social network, or they associated with children who defend and support them. However, female bullies tended to form social networks which included the victims of their harassment, a finding which they relate to the different characteristics of bullying amongst boys and girls.

Few studies have corroborated these predominantly nomination-based studies with naturalistic observations. In England, Boulton (1995b) directly observed peer interaction in the playground by boys classified as either bullies, victims, or not involved. There was no difference between the three groups in terms of their social network size (how many different children each target interacted with in a non-aggressive way). However, bullies tended to have a significantly larger mean number of companions at any one time, than the other two groups, while victims tended to be in smaller groups than bullies and were more likely to spend time alone than either bullies or not involved children. Pepler, Craig, and Roberts (1998) made naturalistic observations of children in Canadian playgrounds. They reported that teacher- and peer-rated aggressive children did indeed display more physical and verbal aggression in the playground, but also generally had high rates of interaction including also prosocial behavior.

There are relatively few data on bully/victims. Perren and Alsaker (1998) examined the friendships and popularity, as rated by peers and teachers, of children involved in bully/victim problems at kindergarten. They report that victims were least popular and received the least nominations as playmate and as best friend. Bullies were quite popular and had many playmates and were often nominated as best friend. Bully/victim status was not as clear-cut; teachers saw them in a similar light to victims, having poor peer relations, whereas peers did not view them as poorly as victims.

Social Skills

Social status and friendship are often related to social skills. The dominant model here has been Crick and Dodge's (1994) social information-processing model, which suggests that children follow a series of sequential steps when processing social information: (1) encoding of cues (both internal and external); (2) interpretation and mental representation of those cues; (3) clarification or selection of a goal; (4) generation of possible responses; (5) choice of most appropriate response; and (6) behavioral enactment.

Crick and Dodge (1996) argue that skilled processing of these steps leads to competent social performance, whereas distorted or deviant processing can lead to socially inappropriate behavior including aggression. Several of the processing steps have been found to be different in aggressive children, For example, at step (1), aggressive children tend to attend to fewer cues before making attributions of others' intent than non-aggressive children (Dodge, 1986).

At step (2), when presented with hypothetical situations in which a negative outcome occurs, although with an ambiguous intent on the part of the provocateur, aggressive children are more likely than non-aggressive children to infer that the intention was hostile; this is known as a "hostile attribution bias" (Quiggle, Garber, Panak, & Dodge, 1992; Graham & Hudley, 1994).

At step (5), aggressive children are also more likely to opt for aggressive solutions than their non-aggressive peers. Trachtenberg and Viken (1994) report that aggressive boys were more likely to choose aggressive solutions to problems and to judge those solutions as competent than non-aggressive boys. Rubin, Bream, and Rose-Krasnor (1991) reported that aggressive children are not only more likely to suggest aggressive solutions to hypothetical scenarios, but are also more likely to use aggression to meet their social goals in an observed social problem-solving setting.

Some studies have attempted to examine the differences in processing of individuals who display different types of aggressive behavior, most notably proactive (instrumental) and reactive (hostile) aggression. Proactive aggression is a deliberate form of aggressive behavior which is instrumental in that it is a means for obtaining a goal (be that a teddy bear or social status within the group). Reactive aggression is an aggressive response to provocation or frustration. Although positively correlated with one another, Crick and Dodge (1996) note that it is possible to identify distinctly proactively aggressive and reactively aggressive groups of children with "a sufficiently large sample". Bullying has been described as, on the whole, a form of proactive aggression (Dodge & Coie, 1987).

Dodge and Coie (1987) examined whether proactively and reactively aggressive boys exhibited similar hostile attributional biases. The boys were shown a video recording of a series of vignettes depicting provocations by peers and asked to interpret the intentions. Only the reactively aggressive boys exhibited "hostile attribution biases". Attributional biases correlated positively with the rate of reactive aggression, but not with proactive aggression which was observed in free play with peers.

Crick and Dodge (1996) found that proactively aggressive children viewed both physical and verbal forms of aggression in a more positive way than other children who were not proactively aggressive (including a group of children who displayed reactive patterns of aggression). They also viewed instrumental goals in social situations more positively than other children, which would suggest a type of processing at step (3) in Crick and Dodge's (1994) model that would contribute to their use of aggressive behavior in social situations. In contrast, older reactively aggressive children tended to attribute more hostile intent in an ambiguous situation than other children, consistent with the hypothesis that reactively aggressive children view other children as hostile and then react aggressively toward them. Reactively aggressive children do not view instrumental aggression positively, which is also consistent with the suggestion that aggressive behavior for reactively aggressive children is not used as a way of achieving instrumental goals and is a reaction to the (perceived) hostility of others.

A few studies have reported on the actual behavioral strategies used by victims of bullying (usually on the basis of self- or peer-report). Kochenderfer and Ladd (1997) looked at the success of different strategies in a longitudinal study of 5- to 6-year-olds. They found that telling a teacher, and having a friend help, were used more by pupils whose victimization scores decreased over time. Fighting back, and walking away, were used more by pupils whose victimization scores increased over time. Salmivalli, Karhunen and Lagerspetz (1996) found that 12–13-year-old Finnish pupils rated non-chalance as being a more constructive response to bullying than either counter-aggression or helplessness.

Roles Taken in Bullying and Social Cognition

Although the prevailing view according to the social information-processing model is that both bullies and victims have some deficiencies or deficits, recent work has questioned this so far as bullies are concerned. Sutton, Smith, and Swettenham (1999) argued that ringleader bullies would need considerable skills to be successful; they needed to organise a gang, choose a suitable victim and way to victimize, and a time and venue to minimize detection or its consequences. They suggested that ringleader bullies should score high on theory of mind tasks, involving understanding someone else's perspective (rather than poorly, as might be predicted on a deficit view).

In a study with 8–11-year-old children, Sutton, Smith, and Swettenham (1999b) found that ringleader bullies were superior to any of the participant roles (of Salimivalli et al., 1996) in their ability to read the mind of others (good theory of mind) and to use this to manipulate and dominate others. Bullies were high in their social cognition scores but showed a deficit in feeling for others (empathy). Victims showed the poorest performance in the social cognition tasks. Bullies (ringleaders) and controls (outsiders, de-fenders) scored significantly higher than victims, with assistants and rein-forcers taking an intermediate place. This finding held for girl as well as boy bullies; indeed, the indirect bullying more characteristic of older girls may require theory of mind skills more than straightforward physical attack.

Self-esteem

Self-esteem may be an important contributory factor in the pathway to victim-ization. Egan and Perry (1998) suggest that low self-esteem may contribute to victimization by peers for three main reasons:

- Children with low self-esteem may hesitate to defend themselves during conflict due to their low self-worth.
- Individuals with low self-esteem expect and accept negative social feedback.
- Low self-esteem has been related to depression, cautiousness, and poor self-regulation; all of which may make a child vulnerable to aggressors.

They postulate that the level of self-regard would mediate the impact of behavioral vulnerabilities on pupils' victimization. A study of 189 children examined these hypotheses. It was found that low self-regard did contribute to victimization by peers. It was also found that behavioral problems such as physical weakness, manifest anxiety, and poor social skills were more likely to lead to victimization over time when the children had low self-regard.

A quite different picture emerges with self-esteem of bullies. Slee and Rigby (1993) found that children's tendency to bully others was not associated with low self-esteem. They suggest that the bully's level of self-esteem is maintained by the sense of power they gain through dominating and humiliating those "weaker" than themselves. These findings are consistent with the views of Olweus (1993a) and Boulton and Smith (1994), who also report that bullies do not suffer from poor self-esteem, at least at a global level. Some other studies, such as O'Moore and Hillery (1989) do report lower self-esteem in bullies; the disagreement here may reflect the proportion of bully/victims (predicted to have low self-esteem) included in the bully category, as well as the precise measures of self-esteem used (e.g., the inclusion of scales directly reflecting antisocial behavior).

Salmivalli, Kaukiainen, Kaistaniemi, and Lagerspetz (1999) used multiple measures of self-esteem, involving peer and self-evaluated self-esteem and defensive egotism in order to investigate the relationship between the roles taken in bullying behavior and self-esteem in a group of 14–15-year-olds. Defensive egotism refers to the "narcissistic, self-aggrandising tendencies" in self-esteem. This was included, as it has been suggested that high self-esteem may reflect an inflated view of oneself and may be a form of defensiveness rather than a "true" measure of self-worth.

Adolescents' self-esteem profiles were associated with their behavior in bullying situations, although the relationships were stronger for boys than girls. Bullying others as well as reinforcing the bullying behavior or assisting the bully were associated with what Salmivalli et al. (1999) describe as "Defensive Self-Esteem". This refers to a pattern of self-esteem which is characterised by high levels of defensive egotism and only slightly above-average self- and peer-evaluated self-esteem.

Adolescents who were nominated as exhibiting prosocial behaviors, such as defending the victims of bullying, were found to be characterized as having "Genuine High Self-Esteem". Salmivalli et al. (1999) suggest that it may be that pupils require a good level of self-esteem before they feel able to stand up to the bullies.

Being victimized was associated with "Low Self-Esteem" for boys and girls, by both peer- and self-rated evaluations. For girls, an additional profile of self-esteem was found to be associated with victimization, that of "Humble Pride". "Humble Pride" is characterised by high self-reported self-esteem and low peer-reported self-esteem. The authors suggest that the "Humble Pride" group may find it difficult to admit to being victimized (the levels of victimization were based on peer nominations) and having low self-regard. Yet another self-esteem profile, that of "Defensive Self-Enhancers", was associated with moderate victimization in boys. There may be links here with the "paranoids" and "deniers" of Graham and Juvonen (1998), which remain to be further explored.

BULLY/VICTIM RELATIONSHIPS OVER TIME

Case studies of individuals who have been bullied severely at school indicate that sometimes the bullying can extend over many years (Smith & Sharp, 1994). In a survey of 2300 pupils of 10 to 14 years of age, in 19 English schools, Smith and Shu (1998) found that for those bullied, in about one half of cases (47%) the bullying only lasted about a week, and for another 17% about a month; but for 9% it had lasted about a year, and for 13% it had gone on for several years. Thus, the experience of victimization is rather brief for many pupils, but can be very prolonged for a minority.

This finding should be put together with the age trends in victimization, which show a decrease in self-reports of being victimized (but no systematic change in self-reports of bullying others). These trends have been discussed by Madsen (1997) and Smith, Madsen, and Moody (1999). While some changes may be due to differing interpretations of the term "bullying" with age, the two most powerful explanations appear to be (a) the increasing social skills of children who might be victims, and (b) the greater opportunity for bullies to pick on younger (usually weaker) children.

So far as social skills are concerned, several researchers (Kochenderfer & Ladd, 1997; Hodges, Malone, & Perry, 1997; Smith, Madsen, & Moody, 1999) propose that most or all children will experience some teasing and (often mild) bullying during their early years at school, when they are in large peer groups. Much of this will be short in duration; and much of it children will cope with in a way which does not reward the bully and discourages further bullying. However, some children will respond less skilfully, and the bullying children will focus on them for further harassment. This model sees some children (potential bullies) as "sampling" the peer group for children who can be bullied with relative success and impunity.

This model is compatible with many of the other areas of knowledge reviewed. Firstly, the potential bullies are likely to be those who have experienced similar relationships at home, and have a hot-headed temperament. This leads them to see relationships in an exploitative way and to value dominance and abusive use of power. In this sense their social skills are "deviant" but not necessarily "defective" (Sutton, Smith, & Swettenham, 1999a,c). Indeed, ringleader bullies may exercise considerable social skill and understanding of others in their manipulation of situations, of their cronies, and of the victims' weaknesses. Since most children dislike bullying, bullies are not particularly popular; but, especially by secondary school, they have gathered around them a network of like-minded children and may have some degree of popularity. This developmental shift is associated with a decrease in sympathetic attitudes to victims, and a decrease in empathetic responses, especially to male victims, most pronounced around 14–15 years of age (Rigby, 1997; Olweus & Endresen, 1998).

Other factors help to single out long-term victims. In addition to dealing less competently with immediate episodes of bullying, victims appear to lack friends and/or to have friends who lack social status and may themselves also be victims. Either way, they get less protection from friends, who can be an obvious support against bullying. In what appears to be a two-way process—a vicious cycle—victims have low self-esteem, which is exacerbated by being victimized and in turn makes them feel less worthy of defending themselves or seeking help for the bullying. Thus, by secondary school, victims are less likely to seek help than they were at primary school.

Being physically weak is a risk factor for boys, since at younger ages, and for boys especially, much bullying is physical. In addition, some external characteristics such as obesity, clumsiness, a stutter, or other kinds of disability, may increase risk—but possibly only via other factors such as friendship and self-esteem. The independent influence of these external factors is still not fully clear. It may interact with wider factors such as school policies in integration and segregation, and attitudes to disability. Being in an ethnic minority group may bring increased risk of racial teasing and harassment, but both the extent of this, and its perception as (individual) bullying or (group) harassment, will also be influenced by wider factors.

It is also clear that boys and girls have rather different kinds of bully/victim relationships, even though there is overlap. Boys tend to use verbal and physical bullying; this can be seen as functioning to damage the victim's status in the peer group, which tends to be tied more to physical strength in boys. By contrast, girls have been found to use more indirect/relational/social forms of aggression and bullying (Crick & Grotpeter, 1995; Crick, 1997; though this may depend partly on culture, see Tomada & Schneider, 1997). These forms of bullying, more or less by definition, tend to damage the victim's reputation in the peer group and the immediate social network (which tends to be more focused and intense in older girls, compared to the larger networks of boys at secondary school).

Olweus and Endresen (1998) have suggested an ultimate evolutionary explanation for these sex differences; bullying is sex-specific in ways which damage the victim most appropriately—physical status in the case of boys, peer reputation/network in the case of girls, especially as puberty is approached and these factors influence desirability vis-à-vis mate choice characteristics. The decreased empathy for male victims of bullying (Olweus & Endresen, 1998) as pupils approach puberty, can be given a similar explanation. In this light, "bully" and "victim" can be seen as roles which result from natural processes: a competition for dominance and status, albeit moderated by friendship, cooperation, and empathy. In most cases, children who bully others, or who do not escape a victim role, can be seen as within a normal range, while acknowledging the "risk factors" identified with each role, as well as the wider influence of institutional and societal factors.

More needs to be done, however, to flesh out the pathways related to different roles or styles (such as ringleader vs. assistant bully, or overt vs.

relational bully). In addition, the particular status of bully/victims (who may overlap considerably with aggressive or provocative victims) deserves more consideration, since some appear to come from quite abusive backgrounds, and to have particularly severe difficulties with peers.

BRIEF IMPLICATIONS FOR INTERVENTION

Existing interventions have been made at the levels of school, class, and individual (Olweus, 1993a; Smith & Sharp, 1994). Schools vary greatly by pupil-reported incidence of bullying. Correlational analyses indicate that neither school size, nor class size, are important variables. In Scandinavia, socioeconomic characteristics (school catchment area) is of no importance (Olweus, 1993a), and in England the effect is minor (Whitney & Smith, 1993). The most likely candidates for explaining school variation are the amount of effort put into anti-bullying work, and the nature, extent, and salience of relevant policy work. Formulation and use of a whole-school anti-bullying policy is now quite widespread in the U.K. and has been found to be effective (Smith & Madsen, 1997).

Eslea and Smith (1998), in a detailed study of four primary schools, found that recency and salience of policy work probably provided the best explanation for the varying trends in rates of bullying over time. However, these authors also found that decreases in bullying were most marked for boys, and small or absent for girls. This may be due to the different types of bullying and pathways of bullying in girls, which have only recently been recognised. Class-level work against bullying (curricular work, role plays, literature) may presently focus more on physical and verbal bullying and neglect the kinds of relational bullying characteristic of girls. Alternatively, these latter kinds of bullying may simply be more difficult to detect and intervene against.

As we learn more about the nature of the children particularly involved as bullies or victims, we may be able to devise and target particular interventions for them. Currently, some such programs for aggressive children follow the social skills model. Coie, Rabiner, and Lochman (1987) developed "social relations training", which focuses on social problem-solving (identifying problems, specifying the goals for that situation and evaluating different solutions). Hudley, Britsch, Wakefield, Smith, Demorat, & Cho (1998) evaluated the effectiveness of an attribution retraining program aimed at reducing aggression in an elementary school. Selman and Schultz (1990) and Selman, Schultz, Nakkula, Barr, Watts, & Richmond (1992) have developed an intervention based on pairing children (often an aggressive child is paired with a shy or withdrawn child) and helping them to conceptualize interpersonal conflict as a four-stage process of negotiation (defining the problem, producing different responses, evaluating these responses, and selecting the best outcome).

These interventions appear to have some limited success. However, those designing such programs need to bear in mind that ringleader bullies may actually have some good social skills. What is needed is a re-orientation of values and empathic consideration, embedded in a comprehensive model of relationships. For younger children, family-based therapeutic work (perhaps based on attachment-theory premises) may be helpful (see van IJzendoorn, Juffer, & Duyvesteyn, 1995). For older children, and given limited resources, creating an environment which minimizes the opportunities for bullying un-detected, and the rewards for bullying, and works on the self-esteem and capabilities of victims and their opportunities to seek help if necessary, may be the best way to break the damaging continuation of bully/victim relationships.

Chapter 8

An Analysis of Sources of Power in Children's Conflict Interactions

Michal Perlman

University of California at Los Angeles

and

Afshan Siddiqui, Avigail Ram, & Hildy S. Ross

University of Waterloo, Ontario, Canada

Social psychologists have conducted research on conflict resolution in contexts such as labor-management negotiations, organizational disputes, and international conflict. Concurrently, developmentalists have focused on conflict resolution within children's close relationships. There has been some bridging of information between these two empirical and theoretical traditions. For example, developmentalists incorporated the distinction between destructive and constructive conflict (Shantz & Hartup, 1992; Vandell & Bailey, 1992), an idea that was introduced in social psychology (Deutsch, 1973). However, for the most part there has been little crossover between these two literatures. In fact, we lack even the most basic terms for comparing the types of relationships examined by investigators within these two research traditions. We adopt the term Formal Relationships to describe non-close relationships studied largely with adults, and Personal Relationships to

The Developmental Psychology of Personal Relationships.
Edited by Rosemary S. L. Mills and Steve Duck. © 2000 John Wiley & Sons Ltd.

designate close relationships, the focus of most studies of children's conflict. The two types of relationships differ largely in terms of the degree of intimacy or emotional closeness. Generally, high-intimacy relationships tend to be affectionate while low-intimacy relationships are more business-like (Emery, 1992).

One possible reason for the limited communication between these traditions is that, until fairly recently, young children's disagreements with others have not been conceptualized as interpersonal conflict (Shantz & Hobart, 1989). When children fought with their peers or friends, child psychologists were interested in the aggressiveness of the antagonists, with little concern for the processes by which issues of contention are resolved. A central construct within the sibling literature has been rivalry, and some theorists have gone so far as to consider sibling disputes to be epiphenomena, whose chief aim is to capture parental attention and affection. Only recently has the realistic nature of children's sibling conflicts come into focus. Developmental psychologists have long studied what we might now consider to be parent–child disputes within the framework of parent–child socialization. When parents discipline, children either comply or defy, internalize or resist their parents' rules. The recent emphasis on the bi-directional nature of parent–child relationships (Lollis & Kuczynski, 1997; Perlman & Ross, 1997b) has led to a re-conceptualization of disciplinary encounters as events of parent–child conflict. It is too early to judge how generative this "conflict" paradigm will be with respect to studying children's fights. What is clear is that this re-conceptualization suggests research issues that have not been part of past traditions. For example, constructs of negotiation, resolution, and power relations emerge as central to a conflict focus.

The goal of the current chapter is to begin to bring what is known about conflict resolution in Formal Relationships together with what is known about how children resolve conflicts in their Personal Relationships. We will provide the reader with a representative, rather than comprehensive, literature review in the hope of stimulating research. We recognize that we have neglected a rich literature on adults' personal conflicts, especially within marital relationships (Gottman, 1979; Holmes & Murray, 1996), that is beyond the scope of this paper. Absent, as well, is a serious developmental and gender analysis of children's conflicts (see Shantz & Hartup, 1992).

In thinking about conflict resolution in Personal vs. Formal Relationships, we began by attempting to define power in the context of negotiation. We quickly realized that we were dissatisfied with the unitary definition commonly used by developmentalists. This definition emphasizes the coercive, aggressive aspects of power. Based on our own work, we differentiated between power based on force and power based on legitimacy. We also drew upon French and Raven's (1959) typology of the bases of social power. According to French and Raven, power is based on: coercion, reward, referents, expertise, information, and legitimacy. These distinctions have rarely been used by Personal Relationships researchers and will be expanded at length later in this chapter. They provide an interesting perspective on conflict and one that we feel extends thinking about power in Personal Relationships. Thus, this review is structured around the concept of power.

The study of conflict resolution has been conducted in different ways in the Formal and Personal Relationships traditions. Formal Relationships research is largely based on laboratory procedures, using undergraduate students as subjects and tasks that involve problem-solving based on hypothetical situations or game theory. Studies that utilize observational or naturalistic procedures are rare. The classic example of a hypothetical problem-solving paradigm is the prisoner's dilemma. In this paradigm two subjects, typically undergraduate students, are interrogated independently. They can either cooperate with one another, or compete. If they both cooperate, they earn a moderate pay-off. If they both compete, they earn very little. Individuals achieve maximum pay-off when they choose to compete but their partner cooperates. In that case the cooperative partner's reward is generally smallest. Thus, the risk of competition is that the other will also compete and reduce the pay-off, and the risk of cooperation is that the other will compete. This is analogous to the interrogation of two suspects who are jointly guilty of a crime. The maximum pay-off is achieved by one partner if the other partner confesses but the first does not. This type of study is quite different from the more diverse methodologies used by developmentalists, methodologies that rely more heavily on naturalistic observations.

There are important differences in the interactions of parties involved in Formal Relationships vs. Personal Relationships. For example, concern for one's opponent is clearly very different in parent–child conflict than it is when a car dealer and a car buyer resolve their differences. Yet, little effort has been made to study the effects of antagonists' concern for one another on the resolution of children's Personal conflicts. Furthermore, there are differences among different types of Personal Relationships. Because our interest lies in children's resolution of conflict in Personal Relationships, we have examined what is known about children's conflict with their parents, friends, and siblings. We will compare findings based on these relationships to findings based on Formal Relationships. Although all three of these categories of children's relationships are "close" (because interaction partners have ongoing, intimate relationships) they differ in meaningful ways. For example, parent–child relations involve power imbalances that friendships are less likely to exhibit. Another relationship that has been examined by developmentalists is that between peers (i.e., non-friends such as classmates). This relationship is interesting in that it approximates the Formal Relationships typically examined by social psychologists.

In the review that follows we examine the sources and the exercise of power within conflict. For each source of power we first present findings from the Formal Relationships literature followed by the relevant findings from research on Personal Relationships. Where possible we have incorporated additional variables that are related to the nature of the opponents' relationship. These include imbalances of power, concern for one's opponents and the extent to which opponents are mutually dependent.

SOURCES OF POWER

Researchers of Personal Relationships have focused on the coercive nature of power. The emphasis has been on forms of verbal and physical aggression. French and Raven's (1959; Raven, 1992) typology elaborates other crucial sources of antagonists' power. Social psychologists have directly manipulated variables related to these sources of power. Findings from the developmental literature require greater extrapolation before they can be understood in terms of this typology.

Coercion and Reward

According to French and Raven (1959), coercion and reward provide one basis for power. These stem from control over personal (e.g., fear of disapproval from someone we value) or impersonal (e.g., withdrawal of privileges) resources. The use of coercive strategies (such as threats) has received much attention from researchers of Formal and Personal Relationships. Generally, such strategies are reciprocated and have negative consequences like decreasing agreement. But, at times, contentious strategies are effective as they can be used to force reluctant parties to negotiate (Pruitt & Carnevale, 1993).

An interesting finding from the Formal Relationships literature relates to use of coercion depending on the power differential between opponents. Generally, more powerful negotiators make fewer concessions, threaten their opponents more frequently (Hornstein, 1965; Michener, Vaske, Schleiffer, Plazewski, & Chapman, 1975), and cooperate less frequently than less powerful negotiators (Lindskold & Bennett, 1973). However, when the power discrepancy between negotiators was small the weaker parties made more threats and fewer agreements were reached (Hornstein, 1965). Thus, mild discrepancy in power may result in "power struggles" as weaker parties are unwilling to accept their lower status while the stronger parties expect to achieve more than their opponents (Pruitt & Carnevale, 1993). This relation between power imbalance and conflict behavior may help account for the finding that sibling conflicts occur far more often than parent–child conflicts.

Parent–Child Conflict

Parents' greater strength and control of the material resources in the family enable them to use coercive and reward power with their children. A flagrant exercise of such power occurs when parents punish or reward their children within one domain for transgressions that occurred within another domain (e.g., you can't go to your friend's house because you talked back to me). Although parents' power to control important resources is almost intrinsic, it is exercised in a variety of ways and to varying degrees in different families (e.g., Baumrind, 1971).

Vuchinich (1986, 1987, 1990) observed disputes between parents and children ranging in age from 3 to 22 years. He found that most disputes end in a standoff and that: "what is somewhat surprising is that parents did not choose to—or were not able to—use their power to win most conflicts with their children. Conflicts did not usually end with parents "putting their children in their place." This does not mean that parental power cannot be exercised in a standoff. Power can be maintained through other mechanisms . . . such as defining the terms and boundaries involved in conflict and controlling the flow of negative affect" (Vuchinich, 1990, p. 136). Power asymmetries may exist between parents and their children, but it seems clear that parents do not simply use coercive strategies to "win" conflicts with their children. Understanding how power imbalances influence parent–child conflict presents an intriguing challenge for researchers.

Children themselves use coercive power in parent–child relationships. Children's defiance of parental authority can set in motion coercive cycles in which parents' nattering and ineffective threats escalate children's aversive defiance, and result in parents' eventual capitulation. This, in turn, rewards children's continuing defiance. Children's coercive behavior has a substantial short-term pay-off in normally functioning families, as 35% of the time family members capitulate to children during conflict. The pay-off increases dramatically to 59% for problem boys from distressed families (Patterson, 1982; Patterson & Capaldi, 1991).

Sibling Conflict

For siblings, the power to coerce or reward one another likely comes from relative maturity. Not surprisingly, findings suggest that older children use higher rates of physical and verbal aggression than younger siblings (Corter, Pepler, & Abramovitch, 1982; Erel, Margolin, & John, 1998; Lamb, 1978; Martin & Ross, 1995). Older, dominant siblings also give more rewards but deprive their younger brothers and sisters of more privileges as well (Sutton-Smith & Rosenberg, 1970). These findings are consistent with findings from the Formal Relationships domain indicating that dominant parties are more likely to use contentious tactics in resolving conflicts (Pruitt & Carnevale, 1993).

Older children "win" more conflicts than their younger siblings. This is especially true when the sibling pairs are young (Felson & Russo, 1988; Ross, Filyer, Lollis, Perlman, & Martin, 1994) and differences in power are more significant. Siblings who are closer in age have smaller power differentials and are more likely to engage frequently in disputes (e.g., Furman & Buhrmester, 1985; Minnett, Vandell, & Santrock, 1983; Vandell & Bailey, 1992). This is consistent with findings from Formal Relationships research indicating that when power differentials are small parties engage in high rates of conflict (Pruitt & Carnevale, 1993).

Because of these power differences, Felson and Russo (1988) argue against parent intervention in the conflicts of their children. They assume that parents intervene in support of their younger (weaker) children, thereby disrupting the power balance that the children would achieve naturally. However, the findings from the Formal Relationships literature suggest that siblings, especially ones close in age (for which the power discrepancy is smaller), will escalate conflict rather than de-escalate it if left to resolve conflict on their own. Thus, parent intervention may be advantageous. In fact, there is evidence that parent intervention in sibling conflict is associated with children fighting in more constructive ways leading to more positive and continued interaction (Perlman & Ross, 1997a; Siddiqui & Ross, 1999).

Friend–Peer Conflict

Toddlers frequently use power tactics to take toys from their peers, while the use of personally aggressive tactics occurs less frequently at this age (Hay & Ross, 1982; Ross & Conant, 1992). None the less, both forms of aggression have implications for children's relationships with others. For example, children's social groups often contain dominance hierarchies, based on consistent patterns of submission to the aggression of peers (Strayer & Strayer, 1980). Dominance hierarchies have been shown to decrease the amount of aggression that occurs between children. Nevertheless, they are based on coercion (LaFreniere & Charlesworth, 1983).

The bully–victim relationship is a form of peer interaction that clearly involves hierarchies of unequal power (see Monks & Smith, in this volume). Bullying makes up a substantial portion of aggression between peers and is associated with delinquency, poor school performance, and peer rejection for both bullies and victims (Olweus, 1993). Bullies are generally stronger physically and have greater social support than their victims (Olweus, 1993). Victims tend to be weaker, less self-confident, and try to avoid conflict. These differences result in relationships that are highly asymmetrical. Aggressive children search for a peer who will not retaliate against them (Patterson, Littman, & Bricker, 1967). Having found such a peer, they continue to direct aggression towards that individual.

Traditionally, bullying research has focused on aggression (Olweus, 1993). Recently, researchers began examining relational aggression as a source of coercive power (Crick & Grotpeter, 1996; Galen & Underwood, 1997; Rys & Bear, 1997). Relational aggression involves social ways of harming others such as excluding victims or gossiping about them. This broader definition of bullying includes control over "social" resources such as access to companionship and public opinion. French and Raven's coercion and reward category accommodates both the original and expanded ways of thinking about bullying. However, little is known about the role of other sources of power in bully–victim relations.

Expert Power

Expert power is evoked when one party has superior knowledge or ability. The expert is able to determine the best outcome for the conflict, and therefore that person's position should be accepted. Mediation provides an interesting example of the impact of expertise in the resolution of conflict in Formal Relationships. Mediators are experts in the process of conflict resolution and have been found to facilitate constructive conflict resolution (Pruitt & Carnevale, 1993). Expertise likely provides mediators with the power to influence the conflict process.

Parent–Child Conflict

Compared to children, parents possess greater knowledge and derive power from their expertise. One characterization of parents is as "local guardians of the social order," or experts on the culture which children gradually acquire (Shweder & Much, 1987, p. 203). By successfully socializing their children, parents can exercise their expert power in the best interests of their children. For example, the earliest rules parents claim to have for their children involve matters of child safety and depend on parents' knowledge of what would endanger their young children (Gralinski & Kopp, 1993).

Parental authority may be limited to domains in which parents are experts. For example, both children and parents accept parents' expertise with respect to the moral (pertaining to the rights and welfare of others) and social conventional domains (pertaining to accepted social and familial practices), but not with respect to issues in the personal domain (pertaining to personal preferences in food, friends, and so on) (Killen & Nucci, 1995; Nucci & Weber, 1995; Smetana & Asquith, 1994). There is, however, overlap between the conventional and personal domains (e.g., conventions regarding appropriate attire), so that it is not always clear when social conventions should apply and when personal choice can be exercised. This ambiguity likely contributes to the finding that parent–adolescent conflict is often centered on issues that children regard as personal and parents regard as conventional (Smetana, 1988, 1996; Smetana & Asquith, 1994). Interestingly, children agree that parents have authority with respect to social conventions, but consider that authority limited to issues in the home, which is the parents' domain of expertise. Observations of mothers and preschoolers also indicated that there is both more negotiation and more compromise on issues that are considered to be both personal and conventional (Nucci & Weber, 1995). We suggest that a potential distinction between personal and conventional issues might lie in the relative degree of expertise all family members attribute to parents with respect to each domain. Conflict arises when parents and children disagree about parents' expertise in a specific domain.

Sibling Conflict

Like coercive power, expert power is advantageous to older brothers and sisters. In a review of the sibling conflict research, Bryant and Litman (1987) note that, overall, older siblings tend to dominate and overpower their younger siblings in dyadic interactions. They argue that this phenomenon should be expected, due to the older child's physical prowess and higher intellectual advancement and competence. Phinney (1986) found that older siblings use more elaborate arguments than their younger counterparts in sibling disputes. She concluded that accounting for this difference, at least partially, is the older sibling's greater cognitive capacity.

Friend–Peer Conflict

Since peer relationships are between children whose physical and intellectual development are fairly equivalent, expertise may play a relatively minor role in their conflicts. Age differences that influence power between peers might be attributed to the greater knowledge of older peers. Children are more likely to take charge of decision-making in a group of younger children than in a group of agemates (French, Waas, Stright, & Baker, 1986). In addition, older children accept younger children's suggestions less often than do younger children (Brody, Stoneman, & MacKinnon, 1982). Moreover, some same-age peers do have acknowledged expertise in some areas. For example, children are often used as tutors for their peers, through peer teaching as well as peer modeling (Hartup, 1996). Children can use this expertise as a source of power. For example, Krappmann and Oswald (1991) found that 41% of requests for help among classmates were disparaged.

   As in Formal Relationships, there is evidence that knowledge of the conflict process itself is a source of expert power. For example, Weingart, Hyder, and Prietula (1996) found that children who had been instructed on how to resolve their differences (i.e., given tactical knowledge) achieved higher joint outcomes. This effect was mediated by opponents' use of integrative behaviors (e.g., trading off across conflict issues). Thus, knowledge of such strategies empowered children in their conflict resolutions.

Referent Power

Referent power influences conflict outcomes when individuals identify with, or feel a sense of oneness with one another. In such circumstances antagonists maintain an interest in the welfare of the other, despite their opposition within a conflict. Concern for conflict opponents can include both a general interest in the other's well-being, and a specific interest in the other's ability to achieve his or her conflict goals. Individuals are more likely to achieve their goals when sympathetic opponents also want them to do so, and thus referent power derives from the concern of another. Negotiations within a social group are more likely to be influenced by referent power than negotiations between different groups. Generally, when people negotiate with members of their own group, they make more concessions and use more problem-solving strategies than those who negotiate with members of another group (Rothbart & Hallmark, 1988). Furthermore, participants in a prisoner's dilemma increase their cooperation when cooperation becomes more valuable to their opponents (Kelley & Grzelak, 1972).

In much of the Formal Relationships research, it is assumed that negotiators have an individualistic orientation and are driven to maximize their gains at the expense of their opponents. Yet, Pruitt and Carnevale (1993) point out that some concern for opponents is always present, though perhaps only as a strategy that serves to maximize personal gains. Thus, concern with the other may develop as a result of insight into a stalemate that is detrimental to all parties (Terhune, 1974). For example, Mnookin, Peppet, and Tulumello (1996) define empathy as "the process of demonstrating an accurate, nonjudgmental understanding of the other side's needs, interests, and positions . . . this enables good perspective-takers to gain strategic advantage" (p.219). The finding that more empathic negotiators achieved more mutually beneficial agreements supports this contention (Neale & Bazerman, 1983). Mnookin, Peppet, and Tulumello (1996) add that "the subtext to good empathy is concern and respect . . ." (p. 220). But this more humane approach to empathy seems secondary to its strategic aspect and differs from the view held by Personal Relationships researchers of empathy as an emotional component of sympathy.

Thinking in the Formal Relationships domain has also extended consideration to the balance of concern for self and other. The dual-concern model posits that individuals concerned only with the other may concede their own conflict goals, whereas those concerned with both self and other will devote greater efforts to finding the kinds of creative solutions that would enable both to achieve their objectives. The dual-concern model integrates the two orientations and predicts that high rates of negotiation will result from their co-occurrence (Pruitt & Carnevale, 1993).

Developmentalists have studied both self- and other-orientations (Eisenberg & Garvey, 1981; Perlman & Ross, 1997a) but have typically treated these as independent, with little acknowledgment of the possibility of co- or dual-existence of the two orientations. Although it seems likely that researchers who have studied other-concern are in effect studying situations of dual concern, this important distinction has not been made in the developmental literature.

Parent–Child Conflict

Positive emotional relationships between parents and children set the stage for responsive problem-solving and lead to more conciliatory resolutions. Hostile emotions appear to preclude productive negotiation. For example, hostile interactions during a general discussion between parents and their adolescent children predicted the use of destructive conflict tactics one year later, which in turn led to less effective resolutions of conflict issues (Rueter & Conger, 1995). Contemporaneous associations have also been found between the affective quality of the parent–child relationship and the processes of conflict resolution. Parental warmth is highly related to toddlers' use of negotiation (Kuczynski, Kochanska, Radke-Yarrow, & Girnius-Brown, 1987) and to preadolescents' use of constructive problem-solving processes with their parents (Vuchinich, Wood, & Vuchinich, 1994). Dunn and Brown (1994) found parallel effects with preschool-aged children, as children who were often negative used fewer other-oriented arguments in their negotiations and were more likely to not reason at all than were children who were less negative.

Compromises occur when antagonists achieve a resolution that is affected by their own goals along with consideration of the other's position. Given that parents are likely to be concerned about the welfare of their children, and given the reasonably high level of children's compliance to parents' requests, one might expect frequent compromises in parent–child conflict, but this is not the case (Kochanska, Kuczynski, Radke-Yarrow, & Welsh, 1987; Vuchinich, 1987). For example, Eisenberg (1992) studied a variety of disputes as mothers and preschoolers traveled by car or baked cookies. These dyads compromised in 3% of their conflicts; submission by one member of the dyad was ten times as frequent.

Why so little compromise, even when caring adults are involved in disputes? Perhaps the parties lack concern with the goals that arise in the context of everyday disputes, despite their more general concern for one another's well-being. There is evidence that mothers lack concern for the property rights of their children (Ross, Tesla, Kenyon, & Lollis, 1990). In this research, mothers were present while toddler dyads played together in one family's home. When conflicts occurred in which the peers' toys were contended, mothers told their own child to yield the toy to the owner. When the peer had taken toys that belonged to their own children, mothers once again addressed their own children, suggested that they once again let the peer have the toy, despite their ownership of it. Ross et al. (1990) argued that these mothers underestimated the importance of their children's goals in property conflicts with their peers.

Sibling Conflict

Affect and emotion influence the types of interactions that siblings exhibit. For example, Minnett, Vandell, & Santrock (1983) reported that affection is less common in more aggressive sibling dyads. Raffaelli (1992) compared the conflict resolution of more vs. less close siblings. He found that children who report high emotional closeness with their siblings also report less sibling-directed violence, spend more time on the process of conflict resolution, and fight about different issues. Close siblings fight about property and power issues more often and non-close siblings tend to fight about betrayal more frequently.

Promoting self-centered conflict outcomes indicates concern with the self rather than with the opponent or with joint benefits. In fact, when young siblings initiate disputes they are less likely to compromise than when someone else initiates the disagreement (Tesla & Dunn, 1992). Therefore, when the children are especially concerned with the outcomes of the conflict (as they likely are when they initiated the issue) they are less likely to yield to

their opponents. At the same time, children do show concern for their siblings. Older siblings are more likely than younger siblings to use conciliatory
arguments in their disputes (Perlman & Ross, 1997a; Tesla & Dunn, 1992) and
make more frequent references to their siblings than to themselves (Howe,
1991). During high conflict periods, older siblings' awareness of their younger
partners' internal states may be the first step in establishing a shared view of
the world, or a position of dual concern (Howe, 1991). Children's use of other-
oriented types of reasoning and explicit verbal consideration of feelings is
associated with less negative feelings and decreased levels of conflict (Dunn &
Brown, 1994; Howe, Petrakos, & Rinaldi, 1998). Thus, expressing concern for
one's opponent during conflict produces positive, constructive outcomes.

Findings from our own investigations (e.g., Ram & Ross, 1998) touch on the
effects of combined self- and other-concern on the management of conflict
between siblings. We asked siblings to divide a set of six toys between them.
Most dyads selected three toys each; however, a substantial minority of the
children reached more creative solutions in which single toys were divided or
shared between the two. Sharing or dividing toys gives both children the
benefit of access to the most desirable resources. Negotiation in pairs that
reached these more integrative solutions took longer and involved more
problem-solving strategies of negotiation. and more speech turns (including
both problem-solving and contentious turns), especially on the part of older
siblings. It was the dual consideration of both the self and other that brought
on the most creative and beneficial outcomes of all.

Friend–Peer Conflict

Conflicts between friends differ in many ways from conflicts with peers, because friends like one another and share a more intimate relationship than do
peers. Because of their shared goals and the greater amount of time they
spend with one another, friends engage in more conflict than peers (Berndt &
Perry, 1986; Hartup, French, Laursen, Johnston, & Ogawa, 1993). At the
same time, they deal with conflict more constructively than do peers. Compared to non-friends, friends show more extended negotiation, compromise,
conciliation, constructive communication, and explanation (Fonzi, Schneider,
Tani, & Tomada, 1997; Krappmann, 1993; Vespo & Caplan, 1993). On the
other hand, non-friends show higher rates of submission, disengagement, and
third-party intervention (Katz, Kramer, & Gottman, 1992). Thus, the strategies that children use to resolve their differences vary depending on the
extent to which they like their opponent.

The outcomes of friend and peer conflicts also differ. Conflicts between
friends are more likely to be resolved in an egalitarian way than those between peers (Newcomb & Bagwell, 1995; Hartup & Laursen, 1991). Finally,
friends are more likely to continue to interact after conflict than non-friends
(Hartup & Laursen, 1991; Hartup, Laursen, Stewart, & Eastonson, 1988).
These differences have important implications for continuing relationships.
Generally, closeness and interdependence are seen as limiting anger and

coercion between opponents and minimizing relationship disruption (Laursen & Koplas, 1995). Therefore, liking among age-mates seems to have a positive effect on conflict management.

The majority of children's conflicts with peers are driven by self-interest. For example, during conflict 90% of students chose to negotiate in a distributive way by maximizing their own outcome at the expense of the other (Johnson & Johnson, 1996). In conflicts with friends, however, a balance between individual and communal goals is usually achieved (Hartup, 1996; Laursen, 1996). Children's goals have an impact on the strategies that are used. For example, children with primarily self-goals (e.g., control goals) strongly preferred hostile/coercive strategies in response to hypothetical vignettes, whereas children whose primary goals were to have good peer relationships, gave in or chose strategies that accommodated the needs of both parties (Chung & Asher, 1996). In addition, friends preserve relationships by avoiding coercive resolutions and anger during some conflicts, averting inequitable outcomes and maintaining social interaction (Hartup, 1992; Laursen & Collins, 1994).

Social status may also affect children's goals and strategies. For example, Black (1992) found that liked children extended the ideas of others and explained play to others when negotiating play. Thus, "they maximized the possibility that their own ideas, dovetailed with those of their peers, would be accepted." There is some evidence that disliked children, on the other hand, rely on self-referent behaviors during social interactions (Black, 1992; Dodge, Schlundt, Schocken, & Delugach, 1983).

Distinguishing between self-, other-, and dual-concern has important implications for our understanding of children's negotiations. Based on findings from Formal Relationships research, each predicts a different pattern of behaviors in conflict. We have found support for this in the Personal Relationships research as well. Personal Relationships researchers should pay special attention to the differences between other- and dual-concern, differences that have been blurred in past research.

Comparing Families and Friends

Families and friendships are reference groups, in that individuals belong to both. Extrapolation from the Formal Relationships research suggests that negotiations should be less contentious within the family or between friends than in other contexts. However, this does not appear to be the case for families. For example, children use more elaborated reasoning with peers than they do with family members (Dunn, Slomkowski, Donelan, & Herrera, 1995; Phinney, 1986) and are more likely to continue to interact after peer than after sibling conflict (Laursen, 1993).

Why is affiliation within the family associated with a different pattern of conflict resolution than affiliation with friends? One explanation stems from the different levels of constraint within these relationships. Family relationships generally have a low risk of dissolution and family members can express greater hostility or walk away at the end of a conflict, without fear of dissolving their relationships (Vandell & Bailey, 1992). In contrast, when interacting with peers, or in Formal Relationships, individuals have a greater need to ensure that differences are resolved positively (Phinney, 1986). The interaction of referent power and constraint imposed on the relationship may explain the different patterns of results observed in studies of conflict resolution between friends, peers, and family members and the differences found in the resolution of conflict in Formal vs. Personal Relationships.

Information Power

According to French and Raven (1959), information is another basis for power that results from the exchange of information or logical argument. Thus, it refers to the use of a broad category of persuasive arguments and reasoning. Raven (1992) suggests that information may be more effective if it is presented indirectly. Indirect persuasion is presumed to be especially useful for lower status individuals trying to influence higher status individuals. Use of persuasive, logical argument during negotiations that take place within Formal Relationships has received substantial attention from researchers. For example, Pruitt and Carnevale (1993) discuss problem-solving, exchange of concessions across different issues, and solving underlying concerns as methods for achieving mutually beneficial conflict outcomes.

Parent–Child Conflict

Information as a source of power is exercised when parents and children reason with one another. Parents' use of reasoning as a discipline technique has long stood in contrast to coercive tactics (Baumrind, 1971; Grusec & Goodnow, 1994; Hoffman, 1975). Reasoning is deemed to be the most effective long-term parenting strategy, leading to greater internalization of moral rules. Clear, redundant, consistent messages that are based on the exchange of information are likely to be the parents' most effective means of socializing their children (Grusec & Goodnow, 1994).

More recently, the value of children's informed arguments has been recognized. Kuczynski and his colleagues (Kuczynski & Kochanska, 1990; Kuczynski et al., 1987; Kuczynski & Hildebrand, 1998) have drawn our attention to the fact that children resist their parents' demands in a variety of ways, including by negotiation. Even young children bargain, propose alternatives to parents' requests, offer and seek explanations for their own or their parents' positions, and successfully resist their parents' wishes (Dunn & Munn, 1987; Eisenberg, 1992; Kuczynski et al., 1987; Perlman & Ross, 1997a). Children's negotiation increases with age and is associated with parents' explanations, bargaining, and affection. When young siblings resolve conflicts in ways that are antithetical to their parents' positions, and especially when parents explicitly change their views, both parents and children are more inclined to reason with one another (Perlman & Ross, 1997b). Thus, children appear to derive power when information exchange is part of their disputes.

Sibling Conflict

Young children learn rapidly about conflict, and use this knowledge in a variety of ways in sibling disputes. Dunn and Munn (1985) note that younger siblings' teasing increases over the second year of life, showing improvements in pragmatic understanding of how to annoy the older sibling. Children also understand how and when to recruit their parents' involvement in their conflicts (Ross & den Bak-Lammers, in press). Children are more likely to appeal to their mothers when they are the victims of their siblings' hostile acts than when they themselves are the instigators of hostility. When tattling, they convey the essence of the siblings' wrongdoing succinctly and focus their reports on issues that parents regard as more serious (e.g., physical aggression, property damage). Thus, siblings use their conflict understanding to increase their effectiveness as opponents.

Knowledge related to particular issues of contention is also used in conflict to persuade the sibling of the merits of a position. Very young children justify their positions during sibling conflict (Dunn & Munn, 1987; Perlman & Ross, 1997a). For example, Perlman and Ross (1997a) found that two-year-old children used both self-oriented (e.g., "Give it to me because it's mine") and other-oriented (e.g., "We should share the paint brushes") justifications during sibling conflict.

Children's justifications become more frequent with age; however, it is the use of self- rather than other-oriented arguments that increases over time (Tesla & Dunn, 1992). Three important developmental changes occur in young children's use of information to persuade their siblings. It becomes more varied (Ross, 1996), more elaborated, and more fact-based (Phinney, 1986). In addition, children are more likely to ignore the simple arguments of younger siblings than the simple arguments of older brothers or sisters. In contrast, they are more likely to ignore elaborate arguments of older siblings than the similar arguments made by younger brothers and sisters (Phinney, 1986). Phinney argues that older, higher-status siblings may not feel obliged to respond to simple, unjustified arguments presented by their younger sibling. Older siblings may feel sufficiently mature to respond to their younger siblings' justifications. In contrast, younger children may feel powerless in attempting to counter the elaborated arguments of their older siblings, while feeling sufficiently competent to counter their older siblings' unjustified arguments.

Friend–Peer Conflict

As children mature cognitively, their use of justification and reasoning develops. Toddlers have been found to vary their communication in simple ways according to their goals (Hay & Ross, 1982), while preschoolers use more elaborate types of communication sequences in their interactions (Phinney, 1986). More elaborate interactions include reasoning, which provides more information about the other's perspective and possible resolutions and is more likely to resolve conflicts (Eisenberg & Garvey, 1981; Ross & Conant, 1992). Also, friends make more use of negotiation and disengagement in their conflict resolutions than peers do (Hartup & Laursen, 1991; Hartup et al., 1988). Greater use of reasoning with friends rather than with peers is thought to occur because of the greater levels of interdependence and liking that friends experience.

Children's ability to argue their positions effectively is also associated with higher social status. Popular children are perceived to be more skilled negotiators who remain calm during conflict and continue interacting until conflicts are resolved positively (Bryant, 1992; Chung & Asher, 1996; Yeates, Schultz, & Selman, 1991). Rejected children are described as frequently using aggression and social withdrawal strategies while rarely using prosocial or calm approaches to resolve differences with peers. Information seems to be an especially important form of power in Personal Relationships because it is one that allows individuals to deal with differences while maintaining a positive relationship.

Legitimate Power

Legitimate power is based on the idea that opposing parties have rights and obligations. Thus, it is closely linked to social norms and moral rules. Formal Relationships researchers have studied the role of social norms in the resolution of conflict. One area that has received particular attention is that of fairness. For example, three broad classes of the fairness principle have been defined (Deutsch, 1973; Lerner, Miller, & Holmes, 1976; Leventhal, 1976). These norms are (1) that all participants should contribute and benefit equally; (2) that benefits should be proportional to contribution; and (3) that benefit should be proportional to need. As Pruitt and Carnevale (1993) state, norms are almost always important in negotiation as "they affect the positions taken, the arguments and concessions made, and the agreements reached" (p. 122). Social norms become relevant only if they can be applied. For example, to apply the norm that benefits should be proportional to need, it must be possible to evaluate the opponents' relative needs (Walster, Walster, & Berscheid, 1978). Adherence to norms is largely voluntary. However, studies using the prisoner's dilemma suggest that increased solidarity, social pressure, and sanctions all enhance compliance with norms (Bonacich, 1972; Yamagishi, 1986)

French and Raven list four types of legitimate power: *position*, *responsibility/dependence*, *reciprocity*, and *equity*. We will discuss these jointly. *Position* refers to the structural relationship between individuals in which mere position empowers one individual (e.g., employer–employee or parent–child). *Responsibility/dependence* stems from a sense of obligation to help the helpless. In extending this basic position to family and peer relationships, we broaden the concept, asking the question: what are the rights and obligations that parents and their offspring, siblings, and friends have with respect to one another simply by virtue of the nature of their specific relationship?

Reciprocity and *equity* are both based on social norms that hold regardless of individual relationships. *Reciprocity* is based on people's understanding of give-and-take (i.e., if you did X to me then I should or can respond with X). *Equity* is based on the idea that individuals should provide reparations for damage they have caused. French and Raven regard these two as independent and particular sources of legitimate power. We regard them as two instances of a more general class of entitlements that depend on moral or social rules. The violation of a rule by one individual empowers the victim to seek and obliges the perpetrator to supply redress for the harm done. Likewise, social norms require the return of a favor.

Reciprocity is found across ages and contexts, both in Formal and Personal Relationships. It interacts with power so that weaker parties are more likely to reciprocate cooperative behaviors (Pruitt & Carnevale, 1993). Reciprocation of negative behaviors such as threats has been found to have negative consequences such as failure to reach agreement and poor relations between parties (Putnam & Jones, 1982; Sillars, 1981). People reliably match their opponent's non-cooperation unless there is some explanation for it (Kerr, 1983). However, there is some evidence that use of a tit-for-tat strategy is perceived negatively in Personal Relationships, as people feel that in that context generosity rather than equity should be the guiding principle (Gottman, 1979).

Parent–Child Conflict

A parent's position is an acknowledged source of power in relation to his or her children. Historically, mere position conferred unquestioned authority to parents (Holden, 1997). These absolute views persist in some fundamental traditions even today (Kuczynski & Hildebrand, 1998). For the most part, however, mere position is no longer thought to be a sufficient basis of parental power, but its influence remains to varying degrees within different families. For example, while children accept the authority of their parents well into adolescence (Smetana, 1996), they tend to limit it to certain domains of influence. Furthermore, children see their parents as exercising legitimate authority with respect to their disputes with siblings, and utilize that authority to their own advantage by tattling on siblings who have transgressed (den Bak & Ross, 1996; Ross & den Bak-Lammers, 1998). Complementary to the parent's positional authority is the child's greater dependency. Parents must serve the needs of developing children, and this responsibility empowers children. This source would empower the newborn most of all. Such utterly dependent individuals have a strong influence, totally changing their parents' lives (Rheingold, 1969).

More general moral principles also play a role in parent–child conflict. Parents' discipline often involves instructing their children in morally and socially acceptable behavior. Thus, the legitimacy of moral rules enhances the power of the parents' positions. When parents intervene in disputes between their children, they tend to address the child who has violated the siblings' rights, they support moral principles, and children tend to resolve conflicts in a way that adheres to the moral principles involved (Ross et al., 1994). A more telling test of the role of equity in conferring power, of course, is when such legitimacy conflicts with other sources of power, such as those conferred by position, coercion, or expertise. Whereas adolescents believe that their parents do have authority in the moral domain, such authority does not extend to prescribing actions that violate moral principles (Smetana, 1996). Moreover, the resolution of young children's property disputes reflects the priority of owners to control their belongings (Ross, 1996). Children endorse this principle in their justifications and in the disputes that they settle without parent involvement. When they intervene, however, parents are more ambiguous, endorsing the rights of possessors equally with those of owners, and urging their children to share. None the less, disputes are resolved in favor of owners when parents intervene.

Sibling Conflict

Schvaneveldt and Ihinger (1979) argue that legitimate power is the type of power most likely to prevail in sibling relationships due to the hierarchical nature of the family system, as well as cultural prescriptions that allot more power based on age and other factors such as wealth and beauty. Frequently, power within sibling relationships is allotted to the older member of the dyad (or group), whether explicitly (through a parent's direction) or implicitly (due to social norms which require younger individuals to obey the directions of older individuals). However, when a parent confers authority on a particular child, sibling compliance increases regardless of the age of the child who is "left in charge" (Laupa, 1995). Generally, however, legitimacy, as well as coercion and expertise, creates power advantages for older siblings. That makes it all the more significant when principles of entitlement redress this balance of power. Property rights may be the earliest legitimacy concerns that mitigate the dominance of older siblings. Disputes over such issues as insults, threats, commands, and physical aggression are most often initiated by older siblings. However, disputes over object ownership are initiated by both older and younger siblings (Corter, Pepler, & Abramoritch, 1982; Ross et al., 1994). Furthermore, owners of an object are more likely to win property disputes, regardless of birth order (Ross, 1996).

Friend–Peer Conflict

Reciprocity in conflict is an important characteristic of children's peer interactions (Garvey & Ben Debba, 1974; Peterson, Hartmann, & Gelfand, 1977; Phinney, 1986; Ross, Cheyne, & Lollis, 1988; Ross, Lollis, & Elliot, 1982). Children reciprocate both positive and negative behaviors during peer–friend conflict (Eisenberg & Garvey, 1981; Phinney, 1986). For example, Phinney writes: "Each move in a dispute strongly influences the following moves. Most simple moves are followed by simple responses and most elaborate moves by elaborate responses" (p. 58). Findings from experimental studies indicate that the rates of positive behaviors such as sharing change depending on the perceived actions of interaction partners (Levitt, Weber, Clark, & McDonnell, 1985; Peterson, Hartmann, & Gelfand, 1977). Reciprocity may be an adaptive, sophisticated pattern of behavior. For example, children with an internal locus of control are thought to show greater reciprocity when solving hypothetical conflicts than children with an external locus of control (Adalbjarnardottir, 1995).

Equality is fundamental to peer and friend relationships, both as a feature of interaction and as the foundation upon which the moral code rests. Most developmental theorists believe that children learn a great deal from their peers because of their egalitarian relationships. Moral development is also strongly influenced by the equality of peers and expectations of reciprocity that follow from that equity (Piaget, 1932). It is within egalitarian relationships that children must learn how to deal with differences of opinion through discussion, debate, argument, negotiation, and compromise (Piaget, 1932; Shantz & Hobart, 1989).

Children respect the rights of their peers because they expect reciprocal respect for their own rights from their peers. As children mature and begin to recognize that they have shared goals, their negotiation strategies become more reciprocal and collaborative (Selman, Beardslee, Schultz, Krupa, & Poderefsky, 1986). When interacting with adults, children attribute moral rules to the authority of the adults and fail to explore the moral basis of obligations not to harm others. Children use more reciprocity in discussing peer-oriented dilemmas than adult-oriented ones and with hypothetical situations that involve personal rather than work-related problems (Selman et al., 1986). Children challenge their partners and request feedback when interacting with peers. Their discussions with adults are more one-sided as adults dominate the interactions and the children are forced into a less reciprocal role (Kruger & Tomasello, 1986). Finally, children also use reciprocity as an excuse, mitigating the responsibility and punishment assigned to a child who violates the rights or welfare of another (Martin & Ross, 1995).

In egalitarian relationships, rules can add legitimacy to different positions during conflict. Bakeman and Brownlee (1982) observed that both toddlers and preschoolers were more successful in taking away an object from another child when they had had possession of it previously. Preschoolers also faced less resistance from their opponent when they had formerly possessed the object. This suggests that even children who are disadvantaged by the possession rule accept it. Ownership also is a right respected in children's peer groups. An object that is "communal," for example, elicits more conflict over refusals to share than one that belongs to a specific child (Eisenberg, Haake, & Bartlett, 1981). Therefore, children appear to have a "systematic set of beliefs about conflict with their peers," often condoning aggression in defense of possessions and preferring the protester to the initiator of such conflicts (Hay, Zahn-Waxler, Cummings, & Iannotti, 1992). Clearly, when opponents present positions that are based on social norms their position can be legitimized. In this way, social norms can act as a source of power.

DISCUSSION

The utility of French and Raven's typology of power to the study of children's Personal Relationships is apparent. It broadens our thinking about the concept of power and its impact on negotiations. The typology provides an interesting structure for organizing findings about children's negotiations. Adopting this more complex perspective on power allows us to evaluate how power interacts with the nature of the opponents' relationships. The analysis above reveals that relationship variables such as the level of constraint placed on a relationship, equality among opponents and so on, influence the way these sources of power are manifested.

When the idea of power is expanded, as it is within the current analysis, it becomes clear that both children and parents derive power from varied sources and a unidirectional perspective begins to seem simplistic. This is illustrated by the assumption that children acquire greater power as they get older. Even as Kuczynski and his colleagues (Kuczynski, Marshall, & Schell, 1997) proposed a bidirectional model of socialization, arguing that power has been a major stumbling block in the acceptance of such models, they stated: "The 7-year-old has much more power than the infant and the adolescent has more power than the 7-year-old. However, even the infant has considerable capacities both to influence the parent and to blunt the parent's impact" (pp. 26–27). If one considers the utter dependency of the infant, the responsibility of the parent for the infant's care, the legitimacy of the infant's needs, and the coercive power of an infant's cry, this statement becomes anything but self-evident. Although very young infants may not be attempting to influence their parents intentionally, in most normal circumstances, infants leave their parents little choice but to provide care, with only limited discretion as to its precise nature. The expanded analysis of power calls for a critical examination of the assumption that parents have greater power in the context of conflict.

One of the advantages of the Formal Relationships approach (e.g., the prisoner's dilemma) is that it enables researchers to control a variety of variables such as conflict outcome (e.g., it is possible to quantify who wins and the extent to which one person wins), the relative power available to subjects, and so on. The greater methodological control afforded by use of more constrained laboratory procedures has allowed Formal Relationships researchers to test important assumptions underlying theories of negotiation. For example, subjects' interdependence can be manipulated using the prisoner's dilemma and its effect on negotiation can be studied (Pruitt, 1967, 1970). In contrast, Personal Relationships research incorporates more diverse methods. Children are often observed in labs, in their homes, and at school. Questionnaires and intensive interviews are also frequently used. The use of vignettes (scenarios that children are told, followed by a set of questions) most closely approximates the use of the prisoner's dilemma in the Formal Relationships research because hypothetical situations are used and subjects' stated responses to these hypothetical situations are thought to represent their behaviors.

A study using a prisoner's dilemma game with preschool-aged children illustrates the potential of combining methodological approaches (Matsumoto, Haan, Yaborve, Theodorou, & Carney, 1986). Preschool-aged children played a simplified version of the game, but were allowed to negotiate future moves with one another. Teachers rated the friendship status of the participants. Researchers observed the quality of the children's negotiations and their emotional reactions and related these to the nature of the children's relationship. This procedure allowed researchers to include interesting new categories, such as betrayal, which occurred when a child promised to cooperate but then made a competitive move. The relationship between children's emotional reactions and their subsequent moves could also be examined. At the same time, the prisoner's dilemma provided a consistent, tangible measure of the quality of conflict outcomes achieved through negotiation.

In conclusion, we set out to bridge what is known about negotiations in Formal and in Personal Relationships. We believe that this goal was useful in several respects. The resulting analysis of power goes beyond the traditional, unitary, thinking about the construct in studies of children's conflict. It reveals important sources of power that have been neglected by researchers of Personal Relationships in children (e.g., the power of the powerless). Furthermore, this framework provides a useful context for understanding findings from research on children's disputes. For example, patterns of parent–adolescent conflict can be explained when we take into account their different definitions of parents' expertise (i.e., they fight about topics where they disagree about the extent of parents' expertise). Findings from Personal Relationships research fit well into French and Raven's typology, highlighting the utility of that typology in understanding children's resolution of conflict. In addition, this exercise revealed relationship variables that are important to our understanding of interpersonal negotiation. For example, the role of self, other, and dual concern during conflict resolution was highlighted. Each of these has important implications for the way individuals resolve their differences. Through this comparative process we were able to highlight areas in our field that need to be clarified and developed. Now we face the exciting and challenging task of addressing these issues empirically.

ACKNOWLEDGMENT

This chapter was prepared with the assistance of a postdoctoral fellowship to the first author and a research grant to the last author from the Social Sciences and Humanities Research Council of Canada. Special thanks to Dean Pruitt for guiding us in our review of the adult conflict resolution literature.

Chapter 9

Connecting Children's Peer Relations with the Surrounding Cultural Context

Barry H. Schneider

University of Ottawa, Canada

and

Andrea Smith, Samantha E. Poisson, & Archie B. Kwan

University of Toronto, Canada

Sweeping political changes in most parts of the world have led to an increase in contacts among people of different cultural backgrounds. Because of emigration, immigration, and urbanization, large subcultures of different ethnocultural origin coexist more than ever before within many major Western societies. As members of these subcultures negotiate their relations with the "host" culture, they are compelled to reexamine the basic features of interpersonal relationships in their culture of origin. Ironically, their cousins who remained at "home" may well be confronting many of the same comparisons and choices. It is impossible to establish at this point how quickly or how completely changes in economic and political reality are translated into

The Developmental Psychology of Personal Relationships.
Edited by Rosemary S. L. Mills and Steve Duck. © 2000 John Wiley & Sons Ltd.

changes in the ways people relate to each other. Many formerly closed societies, once dominated by a single ideology, are becoming more open and complex.

No known lexicon for describing cultural variation is adequate to conceptualize these more complex cultures in any systematic way. The dichotomy between collectivism/individualism has long been seen as the most fundamental dimension of variation among cultures (Kim, 1994; Triandis, 1986), although it is but one of many useful classification systems (see review by Cooper & Denner, 1998). In a collectivistic society, a greater portion of a person's identity is related to his or her membership in the larger group. Many theorists believe that the interpersonal relationships of individuals within a society relate to the degree of individualism or collectivism that characterizes the culture (e.g., Gudykunst & Ting-Toomey, 1988). The collectivism or individualism of a society as a whole is thought to have a profound influence on interpersonal relationships at a small-group or dyadic level. For example, the continuation of a long-term friendship or romantic relationship is typically seen in the literature on adult relationships as depending on individual satisfaction and commitment (see Rusbult & Buunk, 1993). Some theorists have observed that individuals in collectivistic societies do not feel totally free to initiate and terminate relationships according to their individual "calculations" (Lin & Rusbult, 1995), but must take into account the expectations of third parties (Dion & Dion, 1996; Hsu, 1981). This might conceivably contribute to the longevity of relationships in collectivistic societies. Furthermore, Dion and Dion (1996) suggest that in individualistic societies, there may be a certain ambivalence toward interpersonal relationships because commitment to them may be seen as compromising one's own autonomy. Some examples of the implications of individualism/collectivism for children's relationships appear later in this chapter.

Most immigrants move from a collectivistic society to a more individualistic one (Triandis, Bontempo, Villareal, Asai, & Lucca, 1988). With the decline of communism, moreover, most of the sweeping sociopolitical changes of our decade also appear to involve a transition from collectivism to individualism at a broad cultural level. This distinction between collectivism and individualism, however, tends to oversimplify matters. Within one society, subgroups may vary enormously in terms of collectivism/individualism. For example, those urban Koreans most involved in their nation's trend toward industrialization are known to be highly individualistic, in contrast with the collectivistic national norm (Cha, 1994). Societies may be collectivistic in some respects and individualistic in others. Indians, whether living in India or abroad, have been found to combine a collectivistic orientation to family contexts with an individualistic orientation toward interpersonal relationships and economic activity (Sinha & Tripathi, 1994). Philipsen (1987) very aptly described the dynamic interplay of individualism and collectivism within cultures, without denying the utility of this fundamental dichotomy:

> The reality of a culture as experienced by those who live it moves along an axis with two poles at the opposite extremes, one exerting a pull toward the commu-

nal, the other toward the individual, as the dominant themes and warrants of human thought, speech, and action. Locating a culture on this axis reveals a partial truth about it, a kind of cultural snapshot, but in order to perceive a culture fully, one must also know the culture's direction of movement along the axis and the relative strength of the competing forces pushing it one way or another. (p. 245)

Philipsen asserts that the interplay of these forces at the community level in Western societies over the past four centuries has had a profound influence on the beliefs, values, and ideals of members of Western civilizations and on their communicative conduct. Based on literary sources, he documents a progressive shift in the center of moral gravity from the public to the intimate as the standard and the setting for interpersonal interchange. Since individuals in contemporary Western society have relatively little need to be concerned about the evaluation of their speech by peer groups, there is less time spent on forethought and editing and, concomitantly, more time spent talking. The empirical basis for these interesting contentions is not clearly established. Furthermore, they may not fully reflect the cultural heterogeneity of contemporary Western societies.

The collectivism or individualism of a society is known to affect both adult and child cultures within it. Perhaps the best-known documentation of this is Bronfenbrenner's (1970) striking comparison of children's lives in the USA and the Soviet Union during the 1960s. His account depicted a marked collectivism in the USSR, which was propagated as if it were a religion. Collective ideology dictated the rituals of children's groups and permeated the lives of almost all the adults. Within the same culture, however, it is entirely possible that the differences in socialization and acculturation experienced from one generation to the next may be reflected in variations in the degree of their individualism or collectivism. Nevertheless, despite the enormous scope of recent sociopolitical changes, it would be naive to expect any immediate or radical transformations in culturally-ingrained styles of relating. Recent research on relationships in Russia suggests that many of the parents and grandparents observed by Bronfenbrenner may not have subscribed fully to the collectivism that pervaded the era (Goodwin & Emelyanova, 1995). In most modern societies, children attend schools and other institutions which have as one of their goals the instilling of the collectivistic or individualistic values. These values may be mixed; they may also differ from those to which adults are expected to adhere. In individualistic North America, for instance, children are expected to identify at least to some degree with their schools, sports teams, and scout troops. There may, thus, be less latitude for true individualism for American schoolchildren than for their parents.

There are important cross-cultural differences in relationship styles, some of which will be detailed below. These differences must be understood within the context of the many features of social relations that are universal. Several theorists have emphasized that the value of cross-cultural research is not only in discovering differences among cultures, but also in learning about commonalities that are possibly inherent to our species (Segall, 1979).

This chapter is a selective review of theory and research pertaining to cultural influences on children's peer relations. It draws primarily from two bodies of literature. In the first, cultures are regarded as more or less distinct entities. Features of one culture, such as economic activity, religious belief, or ideology, are compared with parallel features of other cultures and these cross-cultural differences are considered as potential sources of differences in interpersonal relations. This deductive style of inquiry may be seen as a far superior basis for the development of a theory of cultural variation in social relations than the hitherto casual comparison of cultures that has often been carried out. In order to use this method optimally, a broad sampling of cultures should be selected for comparison, all of which vary along a particular dimension of interest. For example, one might compare a selection of cultures ranging from very low to very high in deference toward authority figures. This method, which represents only a minuscule fraction of the research, is far more advanced in its application to the social relations of adults, but it has been used in some studies conducted with children. Two countries—China and Italy—in which there have been several studies conducted with children, are considered below as examples of this approach. As is the case in much cross-cultural research, the choice of these two societies is somewhat fortuitous, in that they are the cultures with which the authors are most familiar. Nevertheless, comparison of the marked differences between these two cultures in terms of degree of overall collectivism/ individualism, the priorities established for peer relations in each, and the demands for deference to authority may contribute substantially to the development of theories of cultural difference in peer relations. Despite the pronounced differences between Italy and China, however, the consequences of nonconformity in both cultures take the form of some degree of rejection. Similarities such as these, found within very disparate cultures, demonstrate the importance of theories that can account simultaneously for similarities as well as differences among cultures.

The second body of literature reviewed in this chapter is concerned with relations between members of different subcultures within the same larger culture. Two sets of studies will be reviewed: those that have investigated the sociopolitical context of peer relations among aboriginal children in North America, and those that constitute the substantial literature on inter-ethnic and inter-racial friendship in North America and the UK. The studies conducted with indigenous peoples provide valuable descriptions of the changes in interpersonal relationships that may occur when the values of minority cultures, which are often collectivistic, interact with the individualism of the majority culture. The studies on inter-racial and inter-ethnic friendship illuminate the saliency of culture in determining children's preference for relationship partners. This phenomenon has been widely studied, perhaps because of the world-wide media coverage of the events leading to the racial desegregation of American schools.

The Peer Relations of Chinese Children

The peer relations of Chinese children are influenced by a complex network of age-old traditions and philosophies that assign meaning to social behavior.

There are many sound reasons for the focus on China, in the recent empirical literature, aside from the fact that it is home to such a large proportion of the planet's population. As we shall see, the core values in Chinese society are articulated very clearly. Furthermore, the Chinese population is relatively homogenous culturally, and there is very little mobility (Chen, Rubin, Li, & Li, in press).

Most sources suggest that the social behavior of the Chinese differs from those of individuals living in the West. According to Triandis (1986), China and most Western countries such as the USA occupy opposite ends of the collectivism–individualism dimension, with Chinese society ranking high in collectivism. This polarity has been used frequently to explain the differences in social behavior between these societies. In China, the individual is seen as existing within and being defined by an interactive social context (Bond & Hwang, 1986). The collectivist nature of Chinese culture is seen as providing a structure for social behavior, in which interactions between individuals reflect the needs and expectations of the group. Yang (1981) suggests that the Chinese govern their social behavior according to the anticipated reactions of others. The Chinese concept of "face" is inconsistent with direct confrontations between individuals (Chiu, Tsang, & Yang, 1988). The importance of conflict resolution through mediation and bargaining is reflected in China's non-adversarial or inquisitorial procedural model of community justice (Leung, 1987). The avoidance of conflict, and the rapid resolution of conflict should it occur, serve to preserve the interpersonal relationships that are assigned high priority in the Confucian value system. This value system also emphasizes cooperativeness and altruism.

At the core, Buddhism, Taoism, and Confucianism are seen as dominating and guiding social relationships among the Chinese (Chao, 1983; Ryan, 1985). Buddhist, Taoist and Confucian principles combine to elevate the importance of harmony, social obligations and interrelationships in Chinese culture (Shenkar & Ronen, 1987). In particular, Buddhism represents the "self" or ego as composed of many social components that pertain to family, extended family, community, and country (Ryan, 1985). Taoism promotes the rejection of self-assertiveness and competitiveness (Ryan, 1985). This rejection may influence children's moral and ethical conduct by discouraging behaviors that further their own interests at the expense of others'. Confucian beliefs are guided by four fundamental principles: self-cultivation, maintaining a harmonious relationship with the family, taking responsibility in community affairs, and serving the country (Kong, 1985).

In Confucian precepts, the process of self-cultivation involves the perfection of interpersonal skills and the acceptance of a role in, and moral obligations to, the community (Kong, 1985; Shenkar & Ronen, 1987). Self-cultivation governs relationships and defines the responsibilities of each family member. Through self-cultivation, harmonious relationships within the family can be achieved and role conflicts within the family are avoided. Accordingly, the Chinese extended family has clear role differentiation and structure (Tsui & Schultz, 1988). The Chinese people believe that their family

structure provides for continuity in society because it links successive generations with their ancestors, and thereby assigns a role in history to every
individual (Kong, 1985).

Child-rearing Practices

Traditional child-rearing values and practices in China strongly reflect Confucian principles. Chinese parents are expected to emphasize proper conduct in
the socialization of their children. The Chinese parenting style is largely authoritarian. Lin and Fu (1990) compared child-rearing practices among Chinese (Taiwanese), immigrant Chinese (American) and Caucasian-American
parents. The Chinese parents were found to be more controlling, but, at the
same time, they emphasized independence and achievement more than did
Caucasian-American parents. These patterns were somewhat stronger for
Chinese parents in Taiwan than among immigrant Chinese parents. These
findings have been confirmed by other studies (e.g., Rosenthal & Feldman,
1990). The Chinese responses to control and achievement are consistent with
more traditional Confucian values. Chen and Uttal (1988) suggest that although the Chinese value system encourages deference to the group, it also
promotes a belief in personal control and in the fulfilment of internal goals.
From this perspective, personal control requires independence. Lin and Fu
(1990) speculate that the findings with regard to parental encouragement of
autonomy could also indicate that traditional values of interdependence are
declining.

Nevertheless, child-rearing studies in which Chinese and Western parents
are compared tend to indicate that traditional values and practices rooted in
Confucian principles have been retained among the immigrant group even
within an external host culture (Lin & Fu, 1990). For example, Kelley and
Tseng (1992) found that first-generation Chinese immigrant mothers tended
to express more concern for their child's physical needs whereas American
mothers of the majority culture expressed more concern for their child's
psychological needs. Consistent with traditional practices, the immigrant
mothers reported using more physical control over their children and more
harsh scolding, and were less nurturant and less responsive than were their
American counterparts. In conclusion, we might speculate that Chinese children are prepared by their parents for peer relations that conform closely to a
cultural mould that emphasizes the continuity of relationships and the minim-
ization of conflict. Higher levels of power assertion are used by parents to
regulate their children's peer relations in light of the expectations of tradition
and of society.

Empirical Studies of Children's Peer Relations

The literature on peer relations of Chinese children is still somewhat
fragmented, although some important theory-driven research in this domain
has emerged in the past few years. Domino and Hannah (1987) examined

parallels between cultural value systems and the content of children's stories. They compared the themes of stories told by Chinese and American children between 11 and 13 years of age. The researchers provided story stems that referred to rule-breaking behavior. It was found that Chinese children tended to be more socially oriented than their American counterparts. The Chinese children's stories focused on peer pressure, shame, and group unity to correct deviant behavior. Furthermore, Chinese stories tended to include more authority figures, such as police and adults, than American stories. Consistent with Taoist principles, Chinese children emphasized greater moral and ethical conduct than their American peers. Thus, Chinese children seem to internalize the expectations of adult society with regard to their peer relations.

Orlick, Zhou and Partington (1990) conducted an observational study of cooperation and conflict among 5-year-olds in China and Canada. Eighty-five per cent of the behaviors of Chinese children were classified as cooperative. Chinese kindergartners engaged in many more helping and sharing activities than Canadian children of the same age. In sharp contrast, 78% of the behaviors of Canadian children involved conflict. Orlick, Zhou, and Partington (1990) attributed the findings to differences in socialization processes in Canada and China. In particular, Chinese kindergartners engaged in more helping and sharing activities than was evident in Canadian settings.

Another study focusing on kindergarten children in Canada and China is that of Chen and Rubin (1992). Using self-report scales and sociometric measures, they found that Chinese children were less accepting of one another than their Canadian peers. In some respects, these are surprising findings, given the collectivist nature of Chinese society. However, Chen and Rubin (1992) suggested that Chinese children may be less accepting and prosocial because they tend to form small well-defined "cliques".

There were also many similarities between the two cultures. Children's peer acceptance in both the Chinese and Canadian samples was positively correlated with children's ability to produce numerous alternative problem-solving strategies, with the quality of the parent–child relationship, and with the socioeconomic status of the parents. In another study, Chen, Rubin, and Li (1994) explored in greater depth the social behaviors that were correlates of peer acceptance and rejection among 7–10-year-old Chinese children. Consistent with studies of Western cultures, they found that sociable and prosocial behavior was positively related to social adjustment, while aggressive behavior was positively associated with maladjustment in Chinese children.

As noted by Rubin (1998), the behavioral manifestations of shyness are the same in China and in Western cultures; however, it has a very different cultural meaning. Chen, Rubin, and Sun (1992) found that, whereas shy and sensitive Canadian children (aged 7–9 years) were likely to be rejected by their peers, among 7–10-year-old Chinese children shyness and sensitivity were positively correlated with peer acceptance. Chen, Rubin, and Li (1994) found that shyness-sensitivity in 8- and 10-year-old Chinese children was positively and concurrently related not only to peer acceptance but also to teacher-assessed competence, leadership, and academic achievement.

Furthermore, a recent longitudinal study indicated that Chinese children who are shy during the early elementary-school years continue to show positive psychosocial adjustment when followed into adolescence (Chen et al., in press). This does not apply, however, to those who display shyness in their peer environment during adolescence: by the age of 12, shyness-sensitivity was positively correlated with peer rejection. When internalizing behaviour is severe enough to be diagnosed as depression, which occurs as frequently among Chinese adolescents as among their Western counterparts, it might even be more of a problem than in the West. This is because the depressed adolescent must face not only rejection by peers, but also indifference by adults who are relatively insensitive to moods and who may not notice depression or become concerned about it because they value shyness and modesty (Chen & Li, in press).

Taken together, these findings suggest that, during early and middle childhood at least, there are cultural differences in the meanings assigned to certain social behaviors. Chen, Rubin, and Li (1994) suggest that shy-inhibited 8- and 10-year-olds may be perceived by their peers as soft-spoken, well-mannered and achieving in academic subjects. In the Chinese culture, these characteristics are seen as virtues. However, by the age of 12, Chinese children are faced with different expectations. For example, high-school selection procedures in China place high levels of academic and achievement pressure on the 11–13 age group (Dong, Yang, & Ollendick, 1994). The educational system may reflect the cultural expectation that children attain substantially more independence, responsibility, and control by late childhood. Moreover, Chen, Rubin, and Li (1994) suggest that successful social interaction requires greater degrees of assertiveness and interpersonal maturity in older children. While these expectations are also found in Western cultures, these differences in the shyness-sensitivity dimension raise the possibility that there is a later age for the developmental shift in the Chinese sample. Therefore, by the age of 12, Chinese children are expected to function with greater autonomy in the fulfilment of culturally-defined goals. This has broader implications for cross-cultural research on children's peer relations. The effects of collectivism/individualism may be more evident at particular ages or stages, and may be reflected in the ages at which important transitions in the expectations of groups or individuals take place. This can only be confirmed in a systematic way by researchers who use cross-sectional and cohort-sequential designs.

Ho and Chiu (1994) speculate that, in a changing China, the expectations for collectivistic behaviors may be required more consistently in relationships based on blood and marriage; although the expectations for collectivism in other relationships have by no means been abandoned. Some changes in the traditional pattern of collectivism may also emerge as a result of the current metamorphosis of China's economic system, in which private enterprise is a growing feature. This places a premium on individual initiative and individual educational attainment. Chinese people are well-known for the prominence of educational attainment in their hierarchy of values (Stevenson, Chen, Lee, & Fuligni, 1991). Sociometric studies in the USA have revealed that elementary-school children of the majority Anglo-American culture assign high social status to peers who do well in academic subjects (see Coie, 1985). This respect for academic achievement may be even more evident in China and among overseas Chinese. The intensity of the emphasis on academic prowess by the Chinese indicates that failure to consider its impact on social relations may lead to a very incomplete picture of Chinese peer relations. Udvari, Schneider, Labovitz, and Tassi (1995) studied the influence of various types of competitiveness and competition domains on children's evaluations of their peers' social status. Their study was conducted in a Toronto elementary school with a large East Asian enrollment. In the sociometric choice nominations made by Chinese youngsters (i.e., nominations by Chinese pupils of all their classmates), children who were competitive in *academic tasks* were well liked, whereas children who were competitive in *physical or athletic activities* were disliked. This was very different from the data obtained from pupils who were not of Asian origin. In the non-Asians' nominations, pupils who were competitive in athletic pursuits were chosen more frequently as work or play partners. Competition in the academic domain was unrelated to peer acceptance. These important distinctions would not have emerged if Udvari and his colleagues had failed to consider the East Asian origin of a substantial part of their Canadian sample, and the potential importance of Chinese values to these participants.

Peer Relations in the Shadow of the Italian Family

The study of children's peer relations in Italy is of interest for reasons diametrically opposite to those that might lead the scholar to peruse the literature on children's social interaction in China and other East Asian countries. In sharp contrast to China, the personal identity of Italians is not intertwined with a sense of belonging to a larger collective unit. It has been well-documented that there are strong cultural rules for interpersonal relationships in Italy, but it is abundantly clear that there is one set of rules for the family, clan, or immediate neighbourhood and another for less proximate relationships (Lanaro, 1992). From all available sources, conflict occurs regularly within the interpersonal relationships of Italian adults and children both inside and outside their families (Argyle, Henderson, Bond, Iizuka, & Contarello, 1986; Genta, Menesini, Fonzi, & Costabile, 1996). Accordingly, Italians should have relatively little need to suppress the expression of anger in relationships, and little worry about loss of face in the presence of a stranger or authority figure as a result of such expression.

Young and Ferguson (1981) found that, in Calabria, many parents regarded peer relations as an unnecessary distraction for their adolescent sons; responses of this type were unknown, however, among parents of Calabrian origin living in Rome or Boston. Although Italy has undergone marked economic progress and urbanization since the Second World War, it is commonly held that the primary loyalty to one's extended family, clan, or immediate neighbours is still a core feature of the Italian value structure (New, 1988; Saraceno, 1981). Thus, there is an interesting difference between Italy and the English-speaking countries in that children's peer relations seem to be much less of a priority for Italian families than for those in English-speaking countries.

Argyle et al. (1986) found that Italian adults were quite flexible in their expectations for interpersonal relationships with non-kin. As already mentioned, there was no sharp rule against the expression of conflict. In comparison, respondents in the UK and Hong Kong had clearly defined rules for behavior within relationships, but adults in Italy indicated fewer strict rules for relationships, and were inconsistent among themselves about what rules there were. Argyle and his colleagues discuss this phenomenon as an Italian ambivalence toward interpersonal relationships, but one could easily interpret it in a more positive light as a manifestation of flexibility. Furthermore, the skills learned in harmonious family life, and the security it provides, may enhance relationships outside the family, whatever the relative importance of families and friends for social support. Furthermore, the socialization practices of Italians emphasize perspective-taking, in contrast with other societies in which children are taught to accept unquestioningly the thinking of an individual in authority. New (1988) documented the processes by which Italian parents and teachers encourage children to consider several alternative explanations for a social situation.

Whatever the reasons for them, some data indicate beyond doubt that children's friendships in family-oriented Italy are of higher quality than those in English Canada, where extended families are less predominant as sources of social support. Schneider, Fonzi, Tani, and Tomada (1997) found that a higher proportion of friendships remained intact over a school year among Italian 8-year-olds than among English-speaking Canadian boys and girls of the same age. Schneider, Fonzi, Tomada, and Tani (in press) determined, in an observational study, that Italian 8-year-olds were far more proficient than English Canadians at resolving conflicts and achieving compromises in situations of potential conflict.

One might speculate that if conflict is a normal and expected feature of relationships, there would be relatively little reason for Italian children to reject classmates who are aggressive. Relevant data are available from major urban settings regarding the behavioral correlates of peer status in Italian preschools (Fonzi, Tomada, & Ciucci, 1994) and Grade Two classrooms (Attili, Vermigli, & Schneider, 1997). These studies were conducted with large samples, using measures very similar to those used in most American studies. The results indicate that both the pattern and strength of the behavioral correlates of peer acceptance in Italy are very similar to those of most other countries, with correlations every bit as strong as those found in studies conducted in North America with both preschoolers and elementary school-age children. These data, combined with those from other countries, help establish that many aspects of peer acceptance in children's groups are more or less invariant across cultures, despite plausible reasons for cross-cultural differences. Aggressive/disruptive behavior is associated with rejection by peers, but prosocial behavior is linked with their acceptance. There are some indications, though, that, unlike the results of studies conducted in Central and Northern Italy, youngsters in Southern Italy perceive some forms of aggression as typical of peers they consider sociable (Casiglia, LoCoco, & Zappulla, 1998).

Italian and North American data, among others, indicate that social withdrawal is also a correlate of rejection in the elementary school years. This does not apply to Chinese youngsters, as noted earlier, but the implications of withdrawal seem to change in China from preadolescence on. Whiting and Edwards (1988) emphasize the value of research that demonstrates similarities in social behavior in cultures that have little contact with each other. Such similarities may help us learn about "scripts" that children follow universally in relating to others at various stages of development. The growing cross-cultural literature on patterns of peer acceptance and rejection may eventually be more useful in this way than in underscoring any cross-cultural differences that emerge from disparities among the features of various cultures.

CULTURES IN CONTACT

The examples of China and Italy are useful in understanding the interplay between the economic and social structure of a society and the peer relations of its children. The second part of this chapter is devoted to the peer relations of children of different cultural origins within a larger heterogeneous culture.

Indigenous Peoples in North America

The indigenous peoples of North America, more than most other groups, have undergone rapid social, economic, and political upheaval. As recently as 200 years ago, the indigenous peoples of North America lived free from European involvement, and adhered to their own values and social structure. Today, we are shocked by disturbing statistics about high rates of suicide, drug abuse, alcohol abuse, child abuse, homicide, and suicide (see review by LaFramboise & Low, 1998). The low rates of social interaction observed among aboriginal children and their lack of assertiveness can be interpreted in several ways. They may be a feature of children's lives in these cultures, which is only problematic when interpreted according to the majority culture's view that it is healthy for children to interact socially with both peers and adults. However, it is also possible to interpret their reticent ways in large groups as a symptom of more general social malaise. In any event, this mode of relating may serve as an obstacle in transactions with members of the dominant culture.

It is difficult to identify a cohesive value system common to the aboriginal people of North America because of the sheer number of distinct groups within that classification, each of which adheres to its own specific values and beliefs (LaFramboise & Low, 1998). However, there are some common aboriginal values that can help provide a framework for viewing peer relations among the indigenous peoples. Many aboriginal people believe that there exists an Almighty, a supernatural spirit, whose form can be perceived in the life-power and light of the sun or the strength and fertility of the earth. This spirit, which is conceptualized differently by the various groups, is omnipotent. Maintaining a positive relationship with it is critical. According to Hay (1977), the Ojibwa of Wisconsin value emotional restraint, especially with regard to anger, for fear that the *pawaganak*, or supernatural beings, will look unfavourably upon them if they express themselves. They believe that the expression of anger can result in the imposition of death or illness by the supernatural beings. Another core belief of the aboriginal groups is that animals and plants are not very different from humans, since all are dependent on the life-giving powers of the spirits. Therefore, all should be respected and not dominated. Harmony with the land and with each other, tolerance and non-competitiveness are predominant values. The kinship structure is more egalitarian than in Euro-American families, with clear expectations for kinship, loyalty, and cooperation (Watson, 1989). Therefore, one could expect aboriginal children to be more altruistic and cooperative than their Euro-American counterparts.

These traditional aboriginal values interact almost everywhere with those of the surrounding majority culture. Contemporary aboriginal populations are under pressure to alter their beliefs to accommodate the values of Euro-Americans and Euro-Canadians. For many Native Americans, the incongruities between the traditional value system and the highly individualistic values of the majority culture have been costly. Although it is possible to draw parallels between many of these traditional beliefs and the social reticence known to characterize aboriginal children, this should not be considered the only explanation. Kleinfeld (1973) found that Inuit and Indian children in Alaskan villages felt that they were better off being silent because they believed that, if they spoke, white classmates and teachers would laugh at them.

Values in the Interpersonal Domain

Most native American children wrestle with the incongruities between the collective interdependence that characterizes their culture of origin and the priorities for autonomy and individual achievement that are emphasized in the schools they attend. Some of the research pertaining to this fundamental dissimilarity in world views is discussed in the next few paragraphs. Additional studies are reviewed by LaFramboise and Low (1998).

Powless and Elliott (1993) conducted a study of the social skills of aboriginal preschoolers. They compared 50 preschool children from the Oneida Reservation near Green Bay, Wisconsin, to 50 Caucasian preschoolers from

Madison, Wisconsin. The Native American preschoolers and the Caucasian preschoolers were matched for gender and age. The researchers were interested in the frequency of utilization of social skills, as defined by the Social Skills Rating System (SSRS) and as measured by parent and teacher ratings using the SSRS. Five out of six of the teachers of the Native American preschoolers were Native American and all 10 of the preschool teachers of Caucasian children were Caucasian. The SSRS measures three positive aspects of social behavior (cooperation, assertion, and self-control) and one domain of problem behavior (interfering behavior). A comparison of the reports of the parents and teachers of the two groups indicated that the Native American children were reported to have exhibited those social skills that the SSRS identified as positive less frequently than were the Caucasian preschoolers. The difference was significant for all three positive scales; however, the largest difference between Caucasian preschoolers and Native American preschoolers was in the assertion domain, according to both teacher and parent ratings. There was no significant difference between the groups for the Interfering Behavior subscale. Although generalization of these findings could be problematic because the study was conducted close to a major American city, the passiveness of aboriginal children has been corroborated by many other researchers in several parts of the continent. With regard to assertive behavior, Philips (1972) studied the use of speech in the classroom by Native Americans and found that verbally-initiating responses depended greatly upon the participant structure of the activity. In general, being verbally assertive is not as highly valued a social skill among Native Americans as it is among Caucasian Americans. Non-verbal differences in communication style were reported by Greenbaum (1985), who videotaped the classroom interactions of Choctaw Indians and Anglo-Europeans in Florida. The aboriginal pupils spoke less often, used shorter utterances, and gazed more often at their peers while the teacher was talking.

The results obtained by Powless and Elliott might be misinterpreted if one assumed that more frequent social interaction in public is necessarily an indication of social competence. Asher, Markell, and Hymel (1981) have addressed this issue, arguing that low rates of interaction alone are not enough to conclude that children are lacking in social competence. It is important to look not only at the quantity of social interactions, but also at their quality. These remarks may apply to cultural as well as individual differences.

Acceptance by the peer group may be less important to aboriginal children than their Euro-American counterparts. Withycombe (1973) studied the peer acceptance and self-concept of Paiute Indians in Arizona and their non-aboriginal classmates. She found that popularity was more highly valued in the Anglo-American group. As discussed above, the indigenous children's lower priorities for social competence may reflect the values of their cultures, and may be troublesome only for outsiders. However, social rejection must cause some distress to the aboriginal children themselves because social status was found to be related to the children's self-concepts to some degree.

Attributes of Social Power

Weisfeld, Weisfeld, and Callaghan (1984) examined peer- and self-appraisals of 67 Hopi and 144 Afro-American schoolchildren. These two groups were selected specifically because of their cultural differences. The Hopi, from north-east Arizona, are noted for their non-violence, collectivism, and punishment of violent or aggressive behavior. In fact, their full name means "the little people of peace" (p. 69). Peacefulness and egalitarianism are Hopi ideals, and decisions are usually based on unanimous consent. In contrast, the Afro-American children in the study were from a Chicago private school. Because large American cities such as Chicago are known for high rates of crime and violence, it can be assumed that this group was more tolerant of violent or aggressive behavior than the Hopi group.

Weisfeld et al. noted significant differences in the spontaneous social play of the two groups. The Afro-American children played in sex-segregated groups, with the boys playing softball and football and the girls jumping rope. In contrast, the Hopi boys and girls played a modified version of basketball together. Instead of dividing up into two teams to compete against one another, the object was to play as one team and get as many baskets as possible. There were also marked differences in the rate of conflict observed. The Afro-American children fought at a rate of once per hour per 70 individuals. In contrast, the Hopi children engaged in only one act of aggression in all the many hours of observations. This was a shoving match between two boys, which was quickly broken up by the other Hopi children. Unfortunately, the researchers did not publish any gender-specific information, neither did they indicate which behaviors constituted a fight in their coding system.

The Weisfeld, Weisfeld, and Callaghan (1984) study also sheds some light on the difficulty of conducting cross-cultural studies on peer relations as a result of the differences in meaning a word or phrase may have from one culture to another. In post-questionnaire conversations with the subjects, it was discovered that the notion of acting grown-up meant very different things to the two populations. The Hopi children understood it to mean performing useful labor, whereas African-American participants may have understood it to mean wearing makeup, using profanity, and insulting people. Bennett and Berry (1992) explored the Native American meaning of the word "competence" among a group of Native Americans from Big Trout Lake, Ontario. They discovered that the meaning of competence for this particular native group was highly related to notions of respect, paying attention, and listening. Although this research did not involve a comparison group, we doubt that a Caucasian or Afro-American population would generate similar associations. Semantic differences need to be explored fully before one assumes that a specific question or item has a similar meaning across different cultures. This has not been done in many if not most studies. Therefore, there may be similar problems in many other studies that remain undetected and unreported.

Cooperation and Competition

Miller and Thomas (1972) conducted a study of the cooperative and competitive behaviors of native and non-native school children ranging in age from 7 to 10 years. The researchers compared 48 Blackfoot natives in Alberta, Canada, to 48 non-natives; each group comprised equal numbers of boys and girls. Cooperative and competitive behaviors were measured using the Madsen Cooperation Board, which can be rigged by the experimenter to make it advantageous to play either competitively or cooperatively. The native youngsters, especially the boys, worked cooperatively even when it was not in their interest to do so, illustrating very clearly the survival of the Native American collectivistic orientation of the children in this group.

In summary, most studies indicate that Native American children are cooperative and collectivistic, but more attention needs to be directed at determining whether these characteristics have persisted despite the rapid changes in the social world of the indigenous peoples. One might also wonder whether their recent group assertiveness in demanding adjudication of land claims, their own judicial system, etc., may be reflected eventually in more assertiveness at the individual level. There are some indications that this kind of change is already under way. Crago, Annahatak, and Ningiuruvik (1993) conducted a longitudinal study of the interactions of children and their caretakers in the Kangirsuk and Quaqtaq Inuit communities of Northern Quebec. They found that older women were quite traditional in their expectations for children and in their parenting. Younger mothers were unaware of some traditional customs, and disdainful of others. The younger mothers engaged their children in question-and-answer routines in the hope that their children would not be withdrawn and unexpressive in school.

Inter-ethnic and Inter-racial Friendship

The demise of racial segregation in American schools and the entrance of non-traditional immigrants to urban North American schools have aroused concern about relations among various ethnic and racial groups. It is important to clarify some of the terminology used in this area, which can be misunderstood very easily. Prejudice refers to a stable pattern of evaluating members of another ethnic group in a negative way and behaving in a negative way toward them (Aboud, 1993). Prejudice depends on being able to identify oneself as a member of one's own ethnic group, which even 4- and 5-year-olds can do. Aboud (1993) reviews the theoretical perspectives on the origins of children's prejudice. According to social reflection theories, children become prejudiced because they learn that different ethnic groups are valued differently in society as a whole, or by their parents in particular. Other, more psychodynamic, approaches contend that prejudice emerges in situations where parents or other authority figures punish any attempt by the child at expressing hostility. Members of lower-status ethnic groups become the targets of the displaced hostility. In cognitive-developmental theories, prejudice can be seen as a reflection of the egocentrism of the young child.

Aboud (1993) provides a useful compendium of research on prejudice, including studies that are useful in validating the theories discussed in the preceding paragraph. The following section pertains to studies on the extent and quality of the friendships between members of differing racial and cultural groups. As will be discussed later, the failure to form friendships outside one's own group may or may not be an indication of prejudice, since it may or may not relate to the attribution of negative characteristics to members of other groups and may or may not entail behaving in a negative way toward them. This research is interesting because it helps portray the extent of the meaningful interpersonal relationships between members of different cultural groups in multicultural societies where there is ample opportunity for such relationships to develop. Studies in this area are summarized in Tables 9.1–9.3.

Participant Characteristics

Given that similarity is a basis for interpersonal attraction (Hallinan & Williams, 1987), many authors have theorized that children will over-whelmingly choose friends from their own ethnic or racial group. This expec-tation has been borne out for students in the majority group in many of the studies listed in Table 9.1 (Braha & Rutter, 1980; Clark & Ayers, 1992; De-nscombe, Szulc, Patrick, & Wood 1986; Durojaiye, 1969; Howes & Wu, 1990; Rowley, 1968). In all of the preceding studies, majority students showed a higher preference for friends from their own ethnic or racial group than did minority students. A similar picture emerged in Eshel and Dicker's (1995) exploration of the reasons articulated by Israeli adolescents for their choices of friends: majority-group adolescents (i.e., Israelis of European origin) em-phasized ethnicity in explaining their reasons for the choice of friends, whereas members of the minority group, Israelis of Middle Eastern origin, de-emphasized ethnicity. In contrast, St. John (1964), Jelinek and Brittan (1975), and Hallinan (1982) all found in-group preference to be highest in minority group students. There is no apparent reason why in some studies the majority group was more ethnocentric and in other studies the minority groups were more ethnocentric. Nevertheless, the incidence of cross-race or cross-ethnic friendship choice was much lower than would be expected if race or ethnicity were not a determining factor. Although the relative rarity of cross-ethnic/ cross-race friendship can be seen as a reflection of ethnic/racial prejudice in children, many researchers do not see it that way, and do not regard it as inherently problematic (e.g., Denscombe et al., 1986).

Age/Grade

Aboud and Doyle (1995) found that, although awareness of racial differences increases across the elementary-school years, prejudice tends to decline. This

Table 9.1   Studies investigating participant characteristics in cross-ethnic/cross-race friendship

Study	Country	n	Race/ethnicity	Age/grade	Measure of friendship
1. Studies conducted primarily with younger participants (age 4–11)					
Cross-sectional studies:					
Durojaiye (1969)	UK	312[a]	203 White 109 Coloured	8–11 years	Sociometric
Braha & Rutter (1980)	UK	120	42 White 78 Non-white	4–10 years	Sociometric
Davey & Mullin (1980)	UK	3953	2584 White 731 Black 638 Asian	7–10 years	Sociometric
Denscombe (1983)	UK	107	40 White 18 Sikh 38 Hindu 8 Muslim 2 West Indian 1 Mixed	7–11 years	Sociometric
Howes & Wu (1990)	US	*210	128 Euro-American 33 Spanish-American 37 Afro-American 12 Asian-American	K & Grade 3	Sociometric Observation
Longitudinal studies:[b]					
Singleton & Asher (1979)	US	[c]227 (154)	48 (38) Black 179 (116) White	Grade 3 (6)	Sociometric
Tuma & Hallinan (1979)	US	*445	Black Non-black	Grades 4–6 (to end of school year)	Sociometric
Denscombe, Szulc, Patrick, & Wood (1986)	UK	54 (50)	27 White 11 Hindu 12 Sikh 3 Muslim 1 Buddhist	7–11 years (+6 months)	Sociometric Observation
Studies conducted primarily with older participants (age 7–20):					
Cross-sectional studies:					
Lundberg & Dickson (1952)	US	1360	Jewish Non-Jewish White Japanese Negro Chineses	13–20 years	Sociometric
St. John (1964)	US	*929	166 Black 763 White	High-school juniors	Sociometric
Rowley (1968)	UK	1747	1109 British 358 Indian 245 West Indian 35 Europeans	7–15 years	Sociometric

continued over

Table 9.1   (*continued*)

Study	Country	*n*	Race/ethnicity	Age/grade	Measure of friendship
Jelinek & Brittan (1975)	UK	4300	2093 British 469 Indian 133 Pakistani 816 West Indian 256 Kenyan Asian 221 Cypriot 95 Italian 217 Others	8–14+ years	Sociometric
Ziegler (1980)	Canada	153	51 Anglo-Canadian 51 Chinese-Canadian 51 Italian-Canadian	12–15 years	Observation
Clark & Ayers (1988; 1992)	US	136	44 Non-white 92 White	Grades 7–8	Sociometric
DuBois & Hirsch (1990)	US	292	216 White 76 Black	Grades 7–9	Sociometric
Smith & Schnieder (in press)		72	28 White 17 Black 18 East Asian 9 South Asian	12–14 years	Sociometric
Longitudinal studies:[b]					
Zizman & Wilson (1992)	US	208	81 Black 89 White n/a Hispanics n/a Asians n/a Others	Grades 8 (9)	Observation

*Estimated.
[a]A leadership substudy was carried out with 83 white and 55 coloured students 10–11 years old. All participants were retested six weeks later to check the accuracy of their responses.
[b]Follow-up data are given in parentheses.
[c]A further group of 153 white and 52 black Grade 3 students were used in the last year of the study for time-lag comparison purposes.

has not always been replicated in other studies (e.g., Black-Gutman & Hickson's [1996] cross-sectional investigation of the attitudes of Australians of European origin toward aboriginal Australians). Multiple age groups participated in most of the studies in Table 9.1. Although the findings of the various studies were not consistent, the trend indicates increasing ethnocentricity with increasing age. The high degree of own-group preference, even in very young children (Braha & Rutter, 1980; Jelinek & Brittan, 1975; Rowley, 1968), has surprised many researchers.

Gender

Hallinan and Williams (1989) postulated that "... the pervasiveness of the negative effect of gender on youth's friendships makes it likely that it

Table 9.2 Studies investigating contextual characteristics in relation to cross-group friendship

Study	Country	n	Race/ethnicity	Age/grade	Measure of friendship
Studies conducted primarily with younger participants (Grades 4–7)					
Longitudinal studies:					
Hallinan (1982)	US	*482	239 Black 243 White	Grades 4–7 (to end of school year)	Sociometric
[a]Hallinan & Sorensen (1985); Hallinan & Smith (1985); Hallinan & Teixeira (1987a, 1987b); Hallinan & Williams (1987)[c]	US	1477	658 Black 697 White 75 Asian 47 Chicano	Grades 4–7 (to end of school year)	Sociometric
Studies conducted primarily with older participants (Grade 6 to high school seniors):					
Cross-sectional studies:					
Damico & Sparks (1986)	US	677	White Black	Grades 6–8	Report of verbal interaction
Hallinan & Williams (1989)	US	[b]58 000	Black White	High-school sophomores & seniors	Sociometric
Eshel & Kurman (1990)	Israel	613	296 Ashkenazi Jews 317 Sephardi Jews	Grades 6–8	Sociometric
Longitudinal studies:					
Schofield & Sagar (1977)	US	*800	Black White	Grades 7–8 (+ 5 months)	Observation

*Estimated.
[ac]This group of studies focused on a subset of the 1477 students in the larger longitudinal study. Some of the studies excluded the Asian and Chicano students and others included them with the white students.
[b]Only a subsample of the 58 000 students was used in this study.

transcends race and other background characteristics" (p. 68). Cross-gender friendship in general is rare during the elementary school years, but it does occur. The results summarized in Table 9.1 concerning the effect of gender on cross-race friendship choice revealed inconsistent gender effects and a gender × race interaction. Friendships that crossed racial/ethnic barriers were usually same-gender (Hallinan & Teixeira, 1987a, 1987b). Cross-gender friendships were usually from the choosing participant's own ethnic group (Jelinek & Brittan, 1975). Some studies showed less ethnocentrism in males than in

Table 9.3 Studies of the effects of cooperative learning groups on cross-group friendship

Study	Country	n	Race/ethnicity	Age/grade (Post-test lag)	Measure of friendship
Weigel, Wiser, & Cook (1975)	US	324	231 White 54 Black 39 Mexican-American	Grades 7 & 10	Sociometric
Slavin (1979)	US	294	170 White 157 Black	Grades 7–8	Sociometric
Hansell & Slavin (1981)	US	402	245 White 157 Black	Grades 7–8	Sociometric
Ziegler (1981)	Canada	146	64 Anglo-Canadian 21 Italian-Canadian 18 Chinese-Canadian 12 Greek-Canadian 11 West Indian 20 Other	Grades 5–6 (+10 weeks)	Sociometric
Hansell (1984)	US	317 (301)	168 White 149 Black	Grades 5–6	Sociometric

females (Lundberg & Dickson, 1952; Schofield & Sagar, 1977), while others showed more male ethnocentrism (Denscombe et al., 1986). Hallinan and Teixeira (1987a, 1987b) found that black females had more cross-race friends than black males, while white males had more cross-race friends than white females, though neither finding was statistically significant. St. John (1964) and Howes and Wu (1990), unlike the others, found no major gender differences in inter-racial friendship choices. These studies lead to the tentative conclusion that cross-sex, cross-race friendships are fairly rare and that white females are the least likely to form friendships with members of other races (Hallinan & Teixeira, 1987b).

Contextual Characteristics

Some sociologists, social psychologists, and school administrators believe that simply placing members of different races or ethnic groups in the same school or class will lead to cross-ethnic/cross-race acceptance and friendship formation (Hallinan & Teixeira, 1987a). Their beliefs have not always been confirmed and sometimes mere proximity has served only to increase tension and hostility (Amir, 1969). The contextual characteristics of the schools, such as ability grouping, can act as a barrier to inter-ethnic/inter-racial friendships by limiting the opportunities for different ethnic/racial groups to interact with each other. The studies in Table 9.2 examined school organizational variables that may influence cross-ethnic/cross-race friendship choice, acceptance, communication, and aggregation.

The effect of the racial composition of the classroom or school on friendship choice varies considerably. Hallinan and Smith (1985) found that the numerical minority group had more cross-race friendships than the majority group. Hallinan and Teixeira (1987b) found that racial composition had no effect on the cross-race friendships of blacks but that whites were more likely to choose a black classmate as best friend the more blacks there were in the classroom. Denscombe (1983) found that whites showed a higher degree of ingroup preference in a school with a higher ratio of minorities to whites than they did in other schools. Many qualitative accounts document the phenomenon of "re-segregation" in racially mixed schools with substantial minority enrollments (e.g., Schofield, 1995).

Ability Grouping

Being in the same ability group for instruction had a significant positive effect on whites' choice of blacks according to both studies by Hallinan and Teixera (1987a, 1987b). One of their reports indicates a slight negative effect on blacks' choice of whites (Hallinan & Teixeira, 1987a), while the other indicates no significant effect on the cross-race friendships of blacks (Hallinan & Teixeira, 1987b). Damico and Sparks (1986) found that whites talked with significantly greater frequency to blacks in the school without ability grouping than in the school where ability grouping was employed. Grouping blacks and whites together for instruction affected white students' inter-racial friendships more than it did that of black students. Hallinan and Teixeira (1987b) suggested that structural constraints on cross-race friendships influence whites more than blacks.

Classroom Climate

In classes in which marks were emphasized, whites were significantly less likely to choose blacks as friends but there was no effect on blacks' choice of whites (Hallinan & Teixeira, 1987b). Where there was an emphasis on basic skills and mastery of the curriculum, whites were less likely to choose blacks but blacks were more likely to choose whites (Hallinan & Teixeira, 1987b). When student initiative and enjoyment of learning were stressed, blacks were more likely to choose whites as best friend and there was a weak positive effect on the inter-racial choice of whites (Hallinan & Teixeira, 1987b). The less competitive the classroom was academically, the more likely blacks were to choose whites as best friends. Hallinan and Williams (1987) concluded that the inter-racial friendships of blacks displayed greater responsiveness than those of whites to classroom climates that influence the status hierarchy.

Cooperative Learning

According to Allport (1954), "equal-status contact between majority and minority groups in the pursuit of common goals" (p. 281) is a prerequisite for mutual acceptance. Table 9.3 lists studies on the effects of cooperative learning groups on inter-ethnic/inter-racial friendship choice. These groups contained a mixture of ethnic/racial groups and academic abilities. Students were encouraged to tutor and quiz each other in order to help each other learn the material, and were rewarded as a group for their achievement. All students in the group had an equal chance of contributing points to the group's score (Slavin, 1979). Slavin (1979) found a statistically significant effect for cooperative learning in terms of both the number and proportion of cross-race friends chosen. Ziegler (1981) found a significant increase in casual cross-ethnic friendship for the cooperative learning group in comparison to the control group, which received regular classroom instruction. No effect of the treatment on close other-race friendships was evidenced until 10 weeks after the experiment ended. Cooperative groups had positive effects on students' interaction with others of a different race.

Whether the relatively low incidence of cross-race and cross-ethnic friendship is undesirable depends on one's values and the motives behind the choices. Preference for one's ethnic or racial group does not necessarily mean a rejection of the out-group (Braha & Rutter, 1980; Denscombe, 1983). In Durojaiye's (1969) study, when children were asked why they chose the friends they did, none mentioned race as a reason for their choice. However, it is possible that the children were aware of the reasons for their choice only at a subconscious level, or did not wish to divulge that race or ethnicity played a role in their choices. Denscombe (1983) pointed out that the existence of even a small number of friendships across ethnic lines could be interpreted as an absence of prejudice, despite the more general trend for friends to be selected within one's own group, since even these few choices would indicate children's willingness to form friendships based on personal characteristics rather than ethnicity. On the other hand, it could be argued that if personal factors were more important determinants of choice than ethnicity, there should be more out-group friendships among children, since no one group of people has a monopoly on desirable characteristics. Whether society or schools should be disturbed by the findings depends on one's view of race/ethnic relations. Lundberg and Dickson (1952) believed that "a certain amount of ethnocentrism is a normal and necessary ingredient of all group life," and it is "therefore, not in itself necessarily to be regarded as a problem" (p. 34). Others, of course, may be alarmed by ethnic/racial exclusivity and therefore view the findings with apprehension.

Schofield (1995) noted that, in recent years, more people in more places are coming into contact with substantial proportions of minority-group members. Therefore, it is imperative to expand research on the effects of these demographic trends, and to update the data base continually. It is safe to conclude that, in Western societies where subcultures interact, ethnicity or race is a very important factor in the choice of children's friendships although, as we have seen, there are a number of important variables moderating this general trend.

GENERAL CONCLUSION

As the examples presented above illustrate, many aspects of children's peer relations mirror the social, economic, and spiritual characteristics of their cultural background. Important cultural differences have been found in children's cooperativeness, aggression, assertiveness, and shyness, as well as some similarities. The dimension of individualism/collectivism, long considered the most important element in classifying cultures, still appears somewhat useful in describing these cross-cultural differences. However, the complex structures of nations and peoples require that we elaborate extensively on earlier conceptions of individualism and collectivism, adding qualifiers and new parameters in order to portray differences within cultures among social contexts, generations, socioeconomic classes, and ethnic subgroups.

In accepting these challenges, researchers will have to bring new creativity to their methods and measures. Cross-cultural research has been widely criticized for the widespread use of measures that are not culturally sensitive, samples that are small and not representative of distinctions *within* cultures, such as socioeconomic status and ethnicity, failure to consider developmental differences, and over-reliance on single sources of information (see Schneider, 1993). These flaws are problematic enough if one's goal is to compare two cultures that one believes are very distinct and very homogenous. The repercussions of these shortcomings are greater if one attempts to conduct research that reflects the diversity that exists within many major cultures and the transitions that many of them are undergoing.

As societies undergo rapid change, many of the findings regarding cross-cultural differences in children's social behavior may become outdated. Within the same culture, children reaching the same age at different times may find themselves in very different family, school, and peer contexts. While even cross-sectional designs are not used frequently enough in cross-cultural research, it would be very useful to see cohort-sequential designs, which would better portray both developmental differences and era effects. Given the many obstacles to conducting cross-cultural research, this is probably too much to ask. Although there have been few attempts at comparing styles of social interaction before and after rapid socio-political change, some of the profound transformations in social systems have inspired some *post hoc* studies. For example, Oswald and Krappmann (1994) compared the quality of elementary-school children's friendships in West and East Berlin after the unification of that city. Goodwin (1995) discussed individual differences in self-disclosure as a function of the increased latitude for self- expression in Russia after the disintegration of the Soviet empire. There have been also been recent studies on parents' beliefs and values regarding child-rearing in China (Ruan & Matsumura, 1991), Iran (Tashakkori & Thompson, 1988) and Russia (Goodwin & Emelyanova, 1995). In each case, the research was inspired by the researcher's understanding of connections between societal change and interpersonal interactions.

Although children's peer relations have been studied in many different cultures, the methods used in these studies are usually very similar, and, with very few exceptions, are adaptations of techniques developed in the USA. Without this similarity of method, cross-cultural comparisons of results would be even more complex. Furthermore, American researchers have invested the most energy in this field, and have developed the most sophisticated tools. There is no clear reason to believe that the dimensions of peer relations contained in the American instruments are not valid in other cultures, but it is irresponsible to assume they are valid without demonstrating this. One cannot rule out the possibility that aspects of peer relations considered important in some cultures are being under-represented or mismeasured in some way.

Most peer relations research in America and elsewhere has focused on large groups such as classrooms and schools. As more attention is now being devoted to relationships at the dyadic level, especially relations between friends (see Schneider, Wiener, & Murphy, 1994), it will be useful in future studies to identify patterns of cultural similarity and difference in the ways in which children relate to friends. This knowledge can help refine theory with regard to the influence of culture on behavior in relationships. It may enable us to distinguish between those aspects of child development that may emerge as species-related and universal and those that are sensitive to cultural differences. There may be important practical implications as well. Collett (1971) reported a successful intervention in which Englishmen were taught to understand the social behavior patterns of Arabs. Similar interventions with children may be useful in reducing friction among the cultural groups that interact more and more in schools and neighborhoods around the globe. Dyadic pair therapy has been implemented to assist children from different cultures who have the potential to become friends in enhancing their understanding of each other and their relationships (Karcher & Nakkula, 1997). Knowledge about cultural dimensions of children's social behavior could also inform practitioners contemplating interventions with children of different cultural origins. For example, many standard social skills programs used in the English-speaking countries may target and attempt to modify behaviors that are regarded as socially competent in other countries or communities. Some of these programs seek to modify social withdrawal which, as we have seen, may be normative and even valued by peers and parents in East Asian societies (Kashiwagi & Azuma, 1977). Other social skills interventions focus on the control of anger. These would probably be helpful in most cultures, but could, for example, be less meaningful when implemented with Hispanic children without an understanding of the complex dynamics relating to the expression of anger in many parts of Latin America (Arce & Torres-Matrullo, 1982; Guarnaccia, DeLaCancela, & Carrillo, 1989). Educators who do not understand cultural norms for children's social behaviour may misinterpret the intentions of their pupils and make erroneous inferences about their adjustment. Such misinterpretations are often implicated in portrayals of the alienation of aboriginal children in American schools (e.g., Gallimore, Boggs, & Jordan, 1974). Providing educators with information about the cultural origins of their charges could enhance the schooling experience of all participants.

Chapter 10

A Dynamic-maturational Model of the Function, Development, and Organization of Human Relationships

Patricia M. Crittenden

Family Relations Institute, Miami, FL

Half of all marriages fail. A larger proportion of love affairs fail. In most cases, the separating parties come to believe that they misjudged their partner, that their initial belief that the partner had exceedingly desirable qualities was in error. Indeed, they often come to believe that the partner actually has exceedingly undesirable characteristics and, sometimes, that the partner actively deceived them. How were they (and how are we) deluded?

In this paper, I review several bodies of knowledge to construct a "dynamic-maturational" model of how we learn to differentiate reality from appearance, to accept certain probabilities of error and refuse others, and, on these bases, to establish relationships with a greater or lesser probability of satisfaction. The underlying construct is that of information processing. I choose this because all action, whether reflexive, habitual, or thoughtfully considered, depends on the perception and interpretation of information.

The Developmental Psychology of Personal Relationships.
Edited by Rosemary S. L. Mills and Steve Duck. © 2000 John Wiley & Sons Ltd.

Thus, the adaptiveness of human behavior is constrained by the quality of information underlying it.

I argue that, as a species, we have evolved to perceive and interpret information in particular ways and that, as individuals, we have learned to modify these in ways that reflect our unique circumstances. It is on the outcome of these two levels of modification of information that we organize our behavior with regard to others. I use these propositions to guide a selective review of the literature on mental functioning, development, and relationships to make several points: (1) There are universal principles that can describe the patterning of relationships and these principles operate in a probabilistic manner. (2) A typology of relationships can be described that reflects these principles and that is functionally, developmentally, and clinically meaningful. (3) Underlying the principles are the *evolutionary* issues of safety and reproduction and the *functional* issues of predicting and promoting these. (4) Relationships are central to both protection and reproduction. (5) Much of our brain evolution and mental development is organized around predicting with greater accuracy and promoting with greater skill conditions that are safe and favor reproduction. (6) Because safe conditions and opportunities to reproduce are not always discernible, the issue of appearance and reality is central to relationships. I propose that inaccurate information regarding safety and the opportunity to reproduce is central to failed relationships.

To construct this thesis, I first consider the function of relationships and the importance of inaccurate information to safety and reproduction. I then consider several models of child and adult relationships and offer a "dynamic-maturational" model that is both synthesized from these and tied to the functional principles that I propose. I then offer evidence that adult relationships are tied to early relationship experiences in which children learn what is safe and what is dangerous, what information best identifies safe and dangerous circumstances, and when and how to use falsified behavior to protect oneself. I conclude with a short discussion of the clinical applications of this dynamic-maturational model and a discussion of need for empirical research to test the theory offered.

A. What Are the Principles that Regulate Relationships?

Although relationships accomplish many functions, two are essential to the survival of the human species. These are protection and reproduction. Reproduction formed the basis of Freud's psychoanalytic theory, whereas protection formed the basis of Bowlby's attachment theory. Protection and reproduction also form the base of Maslow's hierarchy of human needs. I propose that together these two "ultimate" functions explain basic aspects of human motivation, behavior, and relationship.

Protection by adult caregivers is essential to the survival of immature humans (Bowlby, 1969/82). Even in adulthood, however, relationships serve a protective function. This function is fulfilled physically when we seek our spouse during real dangers (for example, an attack) and when the risk of danger is higher (for example, when we sleep.) It is fulfilled psychologically when our spouse's support enables us to venture into new activities and roles (for example, parenthood or a challenging job) that, in turn, promote the protection of ourselves, our partners, and our progeny. Adult relationships also enable us to reproduce successfully, that is, with the maximum assurance that our progeny will be genetically fit and well protected.

Knowing when one is safe and with whom one can reproduce is important. Indeed, it is so important that one could argue that a major outcome of brain evolution is to promote transformations of sensory stimuli into meaningful information about safety and reproduction. I offer three sorts of transformations, each of which is vulnerable to predictable sorts of error.

Cognition and the Cerebellum

Animals as evolved as reptiles have a midbrain, one function of which is to attribute causal meaning to sensory information on the basis of temporal order (Green, Irvy, & Woodruff-Pak, 1999). Such sensorimotor learning operates in accordance with the principles of learning theory (Steinmetz, 1998; Thompson, Bas, Chen, Cipriano, Grethe, Kern, Thompson, Tracy, Weninger, & Krupa, 1997). When motor activity yields desirable outcomes, it is maintained or repeated. When undesirable outcomes ensue, behavior is modified or inhibited. Functionally, it is as though predictable, temporally-ordered patterns were used to add causal meaning to sensory information. I call this transformation of sensory stimuli "cognitive" information.

Such information has tremendous protective value. With sensorimotor learning, individuals can adapt to the unique dangerous and safe aspects of their environments. Because such learning is preconscious, it is rapid and efficient; it is also prone to certain types of error. Specifically, causation may be attributed when there is no causal relation. That is, if something dangerous happens, preceding events or conditions may be treated in the future as though they caused the untoward outcome. In addition, in species capable of expectation, behavior that precedes an expected danger that does not occur may come to be treated as protective, i.e., it will be exhibited as though it caused safety. Although repetitions of the preceding events could be used to demonstrate the lack of causal relation, such repetitions are likely to be avoided if the event is dangerous. Indeed, the more dangerous the outcome, the more diligently the organism will avoid repetition.

Single-trial learning is especially likely to reflect false causal attributions and to occur in the context of extreme danger (Gustavson, Garcia, Hankins, & Rusiniak, 1974). Such superstitious learning may become part of a person's behavioral repertoire and be exhibited as inhibitions and compulsions that can no longer be explained (Tracy, Ghose, Strecher, McFall, & Steinmetz, 1999). Thus, I argue that the preconscious, protective function of the cerebellum consists of organizing information temporally in ways that add causal meaning to sensory stimuli. That meaning may be in error and uncorrected error is most likely when conditions are very dangerous.

A second important function of the midbrain is to regulate sexual behavior. Because this is not relevant until puberty, I delay discussion of this function.

The Limbic System

The limbic system has evolved in mammalian species to respond to contextual stimuli by generating feelings of unfocused anxiety (Le Doux, 1995; MacLean, 1990). These feelings motivate the organism to flight (if possible) or prepare it to fight (Selye, 1976). The eliciting stimuli are extreme intensity, for example darkness/brilliant light, suddenness/long delays, loud noises/silence, infinite space/entrapping conditions, crowds/isolation (Bowlby, 1973; Seligman, 1971; Le Doux, 1994). None of these conditions is itself dangerous, but all are associated with increased probability of danger. Having another person present, especially a stronger, wiser, and more experienced person who is intensely interested in our welfare, both makes us feel less anxious and also is a substantial protective advantage (Bowlby, 1973). Put another way, the limbic system transforms sensory stimuli into affective information that enables us to prepare for dangers that we have not yet experienced, thus, reducing the risk of injury or death during the first opportunity for experiential learning. Sometimes, however, feelings of anxiety are elicited when there is no danger. Similarly, feelings of comfort may be experienced in spite of imminent danger. Finally, unconditioned feelings may be generalized to associated conditions. This is particularly likely when there are multiple unconditioned elicitors of anxiety. I refer to this transformed information about context as "affect".

The Cortex

The cortex receives multiple transformations of cognitive and affective information, each leading to a disposition to act (Damasio, 1994). If the dispositions are consistent, responding proceeds rapidly and unimpeded. If, however, the dispositions are discrepant (for example, one feels like fleeing even though previous experience indicates no danger), the mind has the opportunity to become alert and to attempt to resolve the discrepancy (Lashley, 1958/60; Tononi & Edelman, 1998). Three points are important. First, because transformed information is vulnerable to different sources of error, identification of discrepancy enables the mind to correct erroneous information generated by the lower brain. Second, the cortex matures over the course of childhood. Thus, with maturation it becomes better able to identify and resolve discrepancies (Piaget, 1952). Third, if the potential danger is very great, the mind will take protective action rather than run the definitive test to verify the information. Thus, I argue that the mind will choose safety over truth under conditions of danger.

B. How Are These Principles Transformed into Interpersonal Strategies over the Course of Development?

Learning to Use One's Mind

Infants are born ready to transform and integrate information in sensorimotor ways. In addition, infants' affective reflexes provide others with information about infants' well-being. Through interaction, infants learn to attribute meaning to information (Vygotskii, 1987). There are only three patterns of response that caregivers can give to infants' affective behavior (Crittenden, 1995). Caregivers can respond predictably in ways that increase infants' comfort. Such infants are on a schedule of predictable reinforcement of their affective signals. They learn to make cognitive meaning of the relation between their behavior and their caregivers' responses and to associate feelings with meaningful changes in state. Their interpersonal strategy becomes one of open and direct communication of feelings to increase the probability of desired caregiving. In attachment terms (Ainsworth, 1979; Ainsworth, Blehar, Waters, & Wall, 1978), they are securely attached Type B[1] infants (see Fig. 10.1, B1–4.)

Other caregivers respond negatively to infants' affective signals (by shouting, shaking the baby, turning away, etc.). Because such babies are on a schedule of predictable punishment of affective signals, they learn to inhibit display of affect. Thus, they make cognitive meaning of the relation between their behavior and that of their caregivers, but learn that their feelings are both in error and also misleading. Consequently, they tend to attend to cognitive information and to disregard affect; this decreases the probability of punitive outcomes. In attachment terms, they are avoidantly attached (Type A). Nevertheless, most caregivers of Type A children are caring and protective; they simply dislike displays of negative affect that are not necessary to elicit protection. Their infants correctly learn that things work out best if they act as though there were no problem (see Fig. 10.1, A1–2.) However, some parents of avoidant babies are themselves a source of danger to the babies (Crittenden, 1988a). Some are neglectful; when their infants inhibit affective signals, they respond even less to infant needs. Others are violent; display of infant affect increases the probability of danger. In the preschool years, many of these children will develop compulsive strategies (Fig. 1, A3–4).

The third group of caregivers is inconsistent. Their infants are on a schedule of unpredictable, intermittent reinforcement of negative affect. Their infants are unable to organize their behavior around the changing contingencies of parental behavior. Nevertheless, their reinforcement schedule insures that fear (disposition to flee), anger (disposition to attack), and desire for comfort (disposition to approach) will be displayed at high intensity and frequency, for

---

[1]As Bartholomew has pointed out, there are many attachment typologies (Bartholomew, 1993). The ABC "Types" used here refer to how cognitive and affective information is managed rather than to specific patterns of behavior, e.g. avoidance, resistance. Such patterns are age-specific, whereas the patterns of processing information are relevant throughout the life-span.

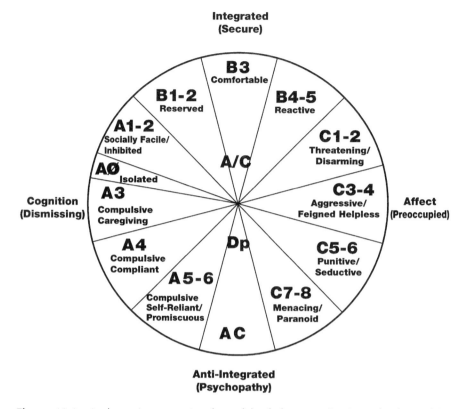

Figure 10.1 A dynamic-maturational model of the organization of relationships (adapted from Crittenden, 1995)

long durations, in spite of punishment, reinforcement of incompatible behavior, or attempts at extinction. Type C infants can make no temporal/causal meaning of information, are affectively aroused and disposed to incompatible actions, and are considered ambivalently attached.

These three patterns, plus a combination A/C pattern (Crittenden, 1985), can be applied to essentially all infants. Nevertheless, even in infancy, there is wide variation in infants' developing personality. It is proposed here that essential mental transformations of information are universal to humans and that the A, B, C and A/C strategies reflect all possible integrations of the mental functions with experience. Personality, on the other hand, includes a second interaction, the interaction of strategies with unique, heritable (but non-essential) characteristics, i.e., temperament (Crittenden, 1999; Tooby & Cosmides, 1990). Personality, thus, varies more greatly than strategies.

The Preschool Years

With preoperational intelligence, children use information in more sophisticated ways and organize their behavior in more complex patterns. Linguistic communication becomes increasingly important and is used to communicate about past and future. As a consequence, internal representational models come to exist in both sensorimotor "procedural" form and, increasingly, in verbal forms that can be discussed with caregivers.

In addition, preschool-aged children use coy behavior to (1) disarm parental aggression (with the non-verbal signals of exposing the [vulnerable] belly and neck and displaying the "no weapons", empty-hands gesture) and (2) elicit parental nurturance (with little, non-threatening glances, an open-mouthed, no-teeth "smile", and a supplicating posture) (Crittenden, 1992; 1995; Eibl-Eibesfeldt, 1979). Together these changes enable many children to modify or change their strategy, i.e., pattern of attachment.

Children who are Type B/secure in the preschool years learn to use language to express feelings and intentions and to negotiate and compromise with caregivers about plans (Marvin, 1977). They are balanced with regard to use of affect and cognition. This pattern is consistent with Baumrind's pattern of authoritative parents and competent children (Baumrind, 1971) and with Erikson's issue of autonomy (Erikson, 1950).

Type A children discover that caregivers use false affect, that is, they express positive affect to conceal negative feelings, especially anger and fear (Crittenden, 1981). Type A/defended children learn to do the same because positive affect elicits the caregiving that they desire. Children with unresponsive parents use false bright affect and entertaining/caregiving behavior to attract attention (Fig. 10.1, A3). This increases the probability of parental protection. Children with dangerously hostile caregivers learn to comply with parental demands, to falsify affective displays in parent-pleasing ways, and to be vigilantly alert; they are compulsively compliant (Fig. 10.1, A4) (Crittenden & DiLalla, 1988). Thus, Type A children learn that there are predictable relations between events (even falsified events) that can be relied on whereas others' affect can deceive. Furthermore, Type A children learn to regulate parental behavior by creating the appearance of happiness to defend against feelings of anger, fear, and desire for comfort. When parents are dissatisfied, such children feel responsibility and shame. This strategy is consistent with, but more elaborated than, Baumrind's pattern of authoritarian parents and socially ineffective children (Baumrind, 1971). It also fits Erikson's notion of preschool-aged children developing feelings of shame (Erikson, 1950).

Type C children show the most dramatic change in behavior. With coy behavior and preoperational intelligence, they organize a coercive strategy of (1) splitting the display of mixed feelings of anger, fear, and desire for comfort into aggressiveness and disarmingly coy behavior, (2) exaggerating the display of one while inhibiting the display of the other, and (3) alternating the displays in concert with changes in adults' angry and placating behavior (Crittenden, 1992). For example, a little boy wants candy in a supermarket. He whines, cries, and then screams in a rapidly escalating tantrum. As long as his parent placates him, he maintains his angry demands. But when his parent becomes fed up and angry, he switches to disarmingly submissive behavior; he looks sweetly innocent, incapable of anger, and in need of nurturance. The parent soothes him. He needs more; he feigns helplessness until the parent gets fed up. Then he meets parental anger with his own anger and his parent, fearing another tantrum, placates him. And so on, in a coercive strategy that transforms parental unpredictableness into child moodiness, volatility, and unpredictableness. Although all children learn the coercive strategy, children of inconsistent parents use it as their primary means of managing the parent–child relationship; see Fig. 10.1, C1–2. This pattern is consistent with Baumrind's pattern of permissive parents and immature, anti-social children (Baumrind, 1971) and Erikson's notion of doubt (Erikson, 1963).

The coercive strategy depends upon the creation of an unresolvable problem that functions to keep parents' attention on the child. Of course, it is also constraining and entrapping for parents. Many overcome the strategy by tricking children regarding the parents' future behavior, i.e., regarding their intentions. For example, they lead children to expect that they are not leaving and then, when the children are not looking, they sneak out. Such parents falsify cognitive information. Because preschool-aged children gauge reality on the basis of appearances (Piaget, 1952), they cannot discern the deception. Children who are repeatedly tricked in this way come to distrust cognitive information.

To conclude, with new cortical potential for organizing information, preschool-aged children organize relationships in more differentiated ways than in infancy. These reflect both extensions of the infant patterns (Egeland & Farber, 1984; Greenberg, Speltz, & DeKlyen, 1993; Stevenson-Hinde & Shouldice, 1995) and, in some, cases changes in strategy (Crittenden, 1992). Thus there is evidence of both continuity and change in children's strategies (Rauh, Ziegenhain, Müller, & Wijnroks, 2000; Teti, Gelfand, Messinger, & Isabella, 1995; Vaughn, Egeland, & Sroufe, 1979). Furthermore, there is clearer differentiation of normative and atypical[2] patterns. Each of the strategies has a normative form; in addition, the A and C strategies have subpatterns (i.e., A3–4 and C3–4) associated with both child behavior disorders and homes that are dangerous (Crittenden & Claussen, 1994; Erickson, Sroufe, & Egeland, 1985; Lyons-Ruth, 1992; Teti et al., 1995).

The School Years

The school years are notable for three processes. First, school-aged children spend increasing amounts of time away from their parents and without adult supervision; consequently, they must depend upon their representations of reality and of others' behavior to assess danger and to regulate their own behavior in ways that promote both safety and exploration. Mentally, they

---

[2]Selecting terminology is difficult. Clinical terminology uses the terms adaptive/maladaptive and functional/dysfunctional to refer to behavior that I have referred to as normative and atypical. In evolutionary terms, all of the strategies and behavior patterns are adaptive and functional, *given the constraints of actual environmental conditions*. The maladaptation occurs when strategies learned in one context are applied without modification to another in which they do not achieve their function (Crittenden, in press c).

become able to integrate diverse sorts of information and to represent diversity in behavior. This enables them to construct internal representational models that are more accurate and flexible because they are differentiated (by person and context) and conditional (as if-then structures.)

Second, school-aged children refine the three basic strategies and subpatterns to create a wider array of ways to manage relationships. For example, among coercive-disarming children, there is a differentiation of silly, clown-like children from persuasive charmers, whiny blamers, submissive victims, and coy, seductive clingers. Among defended children, some develop a public-pleasing, positive presentation that enables them to become socially popular with many children (although, possibly, intimate best friends with none), whereas others become increasingly isolated and lonely. Each new subpattern maximizes some aspect of the underlying strategy in an interaction of person and environment. Although these subpatterns are only sketched here, the important issue is the process of differentiation rather than the details of its outcome (Sroufe, Egeland, & Kreutzer, 1990).

Third, school-aged children learn to deceive others with regard to their intentions. Put another way, they learn to use false cognitive information to cause others to lower their guard against the child's planned treachery. Among coercive-aggressive children, this results in a subgroup of punitive children (C5) who are obsessed with revenge. The pattern is well exemplified by gang-style vendettas and bully–victim relationships (Smith, Bowers, Binney, & Cowie, 1993). Children who are frequently victimized reflect an obsession with rescue (C4).

Adolescence

Adolescence culminates in both mental (cortical) and sexual maturity. The mind becomes capable of sophisticated integrations of information. One function of the mature mind is to identify and correct distortions to create increasingly accurate representations of reality. Having a variety of sources of information permits the mind to perform a multi-method experiment on the nature of reality. In this experiment, errors generated at earlier developmental periods can be corrected. This, of course, increases the probability of revised internal representational models that reflect greater flexibility and complexity of behavior than at younger ages. If, however, danger is perceived as imminent and disguised, the mind may defend the self by presuming the environment to be pervasively malevolent. In this case, false affect may be integrated with false cognition to yield a representation of omnipresent danger. Individuals who hold such representations become exquisitely alert to treachery and constantly prepared to defend themselves. Some cower with paranoia, whereas others menace those who might harm them; see Fig. 10.1, C7–8, AC. Because the best defense is often offense, such individuals become psychopathically dangerous to others.

Sexual maturity activates the second essential motivation of any species, i.e., reproduction. During adolescence and into early adulthood, humans seek partners who function not only as attachment figures but also as reproductive mates. This double function may explain the intensity of these relationships. It also explains some of the relation between early relationship experience with parents and relationship patterns among adults. Adolescents integrate genetically biased patterns of sexual behavior (Buss, 1994) into their existing internal representational models of self and other behavior. In particular, coy behavior is transformed into flirtatious behavior that can be used to negotiate relationships and false positive affect is transformed into promiscuous (A5–6) invitations to intimacy.

This completes the components of a two-dimensional model of both the mental processing of information about safety and danger and also the organization of relationships (see Fig. 10.1.) The horizontal dimension is the source of information used by the mind, i.e., cognitive or affective information, including an array of transformations of these (See Crittenden, 1997c). The vertical dimension is extent of integration of the two sorts of information. Four major patterns are defined by these dimensions: balanced (B), defended (A), coercive (C), and coercive/defended (A/C and AC).

There are three important points about this model. First, it is specifically hypothesized that individuals who have experienced danger, especially danger from caregivers, learn to emphasize the most predictive information and to ignore and/or falsify the least predictive information. Second, the meanings that individuals attribute to information are probabilistic; they do not define how things actually are in all cases, but rather how they might be. Because few things are certain, humans must decide how much certainty is needed before action is taken. The *perception* of danger is critical to making this decision. Third, the more eminent and threatening the danger is perceived to be, the more unreliable information will be distrusted and distorted.

Estimates of the probability of danger, however, are vulnerable to specifiable distortions of reasoning including representativeness, availability, and adjustment and anchoring (Tversky & Kahneman, 1982). By increasing perceived probability, these distortions function to maximize safety. Thus, under dangerous circumstances, humans tend to choose safety over truth. Put concretely, a child who has experienced violence is more likely to perceive danger in neutral stimuli than a child growing up under safer conditions (Dodge & Frame, 1982; Rieder & Cicchetti, 1989).

Selecting a Partner

Selecting a partner is the focus of much adolescent activity. Adolescents advertise themselves in ways they hope will attract desirable partners. The advertisements, however, are not always accurate (Goffman, 1959). For example, flirtatious behavior that becomes seductive may exaggerate interest while underlying anger and fear are hidden. How can one tell? Some people are what they seem whereas others are not. Hypocrisy becomes a cardinal crime for adolescents who want a world in which everyone (else!) displays only accurately predictive information.

What is being predicted is not, however, entirely clear. Although there is a substantial literature on the tendency of males to seek reproductive success and females to seek resources and protection (Buss, 1994), nevertheless, it is unlikely that these ultimate motivations are the sole motivations. To the contrary, immediate rewards may be of considerable importance. Thus a low status, but sweet-talking, male may captivate the mate of a high status, wealthy male with little time for tenderness. In other words, both the motivations underlying relationships and the strategies used to achieve them may be complex.

Adolescents scan potential mates for signs of their suitability. Is the potential mate trustworthy? Protective? A reliable parent for one's progeny? Does he only boast of power or is he powerful? Will she satisfy the insecure boy's desire to feel powerful? Does she really enjoy sex? Will she be faithful? It is not easy to know. As most adolescents discover, appearances can be deceiving. Relationships are tried out. Most fail, but in the process much is learned about appearance and reality, the process of discerning the difference, and the risks of mistaking them. Will the charming boy really be devoted to his girlfriend? Is jealousy a sign of commitment or a warning of violence to come? Is the quiet boy really uncaring? Can he be counted on to do as he promises? What about the seductive girl? Will she be loving and devoted (i.e., submissive) or is she really angry and dangerous? Can one sleep safely with her? Is promiscuity a sign of ready intimacy or of someone so isolated and fearful of intimacy, even when physically close, that there may be no other way for them to reproduce? Adolescents must learn to discriminate real predictive information from information that is too good to be true. Indeed, as astute shoppers and evolutionary biologists have discovered, the less one has to offer, the more one must promise (Margulis & Sagan, 1991; Tooke & Camire, 1991; Trivers, 1985). In love ruses deceive potential partners, thus, improving mating prospects.

It's tricky, and apparently many of us aren't so good at it. This has implications for the many women who are battered by spouses and lovers, for the men who are killed or injured by attacking partners, for the half of adults who will divorce, for all those who live in embattled disharmony or silent separateness, and for all the children of these troubled adult relationships. Relationships are essential for reproduction and they greatly promote personal survival and the survival of children. For all of us, however, relationships represent both our haven of safety and the ultimate danger. Being able to tell these apart is very important.

Who will make errors? Ironically, it may be those who skew their processing of information specifically to prevent errors (for a fuller discussion, see Crittenden, 1997b). If, in our prior experience, errors of judgment or action have been minor, temporary setbacks that allowed us to learn new discriminations, to revise representational models, and to reorganize our behavior more adaptively, then risk can be accepted fairly often. If, on the other hand, risk has been associated with dangerous outcomes, then we must learn to identify the signals of risk, to construct representational models that maximize the avoidance of risk, and to behave in ways that preclude risk (Crittenden, 1998b). Much less can be ventured in such circumstances and much less will be learned.

What kinds of errors will be made? Most models of personality or relationship are silent on this issue, but jails, child protection services, and mental hospitals are clear. Repeatedly, those who have experienced the most treachery in the past select partners who will be the most treacherous (Cowan & Kinder, 1985). Often this is true even when adults are aware of the problem and actively seek a partner who is completely unlike their previous partner. If this model is reasonably accurate, choosing the opposite pattern is both very probable and also very dangerous because the new partner is likely to falsify the very information that is most trusted. Indeed, data suggest that, although Type B secure/balanced individuals are most likely to select a similar partner, Types A and C are equally likely to select the same or the opposite pattern (Crittenden, Partridge, & Claussen, 1991). When partners' strategies are organized in opposite ways, there is risk that selecting an "opposite" partner will result in severe disappointments, unnecessary provocation when strategies misfire, and, potentially, violence. However, nothing is simple. Choosing a partner with an opposite strategy also gives the dyad the advantages of both sorts of truth. It may work—sometimes in exciting and creative ways (Crittenden, 1997a).

C. How Do These Principles Affect the Patterning of Relationships?

Many researchers have created models of human personality and/or relationship. I have already referenced two for which there are substantial empirical data in childhood. Baumrind's model of three types of parental styles with matching types of child functioning is quite similar to Ainsworth's model of secure, avoidant, and ambivalent attachment. The constructs emphasized by Baumrind and Ainsworth are different, but compatible. Moreover, the two approaches would cluster dyads similarly. I have tried in the discussion above to tie the models together with the glue of evolutionary biology, social learning theory, cognitive development theory (both Piagetian and Vygotskiian), and information processing theory. In this section, I attempt to relate this developmental model to several well-known models of adult relationship. I discuss three: Gottman's empirical model, Satir's clinical model, and Olson's more theoretical circumplex model. These are selected because they reflect three academic disciplines, have substantial empirical evidence, and focus on dyads, individuals, and families, respectively.

Gottman's Empirical Model

Gottman's analyses of spousal interaction have yielded three patterns of stable marriages: validating, volatile, conflict-avoiding (Gottman, 1993). These are highly analogous to the attachment Types B, C, and A, respectively.

Gottman also found two unstable patterns that often result in divorce or separation; these are best described as negative extensions of the volatile and conflict-avoiding patterns: hostile and hostile-detached, respectively.

Gottman's empirically-based conceptualization fits quite closely the developmental theory offered here in which the more extreme edges of the A and C patterns become progressively more distorted. There are some important differences, however. In the model offered here, false information is considered critical to understanding the meaning of dyadic communications; Gottman addresses only displayed (and, presumably, true) affect. Second, the patterns presented here reflect the outcome of a developmental process; this process, although not necessarily linear, is helpful in understanding the learning history and motivation behind apparently "dysfunctional" behavior. Finally, Gottman studied patterns that can be discerned in a single session of interaction. The perspective being offered here suggests that these interactions form larger patterns that function to promote protection and reproduction, given conditions as they are represented in each partner's mind. Discerning the two-sided, threatening-disarming coercive strategy, in particular, may require a larger time frame than an interaction. Nevertheless, Gottman's model, unlike most other models, does not make the implicit presumption that all marriages occur under favorable circumstances, nor that the validating/Type B pattern is necessarily best for everyone. If Gottman's model were expanded to address the situation of couples with histories of danger before and during marriage, then the interactive effects of development, maturation, information processing, and current conditions to patterns of relationship might become clearer. In addition, application of the study of the physiological correlates of affect (Levenson, Carstensen, & Gottman, 1994) to false affect might help to identify the internal process underlying the patterns.

Satir's Clinical Model

Satir's "model" is less formal than those of the other theorists considered here (Satir, 1972). On the other hand, it has the detail and complexity typical of real people that are often missing from highly structured models. Of particular interest are Satir's four patterns of communication: blaming, placating, distracting, and computing; the physical stances that she associates with these patterns are highly consistent with the non-verbal behaviors that I have found in preschool-age threatening, disarming, and defended children, respectively. Satir proposes that the blaming and placating patterns are frequently found together in parent–child and spousal dyads, whereas the computing pattern is affectively distancing. This is compatible with my notion of the coercive strategy of threats and bribes (with humor or incompetence functioning as distractors in a coercive-disarming pattern) and of the defended strategy as a cognitive pattern of inhibition of affect. It is also consistent with Gottman's observations of couples' interactions. In addition, Satir touches on physiological functioning, non-verbal communication, strategies, and deceptive information. Satir seems to have discovered intuitively most of the components of the integrated theory that I offer, even though the components are less fully articulated than in later models.

Olson's Theoretical Circumplex Model

Olson's model is the most abstract and best organized of the three models. Olson proposes that families vary on two dimensions, cohesion and adaptation, and that being extreme on either dimension creates risk (Olson, 1989). Thus, both disengaged and enmeshed families show risk with regard to cohesion, whereas both rigid and chaotic families show risk with regard to adaptation. It is noteworthy that the disengaged/rigid combination is similar to the attachment Type A, the enmeshed/chaotic combination to Type C, and the less frequent disengaged/chaotic and enmeshed/rigid combinations similar to Type A/C. Olson conceptualizes balanced families as most adaptive and families who are extreme on both dimensions as dysfunctional. The organization is quite similar to my proposed two-dimensional model in which both balance and flexibility are desirable. Unlike my model, however, Olson does not consider the family/environment interactions that might give rise to extreme patterns that are adaptive, given their context (see Crittenden & Claussen, in press). Finally, viewed from the family level, Gottman, Satir, and Olson appear to cluster families similarly and in ways that are compatible with Baumrind and Ainsworth.

A More Comprehensive Model

This review of models of relationship suggests general agreement on the major dimensions differentiating relationships. The models described here as well as other empirical data and models (e.g., Block & Block, 1980; Caspi, Bem, & Elder, 1989; Caspi & Silva, in press; Hazan & Shaver, 1987; Pulkkinen, 1995) all identify well-functioning relationships as having both warmth/closeness (affect) and predictable structure (cognition). Patterson's social-interactional model (Patterson, 1982) is even more similar to the dynamic-maturational approach. The process that Patterson describes from early childhood to early adulthood is compatible with that offered here as is the bi-directional approach to effects within families. Missing from Patterson's model is the notion of coercion including disarming behavior and the underlying perspective of organization around predicting and preventing danger. These notions are not, however, incompatible with Patterson's thinking.

My second dimension of integration enters several of the models as the notion of balance. There is less agreement on the pattern of organization and little attention to the evaluative aspect of the models (i.e., defining a "good" relationship). In addition, the models do not explain pathological behavior well or the complexity of relations among relationships (within families, across the life span, or cross-generationally.)

One advantage of the conceptualization that I offer is that it accounts for deception (false information) with regard to both feelings and intentions in ways that (1) reflect familiar patterns of pathological behavior and (2) suggest the contexts in which these patterns represent successful adaptations. Because it was constructed from a developmental perspective, it encourages open-ended consideration of the issue of change and continuity. Furthermore, it focuses on the two functional issues of protection and reproduction, thus creating a relatively unbiased, culture-free, non-pejorative means of evaluating relationship strategies (Crittenden, 2000b).

Finally, the model that I propose is probabilistic rather than deterministic. Organisms use strategies that have probabilities of achieving their function. When the function is not fulfilled, when the organism changes as a function of maturation, or when the environment changes, both the behaviors used to implement strategies and the strategies themselves may change. This creates both continuity and change such that early relationships have a clear effect on the organization of later relationships without the effect necessarily being linear or accounting for all of the variance. With a wider range of variation in patterns, more reliable and valid classificatory procedures, and acceptance of the meshing of opposite patterns (i.e., Type A with Type C), the amount of variance accounted for should increase, but is still unlikely to be fully predictive. Chance occurrences, unique genetic influences, changing environmental conditions (not tied to individuals' functioning), and maturation all influence the development of relationships in dynamic (but lawful) ways.

D. How Do Childhood Experiences in Relationships Affect the Pattern of Later Relationships?

A central issue in the study of development and psychopathology has been the extent to which early experience in relationships affects the pattern of later relationships. This can be approached in several ways. The least complex is to ask if early experience with troubled relationships has predictable and detrimental outcomes at later ages. Another approach is to ask whether patterning of relationship is tied predictably to patterning later in life. Finally, one can ask whether parents' patterns are predictive of children's patterns.

Negative Relationship Events in Early Life

There are many studies demonstrating that poor family relationships in childhood are related to less optimal outcomes later in life. For example, families with high conflict have adolescents with higher anxiety, depression, and stress-related psychosomatic symptoms in adolescence (Mechanic & Hansell, 1989). Similarly, children, especially girls, whose parents divorced are likely to marry at younger ages, have children at younger ages, and have more children out of wedlock (McLanahan & Bumpass, 1988). There are similar outcomes for children whose parents engaged in spousal violence (Seltzer & Kalmuss, 1988); moreover, in some cases, parental violence results in adolescent violence to the parents (Peek, Fischer, & Kidwell, 1985). Viewing relationships from children's contributions produces similar findings: children showing anti-social behavior in childhood disproportionately experience alcoholism, divorce, mental illness, criminality, family violence, and welfare dependency (Caspi, Elder, & Bem, 1987; Farrington, 1983; Robins & Ratcliff, 1979). A pervasive hypothesis is that experiencing abuse as a child leads to being abusive as an adult. Nevertheless, it is clear that most abused children do not abuse their own children (Starr, 1979). Although Emery's (1988) conclusion that most families have multiple problems and the causal relation among these is unclear, it appears that whenever safety or reproduction are threatened, the risk of undesirable outcomes is increased.

Patterning of Relationships

The broad empirical base of studies of infant attachment has made clear the relation between anxious attachment in infancy and undesirable outcomes later (Ainsworth, 1985). These include reduced problem-solving competence (Matas, Arhend, & Sroufe, 1978), increased tantrumming, aggression, and ignoring of mothers (Sroufe, 1982), greater emotional dependence and need for attention (Sroufe, Fox, & Pancake, 1983), and greater risk for attentional disorders (Jacobvitz & Sroufe, 1987).

Findings of continuity are not limited to studies of attachment. There are a number of studies that compare the patterns of parental behavior with children's resulting behavior and personality. An early study of character development found that parents who were (a) consistent, warm, and predictable had well-adjusted, rational, and altruistic children, whereas those who were (b) inconsistent had expedient, manipulative children, (c) consistently autocratic had conforming children, and (d) rejecting and inconsistent had amoral children (Peck & Havighurst, 1960). Again, these findings are consistent with the Types B, C, A, and A/C, respectively, as well as with Baumrind's patterns in adolescence when the mixed rejecting/neglecting pattern is added (Baumrind, 1991). The power of the combination of negative styles (i.e., A/C styled patterns) to leave children unprepared for reciprocal, supportive relationships has been replicated in the literature on conduct-disordered and delinquent boys (Patterson, DeBaryshe, & Ramsey, 1989), child maltreatment (Crittenden, 1985, 1988), and bi-polar depression (Radke-Yarrow, Cummings, Kuczynski, Chapman, 1985).

Thus, there is strong evidence that patterns of parental behavior have predictable effects on later child functioning when child outcomes are clustered functionally. That is, everyone finds that (a) predictable parental harshness yields conforming, rule-abiding, inhibited children and adolescents whereas (b) inconsistent, permissive parenting yields acting out, hyperactive, conduct-disordered children and (c) children who experience both conditions become antisocial in ways that may become dangerous. Nevertheless, there are three important limitations to these studies. First, they do not account for all the variance; not all children show the predicted problems. Second, they do not clarify which behavior, within a functional class, will be shown by a given child. Finally, they do not explain the motivation or internal process for either parents or children. Because it is clear that the patterns, especially the less desirable patterns, are very difficult to change, understanding the motivation and process behind the patterns is very important.

Child and Parent Patterns

A number of investigations using the attachment model have explored the direct effect of parents' pattern of attachment on children's pattern of attachment. Many have found evidence of continuity from adulthood to childhood in the next generation (Benoit & Parker, 1994; Crittenden, 1985; Crittenden, Partridge, & Claussen, 1991; Fonagy, Steele, & Steele, Leigh, Kennedy, & Target, 1995; Grossmann, Fremmer-Bombik, Rudolph, & Grossmann, 1988; Main, Kaplan, & Cassidy, 1985). Based on van IJzendoorn's meta-analysis of 18 samples, approximately 22% of the variance in infant pattern could be accounted for by parental *Adult Attachment Interview* patterns (van IJzendoorn, 1995). Nevertheless, there are reasons for caution in interpreting these data. First, the proportion of variance accounted for by the continuity hypothesis is meaningful, but insufficient to preclude additional hypotheses. For example, my colleagues and I point to the "opposites" effect, i.e., children having the opposite pattern from adults (Crittenden, Partridge, & Clausen, 1991). Second, the *Adult Attachment Interview* (Main & Goldwyn, in press) is not a measure of adult attachments; on the contrary, it was *constructed* to match the known patterns of adults' children. A true assessment of adult relationships with partners, parents, or children might yield a different pattern of relations with child attachment. Third, the Main and Goldwyn attachment classificatory system in adulthood is based directly on the infancy system and does not reflect changes in the organization of attachment that may occur after infancy. Further exploration of the nature of relationships after infancy and, especially, after puberty is needed. In particular, I recommend attending to the possibility of increasing complexity in organization and the use of various sorts of deception (of both self and others). For a dynamic-maturational approach, see Crittenden (1998a). Finally, the *Adult Attachment Interview* assesses verbal responses to an interview whereas children experience the effects of parental behavior; the relation between what parents believe and remember and what they do may not be exact. In conclusion, there is good reason to believe that parents' management of relationships affects children's strategies for managing relationships, but the scope of the relation is probably more complex than a simple linear effect of continuity (Crittenden, 2000a).

E. How Can This Theory Inform Clinical Intervention?

Troubled relationships usually involve both distorted patterns of behavior and shattered expectations. Behavioral therapies that change behavior by changing eliciting and reinforcing conditions are often used to modify interactive patterns. Such interventions are, however, quite fragile. In fact, the recommended method of testing such an intervention, the ABAB design, is itself proof that the change is in temporal contingencies and not in individuals or relationships. Interventions are needed that change the participants in enduring ways.

Changing expectations, i.e., internal representational models, may help to accomplish this. Many therapies, including in particular the cognitive therapies, attempt to identify and change generalized belief and value systems. A risk is that the client will emerge from therapy well-adjusted to current circumstances, i.e., with reasonably accurate internal representations models of self and other, only to find that new life changes unsettle the balance and problems reappear. On the other hand, if internal representational models are framed as working approximations of an ever-changing reality and if clients are taught how to perceive new and important information and how to use it to reorganize both models and behavior, they may learn mental processes of assimilation and accommodation that will promote an evolving, synergetic balance between self and environment. Such a balance, one that is constantly being remade, may promote both enduring relationships and also safety and opportunity to reproduce in changing circumstances. The focus must, however, be on the process of opening models to new information and change rather than on correcting their content.[3]

Changing strategies requires that one knows the goal or function of the strategy. This chapter has focused on the functions of protection and reproduction as central to intimate relationships. Framing relationship disorders as attempts to maximize protection and reproductive opportunity, given the prior experience of the individual, can focus therapists on demonstrating to clients that historical conditions are no longer applicable and why, therefore, new strategies are needed. Diagnostically, knowledge of the strategies and of false affect and cognition can enable therapists to interpret accurately the presence of fear, anger, and desire for comfort, even when these are not overtly apparent. Cognitive-behavioral therapies accomplish some of this, but do not adequately account for the evolved function of affect: indeed, they are often too rational, even about affect.

Clinically, troubled couples and parent–child dyads need to understand one another's strategies, to develop compassion for the conditions that elicited partners' strategies, and to behave in ways that create comfort and the opportunity to relinquish the strategy. This does not mean behaving in ways that thwart the strategy. Finally, adults who have repeatedly engaged in destructive relationships could be helped by understanding the two sides of the coercive pattern and the tendency of Type A and C adults to be attracted to one another. In both cases, appearances are deceiving. When adults better

---

[3]The attachment literature often refers to "working" models, i.e., models used to make predictions. I have avoided that term and used the more specific terms "dispositional" and "internal representational" models because most models, including very distorted models, are working models (Crittenden, 1997b)

understand both their own strategy and the strategies of those whom they are likely to attract, they become better able to make balanced decisions about relationships. This is especially true if they learn to recognize the ways in which they distort information. It is important, however, for therapists to realize that these distortions and the strategies serve a purpose. If that purpose remains valid, the distortions and strategies will be maintained.

E. An Overview of a Theory of Relationship and Continuity in Relationship

In this paper I offer a dynamic-maturational theory regarding the development of relationships. Of course, there are already many such theories and typologies. One might wonder if yet another is needed. I propose that further theory development may be valuable if the theory (a) explains commonalities among a variety of empirically, clinically, and theoretically derived theories, (b) offers a simple structure while, nevertheless, accounting for wide variation in human behavior, (c) is developmental in nature such that it not only accounts for incremental change over time, but also accounts for periods of rapid maturational change, (d) is framed in terms of processes rather than traits, events, or conditions, (e) is interactional in accounting for human evolution, genetic variation, child-rearing contexts, and cultural variations, (f) addresses the development of both typical and atypical personalities, and (g) has implications for parenting, under both normative and risk conditions, and for treatment under conditions of maladaptation. I am proposing, in other words, theory that is both familiar in that it is drawn from existing research and theory and novel in that it integrates these in new ways that have implications for further research and for practical applications.

The dynamic-maturational theory that I offer proposes a model of human adaptation with two dimensions, source of information (i.e., cognition and affect) and degree of integration. These two dimensions interact around the functions of protection and reproduction. Evolved brain structures function to transform sensory stimulation into meaningful cognitive information about causal relations and affective information about contexts, whereas experiential learning enables organisms to adapt these to unique life circumstances. The process of learning occurs in the context of relationships, and its outcomes, internal representational models and patterns of behavior, are repeatedly modified both by maturation and by change in circumstances. The modifications, however, are biased by innate and universal tendencies of mental functioning. These biases make early conditions disproportionately important to interpretation of present conditions and present conditions disproportionately important to current modeling and behavior. As a consequence, internal representational models become emergent phenomena to be assessed as processes rather than static conditions that can be defined finitely; indeed, models should be evaluated in terms of openness to discrepant information. Viewed this way, security is not a state; it is a particular strategy of open and direct communication and mental processing in which minor adjustments to internal representational models and behavioral strategies are constantly being made to maintain a dynamic balance between self and context. Adaptation, on the other hand, implies recognition of all the transformations of information and use of all the strategies, at the appropriate time and in the appropriate context.

Thus, the overall model is one of dynamic balance among sources of information and response strategies that, when adaptive, maximizes the flexibility of human response, thus promoting protection and reproduction under varying conditions (Crittenden, in press c). In addition, the model differentiates behavior from the functions that it serves, thus permitting wide variation in behavior as a consequence of variation in both heritable characteristics and environmental contexts. Three basic relationship strategies are proposed: balanced, defended, and coercive, together with a fourth, defended/coercive. As with all systems theories, functional organization, and not specific behaviors, is the central focus. Various levels of analysis, including genes, neurological structures, mental structures (e.g., dispositional models), behavior, individuals, dyads, families, and contexts are integrated into a hierarchy of interrelated systems. Finally, an important contribution of the model is to include the notion of false information, thus addressing both normative problems of whom to trust and with whom to form enduring relationships and also issues of psychopathology. Of course, full integration of these ideas cannot be accomplished in a chapter.

Nevertheless, something can be said that may be useful to all the relationships that end in disappointment. If the perspective offered here reflects a somewhat more accurate representation of human relationships than the models from which it has been derived, then we might conclude that individuals using coercive or defended strategies are more likely to delude both themselves and their partners. They are also more likely to misconstrue information and to do so in ways that heighten their perception of danger. If this is accurate, they would also be likely to respond in protective ways to the perceived threat. Finally, they, more than individuals using a balanced strategy, would desire to achieve a state of unchanging safety. Thus, they would expect their partners to remain the same and they would fail to adjust to change until the evidence of change was too discrepant to ignore. The change when noticed might well be perceived as alarming and elicit protective efforts to regain the prior balance. However, nothing stays the same and nothing goes backwards. Put in the abstract language of theory, healthy couples and healthy parent–child relationships are more "open" to new information and change than models in less healthy relationships. Thus, the "openness" of mental functioning may be critical to behavioral harmony and ultimate adaptiveness.

I cannot prove all of these assertions. That was never the goal. Instead, the goal was to use the existing literature to generate an integrative theory regarding the effect of early relationships on later relationships. I have tried to make the dynamic-maturational theory that I offer internally consistent and testable. Hopefully, enough empirical support has been offered to suggest the plausibility of the theory and enough applications suggested to indicate the importance of empirical testing and refinement of the theory.

REFERENCES

Aboud, F. E. (1993). The developmental psychology of racial prejudice. *Transcultural Psychiatric Research Review*, **30**, 229–242.

Aboud, F. E., & Doyle, A. B. (1995). The development of in-group pride in Black Canadians. *Journal of Cross-Cultural Psychology*, **26**, 243–254.

Abramovitch, R., Corter, C., Pepler, D. J., & Stanhope, L. (1986). Sibling and peer interaction: A final follow-up and a comparison. *Child Development*, **57**, 217–229.

Acitelli, L. K. (1988). When spouses talk to each other about their relationship. *Journal of Social and Personal Relationships*, **5**, 185–199

Acitelli, L. K. (1993). You, me, and us: Perspectives on relationship awareness. In S. W. Duck (Ed.), *Understanding relationship processes 1: Individuals in relationships.* (pp. 144–174.). Newbury Park, CA: Sage.

Acitelli, L. K. (1995). Disciplines at parallel play. *Journal of Social and Personal Relationships*, **12**, 589–596.

Adalbjarnardottir, S. (1995). How schoolchildren propose to negotiate: The role of social withdrawal, social anxiety, and locus of control. *Child Development*, **66**, 1739–1751.

Ainsworth, M. D. S. (1979). Infant–mother attachment. *American Psychologist*, **34**, 932–937.

Ainsworth, M. D. S. (1985). Patterns of infant–mother attachment: antecedents and effects on development. *Bulletin of the New York Academy of Medicine*, **61**, 771–791.

Ainsworth, M. D. S., Blehar, M. C., Waters, E., & Wall, S. (1978). *Patterns of attachment: Assessed in the strange situation and at home.* Hillsdale, NJ: Erlbaum.

Alessandri, S. M., & Lewis, M. (1993). Parental evaluation and its relation to shame and pride in young children. *Sex Roles*, **29**, 335–343.

Alessandri, S. M., & Lewis, M. (1996). Differences in pride and shame in maltreated and nonmaltreated preschoolers. *Child Development*, **67**, 1857–1869.

Allan, G. A. (1993). *Social contexts of relationships (Understanding relationship processes 3)* (pp. 1–25). Newbury Park, CA: Sage.

Allan, G. A. (1995, June). Friendship, class, status and identity. Paper presented at the meeting of the International Network on Personal Relationships, Williamsburg, VA.

Allport, G. W. (1954). *The nature of prejudice.* Cambridge, MA: Addison-Wesley.

Altshuler, J. L., & Ruble, D.N. (1989). Developmental changes in children's awareness of strategies for coping with uncontrollable stress. *Child Development*, **60**, 1337–1349.

Amir, Y. (1969). Contact hypothesis in ethnic relations. *Psychological Bulletin*, **71**, 319–342.

Arce, A. A., & Torres-Matrullo, C. (1982). Application of cognitive behavioral techniques in the treatment of Hispanic patients. *Psychiatric Quarterly*, **54**, 230–236.

Argyle, M., Furnham, A., & Graham, J. (1981). *Social situations.* Cambridge: Cambridge University Press.

Argyle, M., Henderson, M., Bond, M., Iizuka, Y.R., & Contarello, A. (1986). Cross-cultural variations in relationship rules. *International Journal of Psychology*, **21**, 287–315.

Aries, E. (1987). Gender and communication. In P. Shaver & C. Hendrick (Eds). *Review of personality and social psychology: Vol. 7. Sex and gender* (pp. 149–176). Newbury Park, CA: Sage.

Aronfreed, J. (1968). *Conduct and conscience*. New York: Academic Press.

Asendorpf, J. B., & Baudonniere, P. M. (1993). Self-awareness and other awareness: Mirror self-recognition and synchronic imitation among unfamiliar peers. *Developmental Psychology*, **29**, 88–93.

Asher, S. R., & Coie, J. D. (1990). *Peer rejection in childhood*. Cambridge: Cambridge University Press.

Asher, S. R., Markell, R.A., & Hymel, S. (1981). Identifying children at risk in peer relations: A critique of the rate-of-interaction approach to assessment. *Child Development*, **52**, 1239–1245.

Attili, G., Vermigli, P., & Schneider, B. H. (1997). Peer acceptance and friendship patterns of Italian elementary-school children within a cross-cultural perspective. *International Journal of Behavioral Development*, **21**, 277–298.

Ausubel, D. P. (1955). Relationship between shame and guilt in the socialization process. *Psychological Review*, **62**, 378–390.

Averill, J. (1982). *Anger and aggression. An essay on emotion*. New York: Springer.

Bagwell, C. L., Newcomb, A. F., & Bukowski, W. M. (1998). Preadolescent friendship and peer rejection as predictors of adult adjustment. *Child Development*, **69**, 140–153.

Bakan, D. (1966). *The duality of human existence*. Chicago, IL: Rand McNally.

Bakeman, R., & Brownlee, J. R. (1982). Social rules governing object conflicts in toddlers and preschoolers. In K. H. Rubin & H. S. Ross (Eds.), *Peer relationships and social skills in childhood*. New York: Springer-Verlag.

Bank, S., & Kahn, M. (1982). *The sibling bond*. New York: Basic Books.

Barnett, M. A. (1987). Empathy and related responses in children. In N. Eisenberg & J. Strayer (Eds.), *Empathy and its development* (pp. 146–162). Cambridge: Cambridge University Press.

Barrett, D. E. (1979). A naturalistic study of sex differences in children's aggression. *Merrill-Palmer Quarterly*, **25**, 193–203.

Barrett, D. E., & Yarrow, M.R. (1977). Prosocial behavior, social inferential ability, and assertiveness in children. *Child Development*, **48**, 475–481.

Barrett, K. C. (1995). A functionalist approach to shame and guilt. In J.P. Tangney & K.W. Fischer (Eds.), *Self-conscious emotions: The psychology of shame, guilt, embarrassment, and pride (pp. 25–63)*. New York: Guilford.

Barrett, K. C., & Campos, J. J. (1987). Perspectives on emotional development: II. A functionalist approach to emotions. In J. Osofsky (Ed.), *Handbook of infant development* (2nd ed., pp. 555–578). New York: Wiley.

Barrett, K. C., Zahn-Waxler, C., & Cole, P.M. (1993). Avoiders versus amenders—Implications for the investigation of guilt and shame during toddlerhood? *Cognition and Emotion*, **7**, 481–505.

Barrett, P. M., Rapee, R. M., Dadds, M. M., & Ryan, S. M. (1996). Family enhancement of cognitive style in anxious and aggressive children. *Journal of Abnormal Child Psychology*, **24**, 187–203.

Barth, J. M., & Parke, R. D. (1993). Parent–child relationship influences on children's transition to school. *Merrill-Palmer Quarterly*, **39**, 173–195.

Bartholomew, K. (1993). From childhood to adult relationships: Attachment theory and research. In S. Duck (Ed.), *Learning about relationships (Understanding relationship processes series*, Vol. 2, pp. 30–62). Newbury Park, CA: Sage.

Batsche, G. M., & Knoff, H. M. (1994). Bullies and their victims: Understanding a pervasive problem in the schools. *School Psychology Review*, **23**, 165–174.

Baumeister, R. F., & Leary, M. R. (1995). The need to belong: Desire for interpersonal attachments as a fundamental human motivation. *Psychological Bulletin*, **117**, 497–529.

Baumeister, R. F., Stillwell, A. M., & Heatherton, T. F. (1995). Interpersonal aspects of guilt: Evidence from narrative studies. In J. P. Tangney & K. W. Fischer (Eds.), *Self-conscious emotions: The psychology of shame, guilt, embarrassment, and pride (pp. 255–273)*. New York: Guilford.

Baumrind, D. (1967). Child care practices anteceding three patterns of preschool behavior. *Genetic Psychology Monographs*, **75**, 43–88.

Baumrind, D. (1971). Current patterns of parental authority. *Developmental Psychology Monographs*, **4** (No. 1, Pt. 2), 1–103.

Baumrind, D. (1973). The development of instrumental competence through socialization. In A. D. Pick (Ed.), *Minnesota Symposium on Child Psychology*, Vol 7 (pp. 3–46). Minneapolis, MN: University of Minnesota Press.

Baumrind, D. (1991). The influence of parenting style on adolescent competence and substance abuse. *Journal of Early Adolescence*, **11**, 56–95.

Baxter, L. A., & Montgomery, B. M. (1996). *Relating: Dialogues and dialectics*. New York: Guilford.

Baxter, L. A., Mazanec, M., Nicholson, L., Pittman, G., Smith, K., & West, L. (1996). Everyday loyalties and betrayals in personal relationships: A dialectical perspective. *Journal of Social and Personal Relationships*, **14**, 655–678.

Beitel, A., & Parke, R. D. (1985). *Relationships between preschoolers' sociometric factors and emotional decoding ability*. Unpublished manuscript, University of Illinois at Champaign-Urbana, IL.

Bell, D. C., & Bell, L. G. (1989). Micro and macro measurement of family systems concepts. *Journal of Family Psychology*, **3**, 137–157.

Belsky, J. (1984). The determinants of parenting: A process model. *Child Development*, **55**, 83–96.

Bem, S. L. (1985). Androgyny and gender schema theory: A conceptual and empirical integration. In T. B. Sonderegger (Ed.), *Nebraska Symposium on Motivation: Vol. 32. Psychology and gender* (pp. 179–226). Lincoln: University of Nebraska Press.

Benedict, R. (1946). *The chrysanthemum and the sword: Patterns of Japanese culture*. Boston, MA: Houghton-Mifflin.

Benenson, J. F. (1990). Gender differences in social networks. *Journal of Early Adolescence*, **10**, 472–495.

Benenson, J. F., Apostoleris, N. H., & Parnass, J. (1997). Age and sex differences in dyadic and group interaction. *Developmental Psychology*, **33**, 538–543.

Bennett, J., & Berry, J. W. (1992). Notions of competence in people of Northern Ontario. *Papers of the Twenty-Third Algonquin Conference*, 36–50.

Benoit, D., & Parker, K. C. H. (1994). Stability and transmission of attachment across three generations. *Child Development*, **65**, 1444–1457.

Berndt, T. J. (1989). Obtaining support from friends during childhood and adolescence. In D. Belle (Ed.), *Children's social networks and social supports* (pp. 308–331). New York: Wiley.

Berndt, T. J. & Perry, T. B. (1986). Children's perceptions of friendships as supportive relationships. *Developmental Psychology*, **22**, 640–648.

Berscheid, E., & Walster [Hatfield], E. (1969). *Interpersonal attraction*. Reading, MA: Addison-Wesley.

Berscheid, E., & Walster [Hatfield], E. (1978). *Interpersonal attraction, second edition*. Reading, MA: Addison-Wesley.

Berthelson, D., Smith, J., & O'Connor, I. (1996). Young children's adjustment and domestic violence. *Australian Research in Early Childhood Education*, **2**, 1–15.

Bhavnagri, N. (1987). *Parents as facilitators of preschool children's peer relationships*. Unpublished doctoral dissertation, University of Illinois at Champaign-Urbana, IL.

Bhavnagri, N., & Parke, R. D. (1991). Parents as direct facilitators of children's peer relationships: Effects of age of child and sex of parent. *Journal of Personal and Social Relationships*, **8**, 423–440.

Bigelow, B. J. (1977). Children's friendship expectations: A cognitive developmental study. *Child Development*, **48**, 246–253.

Bigelow, B. J., & La Gaipa, J. J. (1980). The development of friendship values and choice. In H. C. Foot, A. J. Chapman, & J. R. Smith (Eds.), *Friendship and social relations in children*. Chichester, UK: Wiley.

Bigelow, B. J., Tesson, G., & Lewko, J. (1996). *Children's rules of friendship*. New York: Guilford.

Biringen, Z., Robinson, J. L., & Emde, R. N. (1994). Maternal sensitivity in the second year: Gender-based relations in the dyadic balance of control. *American Journal of Orthopsychiatry*, **64**, 78–90.

Birnbaum, D. W., & Croll, W. L. (1984). The etiology of children's stereotypes about sex differences in emotionality. *Sex Roles*, **10**, 677–691.

Bischof-Kohler, D. (1988). Uber den Zusammenhang von Empathie und der Fahigkeit, sich im Spiegel zu erkennen [The relationship between empathy and mirror self-recognition]. *Schweizerische Zeitschrift fur Psychologie*, **47**, 147–159, cited in Asendorpf, J.B. & Baudonniere, P. (1993). Self-awareness and other awareness: Mirror self-recognition and synchronic imitation among unfamiliar peers. *Developmental Psychology*, **29**, 88–93.

Bischof-Kohler, D. (1991). The development of empathy in infants. In M. E. Lamb & H. Keller (Eds.), *Infant development: Perspectives from German-speaking countries* (pp. 1–33). Hillsdale, NJ: Erlbaum.

Bjorkqvist, K., Lagerspetz, K. M. J., & Kaukiainen, A. (1992). Do girls manipulate and boys fight? Developmental trends in regard to direct and indirect aggression. *Aggressive Behavior*, **18**, 117–127.

Black, B. (1989). Interactive pretense: Social and symbolic skills in preschool play groups. *Merrill-Palmer Quarterly*, **35**, 379–397.

Black, B. (1992). Negotiating social pretend play: Communication differences related to social status and sex. *Merrill-Palmer Quarterly*, **38(2)**, 212–232.

Black, B., & Hazen, N. L. (1990). Social status and patterns of communication in acquainted and unacquainted preschool children. *Developmental Psychology*, **26**, 379–387.

Black, B., & Logan, A. (1995). Links between communcation patterns in mother–child, father–child, and child–peer interactions and children's social competence. *Child Development*, **66**, 255–271.

Black-Gutman, D., & Hickson, F. (1996). The relationship between racial attitudes and social-cognitive development in children: An Australian study. *Developmental Psychology*, **32**, 448–456.

Block, J. H. (1983). Differential premises arising from differential socialization of the sexes: Some conjectures. *Child Development*, **54**, 1335–1354.

Block, J. H., & Block, J. (1980). The role of ego-control and ego-resiliency in the organization of behavior. In W. A. Collins (Ed.), *Minnesota Symposium on Child Psychology* (Vol. 13, pp. 39–70). Hillsdale, NJ: Erlbaum.

Bolger, K. E., Patterson, C., & Kupersmidt, J. (1998). Peer relationships and self-esteem among children who have been maltreated. *Child Development*, **89**, 1171–1197.

Bolger, N., & Kelleher, S. (1993). Daily life in relationships. *Social contexts of relationships (Understanding relationship processes 3)* (pp. 100–109). Newbury Park, CA: Sage.

Bonacich, P. (1972). Norms and cohesion as adaptive responses to potential conflict: An experimental study. *Sociometry*, **35**, 357–375.

Bond, M. H., & Hwang, K. K. (1986). The social psychology of Chinese people. In M. H. Bond (Ed.), *The psychology of the Chinese people* (pp. 213–266). Oxford: Oxford University Press.

Booth, C., Rubin, K., & Rose-Krasnor, L. (1998). Perceptions of emotional support from mother and friend in middle childhood: Links with social-emotional adaptation and preschool attachment security. *Child Development*, **69**, 427–442.

Bost, K. K., Vaughn, B. E., Newell-Washington, W., Ciclinski, K. L., & Bradbard, M. R. (1998). Social competence, social support, and attachment: Demarcation of construct domains, measurement, and paths of influence for preschool children attending Head Start. *Child Development*, **69**, 192–218.

Boulton, J. B., & Underwood, K. (1992). Bully/victim problems among middle school children. *British Journal of Educational Psychology*, **62**, 73–87.

Boulton, M. J. (1995a). Patterns of bully/victim problems in mixed race groups of children. *Social Development*, **4**, 277–293.

Boulton, M. J. (1995b). Playground behavior and peer interaction patterns of primary school boys classified as bullies, victims, and not involved. *British Journal of Educational Psychology*, **65**, 165–177.

Boulton, M. J., & Smith, P. K. (1994). Bully/victim problems in middle-school children: Stability, self-perceived competence, peer perceptions, and peer acceptance. *British Journal of Developmental Psychology*, **12**, 315–329.

Bowers, L., Smith, P. K., & Binney, V. A. (1992). Cohesion and power in the families of children involved in bully/victim problems at school. *Journal of Family Therapy*, **14**, 371–387.

Bowers, L., Smith, P. K., & Binney, V. A. (1994). Perceived family relationships of bullies, victims and bully/victims in middle childhood. *Journal of Social and Personal Relationships*, **11**, 215–232.

Bowlby, J. (1969/1982). *Attachment and loss, Vol. I. Attachment.* (2nd ed.) New York: Basic Books.

Bowlby, J. (1973). *Attachment and loss, Vol. II. Separation: Anxiety and anger.* New York: Basic Books.

Bowlby, J. (1980). *Attachment and loss: Vol. III. Loss, sadness and depression.* New York: Basic Books.

Bowlby, J. (1988). *A secure base: Parent–child attachment and healthy human development.* New York: Basic Books.

Boyum, L., & Parke, R. D. (1995). Family emotional expressiveness and children's social competence. *Journal of Marriage and Family*, **57**, 593–608.

Bradbury, T. N., & Fincham, F. D. (1989). Behavior and satisfaction in marriage: Prospective mediating processes. *Review of Personality and Social Psychology*, **10**, 119–143.

Braha, V., & Rutter, D. R. (1980). Friendship choice in a mixed-race primary school. *Educational Studies*, **6**, 217–223.

Bretherton, I. (1987). New perspectives on attachment relations: Security, communication, and internal working models. In J. D. Osofsky (Ed.), *Handbook of infant development* (pp. 1061–1100). New York: Wiley.

Bretherton, I. (1990). Open communication and internal working models: Their role in the development of attachment relationships. In R. A. Thompson (Ed.), *Nebraska Symposium on Motivation: Vol. 36. Socioemotional development* (pp. 57–113). Lincoln, NB: University of Nebraska Press.

Bretherton, I., & Waters, E. (Eds.). (1985). Growing points of attachment theory and research. *Monographs of the Society for Research in Child Development*, **50**(1–2, Serial No. 209).

Bretherton, I., Fritz, J., Zahn-Waxler, C., & Ridgeway, D. (1986). Learning to talk about emotions: A functionalist perspective. *Child Development*, **57**, 529–548.

Bridges, L. J., Connell, J. P., & Belsky, J. (1988). Similarities and differences in infant–mother and infant–father interaction in the Strange Situation: A component process analysis. *Developmental Psychology*, **24**, 92–100.

Brody, G. H., Stoneman, Z., & McCoy, J. K. (1994). Forecasting sibling relationships in early adolescence from child temperaments and family process in middle childhood. *Child Development*, **65**, 771–784.

Brody, G. H., Stoneman, Z., & MacKinnon, C. E. (1982). Role asymmetries in interactions among school-aged children, their younger siblings, and their friends. *Child Development*, **53**, 1364–1370.

Brody, G. H., Stoneman, Z., McCoy, J. K., & Forehand, R. (1992). Contemporaneous and longitudinal associations of sibling conflict with family relationship assessments and family discussions about sibling problems. *Child Development*, **63**, 391–400.

Brody, L. R., & Hall, J. A. (1993). Gender and emotion. In M. Lewis & J. M. Haviland (Eds.), *Handbook of emotions* (pp. 447–460). New York: Guilford.

Bronfenbrenner, U. (1970). *Two worlds of childhood: U.S. and U.S.S.R.* New York: Russell Sage.

Bronfenbrenner, U. (1979). *The ecology of human development*. New York: Harvard University Press.

Bronfenbrenner, U., & Morris, P. A. (1998). The ecology of developmental processes. In W. Damon (Series Ed.) & R. M. Lerner (Vol. Ed.), *Handbook of child psychology: Vol. 1. Theoretical models of human development* 5th ed., pp. 993–1028). New York: Wiley.

Brown, J., & Dunn, J. (1992). Talk with your mother or your sibling? Developmental changes in early family conversations about feelings. *Child Development*, **63**, 336–349.

Brown, J., Donelan-McCall, M., & Dunn, J. (1996). Why talk about mental states? The significance of children's conversations with friends, siblings, and mothers. *Child Development*, **67**, 836–849.

Brownell, C. A., & Carriger, M. S. (1990). Changes in cooperation and self-other differentiation during the second year. *Child Development*, **61**, 1164–1174.

Bruner, J. (1990). *Acts of meaning*. Cambridge, MA: Harvard University Press.

Bryant, B. K. (1985). The neighborhood walk: Sources of support in middle childhood. *Monographs of the Society for Research in Child Development*, **50** (3, Serial No. 210). Chicago, IL: University of Chicago Press.

Bryant, B. K. (1989). The child's perspective of sibling caretaking and its relevance to understanding social-emotional functioning and development. In P. G. Zukow (Ed.), *Sibling interaction across cultures: Theoretical and methodological issues*. New York: Springer-Verlag.

Bryant, B. K. (1992). Conflict resolution strategies in relation to children's peer relations. *Journal of Applied Developmental Psychology*, **13**, 35–50.

Bryant, B. K., & Litman, C. (1987). Siblings as teachers and therapists. *Journal of Children in Contemporary Society*, **19**, 185–205.

Bryant, B., & Crockenberg, S. (1980). Correlates and dimensions of prosocial behavior: A study of female siblings with their mothers. *Child Development*, **51**, 529–544.

Buck, R. (1975). Nonverbal communication of affect in children. *Journal of Personality and Social Psychology*, **31**, 644–653.

Bugental, D. B. (1992). Affective and cognitive process within threat-oriented family systems. In I. Sigel, A. V. McGillicuddy-Delisi, & J. J. Goodnow (Eds.), *Parental belief systems: The psychological consequences for children* (2nd ed., pp. 219–248). Hillsdale, NJ: Erlbaum.

Bugental, D. B., & Goodnow, J. J. (1998). Socialization processes. In W. Damon (Series Ed.) & N. Eisenberg (Vol. Ed.), *Handbook of child psychology: Vol. 3. Social, emotional, and personality development* (5th ed., pp. 389–462). New York: Wiley.

Bugental, D. B., & Happaney, K. H. (in press). Parent–child interaction as a power contest. *Journal of Applied Developmental Psychology*.

Bugental, D. B., & Lin, E. K. (1997). Attention-grabbing vocal signals: Impact on information processing and expectations. *Personality and Social Psychology Bulletin*, **23**, 965–973.

Bugental, D. B., Blue, J., Cortez, V., Fleck, K., & Rodriguez, A. (1992). Influences of witnessed affect on information processing in children. *Child Development*, **63**, 774–786.

Bugental, D. B., Blue, J., Cortez, V., Fleck, K., Kopeikin, H., Lewis, J. D., & Lyon, J. (1993). Social cognitions as organizers of autonomic and affective responses to social challenge. *Journal of Personality and Social Psychology*, **64**, 1–10.

Bugental, D. B., Brown, M., & Reiss, C. (1996). Cognitive representations of power in caregiving relationships: Biasing effects on interpersonal interaction and information processing. *Journal of Family Psychology*, **10**, 397–407.

Bugental, D. B., Lyon, J. E., Lin, E. K., McGrath, E. P., & Bimbela, A. (1999). Children "tune out" in response to the ambiguous communication style of powerless adults. *Child Development*, **70**, 214–230.

Buhrmester, D. (1990). Intimacy of friendship, interpersonal competence, and adjustment during preadolescence and adolescence. *Child Development*, **61**, 1101–1111.

Buhrmester, D., & Furman, W. (1987). The development of companionship and intimacy. *Child Development*, **58**, 1101–1113.

Buhrmester, D., & Furman, W. (1990). Perceptions of sibling relationships during middle childhood and adolescence. *Child Development*, **61**, 1387–1398.

Burks, V. M., & Parke, R. D. (1996). Parent and child representations of social relationships: Linkages between families and peers. *Merrill-Palmer Quarterly*, **42**, 358–378.

Burks, V. M., Carson, J. L., & Parke, R. D. (1987). *Parent–child interactional styles of popular and rejected children*. Unpublished manuscript, University of Illinois at Champaign-Urbana, IL.

Buss, A. (1980). *Self-consciousness and social anxiety*. San Francisco, CA: W. H. Freeman.

Buss, A. H. (1989). Temperament as personality trait. In G. A. Kohnstamm, J. E. Bates, & M. K. Rothbart (Eds.), *Temperament in childhood* (pp. 49–58). Chichester, UK: Wiley.

Buss, D. M. (1994). *The evolution of desire: Strategies of human mating*. New York: Basic Books.

Byrne, B. J. (1994). Bullies and victims in a school setting with reference to some Dublin schools. *Irish Journal of Psychology*, **15**, 574–586.

Cairns, R. B., Cairns, B. D., Neckerman, H. J., Gest, S. D., & Gariepy, J. L. (1988). Social networks and aggressive behavior: Peer support or peer rejection? *Developmental Psychology*, **24**, 815–823.

Callondann, A. (1995). *Geschwister und Ärger—Eine Untersuchung zur Ärgerregulierung im Zusammenhang mit der Qualität der Geschwisterbeziehung*. Unpublished MA Thesis, Freie Universität Berlin.

Campos, J. J., Campos, R., & Barrett, K. C. (1990). Emergent themes in the study of emotional development and emotion regulation. *Developmental Psychology*, **25**, 394–402.

Camras, L. (1977). Facial expressions used by children in a conflict situation. *Child Development*, **48**, 1431–1435.

Canary, D. J., & Dindia, K. (Eds.). (1998). *Sex differences and similarities in communication*. Mahwah, NJ: Erlbaum.

Canary, D. J., & Emmers-Sommer, T. M. (1997). *Sex differences in personal relationships*. New York: Guilford.

Carson, J., & Parke, R. D. (1996). Reciprocal negative affect in parent–child interactions and children's peer competency. *Child Development*, **67**, 2217–2226.

Carson, J., & Parke, R. D. (1998). Children's production and recognition of emotion: Family vs. outsider views. Unpublished manuscript. University of California at Riverside, CA.

Case, R. (1991). Stages in the development of the young child's first sense of self. *Developmental Review*, **11**, 210–230.

Casiglia, A. C., LoCoco, A., & Zappulla, C. (1998). Aspects of social reputation and peer relationships in Italian children: A cross-cultural perspective. *Developmental Psychology*, **34**, 723–730.

Caspi, A. (1998). Personality development across the life course. In W. Damon (Series Ed.) & N. Eisenberg (Vol. Ed.), *Handbook of child psychology: Volume 3. Social, emotional, and personality development* (5th ed., pp. 311–388). New York: Wiley.

Caspi, A., & Silva, P. A. (1995). Temperamental qualities at age three predict personality traits in young adulthood: Longitudinal evidence from a birth cohort. *Child Development*, **66**, 486–498.

Caspi, A., Bem, D. J., & Elder, G. H. (1989). Continuities and consequences of interactional styles across the life course. *Journal of Personality*, **57**, 375–406.

Caspi, G. H., Elder, G. H., & Bem, D. J. (1987). Moving against the world: Life courses of explosive children. *Developmental Psychology*, **23**, 308–313.

Cassidy, J. (1994). Emotion regulation: Influences of attachment relationships. In N. A. Fox (Ed.), The development of emotion regulation: Biological and behavioral considerations. *Monographs of the Society for Research in Child Development*, **59**(2–3, Serial No. 240), 216–233.

Cassidy, J., Kirsh, S. J., Scolton, K. L., & Parke, R. D. (1996). Attachment and representations of peer relationships. *Developmental Psychology*, **32**, 892–904.

Cassidy, J., Parke, R. D., Butkovsky, L., & Braungart, J. (1992). Family–peer connections: The roles of emotional expressiveness within the family and children's understanding of emotions. *Child Development*, **63**, 603–618.

Cavell, T. A. (1990). Social adjustment, social performance, and social skills: A tricomponent model of social competence. *Journal of Clinical Child Psychology*, **19**, 111–122.

Cervantes, C. A., & Callanan, M. A. (1998). Labels and explanations in mother-child emotion talk: Age and gender differentiation. *Developmental Psychology*, **34**, 88–98.

Cha, J. H. (1994). Aspects of individualism and collectivism in Korea. In U. Kim, H. C. Triandis, C. Kagitcibasi, S. Choi, & G. Yoon (Eds.), *Individualism and collectivism: Theory, methods, and applications* (pp.157–174). Thousand Oaks, CA: Sage.

Chao, P. (1983). *Chinese kinship*. London: Kegan Paul.

Chapman, A. J. (1976). Social aspects of humorous laughter. In A. J. Chapman & H. C. Foot (Eds.), *Humour and laughter: Theory, research and applications* (pp 51–78). London: Wiley.

Chapman, A. J., Smith, J. R., & Foot, H. C. (1980). Humor, laughter and social interaction. In P. McGhee & A. Chapman (Eds.), *Children's humour* (pp 21–39). New York: Wiley.

Chen, C., & Uttal, D. H. (1988). Cultural values, parents' beliefs, and children's achievement in the United Sates and China. *Human Development*, **31**, 351–358.

Chen, X., & Li, B. (in press). Depressed mood in Chinese children: Developmental significance for social and school adjustment. *International Journal of Behavioral Development*.

Chen, X., & Rubin, K. H. (1992). Correlates of peer acceptance in a Chinese sample of six-year olds. *International Journal of Behavioral Development*, **15**, 259–273.

Chen, X., Rubin, K. H., & Li, Z. Y. (1994, July). *Social functioning and adjustment in Chinese children: A longitudinal study*. Paper presented at the meeting of the International Society for the Study of Behavioural Development, Amsterdam, Netherlands.

Chen, X., Rubin, K. H., & Sun, Y. (1992). Social reputation and peer relationships in Chinese and Canadian children: A cross-cultural study. *Child Development*, **63**, 1336–1343.

Chen, X., Rubin, K. H., Li, B., & Li, D. (in press). Academic outcomes and social functioning in Chinese children. *Developmental Psychology*.

Chiu, C. Y., Tsang, S. C., & Yang, C. F. (1988). The role of face situation and attitudinal antecedents in Chinese consumer complaint behavior. *The Journal of Social Psychology*, **128**, 173–180.

Chodorow, N. (1978). *The reproduction of mothering: Psychoanalysis and the sociology of gender*. Berkeley, CA: University of California Press.

Chung, T-Y., & Asher, S. R. (1996). Children's goals and strategies in peer conflict situations. *Merrill-Palmer Quarterly*, **42**, 125–147.

Clark, M. L. & Ayers, M. (1988). The role of reciprocity and proximity in junior high school friendships. *Journal of Youth & Adolescence*, **17**, 403–407.

Clark, M. L., & Ayers, M. (1992). Friendship similarity during early adolescence: Gender and racial patterns. *Journal of Psychology*, **126**, 393–405.

Clark, M. S., & Mills, J. (1979). Interpersonal attraction in exchange and communal relationships. *Journal of Personality and Social Psychology*, **54**, 1201–1226.

Cochran, M., & Niego, S. (1995). Parenting and social networks. In M. C. Bornstein (Ed.), *Handbook of parenting* (Vol.3., pp. 393–418). Mahwah, NJ: Erlbaum.

Cochran, M., Larner, M., Riley, D., Gunnarsson, L., & Henderson, C. R. (1990). *Extending families*. New York: Cambridge University Press.

Cohn, J. F., & Elmore, M. (1988). Effect of contingent changes in mothers' affective expression on the organization of behavior in 3-month-old infants. *Infant Behavior and Development*, **11**, 493–505.

Coie, J. D. (1985). Fitting social skills intervention to the target group. In B. H. Schneider, K. H. Rubin, & J. E. Ledingham (Eds.), *Children's peer relations: Issues in assessment* (pp. 141–171). New York: Springer-Verlag.

Coie, J. D., Dodge, K. A., & Coppotelli, H. (1982). Dimensions and types of social status: A cross-age perspective. *Developmental Psychology*, **18**, 557–570.

Coie, J. D., Rabiner, D., & Lochman, J. (1987). Promoting peer relations in a school setting. In L. Bond & B. Compas (Eds.), *Primary prevention and promotion in the schools* (pp. 207–234). Newbury Park, CA: Sage.

Coleman, J. (1988). Social capital in the creation of human capital. *American Journal of Sociology*, **94**, 95–120.

Coleman, M., & Ganong, L. H. (1995). Family reconfiguring following divorce. In S. W. Duck & J. T. Wood (Eds.), *Confronting relationship challenges (Understanding relationship processes 5)* (pp. 73–108). Thousand Oaks, CA: Sage.

Collett, P. (1971). Training Englishmen in the non-verbal behaviour of Arabs: An experiment on intercultural communication. *International Journal of Psychology*, **6**, 209–215.

Collins, W. A., & Russell, A. (1991). Mother–child and father–child relationships in middle childhood and adolescence: A developmental analysis. *Developmental Review*, **11**, 96–136.

Conger, R. D., & Elder, G. H. (1994). *Families in troubled times: Adapting to change in rural America*. Chicago, IL: Aldine.

Cooper, C. R., & Denner, J. (1998). Theories linking culture and psychology: Universal and community specific processes. *Annual Review of Psychology*, **49**, 559–584.

Corter, C., Pepler, D., & Abramovitch, R. (1982). The effects of situation and sibling status on sibling interaction. *Canadian Journal of Behavioural Science*, **14**, 380–392.

Cowan, C., & Kinder, M. (1985). *Smart women; Foolish choices*. New York: Clarkson N. Potter.

Cowan, P. A., Cowan, C. P., Shulz, M. S., & Hemming, G. (1994). Prebirth to preschool family factors in children's adaptation to kindergarten. In R. D. Parke & S. G.

Kellam (Eds.), *Exploring family relationships with other social contexts* (pp. 75–114). Hillsdale, NJ: Erlbaum.

Crago, M. B., Annahatak, B., & Ningiuruvik, L. (1993). Changing patterns of language socialization in Inuit homes. *Anthropology & Education Quarterly*, **24**, 205–223.

Creighton, M. (1990). Revisiting shame and guilt cultures: A forty-year pilgrimage. *Ethos*, **18**, 279–307.

Crick, N. R. (1996). The role of overt aggression, relational aggression, and prosocial behavior in the prediction of children's future social adjustment. *Child Development*, **67**, 2317–2327.

Crick, N. R. (1997). Engagement in gender normative versus nonnormative forms of aggression: Links to social-psychological adjustment. *Developmental Psychology*, **33**, 610–617.

Crick, N. R., & Dodge, K. A. (1994). A review and reformulation of social information-processing mechanisms in children's social adjustment. *Psychological Bulletin*, **115**, 74–101.

Crick, N. R., & Dodge, K. A. (1996). Social information-processing mechanisms in reactive and proactive aggression. *Child Development*, **67**, 993–1002.

Crick, N. R., & Grotpeter, J. K. (1995). Relational aggression, gender, and social-psychological adjustment. *Child Development*, **66**, 710–722.

Crick, N. R., & Grotpeter, J. K. (1996). Children's treatment by peers: Victims of relational and overt aggression. *Development and Psychopathology*, **8**, 367–380.

Crick, N. R., Casas, J. F., & Mosher, M. (1997). Relational and overt aggression in preschool. *Developmental Psychology*, **33**, 579–588.

Crittenden, P. M. (1981). Abusing, neglecting, problematic, and adequate dyads: Differentiating by patterns of interaction. *Merrill-Palmer Quarterly*, **27**, 201–218.

Crittenden, P. M. (1985). Social networks, quality of parenting, and child development. *Child Development*, **56**, 1299–1313.

Crittenden, P. M. (1988a). Relationships at risk. In J. Belsky & T. Nezworski (Eds.), *Clinical implications of attachment* (pp. 136–174). Hillsdale, NJ: Erlbaum.

Crittenden, P. M. (1988b). Distorted patterns of relationships in maltreating families: The role of internal representational models. *Journal of Reproductive and Infant Psychology*, **6**, 183–199.

Crittenden, P. M. (1990). Internal representational models of attachment relationships. *Infant Mental Health Journal*, **11**, 259–277.

Crittenden, P. M. (1992). Quality of attachment in the preschool years. *Development & Psychopathology*, **4**, 209–241.

Crittenden, P. M. (1995). Attachment and psychopathology. In S. Goldberg, R. Muir, & J. Kerr (Eds.), *Attachment theory: Social, developmental, and clinical perspectives* (pp. 367–405). Hillsdale, NJ: The Analytic Press.

Crittenden, P. M. (1997a). The A/C pattern of attachment: Risk of dysfunction versus opportunity for creative integration. In L. Atkinson & K. J. Zuckerman (Eds.), *Attachment and psychopathology* (pp. 47–93). New York: Guilford.

Crittenden, P. M. (1997b). Toward an integrative theory of trauma: A dynamic-maturational approach. In D. Cicchetti and S. Toth (Eds.), *The Rochester Symposium on Developmental Psychopathology, Vol. 10. Risk, Trauma, and Mental Processes* (pp. 34–84). Rochester, NY: University of Rochester Press.

Crittenden, P. M. (1997c). Truth, error, omission, distortion, and deception: The application of attachment theory to the assessment and treatment of psychological disorder. In S. M. C. Dollinger & L. F. DiLalla (Eds.), *Assessment and intervention across the lifespan* (pp. 35–76). Hillsdale, NJ: Erlbaum.

Crittenden, P. M. (1998a). *Adult Attachment Interview: Coding Manual for the Dynamic-Maturational Method*. Unpublished manuscript, available from the author.

Crittenden, P. M. (1998b). Dangerous behavior and dangerous contexts: A thirty-five year perspective on research on the developmental effects of child physical abuse. In

P. Trickett (Ed.), *Violence to children* (pp. 11–38). Washington, DC: American Psychological Association.

Crittenden, P. M. (1999). Danger and development: The organization of self-protective strategies. In J. I. Vondra & D. Barnett (Eds.), Atypical attachment in infancy and early childhood among children at developmental risk. *Monographs of the Society for Research on Child Development* (pp. 145–171).

Crittenden, P. M. (2000a). A dynamic-maturational approach to continuity and change in pattern of attachment. In P. M. Crittenden and A. H. Claussen (Eds.), *The organization of attachment relationships: Maturation, culture, and context* (pp. 343–357). New York: Cambridge University Press.

Crittenden, P. M. (2000b). A dynamic-maturational exploration of the meaning of security and adaptation: Empirical, cultural, and theoretical considerations. In P. M. Crittenden and A. H. Claussen (Eds.), *The organization of attachment relationships: Maturation, culture, and context* (pp. 358–384). New York: Cambridge University Press.

Crittenden, P. M., & Claussen, A. L. (June, 1994). Quality of attachment in the preschool years: Alternative perspectives. Paper presented in the symposium "Quality of attachment in the preschool years," P. M. Crittenden, Chair, International Conference on Infant Studies, Paris, France.

Crittenden, P. M., & Claussen, A. H. (2000). Adaptation to varied environments. In P. M. Crittenden & A. H. Claussen (Eds.), *The organization of attachment relationships: Maturation, culture, and context* (pp. 234–250). New York: Cambridge University Press.

Crittenden, P. M., & DiLalla, D. (1988). Compulsive compliance: The development of an inhibitory coping strategy in infancy. *Journal of Abnormal Child Psychology*, **16**, 585–599.

Crittenden, P. M., Partridge, M. F., & Claussen, A. H. (1991). Family patterns of relationship in normative and dysfunctional families. *Development and Psychopathology*, **3**, 491–512.

Crockenberg, S., & Forgays, D. K. (1996). The role of emotion in children's understanding and emotional reactions to marital conflict. *Merrill-Palmer Quarterly*, **42**, 22–47.

Crockenberg, S., & Litman, C. (1990). Autonomy as competence in two-year-olds: Maternal correlates of child defiance, compliance, and self-assertion. *Developmental Psychology*, **26**, 961–971.

Cross, S. E., & Madson, L. (1997). Models of the self: Self-construals and gender. *Psychological Bulletin*, **122**, 5–37.

Crouter, A. C., & Helms-Erikson, H. (1997). Work and family from a dyadic perspective: Variations in inequality. In S. W. Duck, K. Dindia, W. Ickes, R. Milardo, R. S. L. Mills, & B. Sarason (Eds.), *Handbook of personal relationships: Theory, research, and interventions* (2nd ed., pp. 487–504). Chichester, UK: Wiley.

Cummings, E. M., & Cummings, J. L. (1988). A process-oriented approach to children's coping with adults' angry behavior. *Developmental Review*, **8**, 296–321.

Cummings, E. M., & Davies, P. T. (1994). *Children and marital conflict: The impact of family dispute and resolution.* New York: Guilford.

Cummings, E. M., & Smith, D. (1993). The impact of anger between adults on siblings' emotions and social behavior. *Journal of Child Psychology and Psychiatry*, **34**, 1425–1433.

Cummings, E. M., Ballard, M., El-Sheikh, M., & Lake, M. (1991). Resolution and children's responses to interadult anger. *Developmental Psychology*, **27**, 462–470.

Cummings, E. M., Davies, P. T., & Simpson, K. S. (1994). Marital conflict, gender, and children's appraisals and coping efficacy as mediators of child adjustment. *Journal of Family Psychology*, **8**, 141–149.

Cummings, E. M., Iannotti, R. J., & Zahn-Waxler, C. (1985). Influence of conflict between adults on the emotions and aggression of young children. *Developmental Psychology*, **21**, 495–507.

Damasio, A. R. (1994). *Descartes' error: Emotion. reason, and the human brain*. New York: Avon Books.

Damico, S. B., & Sparks, C. (1986). Cross-group contact opportunities: Impact on interpersonal relationship in desegregated middle schools. *Sociology of Education*, **59**, 113–123.

Daniels, P., & Weingarten, K. (1982). *Sooner or later: The timing of parenthood in adult lives*. New York: Norton.

Darling, N., Steinberg, L., Gringlas, M. B., & Dornbusch, S. (1995). *Community influences on adolescent achievement and deviance: A test of the functional community hypothesis*. Unpublished manuscript, Temple University, Philadelphia, PA.

Darwin, C. (1965). *The expression of the emotions in man and animals*. Chicago, IL: University of Chicago Press. (Original work published 1872.)

Davey, A. G., & Mullin, P. N. (1980). Ethnic identification and preference of British primary school children. *Journal of Child Psychology & Psychiatry & Allied Disciplines*, **21**, 241–251.

Davies, P. T., & Cummings, E. M. (1994). Marital conflict and child adjustment: An emotional security hypothesis. *Psychological Bulletin*, **116**, 387–411.

Davies, P. T., & Cummings, E. M. (1998). Exploring children's emotional security as a mediator of the link between marital relations and child adjustment. *Child Development*, **69**, 124–139.

Dawkins, J. L. (1996). Bullying, physical disability and the paediatric patient. *Developmental Medicine and Child Neurology*, **38**, 603–612.

Deaux, K. (1984). From individual differences to social categories: Analysis of a decade's research on gender. *American Psychologist*, **39**, 105–116.

Deaux, K., & Major, B. (1987). Putting gender into context: An interactive model of gender-related behavior. *Psychological Review*, **94**, 369–389.

DeCasper, A. J., & Fifer, W. (1980). Of human bonding: Newborns prefer their mothers' voices. *Science*, **208**, 1174–1176.

den Bak, I. M., & Ross, H. S. (1996). I'm telling: The content, context, and consequences of children's tattling on their siblings. *Social Development*, **5**, 292–309.

Denham, S. A. (1998). *Emotional development in young children*. New York: Guilford.

Denham, S. A., McKinley, M., Couchoud, E., & Holt, R. (1990). Emotional and behavioral predictors of preschool peer ratings. *Child Development*, **61**, 1145–1152.

Denscombe, M. (1983). Ethnic group and friendship choice in the primary school. *Educational Research*, **25**, 184–190.

Denscombe, M., Szulc, H., Patrick, C., & Wood, A. (1986). Ethnicity and friendship: The contrast between sociometric research and fieldwork observation in primary school classrooms. *British Educational Research Journal*, **12**, 221–235.

Denton, K., & Zarbatany, L. (1996). Age differences in support processes in conversations between friends. *Child Development*, **67**, 1360–1373.

Deutsch, M. (1973). *The resolution of conflict*. New Haven, CT: Yale University Press.

Dickstein, S., Siefer, R., Hayden, L. C., Schiller, M., Sameroff, A. J., Keitner, G., Miller, I., Rasmussen, S., Matzko, M., & Magee, K. D. (1998). Levels of family assessment: II. Impact of maternal psychopathology on family functioning. *Journal of Family Psychology*, **12**, 23–40.

Dindia, K. (1997). Self-disclosure, self-identity, and relationship development: A transactional/dialectical perspective. *Handbook of personal relationships: Theory, research, and interventions* (2nd ed., pp. 411–425). Chichester, UK: Wiley.

Dion, K. K., & Dion, K. L. (1996). Cultural perspectives on romantic love. *Personal Relationships*, **3**, 5–17.

Dishion, T. J. (1990). The peer context of troublesome child and adolescent behavior. In P. E. Leone (Ed.), *Understanding troubled and troubling youth: A multidisciplinary perspective* (pp. 128–153). Newbury Park, CA: Sage.

Dishion, T. J., Andrews, D., & Crosby, L. (1995). Antisocial boys and their friends in early adolescence: Relationship characteristics, quality, and interactional processes. *Child Development*, **66**, 139–151.

Dixson, M. D., & Duck, S. W. (1993). *Individuals in relationships (Understanding relationship processes series*, Vol. 1, pp. 175–206). Newbury Park, CA: Sage.

Dodge, K. A. (1986). A social information-processing model of social competence in children. In M. Perlmutter (Ed.), *Minnesota Symposia on Child Psychology* (Vol. 18, pp. 77–125). Hillsdale, NJ: Erlbaum.

Dodge, K. A. (1991). Emotion and social information processing. In J. Garber & K. A. Dodge (Eds.), *The development of emotion regulation and dysregulation* (pp. 159–181). Cambridge: Cambridge University Press.

Dodge, K. A., & Coie, J. D. (1987). Social information-processing factors in reactive and proactive aggression in children's peer groups. *Journal of Personality and Social Psychology*, **53**, 1146–1158.

Dodge, K. A., & Frame, C. L. (1982). Social cognitive biases and deficits in aggressive boys. *Child Development*, **53**, 620–635.

Dodge, K. A., Coie, J. D., Pettit, G. S., & Price, J. M. (1990). Peer status and aggression in boys' groups: Developmental and contextual analyses. *Child Development*, **61**, 1289–1309.

Dodge, K. A., Pettit, G. S., McClaskey, C. L., & Brown, M. (1986). Social competence in children. *Monographs of the Society for Research in Child Development*, **51**(2, Serial No. 213).

Dodge, K. A., Schlundt, D. C., Schocken, I., & Delugach, J. D. (1983). Social competence and children's sociometric status: The role of peer group entry strategies. *Merrill-Palmer Quarterly*, **29**, 309–336.

Domino, G., & Hannah, M.T. (1987). A comparative analysis of social values of Chinese and American Children. *Journal of Cross-Cultural Psychology*, **18**, 58–77.

Dong, Q., Yang, B., & Ollendick, T. I. (1994). Fears in Chinese children and adolescents and their relations to anxiety and depression. *Journal of Child Psychology and Psychiatry*, **35**, 351–363.

Doyle, A. B., & Markiewicz, D. (1996). Parents' interpersonal relationships and children's friendships. In W. M. Bukowski, A. F. Newcomb, & W. W. Hartup (Eds.), *The company they keep: Friendship in chilhood and adolescence* (pp. 115–137). New York: Cambridge University Press.

Dubois, D. L., & Hirsch, B. J. (1990). School and neighborhood friendship patterns of Blacks and Whites in early adolescence. *Child Development*, **61**, 524–536.

Dubow, E., Tisak, J., Causey, D., Hryshko, A., & Reid, G. (1991). A two-year longitudinal study of stressful life events, social support, and social problem-solving skills: Contributions to children's behavioral and academic adjustment. *Child Development*, **62**, 583–599.

Duck, S. W. (1982). A topography of relationship disengagement and dissolution. In S. W. Duck (Ed.), *Personal relationships 4: Dissolving personal relationships* (pp. 1–30). London: Academic Press.

Duck, S. W. (1990). Relationships as unfinished business: Out of the frying pan and into the 1990s. *Journal of Social and Personal Relationships*, **7**, 5–29.

Duck, S. W. (1993). Preface on social contexts. In S. W. Duck (Ed.), *Social context and relationships (Understanding relationship processes series*, Vol. 3). Newbury Park, CA: Sage.

Duck, S. W. (1994a). *Meaningful relationships: Talking, sense, and relating*. Thousand Oaks, CA: Sage.

Duck, S. W. (1994b). Stratagems, spoils and a serpent's tooth: On the delights and dilemmas of personal relationships. In W. R. Cupach & B. H. Spitzberg (Eds.) *The dark side of interpersonal communication* (pp. 3–24). Hillsdale, NJ: Erlbaum.

Duck, S. W. (1997) (Ed.). *Handbook of personal relationships: Theory, research, and interventions (2nd ed.)*. Chichester, UK: Wiley.

Duck, S. W. (1998). *Human relationships* (3rd ed.). London: Sage.

Duck, S. W., & Pond, K. (1989). Friends, Romans, Countrymen; lend me your retrospective data: Rhetoric and reality in personal relationships. In C. Hendrick (Ed.), *Close relationships* (Vol. 10, pp. 17–38). Newbury Park, CA: Sage.

Duck, S. W., & Sants, H. K. A. (1983). On the origin of the specious: Are personal relationships really interpersonal states? *Journal of Social and Clinical Psychology*, **1**, 27–41.

Duck, S. W., & Wood, J. T. (1995). *Confronting relationship challenges (Understanding relationship processes 5)*. Newbury Park, CA: Sage.

Duck, S. W., & Wright, P. H. (1993). Reexamining sex differences in same-sex friendships: A close look at two kinds of data. *Sex Roles*, **28**, 709–727.

Duck, S. W., Pond. K., & Leatham, G. B. (1994). Loneliness and the evaluation of relational events. *Journal of Social and Personal Relationships*, **11**, 235–260.

Duck, S. W., Rutt, D. J., Hurst, M., & Strejc, H. (1991). Some evident truths about communication in everyday relationships: All communication is not created equal. *Human Communication Research*, **18**, 228–267.

Duck, S. W., West, L., & Acitelli, L. K. (1997). Sewing the field: the tapestry of relationships in life and research. In S. W. Duck (Ed.), *Handbook of personal relationships* (2nd ed., pp. 1–23). Chichester, UK: Wiley.

Dunn, J. (1983). Sibling relationships in early childhood. *Child Development*, **54**, 787–811.

Dunn, J. (1988a). Relations among relationships. In S. W. Duck, D. F. Hay, S. E. Hobfoll, W. Ickes, & B. Montgomery (Eds.), *Handbook of personal relationships*. Chichester, UK: Wiley.

Dunn, J. (1988b). *The beginnings of social understanding.* Oxford: Basil Blackwell.

Dunn, J. (1993). *Young children's close relationships.* Newbury Park, CA: Sage.

Dunn, J. (1996). Siblings: The first society. In N. Vanzetti & S. W. Duck (Eds.), *A lifetime of relationships* (pp. 105–124). Pacific Grove, CA: Brooks/Cole.

Dunn, J. (1997). Lessons from the study of bi-directional effects. *Journal of Social and Personal Relationships*, **14**, 565–573.

Dunn, J., & Brown, J. (1991). Relationships, talk about feelings, and the development of affect regulation in early childhood. In J. Garber & K. A. Dodge (Eds.), *The development of emotion regulation and dysregulation* (pp. 89–108). Cambridge: Cambridge University Press.

Dunn, J., & Brown, J. (1994). Affect expression in the family, children's understanding of emotions, and their interactions with others. *Merrill-Palmer Quarterly*, **40**, 120–137.

Dunn, J., & Kendrick, C. (1982). *Siblings: Love, envy and understanding.* New York: Academic Press.

Dunn, J., & Munn, P. (1985). Becoming a family member: Family conflict and the development of social understanding in the second year. *Child Development*, **56**, 480–492.

Dunn, J., & Munn, P. (1986). Siblings and the development of prosocial behavior. *International Journal of Behavioral Development*, **9**, 265–284.

Dunn, J., & Munn, P. (1987). Development of justification in disputes with mothers and sibling. *Developmental Psychology*, **23**, 791–798.

Dunn, J., Bretherton, I., & Munn, P. (1987). Conversations about feeling states between mothers and their young children. *Developmental Psychology*, **23**, 132–139.

Dunn, J., Brown, J., & Maguire, M. (1995). The development of children's moral sensibility: Individual differences and emotional understanding. *Developmental Psychology*, **31**, 649–659.

Dunn, J., Brown, J., & Beardsall, L. (1991). Family talk about feeling states and children's later understanding of others' emotions. *Developmental Psychology*, **27**, 448–455.

Dunn, J., Brown, J., Slomkowski, C., Tesla, C., & Youngblade, L. (1991). Young children's understanding of other people's feelings and beliefs: Individual differences and their antecedents. *Child Development, 62*, 1352–1366.

Dunn, J., Creps, C., & Brown, J. (1996). Children's family relationships between two and five: Developmental changes and individual differences. *Social Development, 5*, 230–250.

Dunn, J., Slomkowski, C., & Beardsall, L. (1994). Sibling relationships from the preschool period through middle childhood and early adolescence. *Developmental Psychology, 30*, 315–324.

Dunn, J., Slomkowski, C., Beardsall, L., & Rende, R. (1994). Adjustment in middle childhood and early adolescence: Links with earlier and contemporary sibling relationships. *Journal of Child Psychology and Psychiatry, 35*, 491–504.

Dunn, J., Slomkowski, C., Donelan, N., & Herrera, C. (1995). Conflict, understanding, and relationships: Developments and differences in the preschool years. *Early Education and Development, 6*, 303–316.

Durojaiye, M. O. A. (1969). Race relations among junior school children. *Educational Research, 11*, 226–228.

Eagly, A. H. (1987). *Sex differences in social behavior: A social-role interpretation.* Hillsdale, NJ: Erlbaum.

East, P. L., & Rook, K. S. (1992). Compensatory patterns of support among children's peer relationships: A test using school friends, nonschool friends, and siblings. *Developmental Psychology, 28*, 163–172.

Easterbrooks, M. A., & Emde, R. N. (1988). Marital and parent–child relationships: The role of affect in the family system. In R. Hinde & J. Stevenson-Hinde (Eds.), *Relationships within families* (pp. 83–103). Oxford: Clarendon Press.

Easterbrooks, M. A., Cummings, E. M., & Emde, R. N. (1994). Young children's responses to constructive marital disputes. *Journal of Family Psychology, 8*, 160–169.

Ebata, A. T., & Moos, R. H. (1991). Coping and adjustment in distressed and healthy adolescents. *Journal of Applied Developmental Psychology, 12*, 33–54.

Edelmann, R. J. (1987). *The psychology of embarrassment.* Chichester, UK: Wiley.

Edwards, C. P., & Whiting, B. B. (1993). "Mother, Older Sibling and Me:" The overlapping roles of caregivers and companions in the social world of two- and three-year-olds in Ngeca, Kenya. In K. MacDonald (Ed.), *Parent–child play: descriptions and implications* (pp. 305–329). Albany, NY: SUNY Press.

Egan, S. K., & Perry, D. G. (1998). Does low self-regard invite victimization? *Developmental Psychology, 34*, 299–309.

Egeland, B., & Farber, E. A. (1984). Infant–mother attachment: Factors related to its development and changes over time. *Child Development, 55*, 753–771.

Eibl-Eibesfeldt, I. (1979). Human ethology: Concepts and implications for the sciences of man. *Behavior and Brain Sciences, 2*, 1–57.

Eisenberg, A. R. (1992). Conflict between mothers and their young children. *Merrill-Palmer Quarterly, 38*, 21–44.

Eisenberg, A. R. (1996). The conflict talk of mothers and children: Patterns related to culture, SES, and gender of child. *Merrill-Palmer Quarterly, 42*, 438–452.

Eisenberg, A., & Garvey, C. (1981). Children's use of verbal strategies in resolving conflicts. *Discourse Processes, 4*, 149–170.

Eisenberg, N., & Fabes, R. A. (1992a). Emotion, regulation, and the development of social competence. In M. S. Clark (Ed.), *Review of personality and social psychology: Vol. 14. Emotion and social behavior* (pp. 119–150). Newbury Park, CA: Sage.

Eisenberg, N., & Fabes, R. A. (1992b). Young children's coping with interpersonal anger. *Child Development, 63*, 116–128.

Eisenberg, N., & Fabes, R. A. (1998). Prosocial development. In W. Damon (Series Ed.) & N. Eisenberg (Vol. Ed.), *Handbook of child psychology: Vol. 3. Social, emotional, and personality development* (5th ed., pp. 701–778). New York: Wiley.

Eisenberg, N., Fabes, R. A., Carlo, G., Troyer, D., Speer, A. L., Karbon, M., & Switzer, G. (1992). The relations of maternal practices and characteristics to childen's vicarious emotional responsiveness. *Child Development*, **63**, 583–602.

Eisenberg, N., Fabes, R. A., Miller, P. A., Shell, C., Shea, R., & May-Plumlee, T. (1990). Preschoolers' vicarious emotional responding and their situational and dispositional prosocial behavior. *Merrill-Palmer Quarterly*, **36**, 507–529.

Eisenberg, N., Fabes, R. A., Schaller, M., & Miller, P. (1991). Personality and socialization correlates of vicarious emotional responding. *Journal of Personality and Social Psychology*, **61**, 459–470.

Eisenberg, N., Fabes, R. A., Shepard, S. A., Murphy, B. C., Guthrie, I. K., Jones, S., Friedman, J., Poulin, R., & Maszk, P. (1997). Contemporaneous and longitudinal prediction of children's social functioning from regulation and emotionality. *Child Development*, **68**, 642–664.

Eisenberg, N., Fabes, R., Bernzweig, J., Karbon, M., Poulin, R., & Hanish, L. (1993). The relations of emotionality and regulation to preschoolers' social skills and sociometric status. *Child Development*, **64**, 1418–1438.

Eisenberg, N., Fabes, R., Nyman, M., Bernzweig, J., & Pinuelas, A. (1994). The relations of emotionality and regulation to children's anger-related reactions. *Child Development*, **65**, 109–128.

Eisenberg, N., Haake, R. J., & Bartlett, K. (1981). The effects of possession and ownership on the sharing and proprietary behaviors of preschool children. *Merrill-Palmer Quarterly*, **27**, 61–67.

Eisenberg, N., McCreath, H., & Ahn, R. (1988). Vicarious emotional responsiveness and prosocial behavior: Their interrelations in young children. *Personality and Social Psychology Bulletin*, **14**, 298–311.

Ekman, P. (1985). *Telling lies: Clues to deceit in the marketplace, politics, and marriage.* New York: Norton.

Ekman, P., Davidson, R., & Friesen, W. (1990). The Duchenne smile: Emotional expression and brain physiology II. *Journal of Personality and Social Psychology*, **58**, 343–353.

El-Sheikh, M., Cummings, E. M., & Goetsch, V. (1989). Coping with adults' angry behavior: Behavioral, physiological, and self-reported responding in preschoolers. *Developmental Psychology*, **25**, 490–498.

El-Sheikh, M., Cummings, E. M., & Reiter, S. (1996). Preschoolers' responses to ongoing interadult conflict: The role of prior exposure to resolved versus unresolved arguments. *Journal of Abnormal Child Psychology*, **24**, 665–679.

Elder, G. H. (1998). The life course as developmental theory. *Child Development*, **69**, 1–12.

Elder, G. H. (1999). *Children of the Great Depression: Social change in life experience.* Boulder, CO: Westview Press.

Elder, G. H., Modell, J., & Parke, R. D. (1993). Epilogue: An emerging framework for dialogue between history and developmental psychology. In G. H. Elder, J. Modell, & R. D. Parke (Eds.) *Children in time and place: Developmental and historical insights* (pp. 241–249). New York: Cambridge University Press.

Elicker, J., Egeland, M., & Sroufe, A. (1992). Predicting peer competence in childhood from early parent-child relationships. In R. Parke & G. W. Ladd (Eds.), *Family and peer relationships: Modes of linkage* (pp. 77–106). Hillsdale, NJ: Erlbaum.

Ellis, S., & Rogoff, B. (1982). The strategies and efficacy of child versus adult teachers. *Child Development*, **53**, 730–735.

Emery, R. E. (1988). *Marriage, divorce, and children's adjustment.* Newbury Park, CA: Sage.

Emery, R. E. (1992). Family conflicts and their developmental implications: A conceptual analysis of meaning for the structure of relationships. In C. U. Shantz & W. W. Hartup (Eds.), *Conflict in child and adolescent development* (pp. 453–470). New York: Cambridge University Press.

Erel, O., & Burman, B. (1995). Interrelatedness of marital relations and parent-child relations: A meta-analytic review. *Psychological Bulletin*, **118**, 108–132.

Erel, O., Margolin, G., & John, R. S. (1998). Observed sibling interaction: Links with the marital and the mother–child relationship. *Developmental Psychology*, **34**, 288–298.

Erickson, M. F., Sroufe, L. A., & Egeland, B. (1985). The relationship between quality of attachment and behavior problems in preschool in a high risk sample. In I. Bretherton & E. Waters (Eds.), *Growing points in attachment theory and research* (pp. 147–186). *Monographs of the Society for Research in Child Development*, **50** (1–2, Serial No. 209).

Erikson, E. H. (1950). *Childhood and society*. New York: Norton.

Erikson, E. H. (1963). *Childhood and society* (2nd ed.). New York: Norton.

Eshel, Y., & Dicker, R. (1995). Congruence and incongruence in perceived ethnic acceptance among Israeli students. *Journal of Social Psychology*, **135**, 251–262.

Eshel, Y., & Kurman, J. (1990). Ethnic equity and asymmetry in peer acceptance. *Journal of Social Psychology*, **130**, 713–723.

Eslea, M., & Smith, P. K. (1998). The long-term effectiveness of anti-bullying work in primary schools. *Educational Research*, **40**, 203–218.

Fabes, R. A., & Eisenberg, N. (1992). Young children's coping with interpersonal anger. *Child Development*, **63**, 116–128.

Fabes, R. A., Eisenberg, N., McCormick, S. E., & Wilson, M. S. (1988). Preschoolers' attribution of the situational determinants of others' naturally occuring emotions. *Developmental Psychology*, **24**, 376–385.

Fabes, R. A., Eisenberg, N., Smith, M., & Murphy, B. (1996). Getting angry at peers: Associations with liking of the provocateur. *Child Development*, **67**, 942–956.

Fagot, B. (1997). Attachment, parenting, and peer interactions of toddler children. *Developmental Psychology*, **33**, 489–499.

Fagot, B., & Kavanagh, K. (1990). The prediction of antisocial behavior from avoidant attachment classifications. *Child Development*, **61**, 864–873.

Farrington, D. P. (1983). Offending from 10–25 years of age. In K. T. Van Dusen & S.A. Mednick (Eds.), *From children to citizens: Vol. III: Families, schools, and delinquency prevention* (pp. 27–51). New York: Springer-Verlag.

Farrington, D. P. (1993). Understanding and preventing bullying. In M. Tonry & N. Morris (Eds.), *Crime and justice: An annual review of research* (Vol 17, pp. 381–458). Chicago, IL: University of Chicago Press.

Fauber, R. L., & Long, N. (1991). Children in context: The role of the family in child psychotherapy. *Journal of Consulting and Clinical Psychology*, **59**, 813–820.

Feingold, A. (1994). Gender differences in personality: A meta-analysis. *Psychological Bulletin*, **116**, 429–456.

Felson, R. B., & Russo, N. J. (1988). Parental punishment and sibling aggression. *Social Psychology Quarterly*, **51**, 11–18.

Ferguson, T. J., & Stegge, H. (1995). Emotional states and traits in children: The case of guilt and shame. In J. P. Tangney & K. W. Fischer (Eds.), *Self-conscious emotions: The psychology of shame, guilt, embarrassment, and pride* (pp. 174–197). New York: Guilford.

Ferguson, T. J., Stegge, H., & Damhuis, I. (1991). Children's understanding of guilt and shame. *Child Development*, **62**, 827–839.

Ferree, M. M. (1990). Beyond separate spheres: Feminism and family research. *Journal of Marriage and the Family*, **52**, 866–884.

Field, T. M., & Walden, T. A. (1982). Production and discrimination of facial expressions by preschool children. *Child Development*, **53**, 1299–1311.

Field, T., Greenwald, P., Morrow, C., Healy, B., Foster, T., Gutherz, M., & Frost, P. (1992). Behavior state matching during interactions of preadolescent friends versus acquaintances. *Developmental Psychology*, **28**, 242–250.

Field, T., Vega-Lahr, N., Scafidi, F., & Goldstein, S. (1986). Effects of maternal un-availability on mother–infant interactions. *Infant Behavior and Development*, **9**, 473–478.

Fincham, F. D. (1995). From the orthogenic principle to the fish scale model of omniscience: Advancing understanding of personal relationships. *Journal of Social and Personal Relationships*, **12**, 523–527.

Fincham, F. D. (1998). Child development and marital relations. *Child Development*, **69**, 543–574.

Finnegan, R. A., Hodges, E. V. E., & Perry, D. G. (1997, April). *Victimization in the peer group: Associations with children's perceptions of mother-child interaction.* Paper presented at the Meeting of the Society for Research in Child Development, Washington, DC.

Fisher, S. W. (1996). *The family and the individual: reciprocal influences.* In N. Vanzetti & S. W. Duck (Eds.), *A lifetime of relationships* (pp. 311–335). Pacific Grove, CA: Brooks/Cole.

Fitch, K. L. (1998). *Speaking relationally: Culture, communication, and interpersonal connection.* New York: Guilford.

Fivush, R. (1989). Exploring sex differences in the emotional content of mother–child conversations about the past. *Sex Roles*, **20**, 675–691.

Fletcher, A. C., Darling, N. E., Steinberg, L., & Dornbusch, S. M. (1995). The company they keep: Relation of adolescents' adjustment and behavior to their friends' perception of authoritative parenting in the social network. *Developmental Psychology*, **31**, 300–310.

Fogel, A. (1995). Relational narratives of the prelinguistic self. In P. Rochat (Ed.), *The self in infancy: Theory and research.* (pp. 117–139). Amsterdam: Elsevier North Holland.

Fogel, A., Diamond, G. R., Langhorst, B. H., & Demos, V. (1982). Affective and cognitive aspects of the two-month-old's participation in face-to-face interaction with its mother. In E. Tronick (Ed.), *Social interchanges in infancy: Affect, cognition, and communication.* Baltimore, MD: University Park Press.

Fonagy, P., Steele, M., Steele, H., Leigh, T., Kennedy, R., & Target, M. (1995). The predictive specificity of Mary Main's Adult Attachment Interview: Implications for psychodynamic theories of normal and pathological emotional development. In S. Goldberg, R. Muir, & J. Kerr (Eds.), *Attachment theory: Social, developmental, and clinical perspectives.* Hillsdale, NJ: The Analytic Press.

Fonzi, A., Schneider, B. H., Tani, F., & Tomada, G. (1997). Predicting children's friendship status from their dyadic interaction in structured situations of potential conflict. *Child Development*, **68**, 496–506.

Fonzi, A., Tomada, G., & Ciucci, E. (1994). Uso di indici informativi nell'interazione tra bambini del nido. *Eta evolutiva*, **47**, 5–13.

Forsythe, C. J., & Compas, B. E. (1987). Interaction of cognitive appraisal of stressful events and coping: Testing the goodness of fit hypothesis. *Cognitive Therapy and Research*, **11**, 473–485.

Foster, S. L., DeLawyer, D. D., & Guevremont, D. C. (1986). A critical incidents analysis of liked and disliked peer behaviors and their situational parameters in childhood and adolescence. *Behavioral Assessment*, **8**, 115–133.

Fox, N. A., Kimmerly, N. L., & Schafer, W. D. (1991). Attachment to mother/attachment to father: A meta-analysis. *Child Development*, **62**, 210–225.

French, D. C., & Underwood, M. K. (1996). Peer relations during middle childhood. In N. Vanzetti & S. W. Duck (Eds.), *A lifetime of relationships* (pp. 155–180). Pacific Grove, CA: Brooks/Cole.

French, D., Waas, G., Stright, A., & Baker, J. (1986). Leadership asymmetries in mixed-age children's groups. *Child Development*, **57**, 1277–1283.

French, J. R. P., & Raven, B. H. (1959). The basis of social power. In D. Cartwright (Ed.), *Studies in social power* (pp. 150–167). Ann Arbor, MI: Institute for Social Research.

Freud, S. (1961). The ego and the id. In J. Strachey (Ed. and Trans.), *The standard edition of the complete psychological works of Sigmund Freud* (Vol. 19, pp. 3–66). London: Hogarth Press (Original work published 1923).

Friedrich, L. K., & Stein, A. H. (1973). Aggressive and prosocial television programs and the natural behavior of preschool children. *Monographs of the Society for Research in Child Development*, **38** (4, Serial No. 151).

Furman, W., & Buhrmester, D. (1985a). Children's perceptions of the qualities of sibling relationships. *Child Development*, **56**, 448–461.

Furman, W., & Buhrmester, D. (1985b). Children's perceptions of the personal relationships in their social networks. *Developmental Psychology*, **21**, 1016–1024.

Furman, W., & Robbins, P. (1985). What's the point? Issues in the selection of treatment objectives. In B. H. Schneider, K. H. Rubin, & J. E. Ledingham (Eds.), *Children's peer relations: Issues in assessment and intervention* (pp. 41–54). New York: Springer.

Galen, B. R., & Underwood, M. K. (1997). A developmental investigation of social aggression among children. *Developmental Psychology*, **33**, 589–600.

Gallimore, R., Boggs, J. W., & Jordan, C. (1974). *Culture, behavior and education: A study of Hawaiian-Americans*. Beverly Hills, CA: Sage.

Garner, P. W. (1996). The relations of emotional role taking, affective/moral attributions, and emotional display rule knowledge to low-income school-age children's social competence. *Journal of Applied Developmental Psychology*, **17**, 19–36.

Garner, P. W., & Power, T. G. (1996). Preschoolers' emotional control in the disappointment paradigm and its relation to temperament, emotional knowledge, and family expressiveness. *Child Development*, **67**, 1406–1419.

Garvey, C., & Ben Debba, M. (1974). Effects of age, sex, and partner on children's dyadic speech. *Child Development*, **33**, 589–600.

Gavin, L. A., & Furman, W. (1996). Adolescent girls' relationships with mothers and best friends. *Child Development*, **67**, 375–386.

Genta, M. L., Menesini, E., Fonzi, A., & Costabile, A. (1996). Bullies and victims in schools in central and southern Italy. *European Journal of Psychology of Education*, **11**, 97–110.

Gilligan, C. (1977). In a different voice: Women's conceptions of self and morality. *Harvard Educational Review*, **47**, 481–517.

Gleason, J. B. (1987). Sex differences in parent–child interaction. In S. U. Philips, S. Steele, & C. Tanz (Eds.), *Language, gender, and sex in comparative perspective* (pp. 189–199). Cambridge: Cambridge University Press.

Goffman, E. (1959). *The presentation of self in everyday life*. New York: Anchor Books.

Goldsmith, H. H., Buss, K. A., & Lemery, K. S. (1997). Toddler and childhood temperament: Expanded content, stronger genetic evidence, new evidence for the importance of environment. *Developmental Psychology*, **33**, 891–905.

Goodenough, F. (1931). *Anger in young children*. Minneapolis, MN: University of Minnesota Press.

Goodnow, J. J., & Collins, A. (1991). *Ideas according to parents*. Hillsdale, NJ: Erlbaum.

Goodnow, J., & Warton, P. M. (1992). Understanding responsibility: Adolescents' views of delegation and follow-through within the family. *Social Development*, **1**, 89–106.

Goodwin, R. (1995). The privatization of the personal?: I. Intimate disclosure in modern-day Russia. *Journal of Social and Personal Relationships*, **12**, 121–131.

Goodwin, R., & Emelyanova, T. (1995). The perestroika of the family? Gender and occupational differences in family values in modern day Russia. *Sex Roles*, **32**, 337–351.

Gottman, J. M. (1979). *Marital interaction: Experimental investigation*. San Diego, CA: Academic Press.

Gottman, J. M. (1983). How children become friends. *Monographs of the Society for Research in Child Development*, **48** (Serial No. 201).

Gottman, J. M. (1994). *What predicts divorce?* Hillsdale, NJ: Erlbaum.

Gottman, J. M. (1986). The world of coordinated play: Same- and cross-sex friendship in young children. In J. M. Gottman & J. Parker (Eds.), *Conversations of friends: Speculations on affective development* (pp. 192–237). Cambridge: Cambridge University Press.

Gottman, J. M. (1993). The roles of conflict engagement, escalation, and avoidance in marital interaction: A longitudinal view of five types of couples. *Journal of Consulting and Clinical Psychology*, **61**, 6–15.

Gottman, J. M., & Katz, L. F. (1989). Effects of marital discord on young children's peer interaction and health. *Developmental Psychology*, **25**, 373–381.

Gottman, J. M., & Mettetal, G. (1986). Speculations about social and affective development: Friendship and acquaintanceship through adolescence. In J. M. Gottman & J. Parker (Eds.), *Conversations of friends: Speculations on affective development* (pp. 91–113). Cambridge: Cambridge University Press.

Gottman, J. M., Katz, L. F., & Hooven, C. (1996). Parental meta-emotion philosophy and the emotional life of families: Theoretical models and preliminary data. *Journal of Family Psychology*, **10**, 243–268.

Gottman, J. M., Katz, L. F., & Hooven, C. (1997). *Meta-emotion: How families communicate emotionally*. Mahwah, NJ: Erlbaum.

Graham, S., & Hudley, C. (1994). Attributions of aggressive and nonaggressive African-American male early adolescents: A study of construct accessibility. *Developmental Psychology*, **30**, 365–373.

Graham, S., & Juvonen, J. (1998). Self-blame and peer victimization in middle school: An attributional analysis. *Developmental Psychology*, **34**, 587–599.

Graham, S., Hudley, C., & Williams, E. (1992). Attributional and emotional determinants of aggression among African, American and Latino young adolescents. *Developmental Psychology*, **28**, 731–740.

Gralinski, J. H., & Kopp, C. B. (1993). Everyday rules for behavior: Mothers' requests to young children. *Developmental Psychology*, **29**, 573–584.

Graziano, W. G., Jensen-Campbell, L. A., & Sullivan-Logan, G. M. (1998). Temperament, activity, and expectations for later personality development. *Journal of Personality and Social Psychology*, **74**, 1266–1277.

Green, J. T., Ivry, R. B., & Woodruff-Pak, D. S. (1999). Timing in eyeblink classical conditioning and timed-interval tapping. *Psychological Science*, **10**, 19–23.

Greenbaum, P. E. (1985). Nonverbal differences in communication style between American Italian and Anglo elementary classrooms. *American Educational Research Journal*, **22**, 1–115.

Greenberg, M. T., Speltz, M. L., & DeKlyen, M. (1993). The role of attachment in the early development of disruptive behavior problems. *Development and Psychopathology*, **5**, 191–213.

Grossmann, K., Fremmer-Bombik, E., Rudolph, J., & Grossmann, K. A. (1988). Maternal attachment representations as related to patterns of infant–mother attachment and maternal care during the first year. In R. A. Hinde & J. Stevenson-Hinde (Eds.), *Relationships between relationships within families* (pp. 241–260). Oxford: Clarendon Press.

Grotpeter, J. K., & Crick, N. (1996). Relational aggression, overt aggression, and friendship. *Child Development*, **67**, 2328–2338.

Grusec, J. E., & Goodnow, J. J. (1994). Impact of parental discipline methods on the child's internalization of values: A reconceptualization of current points of view. *Developmental Psychology*, **30**, 1–19.

Grusec, J. E., Hastings, P., & Mammone, N. (1994). Parenting cognitions and relationship schemes. In J. G. Smetana (Ed.), *Beliefs about parenting: Origins and developmental implications*. San Francisco, CA: Jossey-Bass.

Grych, J. H. (1998). Children's appraisals of interparental conflict: Situational and contextual influences. *Journal of Family Psychology*, **12**, 437–453.

Grych, J. H., & Fincham, F. D. (1990). Marital conflict and children's adjustment: A cognitive-contextual framework. *Psychological Bulletin*, **108**, 267–290.

Grych, J. H., & Fincham, F. D. (1993). Children's appraisals of marital conflict: Initial investigations of the cognitive-contextual framework. *Child Development*, **64**, 215–230.

Grych, J. H., Seid, M., & Fincham F. D. (1992). Assessing marital conflict from the child's perspective: The Children's Perception of Interparental Conflict Scale. *Child Development*, **63**, 558–572.

Guarnaccia, P. J., DeLaCancela, V., & Carrillo, E. (1989). The multiple meanings of ataques de nervios in the Latino community. *Medical Anthropology*, **11**, 47–62.

Gudykunst, W. B., & Ting-Toomey, S. (1988). *Culture and interpersonal communication*. Newbury Park, CA: Sage.

Gustavson, C., Garcia, J., Hankins, W., & Rusiniak, K. (1974). Coyote predation control by aversive stimulus. *Science*, **184**, 581–583.

Hagekull, B., & Bohlin, G. (1998). Preschool temperament and environmental factors related to the Five-Factor model of personality in middle childhood. *Merrill-Palmer Quarterly*, **44**, 194–215.

Hains, S. M. J., & Muir, D. W. (1996). Infant sensitivity to adult eye direction. *Child Development*, **67**, 1940–1951.

Haith, M. M., Bergman, T., & Moore, M. J. (1977). Eye contact and face scanning in early infancy. *Science*, **198**, 853–855.

Halberstadt, A. G. (1991). Toward an ecology of expressiveness: Family socialization in particular and a model in general. In R. S. Feldman & B. Rimé (Eds.), *Fundamentals of nonverbal behavior* (pp. 106–160). Cambridge: University Press.

Hallinan, M. T. (1982). Classroom racial composition and children's friendships. *Social Forces*, **61**, 56–72.

Hallinan, M. T., & Smith, S. S. (1985). The effects of classroom racial composition on students' interracial friendliness. *Social Psychology Quarterly*, **48**, 3–16.

Hallinan, M. T., & Sorensen, A. B. (1985). Ability grouping and student friendships. *American Educational Research Journal*, **22**, 485–499.

Hallinan, M. T., & Teixeira, R. A. (1987a). Students' interracial friendships: Individual characteristics, structural effects, and racial differences. *American Journal of Education*, **95**, 563–583.

Hallinan, M. T., & Teixeira, R. A. (1987b). Opportunities and constraints: Black-white differences in the formation of interracial friendships. *Child Development*, **58**, 1358–1371.

Hallinan, M. T., & Williams, R. A. (1987). The stability of students' interracial friendships. *American Sociological Review*, **52**, 653–664.

Hallinan, M. T., & Williams, R. A. (1989). Interracial friendship choices in secondary schools. *American Sociological Review*, **54**, 67–78.

Hansell, S. (1984). Cooperative groups, weak ties, and the integration of peer friendships. *Social Psychology Quarterly*, **47**, 316–328.

Hansell, S., & Slavin, R. E. (1981). Cooperative learning and the structure of interracial friendships. *Sociology of Education*, **54**, 98–106.

Harold, G. T., Fincham, F. D., Osborne, L. N., & Conger, R. D. (1997). Mom and dad are at it again: Adolescent perceptions of marital conflict and adolescent psychological distress. *Developmental Psychology*, **33**, 333–350.

Harris, J. R. (1995). Where is the child's environment? A group socialization theory of development. *Psychological Review*, **102**, 458–489.

Harris, M. B., & Siebel, C. E. (1975). Affect, aggression, and altruism. *Developmental Psychology*, **11**, 623–627.

Harris, P. L. (1989). *Children and emotions*. Oxford: Blackwell.

Harrist, A. W., Pettit, G. S., Dodge, K. A., & Bates, J. E. (1994). Dyadic synchrony in mother–child interaction—relation with children's subsequent kindergarten adjustment. *Family Relations*, **43**, 417–424.

Harrist, A. W., Zaia, A. F., Bates, J. E., Dodge, K. A., & Pettit, G. S. (1997). Subtypes of social withdrawal in early childhood: Sociometric status and social-cognitive differences across four years. *Child Development*, **68**, 278–294.

Hartup, W. W. (1979). The social worlds of childhood. *American Psychologist*, **34**, 944–950.

Hartup, W. W. (1983). Peer relations. In P. H. Mussen (Ed.), *Handbook of child psychology: Vol. 4. Socialisation, personality and social development* (4th ed., pp. 103–196). New York: Wiley.

Hartup, W. W. (1989). Social relationships and their developmental significance. *American Psychologist*, **44**, 120–126.

Hartup, W. W. (1992). Conflict and friendship relations. In C. U. Shantz & W. W. Hartup (Eds.), *Conflict in child and adolescent development* (pp. 186–215). New York: Cambridge University Press.

Hartup, W. W. (1996). The company they keep: Friendships and their developmental significance. *Child Development*, **67**, 1–13.

Hartup, W. W., & Laursen, B. (1991). Relationships as developmental contexts. In R. Cohen & A. W. Siegel (Eds.), *Context and development* (pp. 253–279) Hillsdale, NJ: Erlbaum.

Hartup, W. W., French, D. C., Laursen, B., Johnston, M. K., & Ogawa., J. R. (1993). Conflict and friendship relations in middle childhood: Behavior in a closed-field situation. *Child Development*, **64**, 445–454.

Hartup, W. W., Laursen, B., Stewart, M. I., & Eastenson, A. (1988). Conflict and the friendship relations of young children. *Child Development*, **59**, 1590–1600.

Hastings, P. D., & Grusec, J. E. (1998). Parenting goals as organizers of responses to parent–child disagreement. *Developmental Psychology*, **34**, 465–479.

Hay, D. F., & Ross, H. S. (1982). The social nature of early conflict. *Child Development*, **53**, 105–113.

Hay, D. F., Zahn-Waxler, C., Cummings, E. M., & Iannotti, R. J. (1992). Young children's views about conflict with peers: A comparison of the daughters and sons of depressed and well women. *Journal of Child Psychiatry*, **33**, 669–683.

Hay, T. H. (1977). The development of some aspects of Ojibwa self and its behavioral environment. *Ethos*, **5**, 71–89.

Hazan, C., & Shaver, P. (1987). Romantic love conceptualized as an attachment process. *Journal of Personality and Social Psychology*, **52**, 511–524.

Henggeler, S. W., Edwards, J. J., Cohen. R., & Summervile, M. B. (1992). Predicting changes in children's popularity: The role of family relations. *Journal of Applied Developmental Psychology*, **12**, 205–218.

Hermans, H. J. M., Kempen, H. J. G., & van Loon, R. J. P. (1992). The dialogical self. *American Psychologist*, **47**, 23–33.

Herrera, C., & Dunn, J. (1997). Early experiences with family conflict: Implications for arguments with a close friend. *Developmental Psychology*, **33**, 869–881.

Herzberger, S., & Hall, J. A. (1993). Consequences of retaliatory aggression against siblings and peers: Urban minority children's expectations. *Child Development*, **64**, 1773–1785.

Hetherington, E. M. (1988). Parents, children, siblings: Six years after divorce. In R. Hinde & J. Stevenson-Hinde (Eds.), *Relationships within families: Mutual influences* (pp. 311–331). New York: Oxford University Press.

Hetherington, E. M. (1989). Coping with family transitions: Winners, losers, and sur-
vivors. *Child Development*, **60**, 1–14.

Hetherington, E. M., Cox, M., & Cox, R. (1979). Play and social interaction in children
following divorce. *Journal of Social Issues*, **35**, 26–49.

Hetherington, E. M., Hagan, M. S., & Anderson, E. R. (1989). Marital transitions: A
child's perspective. *American Psychologist*, **44**, 303–312.

Higgins, E. T. (1989). Continuities and discontinuities in self-regulatory and self-
evaluative processes: A developmental theory relating self and affect. *Journal of
Personality*, **57**, 407–444.

Hinde, R. A. (1981). The bases of a science of interpersonal relationships. In S. W.
Duck & R. Gilmour (Eds.), *Personal relationships 1: Studying personal relationships*
(pp. 1–22). London, Academic Press.

Hinde, R. A. (1987). *Individuals, relationships and culture: Links between ethology and
the social sciences.* Cambridge: Cambridge University Press.

Hinde, R. A., & Stevenson-Hinde, J. (Eds.). (1988). *Relationships within families.*
Oxford: Oxford University Press.

Hinshaw, S. P., Zupan, B. A., Simmel, C., Nigg, J. T., & Melnick, S. (1997). Peer status
in boys with and without attention-deficit hyperactivity disorder: Predictions from
overt and covert antisocial behavior, social isolation, and authoritative parenting
beliefs. *Child Development*, **68**, 880–896.

Hirsch, B. J., & Dubois, D. L. (1989). The school–nonschool ecology of early adolescent friendship. In D. Belle (Ed.), *Children's social networks and social supports* (pp.
260–274). New York: Wiley.

Ho, D. Y. F., & Chiu, C. Y. (1994). Component ideas of individualism, collectivism,
and social organization: An application in the study of Chinese culture. In U. Kim,
H. C. Triandis, C. Kagitcibasi, S. C. Choi, & G. Yoon (Eds.), *Individualism and
collectivism: Theory, method, and applications* (pp. 137–156). Thousand Oaks, CA:
Sage.

Hodges, E. V. E., Malone, M. J., & Perry, D. G. (1997). Individual risk and social risk
as interacting determinants of victimization in the peer group. *Developmental Psychology*, **33**, 1032–1039.

Hoffman, M. (1976). Empathy, role-taking guilt and the development of altruistic
motives. In T. Likona (Ed.), *Moral development: Current theory and research* (pp.
124–143). New York: Holt, Rinehart, & Winston.

Hoffman, M. (1984). Parent discipline, moral internalization, and development of
prosocial motivation. In E. Staub, D. Bar-Tal, J. Karylowski, & J. Reykowski (Eds.),
Development and maintenance of prosocial behavior (pp. 117–137). New York:
Plenum.

Hoffman, M. L. (1970a). Moral development. In P. H. Mussen (Ed.), *Carmichael's
manual of child psychology* (Vol. 2, pp. 457–557). New York: Wiley.

Hoffman, M. L. (1970b). Conscience, personality, and socialization techniques. *Human
Development*, **13**, 90–126.

Hoffman, M. L. (1975). Moral internalization, parental power, and the nature of
parent-child interaction. *Developmental Psychology*, **11**, 228–239.

Hoffman, M. L. (1982). Development of prosocial motivation: Empathy and guilt. In
N. Eisenberg (Ed.), *The development of prosocial behavior* (pp. 218–231). New
York: Academic Press.

Hogan, R., & Cheek, J. (1983). Self-concepts, self-presentations, and moral judgments.
In J. Suls & A. G. Greenwald (Eds.), *Psychological perspectives on self* (Vol. 2, pp.
249–273). Hillsdale, NJ: Erlbaum.

Holden, G. W. (1997). *Parents and the dynamics of child rearing.* Boulder, CO: Westview Press.

Holmes, J. G., & Murray, S. L. (1996). Conflict in close relationships. In E. T. Higgins
& A. Kruglanski (Eds.), *Social psychology: Handbook of basic mechanisms and
processes* (pp. 622–654). New York: Guilford.

Homel, R., Burns, A., & Goodnow, J. J. (1987). Parental social networks and child development. *Journal of Social and Personal Relationships*, **4**, 159–177.

Honeycutt, J. M. (1993). Memory structures for the rise and fall of personal relationships. In S. W. Duck (Ed.), *Individuals in relationships (Understanding relationship processes series*, Vo. 1, pp. 60–86). Newbury Park, CA: Sage.

Hooven, C., & Katz, L. F. (1994). Parents' emotion philosophies and their children's peer and academic success. Unpublished manuscript, University of Washington.

Hopmeyer, A., & Asher, S. R. (1997). Children's responses to peer conflicts involving a rights infraction. *Merrill-Palmer Quarterly*, **43**, 235–254.

Hornstein, H. A. (1965). Effects of different magnitudes of threat upon interpersonal bargaining. *Journal of Experimental Social Psychology*, **1**, 282–293.

Howe, N. (1991). Sibling-directed internal state language, perspective taking, and affective behavior. *Child Development*, **62**, 1503–1512.

Howe, N., & Ross, H. S. (1990). Socialization, perspective taking, and the sibling relationship. *Developmental Psychology*, **26**, 160–165.

Howe, N., Petrakos, H., & Rinaldi, C. M. (1998). "All the sheep are dead. He murdered them": Sibling pretense, negotiation, internal state language, and relationship quality. *Child Development*, **69**, 182–191.

Howes, C., & Wu, F. (1990). Peer interactions and friendships in an ethnically diverse school setting. *Child Development*, **61**, 537–541.

Howes, C., Unger, O., & Matheson, C. (1992). *The collaborative construction of pretend.* Albany, NY: State University of New York Press.

Hsu, F. L. K. (1981). *Americans and Chinese: Passage to differences* (3rd ed.). Honolulu, Hawaii: The University Press of Hawaii.

Hubbard, J. A., & Coie, J. D. (1994). Emotional correlates of social competence in children's peer relationships. *Merrill-Palmer Quarterly*, **40**, 1–20.

Hudley, C., Britsch, B., Wakefield, W. D., Smith, T., Demorat, M., & Cho, S. (1998). An attribution retraining program to reduce aggression in elementary school students. *Psychology in the Schools*, **35**, 271–282.

Hugh-Jones, S., & Smith, P. K. (1999). Self-reports of short and long-term effects of bullying on children who stammer. *British Journal of Educational Psychology*, **69**, 141–158.

Isley, S., O'Neil, R., & Parke, R. D. (1996). The relation of parental affect and control behavior to children's classroom acceptance: A concurrent and predictive analysis. *Early Education and Development*, **7**, 7–23.

Jacklin, C. N. (1989). Female and male: Issues of gender. *American Psychologist*, **44**, 127–133.

Jacobvitz, D., & Sroufe, L. A. (1987). The early caregiver–child relationship and attention deficit disorder with hyperactivity in kindergarten: A prospective study. *Child Development*, **58**, 1488–1495.

Jelinek, M. M., & Brittan, E. M. (1975). Multiracial education: 1. Inter-ethnic friendship patterns. *Educational Research*, **18**, 44–53.

Jenkins, J. M. (1992). Sibling relationships in disharmonious homes: Potential difficulties and protective effects. In F. Boer & J. Dunn (Eds.), *Children's sibling relationships* (pp 125–138). Hillsdale, NJ: Erlbaum.

Jenkins, J. M., & Smith, M. A. (1991). Marital disharmony and children's behavior problems: Aspects of poor marriage that affect children adversely. *Journal of Child Psychology and Psychiatry*, **32**, 793–810.

Johnson, D. B. (1982). Altruistic behavior and the development of the self in infants. *Merrill-Palmer Quarterly*, **28**, 379–388.

Johnson, D. W., & Johnson, R. T. (1996). Conflict resolution and peer mediation programs in elementary and secondary schools: A review of the research. *Review of Educational Research*, **66**, 459–506.

Jones, P. C., Abbey, B. B., & Cumberland, A. (1998). The development of display rule knowledge: Linkages with family expressiveness and social competence. *Child Development*, **69**, 1209–1222.

Jones, S. S., & Hong, H. (1995, March). *On the development of affective sharing from 8 to 12 months of age*. Paper presented at the meeting of the Society for Research in Child Development, Indianapolis, IN.

Jones, W. H., Kugler, K., & Adams, P. (1995). You always hurt the one you love: Guilt and transgressions against relationship partners. In J. P. Tangney & K. W. Fischer (Eds.), *Self-conscious emotions: The psychology of shame, guilt, embarrassment, and pride* (pp. 301–321). New York: Guilford.

Junger, J. (1990). Intergroup bullying and racial harassment in the Netherlands. *Sociology and Social Research*, **74**, 65–72.

Kagan, J. (1991). The theoretical utility of constructs for self. *Developmental Review*, **11**, 244–250.

Kagan, J. (1998). Biology and the child. In W. Damon (Series Ed.) & N. Eisenberg (Vol. Ed.), *Handbook of child psychology: Volume 3. Social, emotional, and personality development* (5th ed., pp. 177–235). New York: Wiley.

Kahen, V., Katz, L. F., & Gottman, J. M. (1994). Linkages between parent–child interaction and conversations of friends. *Social Development*, **3**, 238–254.

Karcher, M. J., & Nakkula, M. J. (1997). Multicultural pair therapy and the development of expanded worldviews. In R. S. Selman, C. L. Watts, & L. S. Schultz (Eds.), *Fostering friendship: Pair therapy for treatment and prevention* (pp. 207–227). New York: Aldine de Gruyter.

Kashiwagi, K., & Azuma, H. (1977). Comparison of opinions on pre-school education and developmental expectation between Japanese and American mothers. *Japanese Journal of Educational Psychology*, **25**, 242–253.

Katz, L. F., & Gottman, J. M. (1991). Marital discord and child outcomes: A social psychophysiological approach. In J. Garber and K. A. Dodge (Eds.), *The development of emotion regulation and dysregulation* (pp. 129–158). Cambridge: Cambridge University Press.

Katz, L. F., & Gottman, J. M. (1993). Patterns of marital conflict predict children's internalizing and externalizing behaviors. *Developmental Psychology*, **29**, 940–950.

Katz, L. F., & Kahen, V. (1993, April). Marital interaction patterns and children's externalizing and internalizing behaviors: The search for mechanisms. Paper presented at the Biennial meetings of Society for Research in Child Development, New Orleans, LA.

Katz, L. F., Kramer, L., & Gottman, J. M. (1992). Conflict and emotions in marital, sibling, and peer relationships. In C. U. Shantz & W. W. Hartup (Eds.), *Conflict in child and adolescent development* (pp. 122–149). New York: Cambridge University Press.

Kaufman, G. (1985). *Shame: The power of caring*, 2nd edn. Cambridge, MA: Schenkman.

Kaufman, G. (1989). *The psychology of shame: Theory and treatment of shame-based syndromes*. New York: Springer.

Keenan, K., & Shaw, D. (1997). Developmental and social influences on young girls' early problem behavior. *Psychological Bulletin*, **121**, 95–113.

Keller, M. (1987). Resolving conflicts in friendship: The development of moral understanding in everyday life. In J. S. Gewintz & W. M. Kurtines (Eds.), *Morality and moral development* (pp. 63–91). New York: Wiley.

Kelley, H. H. (1984). Affect in personal relations. In P. Shaver (Ed.), *Review of Personality and Social Psychology* (Vol. 5, pp. 89–115). Newbury Park, CA: Sage.

Kelley, H. H., & Grzelak, J. (1972). Bargaining. In C. G. McClintock (Ed.), *Experimental social psychology* (pp. 190–197). New York: Holt.

Kelley, H. H., & Thibaut, J. W. (1978). *Interpersonal relations: A theory of interdependence*. New York: Wiley.

Kelley, M. L., & Tseng, H. M. (1992). Cultural differences in child rearing: A comparison of immigrant Chinese and Caucasian American mothers. *Journal of Cross-Cultural Psychology*, **23**, 444–455.

Kelly, G. A. (1955). *The psychology of personal constructs*. New York: Norton.

Kerig, P. K. (1996). Assessing the links between interparental conflict and child adjustment: The conflicts and problem-solving scales. *Journal of Family Psychology*, **10**, 454–473.

Kerig, P. K., Fedorowicz, A. E., Brown, C. A., Patenaude, R. L., & Warren, M. (1998). When warriors are worriers: Gender and children's coping with interparental violence. *Journal of Emotional Abuse*, **1**, 89–114.

Kerns, K. A. (1996). Individual differences in friendship quality and their links to child-mother attachment. In W. M. Bukowski, A. F. Newcomb, & W. W. Hartup (Eds.), *The company they keep: Friendship in childhood and adolescence* (pp. 137–157). New York: Cambridge University Press.

Kerns, K. A., & Barth, J. M. (1995). Attachment and play: Convergence across components of parent–child relationships and their relations to peer competence. *Journal of Social and Personal Relationships*, **12**, 243–260.

Kerns, K. A., Cole, A., & Andrews, P. B. (1998). Attachment security, parent peer management practices, and peer relationships in preschoolers. *Merrill-Palmer Quarterly*, **44**, 504–522.

Kerns, K. A., Klepac, L., & Cole, A. (1996). Peer relationships and preadolescents' perceptions of the child–mother relationship. *Developmental Psychology*, **32**, 457–466.

Kerr, N. L. (1983). Motivation losses in small groups: A social dilemma analysis. *Journal of Social Psychology and Personality*, **45**, 819–828.

Killen, M., & Nucci, L. P. (1995). Morality in everyday life: Developmental perspectives. In M. Killen & D. Hart (Eds.), *Morality, autonomy, and social conflict* (pp. 52–86). New York: Cambridge University Press.

Kim, U. (1994). Individualism and collectivism: Conceptual clarification and elaboration. In U. Kim, H. C. Triandis, C. Kagitcibasi, S. C. Choi, & G. Yoon (Eds.), *Individualism and collectivism: Theory, methods, and applications* (pp. 19–40). Thousand Oaks, CA: Sage.

Kingston, L., & Prior, M. (1995). The development of patterns of stable, transient, and school-age onset aggressive behavior in young children. *Journal of the American Academy of Child and Adolescent Psychiatry*, **34**, 348–358.

Kleinfeld, J. S. (1973). Classroom climate and the verbal participation of Indian and Eskimo students in integrated classrooms. *Journal of Educational Research*, **67**, 51–52.

Kochanska, G. (1991). Socialization and temperament in the development of guilt and conscience. *Child Development*, **62**, 1379–1392.

Kochanska, G. (1993). Toward a synthesis of parental socialization and child temperament in early development of conscience. *Child Development*, **64**, 325–347.

Kochanska, G. (1995). Children's temperament, mothers' discipline, and security of attachment: Multiple pathways to emerging internalization. *Child Development*, **66**, 597–615.

Kochanska, G. (1997a). Multiple pathways to conscience for children with different temperaments: From toddlerhood to age five. *Developmental Psychology*, **33**, 228–240.

Kochanska, G. (1997b). Mutually responsive orientation between mothers and their young children: Implications for early socialization. *Child Development*, **68**, 94–112.

Kochanska, G. (1998). Mother–child relationship, child fearfulness, and emerging attachment: A short-term longitudinal study. *Developmental Psychology*, **34**, 480–490.

Kochanska, G., & Aksan, N. (1995). Mother–child mutually positive affect, the quality of child compliance to requests and prohibitions, and maternal control as correlates of early internalization. *Child Development*, **66**, 236–254.

Kochanska, G., Kuczynski, L., Radke-Yarrow, M., & Welsh, J. D. (1987). Resolutions of control episodes between well and affectively ill mothers and their young children. *Journal of Abnormal Child Psychology*, **15**, 441–456.

Kochenderfer, B. J., & Ladd, G. W. (1997). Victimised children's responses to peers' aggression: Behaviors associated with reduced versus continued victimization. *Development and Psychopathology*, **9**, 59–73.

Kong, S. L. (1985). Counselling Chinese immigrants: Issues and answers. In R. J. Samuda & A. Wolfgang (Eds.), *Intercultural counselling and assessment: Global perspectives* (pp. 181–189). Lewiston: C. J. Hogrefe.

Kopp, C. B. (1982). Antecedents of self-regulation: A developmental perspective. *Developmental Psychology*, **18**, 199–214.

Kopp, C. B., & Wyer, N. (1991). In D. Cicchetti & S. L. Toth (Eds.), *Disorders and dysfunctions of the self (pp. 31–56)*. Rochester, NY: University of Rochester Press.

Kramer, L., & Gottman, J. M. (1992). Becoming a sibling—with a little help from my friends. *Developmental Psychology*, **28**, 685–699.

Krappmann, L. (1993). Threats to the self in the peer world: Observations of twelve-year-old children in natural settings. In G. G. Noam & T. E. Wren (Eds.), *The moral self* (pp. 359–382). Cambridge, MA: MIT Press.

Krappmann, L. (1996). The development of diverse relationships in the social world of childhood. In A. E. Auhagen & M. von Salisch (Eds.), *The diversity of human relationships* (pp. 52–78). New York: Cambridge University Press.

Krappmann, L., & Oswald, H. (1991). Problems of helping among ten-year-old children—Results from a qualitative study in natural settings. In H. W. Bierhoff & L. Montada (Eds.), *Altruism in social systems* (pp. 149–166). Toronto, ON: Hogrefe.

Krevans, J., & Gibbs, J. C. (1996). Parents' use of inductive discipline: Relations to children's empathy and prosocial behavior. *Child Development*, **67**, 3263–3277.

Kruger, A. C., & Tomasello, M. (1986). Transactive discussions with peers and adults. *Developmental Psychology*, **22**, 681–685.

Kuczynski, L., & Hildebrand, N. (1998). Models of conformity and resistance in socialization theory. In J. E. Grusec and L. Kuczynski (Eds.), *Parenting and the internalization of values: A handbook of contemporary theory* (pp. 227–258). New York: Wiley.

Kuczynski, L., & Kochanska, G. (1990). The development of children's noncompliance strategies from toddlerhood to age 5. *Developmental Psychology*, **26**, 398–408.

Kuczynski, L., Kochanska, G., Radke-Yarrow, M., & Girnius-Brown, O. (1987). A developmental interpretation of young children's noncompliance. *Developmental Psychology*, **23**, 799–806.

Kuczynski, L., Marshall, S., & Schell, K. (1997). Value socialization in a bidirectional context. In J. E. Grusec & L. Kuczynski (Eds.), *Parenting and children's internalization of values: A handbook of contemporary theory* (pp. 23–50). New York: Wiley.

L'Abaté, L. (1997). *The self in the family; a classification of personality, criminality, and psychopathology*. New York: Wiley.

Ladd, G. W. (1992). Themes and theories: Perspective on processes in family–peer relationships. In R. D. Parke & G. W. Ladd (Eds.), *Family–peer relationships: Modes of linkage* (pp. 3–34). Hillsdale, NJ: Erlbaum.

Ladd, G. W., & Golter, B. S. (1988). Parents' management of preschoolers' peer relations: Is it related to children's social competence? *Developmental Psychology*, **24**, 109–117.

Ladd, G. W., & Hart, C. H. (1991, July). *Parents' management of children's peer relations: Patterns associated with social competence*. Paper presented at the 11th Meeting of the International Society for Behavioral Development, Minneapolis, MN.

Ladd, G.W., & Kochenderfer-Ladd, B. J. (1998). Parenting behaviors and parent-child relationships: Correlates of peer victimization in kindergarten? *Developmental Psychology*, **34**, 1450–1458.

Ladd, G. W., & LeSieur, K. (1995). Parents' and children's peer relationships. In M. C. Bornstein (Ed.), *Handbook of parenting*, (Vol. 4, pp. 377–409). Mahwah, NJ: Erlbaum.

Ladd, G. W., & Price, J. M. (1986). Promoting children's cognitive and social competence: The relations between parents' perceptions of task difficulty and children's perceived and actual competence. *Child Development*, **57**, 446–460.

Ladd, G. W., Kochenderfer, B. & Coleman, C. (1997). Classroom peer acceptance, friendship, and victimization: Distinct relational systems that contribute uniquely to children's school adjustment. *Child Development*, **68**, 1181–1197.

Ladd, G. W., LeSieur, K., & Profilet, S. M. (1993). Direct parental influences on young children's peer relations. In S. W. Duck (Ed.), *Learning about relationships (Understanding relationship processes, Vol. 2*, pp. 152–183). Newbury Park, CA: Sage.

Ladd, G. W., Hart, C. H., Wadsworth, E. M., & Golter, B. S. (1988). Preschoolers' peer network in nonschool settings: Relationship to family characteristics and school adjustment. In S. Salzinger, J. Antrobus, & M. Hammer (Eds.), *Social networks of children, adolescents, and college students* (pp. 61–92). Hillsdale, NJ: Erlbaum.

LaFramboise, T. D., & Low, K. G. (1998). American Indian children and adolescents. In T. T. Gibbs & L. N. Huang (Eds.), *Children of color: Psychological interventions with culturally diverse youth* (2nd ed. pp. 112- 142). San Francisco, CA: Jossey-Bass.

LaFreniere, P. J., & Charlesworth, W. R. (1983). Dominance, attention, and affiliation in a preschool group: A nine-month longitudinal study. *Ethology and Sociobiology*, **4**, 55–67.

LaFreniere, P. J., & Sroufe, L. A. (1985). Profiles of peer competence in the preschool: Inter-relations between measures, influence of social ecology, and relation to attachment history. *Developmental Psychology*, **21**, 56–69.

Lagerspetz, K. M. J., & Björkqvist, K. (1994). Indirect aggression in girls and boys. In L. R. Huesmann (Ed.), *Aggressive behavior: Current perspectives* (pp. 131–150). New York: Plenum.

Lagerspetz, K. M. J., Björkqvist, K., & Peltonen, T. (1988). Is indirect aggression more typical of females? Gender differences in aggressiveness in 11- to 12-year-old children. *Aggressive Behavior*, **14**, 403–414.

Lagerspetz, K. M. J., Björkqvist, K., Berts, M., & King, E. (1982). Group aggression among school children in three schools. *Scandinavian Journal of Psychology*, **23**, 45–52.

Laible, D. J., & Thompson, R. A. (1998). Attachment and emotional understanding in preschool children. *Developmental Psychology*, **34**, 1038–1045.

Lamb, M. E. (1978). The development of sibling relationships in infancy: A short-term longitudinal study. *Child Development*, **49**, 1189–1196.

Lamb, M. E., & Nash, A. (1989). Infant–mother attachment, sociability, and peer competence. In T. J. Berndt & G. W. Ladd (Eds.), *Peer relationships in child development* (pp. 219–245). New York: Wiley.

Lanaro, S. (1992). *Storia dell'Italia repubblicana dalla fine della guerra agli anni '90.* [History of Republican Italy from the end of the war through the '90's]. Venice, Italy: Marsilio.

Larson, R., & Richards, M. (1991). Daily companionship in late childhood and early adolescence: Changing development contexts. *Child Development*, **62**, 284–300.

Lashley, K. S. (1958/60). Cerebral organization and behavior. In F. A. Beach, D. O. Hebb, C. T. Morgan, & H. W. Nissen, (Eds.), *The neuropsychology of Lashley* (pp. 529–543). New York: McGraw-Hill.

Laupa, M. (1995). Children's reasoning about authority in home and school contexts. *Social Development*, **4**, 1–16.

Laursen, B. (1993). The perceived impact of conflict on adolescent relationships. *Merrill-Palmer Quarterly*, **39**, 535–550.

Laursen, B. (1996). Closeness and conflict in adolescent peer relationships: Interdependence with friends and romantic partners. In W. M. Bukowski, A. F. Newcomb,

& W. W. Hartup (Eds.), *The company they keep: Friendships in childhood and adolescence* (pp. 186–210). New York: Cambridge University Press.

Laursen, B., & Collins, W. A. (1994). Interpersonal conflict during adolescence. *Psychological Bulletin*, **115**, 197–209.

Laursen, B., & Koplas, A. L. (1995). What's important about important conflicts? Adolescents' perceptions of daily disagreements. *Merrill-Palmer Quarterly*, **41**, 536–553.

Lazarus, R. S. (1991). *Emotion and adaptation.* New York: Oxford University Press.

Lazarus, R. S., & Folkman, S. (1984). *Stress, appraisal, and coping.* New York: Springer.

Le Doux, J. E. (1994). Emotion, memory, and the brain: Neural routes underlying the formation of memories about primitive emotional experiences, such as fear, have been traced. *Scientific American*, **270**(6), 50–57.

Le Doux, J. E. (1995). In search of an emotional system in the brain: Leaping from fear to emotion and consciousness. In M. Gazzaniga (Ed.), *The cognitive neurosciences* (pp. 1049–1061). Boston, MA: MIT Press.

Leaper, C. (1991). Influence and involvement in children's discourse: Age, gender, and partner effects. *Child Development*, **62**, 797–811.

Leaper, C. (1994). Exploring the consequences of gender segregation on social relationships. *New Directions for Child Development*, **65**, 67–86.

Leaper, C., Anderson, K. J., & Sanders, P. (1998). Moderators of gender effects on parents' talk to their children: A meta-analysis. *Developmental Psychology*, **34**, 3–27.

Leaper, C., Leve, L., Strasser, T., & Schwartz, R. (1995). Mother–child communication sequences: Play activity, child gender, and marital status effects. *Merrill-Palmer Quarterly*, **41**, 307–327.

Leary, M. R., Springer, C., Negel, L., Ansell, E., & Evans, K. (1998). The causes, phenomenology, and consequences of hurt feelings. *Journal of Personality and Social Psychology*, **74**, 1225–1237.

Lefcourt, H. M., & Martin, R. A. (1986). *Humor and life stress: Antidote to adversity.* New York: Springer.

Lerner, M., Miller, D. T., & Holmes, J. G. (1976). Deserving and the emergence of forms of justice. In L. Berkowitz & E. Walster (Eds.), *Advances in experimental social psychology* (Vol. 9, pp. 133–162). San Diego, CA: Academic Press.

Leung, K. (1987). Some determinants of reactions to procedural models for conflict resolution: A cross-national study. *Journal of Personality and Social Psychology*, **53**, 898–908.

Levenson, R. W., Carstensen, L. L., & Gottman, J. M. (1994). The influence of age and gender on affect, physiology, and their interrelations: A study of long-term relationships. *Journal of Personality and Social Psychology*, **67**, 56–68.

Leventhal, G. S. (1976). *Fairness in social relationships.* Morriston, NJ: General Learning Press.

Levitt, M. H., Weber, R. A., Clark, M. C., & McDonnell, P. (1985). Reciprocity of exchange in toddler sharing behavior. *Developmental Psychology*, **21**, 122–133.

Lewis, H. B. (1971). *Shame and guilt in neurosis.* New York: International Universities Press.

Lewis, M. (1991a). Self-conscious emotions and the development of self. In T. Shapiro & R. N. Emde (Eds.), New perspectives on affect and emotion in psychoanalysis. *Journal of the American Psychoanalytic Association (Suppl.)*, **39**, 45–73.

Lewis, M. (1991b). Ways of knowing: Objective self-awareness or consciousness. *Developmental Review*, **11**, 231–243.

Lewis, M. (1992). *Shame: the exposed self.* New York: The Free Press.

Lewis, M. (1995). Embarrassment: The emotion of self-exposure and evaluation. In J. P. Tangney & K. W. Fischer (Eds.), *Self-conscious emotions: The psychology of shame, guilt, embarrassment, and pride* (pp. 198–218). New York: Guilford.

Lewis, M., Alessandri, S. & Sullivan, M. W. (1990). Violation of expectancy, loss of control and anger expressions in young infants. *Developmental Psychology*, **26**, 745–751.

Lewis, M., Alessandri, S., & Sullivan, M. W. (1992). Differences in shame and pride as a function of children's gender and task difficulty. *Child Development*, **63**, 630–638.

Lewis, M., Sullivan, M., Stanger, C., & Weiss, M. (1989). Self development and self-conscious emotions. *Child Development*, **60**, 146–156.

Lin, C. Y. C., & Fu, V. R. (1990). A comparison of child-rearing practices among Chinese, immigrant Chinese, and Caucasian-American parents. *Child Development*, **61**, 429–433.

Lin, Y. W., & Rusbult, C. E. (1995). Commitment to dating relationships and cross-sex friendships in America and China. *Journal of Social and Personal Relationships*, **12**, 7–26.

Lindman, R., & Sinclair, S. (1989). Social roles and aspirations of bullies and victims. *Aggressive Behavior*, **15**, 80.

Lindsay-Hartz, J., De Rivera, J., & Mascolo, M. F. (1995). Differentiating guilt and shame and their effects on motivation. In J. Tangney & K. Fischer (Eds.), *Self-conscious emotions: The psychology of shame, guilt, embarrassment, and pride* (pp. 274–300). New York: Guilford.

Lindsey, E. W., Mize, J., & Pettit, G. S. (1997). Differential play patterns of mothers and fathers of sons and daughters: Implications for children's gender role development. *Sex Roles*, **37**, 643–661.

Lindskold, S., & Bennett, R. (1973). Attributing trust and conciliatory intent from coercive power capability. *Journal of Personality and Social Psychology*, **28**, 180–186.

Lippa, R. (1995). Gender-related individual differences and psychological adjustment in terms of the Big Five and circumplex models. *Journal of Personality and Social Psychology*, **69**, 1184–1202.

Loeber, R., & Hay, D. F. (1994). Developmental approaches to aggression and conduct problems. In M. Rutter & D. F. Hay (Eds.), *Development through life: A handbook for clinicians* (pp. 488–516). Oxford: Basil Blackwell.

Loehlin. J. C. (1992). *Genes and environment in personality development*. Newbury Park, CA: Sage.

Lollis, S. P., & Kuczynski, L. (1997). Beyond one hand clapping: Seeing bi-directionality in parent-child relations, *Journal of Social and Personal Relationships*, **14**, 441–461.

Lollis, S. P., Ross, H. S., & Tate, E. (1992). Parents' regulation of children's peer interactions: Direct influences. In R. D. Parke & G. W. Ladd (Eds.), *Family–peer relationships: Modes of linkage* (pp. 255–281). Hillsdale, NJ: Erlbaum.

Londerville, S., & Main, M. (1981). Security of attachment, compliance, and maternal training methods in the second year of life. *Developmental Psychology*, **17**, 289–299.

Long, N., Forehand, R., Fauber, R., & Brody, G. H. (1987). Self-perceived and independently observed competence of young adolescents as a function of parental marital conflict and recent divorce. *Journal of Abnormal Child Psychology*, **15**, 15–27.

Lundberg, G. A., & Dickson, L. (1952). Selective association among ethnic groups in a high school population. *American Sociological Review*, **17**, 23–35.

Lyons-Ruth, K. (1992). Maternal depressive symptoms, disorganized infant–mother relationships, and hostile-aggressive behavior in the preschool classroom: A prospective longitudinal view from infancy to age five. In D. Cicchetti & S. L. Toth (Eds.), Rochester Symposium on Developmental Psychopathology: Vol. 4. *Developmental perspectives on depression* (pp. 131–171). Rochester, NY: University of Rochester Press.

Lyons-Ruth, K. (1996). Attachment relationships among children with aggressive behavior problems: The role of disorganized early attachment patterns. *Journal of Consulting and Clinical Psychology*, **64**, 64–73.

Lytton, H., & Romney, D. M. (1991). Parents' differential socialization of boys and girls: A meta-analysis. *Psychological Bulletin*, **109**, 267–296.

Maccoby, E. E. (1988). Gender as a social category. *Developmental Psychology*, **24**, 755–765.

Maccoby, E. E. (1990). Gender and relationships: A developmental account. *American Psychologist*, **45**, 513–520.

Maccoby, E. E., & Jacklin, C. N. (1974). *The psychology of sex differences*. Stanford, CA: Stanford University Press.

Maccoby, E. E., & Martin, J. (1983). Socialization in the context of the family: Parent-child interaction. In P. Mussen (Ed.), *Handbook of child psychology: Vol. 4. Socialization, personality, and social development* (pp. 1–102). New York: Wiley.

MacDonald, K., & Parke, R. D. (1984). Bridging the gap: Parent–child play interaction and peer interactive competence. *Child Development*, **55**, 1265–1277.

MacFarlane, A. (1975). Olfaction in the development of social preferences in the human neonate. In *Parent–infant interaction* (CIBA foundation Symposium No. 33). Amsterdam: Elsevier.

MacKinnon, C. E. (1989). An observational investigation of sibling interactions in married and divorced families. *Developmental Psychology*, **25**, 36–44.

MacKinnon-Lewis, C., Volling, B. L., Lamb, M. E., Dechman, K., Rabiner, D., & Curtner, M. E. (1994). A cross-contextual analysis of boys' social competence: From family to school. *Developmental Psychology*, **30**, 325–333.

MacLean, P. D. (1990). *The triune brain in evolution: Role in paleocerebral functions*. New York: Plenum.

Madsen, K. C. (1997). *Differing perceptions of bullying*. Unpublished doctoral dissertation, University of Sheffield.

Mahler, M. (1958). Autism and symbiosis: Two extreme disturbances of identity. *International Journal of Psychoanalysis*, **39**, 77–83.

Mahler, M. (1968). *On human symbiosis and the vicissitudes of individuation*. New York: International Universities Press.

Main, M., & Goldwyn, R. (in press), Adult attachment classification system. In M. Main (Ed.), *A typology of human attachment organization: Assessed in discourse, drawing, and interviews*. Cambridge: Cambridge University Press.

Main, M., Kaplan, N., & Cassidy, J. (1985). Security in infancy, childhood and adulthood: A move to the level of representation. In I. Bretherton and E. Waters (Eds.), *Growing points of attachment theory and research. Monographs of the Society for Research in Child Development*, **50**(1–2, Serial No. 209), 66–104.

Malatesta, C. Z., & Haviland, J. M. (1982). Learning display rules: The socialization of emotion expression in infancy. *Child Development*, **53**, 991–1003.

Manke, B., & Plomin, R. (1997). Adolescent familial interactions: A genetic extension of the social relations model. *Journal of Social and Personal Relationships*, **14**, 505–522.

Margulis, L., & Sagan, D. (1991). *Mystery dance: On the evolution of sexuality*. New York: Summit Books.

Markus, H. R., & Kitayama, S. (1994). The cultural construction of self and emotion: Implications for social behavior. In S. Kitayama & H. R. Markus (Eds.), *Emotion and culture* (pp. 89–127). Washington, DC: American Psychological Association.

Martin, J. L., & Ross, H. S. (1995). The development of aggression in the family. *Early Education and Development*, **6**, 335–358.

Martlew, M., & Hodson, J. (1991). Children with mild learning difficulties in an integrated and in a special school: Comparisons of behavior, teasing and teachers' attitudes. *British Journal of Educational Psychology*, **61**, 355–372.

Marvin, R. S. (1977). An ethological-cognitive model for attenuation of mother–child attachment behavior. In T. M. Alloway, L. Kramer, & P. Pliner (Eds.), *Advances in the study of communication and affect: The development of social attachments*, (Vol. 3, pp. 25–60). New York: Plenum.

Mascolo, M. F., & Fischer, K. W. (1995). Developmental transformations in appraisals for pride, shame, and guilt. In J. P. Tangney & K. W. Fischer (Eds.), *Self-conscious emotions: The psychology of shame, guilt, embarrassment, and pride* (pp. 64–113). New York: Guilford.

Matas, L., Arend, R., & Sroufe, L. A. (1978). Continuity and adaptation in the second year: The relationship between quality of attachment and later competence. *Child Development*, **49**, 547–556.

Matsumoto, D., Haan, N., Yabrove, G., Theodorou, P., & Carney, C. C. (1986). Preschoolers' moral actions and emotions in prisoner's dilemma. *Developmental Psychology*, **22**, 663–670.

Mayes, L. C., & Carter, A. S. (1990). Emerging social regulatory capacities as seen in the still-face situation. *Child Development*, **61**, 754–763.

McCall, G. J. (1988). The organizational life cycle of relationships. In *Handbook of personal relationships* (pp. 467–486). Chichester, UK: Wiley.

McCoy, J. K., Brody, G. H., & Stoneman, Z. (1994). A longitudinal analysis of sibling relationships as mediators of the link between family processes and youths' best friendships. *Family Relations*, **43**, 400–408.

McDowell, D. J., & Parke, R. D. (in press). Display rule application in a disappointing situation and children's emotional reactivity: Relations with social competence. *Merrill-Palmer Quarterly*.

McDowell, D. J. & Parke, R. D. (submitted for publication). Differential knowledge of display rules and social competence.

McGhee, P. (1979). *Humor: Its origin and development.* San Francisco, CA: W. H. Freeman.

McLanahan, S., & Bumpass, L. (1988). Intergenerational consequences of family disruption. *American Journal of Sociology*, **94**, 130–152.

Mechanic, D., & Hansell, S. (1989). Divorce, family conflict, and adolescents' well-being. *Journal of Health and Social Behavior*, **30**, 105–116.

Mendelson, M. J., & Aboud, F. E. (1991, April). *Kindergartners' personality, popularity, and relationships.* Poster presented at the biennial meeting of the Society for Research in Child Development, Seattle, Washington.

Menesini, E. (1997). Behavioral correlates of friendship status among Italian schoolchildren. *Journal of Social and Personal Relationships*, **14**, 109–121.

Michener, H. A., Vaske, J. J., Schleiffer, S. L., Plazewski, J. G., & Chapman, L. J. (1975). Factors affecting concession rate and threat usage in bilateral conflict. *Sociometry*, **38**, 62–80.

Miell, D. E. (1987). Remembering relationship development: Constructing a context for interactions. In R. Burnett, J. McPhee, & D. D. Clarke (Eds.), *Accounting for Relationships* (pp. 60–73). London: Methuen.

Milardo, R. M., & Wellman, B. (1992). 'The personal is social'. *Journal of Social and Personal Relationships*, **9**, 339–42.

Miller, A. G., & Thomas, R. (1972). Cooperation and competition among Blackfoot Indian and Urban Canadian Children. *Child Development*, **43**, 1104–1110.

Miller, J. B. (1993). Learning from early relationship experience. In S. W. Duck (Ed.), *Learning about relationships (Understanding relationship processes series*, Vol. 2, pp. 1–29). Newbury Park, CA: Sage.

Miller, J. G. (1995, March). Rethinking problems of interdependence associated with individualism as compared with collectivism. In C. Raeff (Chair). *Individualism and collectivism as cultural contexts for developing different modes of independence and interdependence.* Symposium presented at the meeting of the Society for Research in Child Development, Indianapolis, IN.

Miller, P. A., Eisenberg, N., Fabes, R. A., Shell, R., & Gular, S. (1989). Mothers' emotional arousal as a moderator in the socialization of children's empathy. In N. Eisenberg (Ed.), Empathy and related emotional responses. *New Directions for Child Development*, **44**, 65–83.

Miller, P. M., Danaher, D., & Forbes, D. (1986). Sex-related strategies for coping with interpersonal conflict in children aged five and seven. *Developmental Psychology*, **22**, 543–548.

Miller, R. S. (1995). On the nature of embarrassability: Shyness, social evaluation, and social skill. *Journal of Personality*, **63**, 315–339.

Miller, R. S. (1995). Embarrassment and social behavior. In J. P. Tangney & K. W. Fischer (Eds.), *Self-conscious emotions: The psychology of shame, guilt, embarrassment, and pride* (pp. 322–339). New York: Guilford.

Mills, R. S. L. (in press). Exploring the effects of low power schemas in mothers. In P. D. Hastings & C. C. Piotrowski (Eds.), Conflict as a context for understanding maternal beliefs about child-rearing and children's misbehavior. *New Directions for Child Development*, **86**.

Mills, R. S. L., & Rubin, K. H. (1993). Parental ideas as influences on children's social competence. In S. W. Duck (Ed.), *Learning about relationships (Understanding relationship processes, Vol. 2*, pp. 98–117). Newbury Park, CA: Sage.

Minnett, A. M., Vandell, D. L., & Santrock, J. W. (1983). The effects of sibling status on sibling interaction: Influence of birth order, age spacing, sex of child and sex of sibling. *Child Development*, **54**, 1064–1072.

Minuchin, P. (1992). Conflict and child maltreatment. In C. U. Shantz & W. W. Hartup (Eds.), *Conflict in child and adolescent development* (pp. 380–401). Cambridge: University Press.

Mize, J., & Pettit, G. S. (1997). Mothers' social coaching, mother-child relationship style, and children's peer competence: Is the medium the message? *Child Development*, **68**, 312–332.

Mize, J., Pettit, G. S., & Brown, E. G. (1995). Mothers' supervision of their children's peer play: Relations with beliefs, perceptions, and knowledge. *Developmental Psychology*, **31**, 311–321.

Mize, J., Pettit, G. S., & Meece, D. (in press). Explaining the link between parenting behavior and children's peer competence: A critical examination of the "mediating process" hypothesis. In K. A. Kerns, J. M. Contreras, & A. Neal-Barnett (Eds.), *Family and peers: Linking two social worlds*. Westport, CT: Praeger.

Mnookin, R. H., Peppet, S. R., & Tulumello, A. S. (1996). The tension between empathy and assertiveness. *Negotiation Journal*, **12**, 217–230.

Moffitt, T. E., Caspi, A., Dickson, N., Silva, P., & Stanton, W. (1996). Childhood-onset versus adolescent-onset antisocial conduct problems in males: Natural history from age 3 to 18 years. *Development and Psychopathology*, **8**, 399–424.

Montgomery, B. M., & Duck, S. W. (Eds.). (1991). *Studying interpersonal interaction*. New York: Guilford.

Moran, S., Smith, P. K., Thompson, D., & Whitney, I. (1993). Ethnic differences in experiences of bullying: Asian and white children. *British Journal of Educational Psychology*, **63**, 431–440.

Moreno, J. L. (1934). *Who shall survive?* Washington, DC: Nervous and Mental Disease Publishing Co.

Munn, M., & Dunn, J. (1989). Temperament and the developing relationship between siblings. *International Journal of Behavioral Development*, **12**, 433–451.

Murphy, B. C., & Eisenberg, N. (1996). Provoked by a peer: Children's anger-related responses and their relations to social functioning. *Merrill-Palmer Quarterly*, **42**, 103–124.

Murphy, L. B. (1937). *Social behavior and child personality*. New York: Columbia University Press.

Murray, L., & Trevarthen, C. (1985). Emotional regulation of interactions between two-month-olds and their mothers. In T. Field & N. Fox (Eds.), *Social perception in infants* (pp. 177–197). Norwood, NJ: Ablex.

Muste, M. J., & Sharpe, D. F. (1947). Some influential factors in the determination of aggressive behavior in preschool children. *Child Development*, **18**, 11–28.

Mynard, H., & Joseph, S. (1997). Bully/victim problems and their association with Eysenck's personality dimensions in 8–13 year olds. *British Journal of Educational Psychology*, **67**, 51–54.

Myron-Wilson, R. (1998). *The family and bullying: Parenting and transgenerational patterns of attachment*. Unpublished doctoral dissertation, Goldsmiths College, University of London.

Nabuzoka, D., & Smith, P. K. (1993). Sociometric status and social behavior of children with and without learning difficulties. *Journal of Child Psychology and Psychiatry*, **34**, 1435–1448.

Neale, M. A., & Bazerman, M. H. (1983). The role of perspective-taking ability in negotiating under different forms of arbitration. *Industrial and Labor Relations*, **36**, 378–388.

Neisser, U. (1991). Two perceptually given aspects of the self and their development. *Developmental Review*, **11**, 197–209.

Nelson, K., & Gruendel, J. (1986). Children's scripts. In K. Nelson (Ed.), *Event knowledge: Structure and function in development*. Hillsdale, NJ: Erlbaum.

Neville, B., & Parke, R. D. (1997). Waiting for paternity: Interpersonal and contextual implications of the timing of fatherhood. *Sex Roles*, **37**, 45–59.

New, R. S. (1988). Parental goals and Italian infant care. In R. A. Levine, P. M. Miller, & M. M. West (Eds.), *Parental behavior in diverse societies*. San Francisco, CA: Jossey-Bass.

Newcomb, A. F., & Bagwell, C. L. (1995). Children's friendship relations: A meta-analytic review. *Psychological Bulletin*, **117**, 306–347.

Newman, D. L., Caspi, A., Silva, P. A., & Moffitt, T. E. (1997). Antecedents of adult interpersonal functioning: Effects of individual differences in age 3 temperament. *Developmental Psychology*, **33**, 206–217.

Newman, J. (1996). The more the merrier? Effects of family size and sibling spacing on sibling relationships. *Child: Care, Health and Development*, **22**, 285–302.

Nicholson, J. H. (1998). Sibling alliances. Unpublished Ph.D. Thesis, University of Iowa.

Nucci, L., & Weber, E. K. (1995). Social interactions in the home and the development of young children's conceptions of the personal. *Child Development*, **66**, 1438–1452.

O'Connor, T. G., Hetherington, E. M., & Clingempeel, W. G. (1997). Systems and bidirectional influences in families. *Journal of Social and Personal Relationships*, **14**, 491–504.

O'Donnell, L., & Stueve, A. (1983). Mothers as social agents: Structuring the community activities of school aged children. In H. Lopata & J. H. Pleck (Eds.), *Research in the interweave of social roles: Jobs and families: Vol. 3. Families and jobs* (pp. 119–133). Greenwich, CT: JAI.

O'Moore, A. M., & Hillery, B. (1989). Bullying in Dublin schools. *Irish Journal of Psychology*, **10**, 426–441.

O'Neil, R., & Parke, R. D. (in press). Family–peer relationships: The role of emotion regulation, cognitive understanding, and attention as mediating processes. In K. A. Kerns & A. M. Contreras (Eds.), *Family and peers: Linking two social worlds*. Westport, CT: Praeger.

O'Neil, R., & Parke, R. D. (submitted for publication). Perceived and objective neighborhood quality: Relations to parental monitoring and children's social competence.

O'Neil, R., Garcia, J., Zavala, A., & Wang, S. (1995). *Parental advice giving and children's competence with peers: A content and stylistic analysis*. Paper presented at the Biennial meeting of the Society for Research in Child Development, Indianapolis, IN.

O'Neil, R., Lee, J., Parke, R. D., & Wang, S. J. (submitted for publication). Parents' and children's social networks: Relations to parental attitudes and social competence in the early school years.

O'Neil, R., Parke, R. D., Isley, S., & Sosa, R. (1997, April). *Parental influences on children's emotion regulation in middle childhood*. Paper presented at the biennial meeting of the Society for Research in Child Development, Washington, DC.

Oatley, K. (1992). *Best laid schemes: The psychology of emotions*. Cambridge: Cambridge University Press.

Oliveri, M. E., & Reiss, D. (1987). Social networks of family members: Distinctive roles of mothers and fathers. *Sex Roles*, **17**, 719–736.

Olson, D. H. (1977). Insiders' and outsiders' views of relationships: Research studies. In G. Serringer & O. Moles (Eds.), *Close relationships: Perspectives on the meaning of intimacy* (pp. 115–135). Amherst, MA: University of Massachusetts Press.

Olson, D. H. (1989). *The circumplex model: Systematic assessment and treatment of families*. New York: Hawthorn Press.

Olthof, T., Ferguson, T., & Luiten, A. (1989). Personal responsibility antecedents of anger and blame reactions in children. *Child Development*, **60**, 1328–1336.

Olweus, D. (1978). *Aggression in the schools: Bullies and whipping boys*. Washington, DC: Hemisphere.

Olweus, D. (1980). Familial and temperamental determinants of aggressive behavior in adolescent boys: A causal analysis. *Developmental Psychology*, **16**, 644–660.

Olweus, D. (1984). Aggressors and their victims: Bullying at school. In N. Frude & H. Gault (Eds.), *Disruptive behavior in schools* (pp. 57–76). New York: Wiley.

Olweus, D. (1991). Bully/victim problems among schoolchildren: Basic facts and effects of a school-based intervention program. In D. J. Pepler and K. H. Rubin (Eds.), *The development and treatment of childhood aggression* (pp. 411–448). Hillsdale, NJ: Erlbaum.

Olweus, D. (1993a). *Bullying at school: What we know and what we can do*. Oxford: Basil Blackwell.

Olweus, D. (1993b). Victimization by peers: Antecedents and long-term outcomes. In K. H. Rubin & J. B. Asendorpf (Eds.), *Social withdrawal, inhibition, and shyness in childhood* (pp. 315–341). Hillsdale, NJ: Erlbaum.

Olweus, D. (1994). Annotation: Bullying at school: Basic facts and effects of a school-based intervention program. *Journal of Child Psychology and Psychiatry*, **35**, 1171–1190.

Olweus, D., & Endresen, I. M. (1998). The importance of sex-of-stimulus object: Age trends and sex differences in empathic responsiveness. *Social Development*, **7**, 370–388.

Orlick, T., Zhou, Q. Y., & Partington, J. (1990). Co-operation and conflict within Chinese and Canadian kindergarten settings. *Canadian Journal of Behavioural Science*, **22**, 20–25.

Oswald, H., & Krappmann, L. (1994). Social life of children in a former bipartite city. In P. Noack, H. Manfred, *et al.* (Eds.), *Psychological responses to social change: Human development in changing environments. Prevention and intervention in childhood and adolescence* (pp. 163–185). Berlin: de Gruyter.

Oswald, H., Krappmann, L., Uhlendorff, H. & Weiss, K. (1994). Social relationships and support among peers during middle childhood. In F. Nestmann & K. Hurrelmann (Eds.), *Social networks and social support* (pp. 171–189). Berlin: de Gruyter.

Park, S-Y., Belsky, J., Putnam, S., & Crnic, K. (1997). Infant emotionality, parenting, and 3-year inhibition: Exploring stability and lawful discontinuity in a male sample. *Developmental Psychology*, **33**, 218–227.

Parke, R. D. (1978). Children's home environments: Social and cognitive effects. In I. Altman & J. F. Wohlwill (Eds.), *Children and the environment* (pp. 33–81). New York: Plenum.

Parke, R. D. (1988). Families in life-span perspective: A multi-level developmental approach. In E. M. Hetherington, R. M. Lerner, & M. Perlmutter (Eds.), *Child development in life span perspective* (pp. 159–190). Hillsdale, NJ: Erlbaum.

Parke, R. D. (1994). Progress, paradigms and unresolved problems: A commentary on recent advances in our understanding of children's emotions. *Merrill Palmer Quarterly*, **40**, 157–169.

Parke, R. D. (1995). Fathers and families. In M. Bornstein (Ed.), *Handbook of parenting* (pp. 27–63). New York: Wiley.

Parke, R. D. (1996). *Fatherhood*. Cambridge, MA: Harvard University Press.

Parke, R. D., & Bhavnagri, N. (1989). Parents as managers of children's peer relationships. In D. Belle (Ed.), *Children's social networks and social supports* (pp. 241–259). New York: Wiley.

Parke, R. D., & Buriel, R. (1998). Socialization in the family: Ethnic and ecological perspectives. In W. Damon (Series Ed.) & N. Eisenberg (Vol. Ed.), *Handbook of child psychology: Vol. 3. Social, emotional, and personality development* (5th ed., pp. 463–552). New York: Wiley.

Parke, R. D., & Ladd, G. W. (Eds.) (1992). *Family–peer relationships: Modes of linkage*. Hillsdale, NJ: Erlbaum.

Parke, R. D., & Neville, B. (1995). Late-timed fatherhood: Determinants and consequences for children and families. In J. Shapiro, M. Diamond, & M. Greenberg (Eds.), *Becoming a father: Social, emotional and psychological perspectives* (pp. 104–116). New York: Springer.

Parke, R. D., & O'Neil, R. (1997). The influence of significant others on learning about relationships. In S. W. Duck (Ed.), *Handbook of personal relationships: Theory, research, and interventions* (2nd ed., pp. 29–60). Chichester, UK: Wiley

Parke, R. D., & O'Neil, R. (1999). Neighborhoods of Southern California children and families. *The future of children*, **9**, 58–63.

Parke, R. D., Burks, V. M., Carson, J. L., & Cassidy, J. (1992). Family contributions to peer relationships among young children. In R. D. Parke & G. Ladd (Eds.), *Family–peer relationships: Modes of linkage* (pp.107–134). Hillsdale, NJ: Erlbaum.

Parke, R. D., Burks, V. M., Carson, J. L., Neville, B., & Boyum, L. A. (1994). Family–peer relationships: A tripartite model. In R. D. Parke & S. G. Kellam (Eds.), *Exploring family relationships with other social constructs* (pp. 115–146). Hillsdale, NJ: Erlbaum.

Parke, R. D., MacDonald, K. B., Burks, V. M., Carson, J., Bhavnagri, N., Barth, J., & Beitel, A. (1989). Family and peer systems: In search of the linkages. In K. Kreppner & R. M. Lerner (Eds.), *Family systems and life span development* (pp. 65–92). Hillsdale, NJ: Erlbaum.

Parker, J. G., & Asher, S.R. (1993). Friendship and friendship quality in middle childhood: Links with peer group acceptance and feelings of loneliness and social dissatisfaction. *Developmental Psychology*, **29**, 611–621.

Parker, J. G., & Herrera, C. (1996). Interpersonal processes in friendship: A comparison of abused and non-abused children's experience. *Developmental Psychology*, **32**, 1025–1038.

Parpal, M., & Maccoby, E. E. (1985). Maternal responsiveness and subsequent child compliance. *Child Development*, **56**, 1326–1334.

Parsons, T., & Bales, R. F. (1955). *Family, socialization and interaction process.* Glencoe, IL: Free Press.

Patterson, C. J., & Stouthamer-Loeber, M. (1984). The correlation of family management practices and delinquency. *Child Development*, **55**, 1299–1306.

Patterson, C. J., Griesler, P. C., Vaden, N. A., & Kupersmidt, J. B. (1992). Family economic circumstances, life transitions, and children's peer relations. In R. D.

Parke & G. W. Ladd (Eds.), *Family–peer relationships: Modes of linkage* (pp. 385–424). Hillsdale, NJ: Erlbaum.

Patterson, C. J., Vaden, N. A., & Kupersmidt, J. B. (1991). Family background, recent life events, and peer rejection during childhood. *Journal of Social and Personal Relationships*, **8**, 347–361.

Patterson, G. R. (1982). *Coercive family processes*. Eugene, OR: Castalia.

Patterson, G. R., & Capaldi, D. M. (1991). Antisocial parents: Unskilled and vulnerable. In P. A. Cowan & E. M. Hetherington (Eds.), *Family transitions: Advances in family research* (Vol. 2, pp. 195–218). Hillsdale, NJ: Erlbaum.

Patterson, G. R., DeBaryshe, B. D., & Ramsey, E. (1989). A developmental perspective on antisocial behavior. *American Psychologist*, **44**, 329–335.

Patterson, G. R., Littman, R. A., & Bricker, W. (1967). Assertive behavior in children: A step toward a theory of aggression. *Monographs of the Society for Research in Child Development*, **32**(5, Serial No. 113).

Peck, R. F., & Havighurst, R. (1960). *The psychology of character development*. New York: Wiley.

Peek, C. W., Fischer, J. J., & Kidwell, J. S. (1985). Teenage violence toward parents: A neglected dimension of family violence. *Journal of Marriage and the Family*, **47**, 1051–1060.

Pepler, D. J., Abramovitch, R., & Corter, C. (1981). Sibling interaction in the home: A longitudinal study. *Child Development*, **52**, 1344–1347.

Pepler, D. J., Craig, W. M., & Roberts, W. L. (1998). Observations of aggressive and nonaggressive children on the school playground. *Merrill-Palmer Quarterly*, **44**, 55–76.

Perlman, M., & Ross, H. S. (1997a). The benefits of parent intervention in children's disputes: An examination of concurrent changes in children's fighting styles. *Child Development*, **64**, 690–700.

Perlman, M., & Ross, H. S. (1997b). Who's the boss? Parents' failed attempts to influence the outcomes of conflicts between their children. *Journal of Social and Personal Relationships*, **14**, 463–480.

Perren, S., & Alsaker, F. (1998, July). *Friendship and popularity status of children involved in bully/victim problems in kindergarten*. Poster presented at the Fifteenth Biennial Meeting of the International Society for the Study of Behavioural Development, Berne.

Perry, D. G., Kusel, S. J., Perry, L. C. (1988). Victims of peer aggression. *Developmental Psychology*, **24**, 807–814.

Peterson, L., Hartmann, D. P., & Gelfand, D. M. (1977). Developmental change in the effects of dependency and reciprocity cues on children's moral judgements and donation rates. *Child Development*, **48**, 1331–1339.

Pettit, G. S., & Clawson, M. A. (1996). Pathways to interpersonal competence: Parenting and children's peer relations. In N. Vanzetti & S. W. Duck (Eds.), *A lifetime of relationships* (pp. 125–154). Pacific Grove, CA: Brooks/Cole.

Pettit, G. S., & Lollis, S. P. (1997). Reciprocity and bidirectionality in parent–child relationships: New approaches to the study of enduring issues. *Journal of Social and Personal Relationships*, **14**, 435–440.

Pettit, G. S., & Mize, J. (1993). Substance and style: Understanding the ways in which parents teach children about social relationships. *Learning about relationships (Understanding relationship processes series*, Vol. 2, pp. 118–157). Newbury Park, CA: Sage.

Pettit, G. S., Brown, E. G., Mize, J., & Lindsey, E. (1998). Mothers' and fathers' socializing behaviors in three contexts: Links with children's peer competence. *Merrill-Palmer Quarterly*, **44**, 173–193.

Pettit, G. S., Dodge, K. A., & Brown, M. M. (1988). Early family experience, social problem solving patterns, and children's social competence. *Child Development*, **59**, 107–120.

Philips, S. V. (1972). Participant structures and communicative competence: Warm Springs children in community and classroom. In C. B. Cazden, V. P. John, & D. Hymes (Eds.), *Functions of language in the classroom* (pp. 370–394). New York: Teachers College Press.

Philipsen, G. (1987). The prospect for cultural communication. In D. Kincaid (Ed.), *Communication theory: Eastern and Western perspectives* (pp. 245–254). New York: Academic Press.

Phinney, J. S. (1986). The structure of 5-year-olds' verbal quarrels with peers and siblings. *The Journal of Genetic Psychology*, **147**, 47–60.

Piaget, J. (1932). *The moral development of the child*. New York: Free Press.

Piaget, J. (1952). *The origins of intelligence*. New York: International Universities Press.

Piaget, J. (1986). *Das moralische Urteil beim Kinde. (2. Aufl.)*. München: Klett-Cotta. (originally 1932: Le jugement moral chez l'enfant).

Pikas, A. (1989). A pure concept of mobbing gives the best results for treatment. *School Psychology International*, **10**, 95–104.

Pinkley, R. (1990). Dimensions of conflict frame. *Journal of Applied Psychology*, **75**, 117–126.

Pipp, S., Easterbrooks, M. A., & Harmon, R. J. (1992). The relation between attachment and knowledge of self and mother in one- to three-year-old infants. *Child Development*, **63**, 738–750.

Pipp, S., Robinson, J. L., Bridges, D., Bartholomew, S. (1997). Sources of individual differences in infant social cognition: Cognitive and affective aspects of self and other. In R. J. Sternberg & E. L. Grigorenko (Eds.), *Intelligence: Heredity and environment* (pp. 505–528). New York: Cambridge University Press.

Pomerantz, E. M., & Ruble, D. N. (1998). The role of maternal control in the development of sex differences in child self-evaluative factors. *Child Development*, **69**, 458–478.

Porter, B., & O'Leary, K. D. (1980). Marital discord and childhood behavior problems. *Journal of Abnormal Child Psychology*, **8**, 287–295.

Poulin, F., Cillessen, A. H. N., Hubbard, J. A., Coie, J. D., Dodge, K. A., & Schwartz, D. (1997). Children's friends and behavioral similarity in two social contexts. *Social Development*, **6**, 224–236.

Power, T. G., McGrath, M. P., Hughes, S. O., & Manire, S. H. (1994). Compliance and self-assertion: Young children's responses to mothers versus fathers. *Developmental Psychology*, **30**, 980–989.

Power, T., & Chapieski, M. L. (1986). Childrearing and impulse control in toddlers: A naturalistic investigation. *Developmental Psychology*, **22**, 271–275.

Powless, D. L., & Elliott, S. N. (1993). Assessment of social skills of Native American preschoolers: Teachers' and parents' ratings. *Journal of School Psychology*, 31, 293–307.

Pratt, M. W., Kerig, P. K., Cowan, P. A., & Cowan, P. A. (1992). Family worlds: Couple satisfaction, parenting style, and mothers' and fathers' speech to young children. *Merrill-Palmer Quarterly*, **38**, 245–262.

Prior, M. R., Sanson, A. V., & Oberklaid, F. (1989). The Australian temperament project. In G. A. Kohnstamm, J. E. Bates, & M. K. Rothbart (Eds.), *Temperament in childhood* (pp. 537–554). Chichester, UK: Wiley.

Prochanska, J. M., & Prochanska, J. O. (1985). Children's views of the causes and cures of sibling rivalry. *Child Welfare*, **64**, 427–433.

Pruitt, D. G. (1967). Reward structure and cooperation: The decomposed prisoner's dilemma. *Journal of Personality and Social Psychology*, **7**, 21–27.

Pruitt, D. G. (1970). Motivational processes in the decomposed prisoner's dilemma game. *Journal of Personality and Social Psychology*, **14**, 227–238.

Pruitt, D. G. (1981). *Negotiation behavior*. New York: Academic Press.

Pruitt, D. G. (1983). Strategic choice in negotiation. *American Behavioral Scientist*, **27**, 167–194.

Pruitt, D. G., & Carnevale, P. J. (1993). *Negotiation in social conflict*. Pacific Grove, CA: Brooks/Cole.

Pulkkinen, L. (1995). Behavioral precursors to accidents and resulting physical impairment. *Child Development*, **66**, 1660–1679.

Pulkkinen, L. (1996). Female and male personality styles: A typological and developmental analysis. *Journal of Personality and Social Psychology*, **70**, 1288–1306.

Putallaz, M. (1987). Maternal behavior and sociometric status. *Child Development*, **58**, 324–340.

Putallaz, M., & Sheppard, B. H. (1992). Conflict management and social competence. In C. U. Shantz & W. W. Hartup (Eds.), *Conflict in child and adolescent development* (pp. 330–355). Cambridge: Cambridge University Press.

Putallaz, M., Costanzo, P. R., & Klein, T. P. (1993). Parental childhood social experiences and their effects on children's relationships. In S. W. Duck (Ed.), *Learning about relationships (Understanding relationship processes series*, Vol. 2, pp. 63–97). Newbury Park, CA: Sage.

Putallaz, M., Costanzo, P. R., & Smith, R. B. (1991). Maternal recollections of childhood peer relationships: Implications for their children's social competence. *Journal of Social and Personal Relationships*, **8**, 403–422.

Putnam, L. L., & Jones, T. S. (1982). Reciprocity in negotiations: An analysis of bargaining interaction. *Communication Monographs*, **49**, 171–191.

Quiggle, N. L., Garber, J., Panak, W. F., & Dodge, K. A. (1992). Social information-processing in aggressive and depressed children. *Child Development*, **62**, 1305–1320.

Radke-Yarrow, M., Cummings, E. M., Kuczynski, L., & Chapman, M. (1985). Patterns of attachment in two and three-year-olds in normal families and families with parental depression. *Child Development*, **56**, 884–893.

Raeff, C. (1997). Individuals in relationships: Cultural values, children's social interactions, and the development of an American individualistic self. *Developmental Review*, **17**, 205–238.

Raffaelli, M. (1990). *Sibling conflict in early adolescence*. Unpublished dissertation, University of Chicago.

Raffaelli, M. (1992). Sibling conflict in early adolescence. *Journal of Marriage and the Family*, **54**, 652–663.

Ram, A., & Ross, H. S. (1998, May). *Contention, problem-solving, and struggle: How do siblings resolve conflicts of interest?* Paper presented at the Biennial Conference on Child Development, Waterloo, ON.

Rauh, H., Ziegenhain,U., Müller, B., & Wijnroks, L. (2000). Stability and change in infant–mother attachment in the second year of life: Relations to parenting quality and varying degrees of daycare experience. In P. M. Crittenden (Ed.), *The organization of attachment relationships: Maturation, culture, and context* (pp. 251–276). New York: Cambridge University Press.

Raven, B. H. (1992). A power/interaction model of interpersonal influence: French and Raven thirty years later. *Journal of Social Behavior and Personality*, **7**, 217–244.

Reid, J. B. (1993). Prevention of conduct disorder before and after school entry: Relation of interventions to developmental findings. *Development and Psychopathology*, **5**, 243–262.

Reid, M., Landesman, S., Treder, R., & Jaccard, J. (1989). "My family and friends": Six-to-twelve-year old children's perception of social support. *Child Development*, **60**, 896–910.

Renshaw, P. D., & Asher, S. R. (1983). Children's goals and strategies for social interaction. *Merrill-Palmer Quarterly*, **29**, 353–374.

Repetti, R. L. (1996). The effects of perceived daily social and academic failure experiences on school-age children's subsequent interactions with parents. *Child Development*, **67**, 1467–1482.

Retzinger, S. M. (1995). Shame and anger in personal relationships. In S. W. Duck & J. T. Wood (Eds.), *Confronting relationship challenges (Understanding relationship processes series*, Vol. 5, pp. 22–42). Thousand Oaks, CA: Sage.

Rheingold, H. L. (1969). The social and socializing infant. In D. A. Goslin (Ed.), *Handbook of socialization theory and research* (pp. 779–790). Chicago, IL: Rand-McNally.

Rican, P. (1995). Sociometric status of the school bullies and their victims. *Studia Psychologica*, **37**, 357–364.

Rieder, C., & Cicchetti, D. (1989). An organizational perspective on cognitive control functioning and cognitive-affective balance in maltreated children. *Developmental Psychology*, **25**, 482–493.

Rigby, K. (1993). School children's perceptions of their families and parents as a function of peer relations. *Journal of Genetic Psychology*, **154**, 501–513.

Rigby, K. (1994). Psychosocial functioning in families of Australian adolescent school children involved in bully/victim problems. *Journal of Family Therapy*, **16**, 173–187.

Rigby, K. (1997). *Bullying in schools and what to do about it*. London: Jessica Kingsley.

Rimé, B., Philippot, P., Boca, S. & Mesquita, B. (1992). Long-lasting cognitive and social consequences of emotion: Social sharing and rumination. In W. Stroebe & M. Hewstone (Eds.), *European Review of Social Psychology* (Vol. 3, pp. 225–258). Chichester, UK: Wiley.

Rivers, I., & Smith, P. K. (1994). Types of bullying behavior and their correlates. *Aggressive Behavior*, **20**, 359–368.

Rizzo, T. (1989). *Friendship development among children in school*. Norwood, NJ: Ablex.

Robins, L. N., & Ratcliff, K. S. (1979). Risk factors in the continuum of childhood anti-social behavior to adulthood. *International Journal of Mental Health*, **7**, 96–116.

Rocissano, L., Slade, A., & Lynch, V. (1987). Dyadic synchrony and toddler compliance. *Developmental Psychology*, **23**, 698–704.

Rogoff, B. (1990). *Apprenticeship in thinking*. New York: Oxford University Press.

Rosenthal, D. A., & Feldman, S. S. (1990). The acculturation of Chinese immigrants: Perceived effects on family functioning of length of residence in two cultural contexts. *The Journal of Genetic Psychology*, **15**, 495–514.

Ross, H. S. (1996). Negotiating principles of entitlement in sibling property disputes. *Developmental Psychology*, **32**, 90–101.

Ross, H. S., & Conant, C. L. (1992). The social structure of early conflict: Interaction, relationships, and alliances. In C. U. Shantz & W. W. Hartup (Eds.), *Conflict in child and adolescent development* (pp. 153–185). New York: Cambridge University Press.

Ross, H. S., & den Bak-Lammers, I. (1998). Consistency and change in children's tattling on their siblings: Children's perspectives on the moral rules and procedures of family life. *Social Development*, **7**, 275–299.

Ross, H. S., & Goldman, B. D. (1976). Establishing new social relations in infancy. In T. Alloway, P. Pliner, & L. Kramer (Eds.), *Advances in the study of communication and affect: Attachment behavior* (Vol. 3, pp 61–79). New York: Plenum.

Ross, H. S., Cheyne, J. A., & Lollis, S. P. (1988). Defining and studying reciprocity in young children. In S. W. Duck (Ed.), *Handbook of personal relationships: Theory, research, and interventions* (pp. 143–160). New York: Wiley.

Ross, H. S., Filyer, R. E., Lollis, S. P., Perlman, M., & Martin, J. L. (1994). Administering justice in the family. *Journal of Family Psychology*, **8**, 254–273.

Ross, H. S., Lollis, S. P., & Elliot, C. (1982). Toddler–peer communication. In K. H. Rubin & H. S. Ross (Eds.), *Peer relationships and social skills in childhood* (pp. 73–98). New York: Springer-Verlag.

Ross, H. S., Tesla, C., Kenyon, B., Lollis, S. P. (1990). Maternal intervention in toddler peer conflict: The socialization of principles of justice. *Developmental Psychology*, **26**, 994–1003.

Rothbart, M. K. (1989). Temperament and development. In G. Kohnstamm, J. E. Bates, & M. K. Rothbart (Eds.), *Temperament in childhood* (pp. 187–248). Chichester, UK: Wiley.

Rothbart, M. K., & Bates, J. (1998). Temperament. In W. Damon (Series Ed.) & N. Eisenberg (Vol. Ed.), *Handbook of child psychology: Vol. 3. Social, emotional, and personality development* (5th ed., pp. 105–176).

Rothbart, M. K., & Hallmark, W. (1988). Ingroup-outgroup differences in the perceived efficacy of coercion and conciliation in resolving social conflict. *Journal of Personality and Social Psychology*, **57**, 435–448.

Rowe, D. C. (1994). *The limits of family influence: Genes, experience, and behavior.* New York: Guilford.

Rowley, K. G. (1968). Social relations between British and immigrant children. *Educational Research*, **10**, 145–148.

Ruan, F. F., & Matsumura, M. (1991). Sex in China: Studies in sexology in Chinese culture. New York: Plenum.

Rubin, J. Z. (1994). Models of conflict management. *Journal of Social Issues*, **50**, 33–45.

Rubin, K. H. (1998). Social and emotional development from a cross-cultural perspective. *Developmental Psychology*, **34**, 611–615.

Rubin, K. H., & Mills, R. S. L. (1990). Maternal beliefs about adaptive and maladaptive social behaviors in normal, aggressive, and withdrawn preschoolers. *Journal of Abnormal Child Psychology*, **18**, 419–435.

Rubin, K. H., Bream, L. A., & Rose-Krasnor, L. (1991). Social problem solving and aggression in childhood. In D. J. Pepler & K. H. Rubin (Eds.), *The development and treatment of childhood aggression* (pp. 219–248). Hillsdale, NJ: Erlbaum.

Rubin, K. H., Bukowski, W., & Parker, J. G. (1998). Peer interactions, relationships, and groups. In W. Damon (Series Ed.) & N. Eisenberg (Vol. Ed.), *Handbook of child psychology: Vol. 3. Social, emotional, and personality development* (5th ed., pp. 619–700). New York: Wiley.

Rubin, K. H., Mills, R. S. L., & Rose-Krasnor, L. (1989). Maternal beliefs and children's competence. In B. H. Schneider, G. Attili, J. Nadel, & R. P. Weissberg (Eds.), *Social competence in developmental perspective* (pp. 313–331). Amsterdam: Klewer Academic.

Rubin, K. H., Stewart, S. L., & Chen, X. (1995). Parents of aggressive and withdrawn children. In M. H. Bornstein (Ed.), *Handbook of parenting* (Vol. 1, pp. 255–284). Mahwah, NJ: Erlbaum.

Ruble, D. N., & Martin, C. L. (1998). Gender development. In W. Damon (Series Ed.) & N. Eisenberg (Vol. Ed.), *Handbook of child psychology: Vol. 3. Social, emotional, and personality development* (5th ed., pp. 933–1016). New York: Wiley.

Ruch, W. (1993). Exhilaration and humor. In M. Lewis & J. M. Haviland (Eds.), *Handbook of emotions* (pp. 605–616). New York: Guilford.

Rueter, M. A., & Conger, R. D. (1995). Antecedents of parent–adolescent disagreements. *Journal of Marriage and the Family*, **57**, 435–448.

Rusbult, C. E., & Buunk, B. P. (1993). Commitment processes in close relationships: An interdependence analysis. *Journal of Social and Personal Relationships*, **10**, 175–204.

Russell, A., & Finnie, V. (1990). Preschool children's social status and maternal instructions to assist group entry. *Developmental Psychology*, **26**, 603–611.

Russell, A., & Russell, G. (1992). Child effects in socialization research: Some conceptual and data analysis issues. *Social Development*, **1**, 163–184.

Russell, A., & Saebel, J. (1997). Mother–son, mother–daughter, father–son, and father–daughter: Are they distinct relationships? *Developmental Review*, **17**, 111–147.

Russell, A., & Searcy, E. (1997). The contribution of affective reactions and relationship qualities to adolescents' reported responses to parents. *Journal of Social and Personal Relationships*, **14**, 539–548.

Russell, A., Aloa, V., Feder, T., Glover, A., Miller, A., & Palmer, G. (1998). Sex-based differences in parenting styles in a sample with preschool children. *Australian Journal of Psychology*, **50**, 89–99.

Russell, A., Mize, J., & Saebel, J. (in press). Coding the social dimensions of parent–toddler play from a vertical/horizontal perspective. In P. Kerig & K. Lindahl (Eds.) *Family observational coding systems: Resources for systematic research.* Hillsdale, NJ: Erlbaum.

Russell, A., Pettit, G. S., & Mize, J. (1998). Horizontal qualities in parent-child relationships: Parallels with and possible consequences for children's peer relationships. *Developmental Review*, **18**, 313–352.

Rutherford, E., & Mussen, P. (1968). Generosity in nursery school boys. *Child Development*, **39**, 755–765.

Rutter, M. (1994). Family discord and conduct disorder: Cause, consequence or correlate? *Journal of Family Psychology*, **8**, 170–186.

Ryan, A. S. (1985). Cultural factors in casework with Chinese-Americans. *Social Casework: The Journal of Contemporary Social Work*, **66**, 333–340.

Rydell, A.-M., Hagekull, B., & Bohlin, G. (1997). Measurement of two social competence aspects in middle childhood. *Developmental Psychology*, **33**, 824–833.

Rys, G. S., & Bear, G. C. (1997). Relational aggression and peer relations: Gender and developmental issues. *Merrill-Palmer Quarterly*, **43**, 87–106.

Saarni, C. (1984). An observational study of children's attempt to monitor their expressive behavior. *Child Development*, **55**, 1504–1513.

Saarni, C. (1995, March). *Coping with aversive feelings.* Paper presented at the Meeting of the Society for Research in Child Development, Indianapolis, IN.

Saarni, C., Mumme, D. L., & Campos, J. J. (1998). Emotional development: Action, communication, and understanding. In W. Damon (Series Ed.) & N. Eisenberg (Vol. Ed.), *Handbook of child psychology: Vol. 3. Social, emotional, and personality development* (5th ed., pp. 237–309). New York: Wiley.

Sachs, L. (1987). Preschool boys' and girls' language use in pretend play. In S. U. Philips, S. Steele, & C. Tanz (Eds.), *Language, gender, and sex in comparative perspective* (pp. 178–188). Cambridge: Cambridge University Press.

Sagi, A., & Hoffman, M. (1976). Empathic distress in the newborn. *Developmental Psychology*, **12**, 175–176.

Salmivalli, C. (1998). Intelligent, attractive, well-behaving, unhappy: The structure of adolescents' self-concept and its relations to their social behavior. *Journal of Research on Adolescence*, **8**, 333–354.

Salmivalli, C., Huttunen, A., & Lagerspetz, K. M. J. (1997). Peer networks and bullying in schools. *Scandinavian Journal of Psychology*, **38**, 305–312.

Salmivalli, C., Karhunen, J., & Lagerspetz, K. M. J. (1996). How do the victims respond to bullying? *Aggressive Behavior*, **22**, 99–109.

Salmivalli, C., Kaukiainen, A., Kaistaniemi, L., & Lagerspetz, K. M. J. (1999). Self-evaluated self-esteem, peer-evaluated self-esteem, and defensive egotism as predictors of adolescents' participation in bullying situations. *Personality and Social Psychology Bulletin*, **25**, 1268–1278.

Salmivalli, C., Lagerspetz, K. M. J., Björkqvist, K., Österman, K., & Kaukiainen, A. (1996). Bullying as a group process: participant roles and their relations to social status within the group. *Aggressive Behavior*, **22**, 1–15.

Salmivalli, C., Lappalainen, M., & Lagerspetz, K. M. J. (1998). Stability and change of behavior in connection with bullying in schools: A two-year follow-up. *Aggressive Behavior*, **24**, 205–218.

Salmon, G., James, A., & Smith, D. M. (1998). Bullying in schools: Self-reported anxiety, depression, and self-esteem in secondary school children. *British Medical Journal*, **317**, 924–925.

Sampson, E. E. (1988). The debate on individualism: Indigenous psychologies of the individual and their role in personal and societal functioning. *American Psychologist*, **43**, 15–22.

Sancilio, M., Plumert, J., & Hartup, W. W. (1989). Friendship and aggressiveness as determinants of conflict outcomes in middle childhood. *Developmental Psychology*, **25**, 812–819.

Sanfilipo, M. P. (1994). Masculinity, femininity, and subjective experiences of depression. *Journal of Clinical Psychology*, **50**, 144–155.

Sanford, S., & Eder, D. (1984). Adolescent humor during peer interaction. *Social Psychology Quarterly*, **47**, 235–243.

Sanson, A., Smart, D., Prior, M., & Oberklaid, F. (1993). Precursors of hyperactivity and aggression. *Journal of the American Academy of Child and Adolescent Psychiatry*, **32**, 1207–1216.

Sants, H. K. A. (1984). Conceptions of friendship, social behavior and school achievement in six-year-old children. *Journal of Social and Personal Relationships*, **1**, 293–309.

Saraceno, C. (1981). *Ritrato di famiglia degli anni '80*. Bari, Italy: Laterza.

Satir, V. (1972). *Peoplemaking*. Palo Alto, CA: Science and Behavior Books.

Scarr, S. (1992). Developmental theories for the 1990s: Development and individual differences. *Child Development*, **63**, 1–19.

Schachter, D., & Tulving, E. (1994). *Memory systems 1994*. Cambridge, MA: MIT Press.

Scheff, T. J. (1995). Conflict in family systems: The role of shame. In J. P. Tangney & K. W. Fischer (Eds.), *Self-conscious emotions: The psychology of shame, guilt, embarrassment, and pride* (pp. 393–412). New York: Guilford.

Scherer, K. R., Wallbott, H., & Summerfield, A. (Eds.) (1986). *Experiencing emotion: A cross-cultural study*. Cambridge: Cambridge University Press.

Schneider, B. H. (1993). *Children's social competence in context: The contributions of family, school and culture*. Oxford: Pergamon.

Schneider, B. H., Fonzi, A., Tani, F., & Tomada, G. (1997). A cross-cultural exploration of the stability of children's friendships and the predictors of their continuation. *Social Development*, **6**, 322–339.

Schneider, B. H., Fonzi, A., Tomada, G., & Tani, F. (in press). A cross-national comparison of children's behavior with their friends in situations of potential conflict. *Journal of Cross-Cultural Psychology*.

Schneider, B. H., Wiener, J., & Murphy, K. (1994). Children's friendships: The giant step beyond peer acceptance. *Journal of Social and Personal Relationships*, **11**, 323–340.

Schneider, W., & Larzelere, R. (1988, August). *Effects of discipline strategies on delays of reoccurrences of misbehavior in toddlers*. Paper presented at the meeting of the American Psychological Association, Atlanta, GA.

Schneider-Rosen, K., & Cicchetti, D. (1991). Early self-knowledge and emotional development: Visual self-recognition and affective reactions to mirror self-images in maltreated and non-maltreated toddlers. *Developmental Psychology*, **27**, 471–478.

Schofield, J. W. (1995). Promoting positive intergroup relations in school settings. In W. D. Hawley & A. W. Jackson (Eds.), *Toward a common destiny: Improving race and ethnic relations in America* (pp. 71–99). San Francisco, CA: Jossey-Bass.

Schofield, J. W., & Sagar, H. A. (1977). Peer interaction patterns in an integrated middle school. *Sociometry*, **40**, 130–138.

Schvaneveldt, J. D., & Ihinger, M. (1979). Sibling relationships in the family. In W. R. Burr, R. Hill, F. I. Nye, & I. L. Reiss (Eds.), *Contemporary theories about the family: Research-based theories* (Vol. 1, pp. 453–467). London: The Free Press.

Schwartz, D., Dodge, K. A., Pettit, S., & Bates, J. E. (1997). The early socialization of aggressive victims of bullying. *Child Development*, **68**, 665–675.

Segall, M. H. (1979). *Cross-cultural psychology: Human behavior in global perspective.* Monterey, CA: Brooks-Cole.

Seligman, M. (1971). Preparedness and phobias. *Behavior Therapy*, **2**, 307–320.

Selman, R. L. (1980). *The growth of interpersonal understanding.* New York: Academic Press.

Selman, R. L., & Demorest, A. P. (1987). Putting thoughts and feelings into perspective: A developmental view of how children deal with disequilibrium. In D. Bearison & H. Zimiles (Eds.), *Thought and emotion* (pp. 93–128). Hillsdale, NJ: Erlbaum.

Selman, R. L., & Schultz, L. (1990). *Making a friend in youth: Developmental theory and pair therapy.* Chicago, IL: University of Chicago Press.

Selman, R. L., Beardslee, W., Schultz, L. H., Krupa, M., & Poderefsky, D. (1986). Assessing adolescent interpersonal negotiation strategies: Toward the integration of structural and functional models. *Developmental Psychology*, **22**, 450–459.

Selman, R. L., Schultz, L. H., Nakkula, M., Barr, D., Watts, C., & Richmond, J. B. (1992). Friendship and fighting: A developmental approach to the study of risk and the prevention of violence. *Development and Psychopathology*, **4**, 529–558.

Seltzer, J. A., & Kalmuss, D. (1988). Socialization and stress explanations for spousal abuse. *Social Forces*, **67**, 473–491.

Selye, H. (1976). *The stress of life.* New York: McGraw-Hill.

Senchea, J. A. (1998). Adolescent girls' performance of gender through talk about sex. Unpublished Ph.D. thesis, University of Iowa.

Shantz, C. U. (1987). Conflicts between children. *Child Development*, **58**, 283–305.

Shantz, C. U. (1993). Children's conflicts: Representations and lessons learned. In R. R. Coching & K. A. Renninger (Eds.), *The development and meaning of psychological distance* (pp. 63–89). Hillsdale, NJ: Erlbaum.

Shantz, C. U., & Hartup, W. W. (Eds.) (1992). *Conflict in child and adolescent development.* Cambridge: Cambridge University Press.

Shantz, C. U., & Hobart, C. J. (1989). Social conflict and development: Peers and siblings. In T. J. Berndt & G. W. Ladd (Eds.), *Peer relationships in child development* (pp. 71–94). New York: Wiley.

Shantz, C. U., & Shantz, D. (1985). Conflicts between children: Social-cognitive and sociometric correlates. In M. Berkowitz (Ed.), Peer conflict and psychological growth. *New Directions for Child Development*, **29**, 3–21.

Shenkar, O., & Ronen, S. (1987). The cultural context of negotiations: The implications of Chinese interpersonal norms. *Journal of Applied Behavioral Science*, **23**, 263–275.

Shifflet-Simpson, E., & Cummings, E. M. (1996). Mixed message resolution and children's responses to interadult conflict. *Child Development*, **67**, 437–448.

Shotter, J. (1992). What is a "personal" relationship? A rhetorical-responsive account of "unfinished business". In J. H. Harvey, T. L. Orbuch, & A. L. Weber (Eds.), *Attributions, accounts and close relationships* (pp. 19–39). New York: Springer-Verlag.

Shweder, R. A., & Much, N. C. (1987). Determination of meaning: Discourse and moral socialization. In W. M. Kurtines & J. S. Gewirtz (Eds.), *Moral development through social interaction* (pp. 197–233). New York: Wiley.

Shweder, R. A., Mahapatra, M., & Miller, J. (1987). Culture and moral development. In J. Kagan & S. Lamb (Eds.), *The emergence of morality in young children* (pp. 1–82). Chicago, IL: University of Chicago Press.

Siann, G., Callaghan, M., Glissov, P., Lockhart, R., & Rawson, L. (1994). Who gets bullied? The effect of school, gender, and ethnic group. *Educational Research*, **36**, 123–134.

Siddiqui, A., & Ross, H. S. (1999). How do sibling conflicts end? *Early Education and Development*, **10**, 315–332.

Siegal, M. (1987). Are sons and daughters treated more differently by fathers than by mothers? *Developmental Review*, **7**, 183–209.

Sillars, A. L. (1981). Attributions and interpersonal conflict resolution. In J. H. Harvey, W. Ickes, & R.G. Kidd (Eds.), *New directions in attribution research*, **3**, 279–305. Hillsdale, NJ: Erlbaum.

Silverman, I. W., & Ragusa, D. M. (1990). Child and maternal correlates of impulse control in 24-month-old children. *Genetic, Social, and General Psychology Monographs*, **116**, 435–473.

Silverman, I. W., & Ragusa, D. M. (1992). A short-term longitudinal study of the early development of self-regulation. *Journal of Abnormal Child Psychology*, **20**, 415–435.

Silverman, W. K., La Greca, A. & Wasserstein, S. (1995). What do children worry about? Worries and their relation to anxiety. *Child Development*, **66**, 671–686.

Simpkins, S., & Parke, R. D. (submitted for publication). The relations between parental friendships and children's friendships: Self-report and observational analyses.

Singleton, L. C., & Asher, S. R. (1979). Racial integration and children's peer preferences: An investigation of developmental and cohort differences. *Child Development*, **50**, 936–941.

Sinha, J. B. P., & Tripathi, R. C. (1994). Individualism in a collectivistic culture: A case of coexistence of opposites. In U. Kim, H. C. Triandis, C. Kagitcibasi, S.C. Choi, & G. Yoon (Eds.), *Individualism and collectivism: Theory, methods, and applications* (pp. 123–136). Thousand Oaks, CA: Sage.

Slavin, R. E. (1979). Effects of biracial learning teams on cross-racial friendships. *Journal of Educational Psychology*, **71**, 381–387.

Slee, P. T., & Rigby, K. (1993). Australian school children's self-appraisal of interpersonal relations: The bullying experience. *Child Psychiatry and Human Development*, **23**, 273–287.

Slomkowski, C., & Dunn, J. (1996). Young children's understanding of other people's beliefs and feelings and their connected communication with friends. *Developmental Psychology*, **32**, 442–447.

Smetana, J. G. (1988). Adolescents' and parents' conceptions of parental authority. *Child Development*, **59**, 321–335.

Smetana, J. G. (1995). Context, conflict and constraint in adolescent-parent authority relations. In M. Killen & D. Hart (Eds.), *Morality in everyday life: Developmental perspectives* (pp. 225–255). New York: Cambridge University Press.

Smetana, J. G., & Asquith, P. (1994). Adolescents' and parents' conceptions of parental authority and adolescent autonomy. *Child Development*, **65**, 1147–1162.

Smith, A., & Schneider, B. H. (in press). Culture as a factor in friendship selection among Canadian early adolescents. *International Journal of Intercultural Relations*.

Smith, P. K. (1995). Grandparenthood. In M. H. Bornstein (Ed.), *Handbook of Parenting* (pp. 89–112). Hillsdale, NJ: Erlbaum.

Smith, P. K., & Madsen, K. C. (1997). *A follow-up of the DFE Anti-Bullying Pack for schools: Its use, and the development of anti-bullying work in schools*. London: HMSO.

Smith, P. K., & Myron-Wilson, R. (1998). Parenting and school bullying. *Clinical Child Psychology and Psychiatry*, **3**, 405–417.

Smith, P. K., & Sharp, S. (Eds.) (1994). *School bullying: Insights and perspectives*. London: Routledge.

Smith, P. K., & Shu, S. (1998). *Cross-national study of bullying: Final comparative report for England*. Tokyo: Report to Japanese Ministry of Education.

Smith, P. K., Bowers, L., Binney, V., & Cowie, H. (1993). Relationships of children involved in bully/victim relationships. In S. W. Duck (Ed.), Learning about relationships (Understanding relationship processes series. Vol. 2 (pp. 184–212). Newbury Park, CA: Sage.

Smith, P. K., Madsen, K. C., & Moody, J. C. (1999). What causes the age decline in reports of being bullied at school? Towards a developmental analysis of risks of being bullied. *Educational Research*, **41**, 267–285.

Smith, P. K., Morita, Y., Junger-Tas, J., Olweus, D., Catalano, R., & Slee, P. (1999). *The nature of school bullying: A cross-national perspective*. London: Routledge.

Snyder, J. R. (1998). Marital conflict and child adjustment: What about gender? *Developmental Review*, **18**, 390–420.

Sorce, J. F., Emde, R. N., Campos, J. J., & Klinnert, M. D. (1985). Maternal emotional signaling: Its effects on the visual cliff behavior of 1-year-olds. *Developmental Psychology*, **21**, 195–200.

Spence, J. T., & Helmreich, R. L. (1978). *Masculinity and femininity: Their psychological dimensions, correlates, and antecedents*. Austin, TX: University of Texas Press.

Spitzberg, B. H., & Cupach, W. R. (Eds.). (1998). *The dark side of close relationships*. Mahwah, NJ: Erlbaum.

Spitzer, S., & Parke, R. D. (1994, August). Family cognitive representations of social behavior and children's social competence. Paper presented at the meeting of the American Psychological Association, Washington, DC.

Spitzer, S., Estock, S., Cupp, R., Isley-Paradise, S., & Parke, R. D. (1992). *Parental influence and efficacy beliefs and children's social acceptance*. Unpublished manuscript, University of California, Riverside.

Sroufe, L. A. (1979). Socioemotional development. In J. Osofsky (Ed.), *Handbook of infant development* (pp. 462–516). New York: Wiley.

Sroufe, L. A. (1982). Attachment and the roots of competence. In H. E. Fitzgerald & T. H. Carr (Eds.), *Human development: Annual editions*. Guilford, CA: Dushkin.

Sroufe, L. A., & Fleeson, J. (1986). Attachment and the construction of relationships. In W. W. Hartup & Z. Rubin (Eds.), *Relationships and development* (pp. 51–72). Hillsdale, NJ: Erlbaum.

Sroufe, L. A., Carlson, E., & Shulman, S. (1993). Individuals in relationships: Development from infancy through adolescence. In D. C. Funder, R. D. Parke, C. Tomlinson-Keasey, & K. Widaman (Eds.), *Studying lives through time* (pp. 315–342). Washington, DC: American Psychological Association.

Sroufe, L. A., Egeland, B., & Kreutzer, T. (1990). The fate of early experience following developmental change: Longitudinal approaches to individual adaptation in childhood. *Child Development*, **61**, 1363–1373.

Sroufe, L. A., Fox, J., & Pancake, V. (1983). Attachment and dependency in developmental perspective. *Child Development*, **54**, 1615–1527.

St. John, N. H. (1964). De facto segregation and interracial association in high school. *Sociology of Education*, **37**, 326–344.

Stack, D. M., & Muir, D. W. (1990). Tactile stimulation as a component of social interchange: New interpretations for the still-face effect. *British Journal of Developmental Psychology*, **8**, 131–145.

Starr, R. H. (1979). Child abuse. *American Psychologist*, **34**, 872–878.

Steele, H., Steele, M., & Fonagy, P. (1996). Associations among attachment classifications of mothers, fathers, and their infants. *Child Development*, **67**, 541–555.

Steinberg, L. (1986). Latchkey children and susceptibility to peer pressure: An ecological analysis. *Developmental Psychology*, **22**, 433–439.

Steinberg, L., Darling, N. E., & Fletcher, A.C. (1995). Authoritative parenting and adolescent adjustment: An ecological journey. In P. Moen & G. H. Elder (Eds.), *Examining lives in context: Perspectives on the ecology of human development* (pp. 423–466.). Washington, DC: American Psychological Association.

Steinmetz, J. E. (1998). The localization of a simple type of learning and memory: The cerebellum and classical eyeblink conditioning. *Current Directions in Psychological Science*, **7**, 72–77.

Stephens, M. A. P., & Clark, S. L. (1996). Interpersonal relationships in multi-generational families. In N. Vanzetti & S. W. Duck (Eds.), *A lifetime of relationships* (pp. 431–454). Pacific Grove, CA: Brooks/Cole.

Stephenson, P., & Smith, D. (1989). Bullying in the junior school. In D. P. Tattum & D. A. Lane (Eds.), *Bullying in schools* (pp. 45–57). Stoke-on-Trent, UK: Trentham Books.

Stern, D. (1986). *The interpersonal world of the infant.* New York: Basic Books.

Stevenson, H. W., Chen, C., Lee, S., & Fuligni, A. J. (1991). Schooling, culture, and cognitive development. In L. Okagaki, R.J. Sternberg, *et al.* (Eds.), *Directors of development: Influences on the development of children's thinking* (pp. 243–268). Hillsdale, NJ: Erlbaum.

Stevenson, M. B., Leavitt, L. A., Thompson, R. H., & Roach, M. A. (1988). A social relations model analysis of parent and child play. *Developmental Psychology*, **24**, 101–108.

Stevenson-Hinde, J., & Shouldice, A. (1995). Maternal interactions and self-reports related to attachment classification at 4.5 years. *Child Development*, **66**, 583–596.

Stipek, D. J. (1983). A developmental analysis of pride and shame. *Human Development*, **26**, 42–54.

Stipek, D. J. (1995). The development of pride and shame in toddlers. In J. P. Tangney & K. W. Fischer (Eds.), *Self-conscious emotions: The psychology of shame, guilt, embarrassment, and pride* (pp. 237–252). New York: Guilford.

Stipek, D. J., Recchia, S., & McClintic, S. (1992). Self-evaluation in young children. *Monographs of the Society for Research in Child Development*, **57** (1, Serial No. 226).

Stocker, C. M. (1994). Children's perceptions of relationships with siblings, friends, and mothers: Compensatory processes and links with adjustment. *Journal of Child Psychology and Psychiatry*, **35**, 1447–1459.

Stocker, C., & Dunn, J. (1990). Sibling relationships in childhood: Links with friendship and peer relationships. *British Journal of Developmental Psychology*, **8**, 227–244.

Stocker. C., Ahmed, K., & Stall, M. (1997). Marital satisfaction and maternal emotional expressiveness: Links with children's sibling relationship. *Social Development*, **6**, 373–385.

Stoneman, Z., & Brody, G. H. (1993). Sibling temperaments, conflict, warmth, and role asymmetry. *Child Development*, **64**, 1786–1800.

Stoneman, Z., Brody, G. H., & MacKinnon, C. (1985). Naturalistic observations of children's activities and roles while playing with their siblings and friends. *Child Development*, **55**, 617–627.

Stormshak, E., Bellanti, C., Bierman, K., & Conduct Problems Prevention Research Group (1996). The quality of sibling relationships and the development of social competence and behavioral control in aggressive children. *Developmental Psychology*, **32**, 79–89.

Strayer, F. F., & Strayer, J. (1980). Preschool conflict and the assessment of social dominance. In D. O. Omark, F. F. Strayer, & D.G . Freedman (Eds.), *Dominance relations: An ethological view of human conflict and social interaction* (pp. 137–159). New York: Garland.

Suess, G. J., Grossman, K. E., & Sroufe, L. A. (1992). Effects of infant attachment to mother and father on quality of adaptation in preschool: From dyadic to individual organisation of self. *International Journal of Behavioral Development*, **15**, 43–65.

Sullivan, H. S. (1953). *The interpersonal theory of psychiatry.* New York: Norton.

Surra, C. A., & Ridley, C. (1991). Multiple perspectives on interaction: Participants, peers and observers. In B. M. Montgomery & S. W. Duck (Eds.), *Studying interpersonal interaction* (pp. 35–55). New York: Guilford.

Sutton, J., & Smith, P. K. (1999). Bullying as a group process: An adaptation of the participant role approach. *Aggressive Behavior*, **25**, 97–111.

Sutton, J., Smith, P. K., & Swettenham, J. (1999a). Bullying and "theory of mind": a critique of the "social skills deficit" view of anti-social behavior. *Social Development*, **8**, 117–127.

Sutton, J., Smith, P. K., & Swettenham, J. (1999b). Social cognition and bullying: Social inadequacy or skilled manipulation? *British Journal of Developmental Psychology*, **17**, 435–450.

Sutton, J., Smith, P. K., & Swettenham, J. (1999c). Socially undesirable need not be incompetent: A response to Crick and Dodge. *Social Development*, **8**, 132–134.

Sutton-Smith, B., & Rosenberg, B. G. (1970). *The sibling.* New York: Holt, Rinehart & Winston.

Tangney, J. P. (1995). Shame and guilt in interpersonal relationships. In J. P. Tangney & K. W. Fischer (Eds.), *Self-conscious emotions: The psychology of shame, guilt, embarrassment, and pride* (pp. 114–139). New York: Guilford.

Tangney, J. P., & Fischer, K.W. (Eds.). (1995). *Self-conscious emotions: The psychology of shame, guilt, embarrassment, and pride.* New York: Guilford.

Tashakkori, A., & Thompson, V. (1988). Cultural change and attitude change: An assessment of postrevolutionary marriage and attitudes in Iran. *Population Research and Policy Review*, **7**, 3–27.

Terhune, K. W. (1974). "Wash-in", "wash-out", and systemic effects in extended prisoner's dilemma. *Journal of Conflict Resolution*, **18**, 656–685.

Tesla, C., & Dunn, J. (1992). Getting along or getting your own way: The development of young children's use of arguments in conflicts with mother and sibling. *Social Development*, **1**, 107–121.

Teti, D. M., & Ablard, K. E. (1989). Security of attachment and infant–sibling relationships: A laboratory study. *Child Development*, **60**, 1519–1528.

Teti, D. M., & Teti, L. (1996). Infant–parent relationships. In N. Vanzetti & S. W. Duck (Eds.), *A lifetime of relationships* (pp. 77–104). Pacific Grove, CA.: Brooks/ Cole.

Teti, D. M., Gelfand, D. M., Messinger, D. S., & Isabella, R. (1995). Correlates of preschool attachment security in a sample of depressed and non-depressed mothers. *Developmental Psychology*, **31**, 364–376.

Thompson, L., & Walker, A. J. (1989). Gender in families: Women and men in marriage, work, and parenthood. *Journal of Marriage and the Family*, **51**, 845–871.

Thompson, R. A. (1994). Emotion regulation: A theme in search of definition. In N. A. Fox (Ed.), The development of emotion regulation: Biological and behavioral considerations. *Monographs of the Society for Research in Child Development*, **59** (Serial No. 240), 25–52.

Thompson, R. F., Bao, S., Chen, L., Cipriano, B. D., Grethe, J. S., Kim, J. J., Thompson, J. K., Tracy, J. A., Weninger, M. S., & Krupa, D. J. (1997). Associative learning. In R. J. Bradley, R. A. Harris, & P. Jenner (Series Eds.) & J. D. Schmahmann (Vol. Ed.), *International Review of Neurobiology: Vol. 41. The cerebellum and cognition* (pp. 152–189). San Diego, CA: Academic Press.

Tietjen, A. (1985). Relationships between the social networks of Swedish mothers and their children. *International Journal of Behavioral Development*, **8**, 195–216.

Tinsley, B. R., & Parke, R. D. (1984). Grandparents as support and socialization agents. In M. Lewis (Ed.), *Beyond the dyad* (pp. 161–194). New York: Plenum.

Tizard, B., Blatchford, P., Burke, J., Farquhar, C., & Plewis, I. (1988). *Young children at school in the inner city.* Hove, UK: Erlbaum.

Tomada, G., & Schneider, B. H. (1997). Relational aggression, gender, and peer acceptance: Invariance across culture, stability over time, and concordance among informants. *Developmental Psychology*, **33**, 601–609.

Tononi, G., & Edelman, G. M. (1998). Consciousness and complexity. *Science*, **282**, 1846–1851.

Tooby, J., & Cosmides, L. (1990). On the universality of human nature and the uniqueness of the individual: The role of genetics and adaptation. *Journal of Personality*, **58**, 17–67.

Tooke, J., & Camire, L. (1991). Patterns of deception in intersexual and intrasexual mating strategies. *Ethology and Sociobiology*, **12**, 345–364.

Trachtenberg, S., & Viken, R. J. (1994). Aggressive boys in the classroom: Biased attributions or shared perceptions? *Child Development*, **65**, 829–835.

Tracy, J. A., Ghose, S. S., Strecher, T., McFall, R. M., & Steinmetz, J. E. (1999). Classical conditioning in a non-clinical obsessive-compulsive population. *Psychological Science*, **10**, 9–13.

Triandis, H. C. (1986). Collectivism and individualism: A reconceptualization of a basic concept in cross-cultural psychology. In C. Bagley & G. Verma (Eds.), *Personality, congnition, and values: Cross-cultural perspectives of childhood and adolescence*. London: Macmillan.

Triandis, H. C. (1995). *Individualism and collectivism*. Boulder, CO: Westview.

Triandis, H. C., Bontempo, R., Villareal, M. J., Asai, M., & Lucca, N. (1988). Individualism and collectivism: Cross-cultural perspectives on self-ingroup relationships. *Journal of Personality and Social Psychology*, **52**, 323–338.

Trivers, R. (1985). *Social evolution*. Menlo Park, CA: Benjamin/Cummings Publishing.

Troy, M., & Sroufe, A.L. (1987). Victimization among preschoolers: Role of attachment relationships history. *Journal of the American Academy of Child and Adolescent Psychiatry*, **26**, 166–172.

Tsui, P., & Schultz, G. L. (1988). Ethnic factors in group process: Cultural dynamics in multi-ethnic therapy groups. *American Journal of Orthopsychiatry*, **58**, 136–142.

Tuma, N. B., & Hallinan, M. T. (1979). The effects of sex, race and achievement on schoolchildren's friendships. *Social Forces*, **57**, 1265–1285.

Turner, P. J. (1991). Relations between attachment, gender, and behavior with peers in preschool. *Child Development*, **62**, 1475–1488.

Tversky, A., & Kahneman, D. (1982). Judgment under uncertainty: Heuristics and biases. In D. Kahneman & A. Tversky (Eds.), *Judgment under uncertainty: Heuristics and biases* (pp. 3–20). Cambridge: Cambridge University Press.

Udvari, S., Schneider, B. H., Labovitz, G., & Tassi, F. (1995, August). *A multidimensional view of competition in relation to children's peer relations*. Paper presented at the meeting of the American Psychological Association, New York.

Underwood, M. K., Coie, J. D., & Herbsman, C. R. (1992). Display rules for anger and aggression in school-age children. *Child Development*, **63**, 366–380.

van Aken, M., & Asendorpf, J. (1997). Support by parents, classmates, friends and siblings in preadolescence: Covariation and compensation across relationships. *Journal of Social and Personal Relationships*, **14**, 79–93.

van IJzendoorn, M. H. (1995). Adult attachment representations, parental responsiveness, and infant attachment: A meta-analysis on the predictive validity of the Adult Attachment Interview. *Psychological Bulletin*, **117**, 387–403.

van IJzendoorn, M. H., Juffer, F., & Duyvesteyn, M. G. C. (1995). Breaking the intergenerational cycle of insecure attachment: A review of the effects of attachment-based interventions on maternal sensitivity and infant security. *Journal of Child Psychology and Psychiatry*, **36**, 225–248.

van IJzendoorn, M. H., Kranenburg, M. J., Zwart-Woudstra, H. A., van Busschbach, A. M., & Lambermon, M. W. E. (1991). Parental attachment and children's socio-emotional development: Some findings on the validity of the adult attachment interview in The Netherlands. *International Journal of Behavioral Development*, **14**, 375–394.

Vandell, D. L., & Bailey, M. D. (1992). Conflicts between siblings. In C. U. Shantz & W. W. Hartup (Eds.), *Conflict in child and adolescent development* (pp. 153–185). New York: Cambridge University Press.

Vangelisti, A. L. (1994). Messages that hurt. In W. R. Cupach & B. H. Spitzberg (Eds.), *The dark side of interpersonal communication* (pp. 53–82). Hillsdale, NJ: Erlbaum.

Vangelisti, A. L., & Crumley, L. P. (1998). Reactions to messages that hurt: The influence of relational contexts. *Communication Monographs*, **65**, 173–196.

Vangelisti, A. L., & Sprague, R. J. (1998). Guilt and hurt: Similarities, distinctions, and conversational strategies. In P. A. Andersen & L. K. Guerrero (Eds.), *Handbook of communication and emotion: Research, theory, applications, and contexts* (pp. 123–154). San Diego, CA: Academic Press.

Vangelisti, A. L., Daly, J. A., & Rudnick, J. R. (1991). Making people feel guilty in conversations: Techniques and correlates. *Human Communication Research, 18*, 3–39.

van Hoof, J. A. R. A. M. (1972). A comparative approach to the phylogeny of laughter and smiling. In R. A. Hinde (Ed.), *Nonverbal communication* (pp. 209–238). Cambridge: Cambridge University Press.

Vaughn, B., Egeland, B., & Sroufe, L. A. (1979). Individual differences in infant–mother attachment at twelve and eighteen months: Stability and change in families under stress. *Child Development, 50*, 971–975.

Vespo, J. E., & Caplan, M. (1993). Preschoolers' differential conflict behavior with friends and acquaintances. *Early Education and Development, 4*, 45–53.

Vitaro, F., Gendreau, P. L., Tremblay, R. E., & Oligny, P. (1998). Reactive and proactive aggression differentially predict later conduct problems. *Journal of Child Psychology and Psychiatry, 39*, 377–385.

Vitz, P. C., & Kite, W. R. (1970). Factors affecting conflict and negotiation within an alliance. *Journal of Experimental Social Psychology, 5*, 233–247.

Volling, B. L., & Belsky, J. (1992a). Infant, father, and marital antecedents of infant–father attachment security in dual-earner and single-earner families. *International Journal of Behavioral Development, 15*, 83–100.

Volling, B., & Belsky, J. (1992b). The contribution of the mother–child and the father–child relationship to the quality of sibling interaction: A longitudinal study. *Child Development, 63*, 1209–1222.

von Salisch, M. (1989). *Equality versus dominance within pairs of friends.* Paper presented at the Meeting of the Society for Research in Child Development, Kansas City, MI.

von Salisch, M. (1991). *Kinderfreundschaften. Emotionale Kommunikation im Konflikt.* Göttingen: Hogrefe Verlag.

von Salisch, M. (1996). Child–child relationships: Symmetry and asymmetry among peers, friends and siblings. In A. E. Auhagen & M. von Salisch (Eds.), *The diversity of human relationships* (pp 56–72). New York: Cambridge University Press.

von Salisch, M. (1997). Emotional processes in children's relationships with siblings and friends. In *Handbook of personal relationships: Theory, research and interventions* (2nd ed., pp. 61–80). Chichester UK: Wiley.

von Salisch, M. (2000). *Wenn Kinder sich ärgern . . . Emotionsregulierung in der Entwicklung.* Göttingen: Hogrefe Verlag.

von Salisch, M., & Bänninger-Huber, E. (1994). Investigating facial expression of emotion in face-to-face interaction. In N. Frijda (Ed.), *Proceedings of the 8th Conference of the International Society for Research on Emotions* (pp. 176–180). Storrs, CT: ISRE Publications.

von Salisch, M., & Uhlendorff, H. (1998). *Peer rejection, angry aggressive behavior and scorn.* Unpublished Ms, Freie Universität Berlin, Berlin.

Vuchinich, S. (1986). On attenuation in verbal family conflict. *Social Psychology Quarterly, 49*, 281–293.

Vuchinich, S. (1987). Starting and stopping spontaneous family conflicts. *Journal of Marriage and the Family, 49*, 591–601.

Vuchinich, S. (1990). The sequential organization of closing in verbal family conflict. In A. D. Grimshaw (Ed.), *Family talk* (pp. 118–138). New York: Cambridge University Press.

Vuchinich, S., Wood, B., & Vuchinich, R. (1994). Coalitions and family problem-solving with preadolescents in referred, at-risk, and comparison families. *Family Process, 33*, 409–424.

Vygotskii, L. S. (1987). R. W. Rieber & A. S. Carlton (Eds.), *The collected works of L. S. Vygotskii*, translated by N. Minick. New York: Plenum Press.

Walker, A. (1982). Intermodal perception of expressive behaviors by human infants. *Journal of Experimental Child Psychology*, **33**, 514–535.

Walster, E. H., Walster, G. W., & Berscheid, E. (1978). *Equity: Theory and research.* Boston, MA: Allyn & Bacon.

Wang, S. (1998). The relations among parental advice giving and social competence in middle childhood. Unpublished doctoral dissertation, University of California, Riverside.

Wang, S. J., & McDowell, D. J. (1996, April). *Parental advice-giving: Relations to child social competence and psychosocial functioning.* Poster presented at the annual meeting of the Western Psychological Association, San Jose, CA.

Washburn, M. (1994). Reflections on a psychoanalytic theory of gender differences. *Journal of American Academy of Psychoanalysis*, **22**, 1–28.

Waters, E., Vaughn, B. E., Posada, G., & Kondo-Ikemura, K. (Eds.) (1995). Caregiving, cultural, and cognitive perspectives on secure-base behavior and working models: New growing points of attachment theory and research. *Monographs of the Society for Research in Child Development*, **60**(2–3, Serial No. 244).

Watson, L. (1989). The affirmation of indigenous values in Colonial education system. *Journal of Indigenous Studies*, **1**, 9–20.

Weigel, R. H., Wiser, P. L., & Cook, S. W. (1975). The impact of cooperative learning experiences on cross-ethnic relations and attitudes. *Journal of Social Issues*, **31** 219–244.

Weingart, L. R., Hyder, E. B., & Prietula, M. J. (1996). Knowledge matters: The effect of tactical descriptions of negotiation behavior and outcome. *Journal of Personality and Social Psychology*, **70**, 1205–1217.

Weisfeld, G. E., Weisfeld, C., & Callaghan, J. W. (1984). Peer and self perceptions in Hopi and Afro-American third- and sixth-graders. *Ethos*, **12**, 64–85.

Wellman, B. (1985). Domestic work, paid work and net work. In S. W. Duck & D. Perlman (Eds.), *Understanding personal relationships.* Beverly Hills, CA: Sage.

Wentzel, K. R., & Caldwell, K. (1997). Friendship, peer acceptance, and group membership: Relations to academic achievement in middle school. *Child Development*, **68**, 1198–1209.

Werner, C., Altman, I., Brown, B., & Ginat, J. (1993). Celebrations in personal relationships: A transactional/dialectical perspective. In. S. W. Duck (Ed.), *Social contexts and relationships (Understanding relationship processes series*, Vol. 3, pp. 109–138). Newbury Park, CA: Sage.

West, C., & Zimmerman, D. (1987). Doing gender. *Gender & Society*, **1**, 125–151.

Westerman, M. A., & Schonholtz, J. (1993). Marital adjustment, joint parental support in a triadic problem-solving task, and child behavior problems. *Journal of Clinical Child Psychology*, **22**, 97–106.

Whitesell, N. R., & Harter, S. (1996). The interpersonal context of emotion: Anger with close friends and classmates. *Child Development*, **67,** 1345–1359.

Whiting, B. B., & Edwards, C. P. (1988). *Children of different worlds: The formation of social behavior.* Cambridge, MA: Harvard.

Whiting, B., & Whiting, J. (1975). *Children of six cultures.* Cambridge, MA: Harvard University Press.

Whitney, I., & Smith, P. K. (1993). A survey of the nature and extent of bullying in junior/middle and secondary schools. *Educational Research*, **35**, 3–25.

Whitney, I., Nabuzoka, D., & Smith, P. K. (1992). Bullying in schools: Mainstream and special needs. *Support for Learning*, **17**, 3–7.

Whitney, I., Smith, P. K., & Thompson, P. (1994). Bullying and children with special educational needs. In P. K. Smith & S. Sharp (Eds.), *School bullying: Insights and perspectives* (pp. 213–240). London: Routledge.

Williams, K. D., Shore, W. J., & Grahe, J. E. (1998). The silent treatment: Perceptions of its behaviors and associated feelings. *Group Processes & Intergroup Relations*, **1**, 117–141.

Wilson, B. (1998). Entry behavior and emotion regulation abilities of developmentally delayed boys. *Developmental Psychology*, **35**, 214–222.

Windle, M. (1994). A study of friendship characteristics and problem behavior among middle adolescents. *Child Development*, **65**, 1764–1777.

Wiseman, J. P., & Duck, S. W. (1995). Having and managing enemies: A very challenging relationship. In S. W. Duck & J. T. Wood (Eds.), *Relationship challenges (Understanding relationship processes series*, Vol. 5, pp. 43–72). Thousand Oaks, CA: Sage.

Withycombe, J.S. (1973). Relationships of self-concept, social status, and self-perceived social status and racial differences of Paiute Indian and white elementary school children. *Journal of Social Psychology*, **91**, 337–338.

Wolke, D., & Schulz, H. (1997). Bullying bei Grundschulkindern: Prävalenz, Schulfaktoren und Täter-Opfer Charakteristiken. In J. Glück (Ed.), *13. Tagung fuer Entwicklungspsychologie: Kurzfassungen* (pp. 320–321). Wien: Abtlg. fuer Entwicklungspsychologie und Pädagogische Psychologie, Institut fuer Psychologie.

Wood, J. T. (1995). *Relational communication: Continuity and change in personal relationships*. Belmont, CA: Wadsworth.

Wood, J. T. (Ed.) (1996a). *Gendered relationships*. Mountain View, CA: Mayfield.

Wood, J. T. (1996b). Gender, relationships, and communication. In J. T. Wood (Ed.), *Gendered relationships* (pp. 3–19). Mountain View, CA: Mayfield.

Wood, J. T., & Cox, J. R. (1993). Rethinking critical voice: Materiality and situated knowledge. *Western Journal of Communication*, **57**, 278–287.

Wood, J. T., & Duck, S. W. (1995). Off the beaten track: New shores for relationship research. In J. T. Wood & S. W. Duck (Eds.), *Understudied relationships: Off the beaten track (Understanding relationship processes series*, Vol. 6, pp. 1–21). Thousand Oaks, CA: Sage.

Wurmser, L. (1987). Shame: The veiled companion of narcissism. In D. Nathanson (Ed.), *The many faces of shame* (pp. 64–92). New York: Guilford.

Yamagishi, T. (1986). The provision of a sanctioning system as public good. *Journal of Personality and Social Psychology*, **50**, 110–116.

Yang, K. S. (1981). Social orientation and individual modernity among Chinese students in Taiwan. *Journal of Social Psychology*, **113**, 159–170.

Yarrow, M. R., & Waxler, C. Z. (1976). Dimensions and correlates of prosocial behavior in young children. *Child Development*, **47**, 118–125.

Yeates, K. O., Schultz, L. H., & Selman, R. L. (1991). The development of interpersonal negotiation strategies in thought and action: A social-cognitive link to behavioral adjustment and social status. *Merrill-Palmer Quarterly*, **37**, 369–405.

Young, H. B., & Ferguson, J. (1981). *Puberty to manhood in Italy and America*. New York, NY: Academic Press.

Youngblade, L., & Belsky, J. (1992). Parent–child antecedents of five-year-olds' close friendships: A longitudinal analysis. *Developmental Psychology*, **28**, 700–713.

Youniss, J. (1980). *Parents and peers in social development*. Chicago, IL: University of Chicago Press.

Youniss, J., & Smollar, J. (1985). *Adolescent relations with mothers, fathers and friends*. Chicago, IL: University of Chicago Press.

Zahn-Waxler, C., & Kochanska, G. (1990). The origins of guilt. In R. A. Thompson (Ed.), *Nebraska Symposium on Motivation: Vol. 36. Socioemotional development* (pp. 183–258). Lincoln, NB: University of Nebraska Press.

Zahn-Waxler, C., Radke-Yarrow, M., & King, R. (1979). Child rearing and children's prosocial initiations toward victims of distress. *Child Development*, **50**, 319–330.

Zahn-Waxler, C., Radke-Yarrow, M., Wagner, E., & Chapman, M. (1992). Development of concern for others. *Developmental Psychology*, **28**, 126–136.

Zarbatany, L., Hartmann, D., & Rankin, B. (1990). The psychological functions of preadolescent peer activities. *Child Development*, **61**, 1067–1080.

Zeifman, D., & Hazan, C. (1997). A process model of adult attachment formation. In S. W. Duck (Ed.), *Handbook of personal relationships: Theory, research and interventions* (2nd ed., pp. 179–195). Chichester, UK: Wiley.

Zelkowitz, P. (1989). Parents and children as informants concerning children's social networks. In D. Belle (Ed.), *Children's social networks and social supports* (pp 221–237). New York: Wiley.

Ziegler, S. (1980). Report from Canada: Adolescents' inter-ethnic friendships. *Children Today*, **9**, 22–24.

Ziegler, S. (1981). The effectiveness of cooperative learning teams for increasing cross-ethnic friendship: Additional evidence. *Human Organization*, **40**, 264–268.

Zisman, P. & Wilson, V. (1992). Table hopping in the cafeteria: An exploration of "racial" integration in early adolescent social groups. *Anthropology & Education Quarterly*, **23**, 199–220.

AUTHOR INDEX

SUBJECT INDEX

Related titles of interest...

Life-Span Developmental Psychology
Edited by ANDREAS DEMETRIOU, WILLEM DOISE and
CORNELIS F. M. VAN LIESHOUT
Offers a broad coverage of all sub-fields of developmental psychology,
including: the biological bases of development; perceptual and motor
development; cognitive development; communication and language
development; social development; personality and emotional development;
moral development and wisdom; and developmental psychopathology.
0471 97078 6 536pp July 1998 Paperback

Infant and Child Development
An International Journal of Research
Edited by BRIAN HOPKINS and CHARLIE LEWIS
Infant & Child Development, formerly known as *Early Development and
Parenting*, publishes empirical, theoretical and methodological papers
dealing with psychological development during infancy and childhood, up to
and including adolescence. Areas covered by the journal include caregiver-
child interaction, cognitive development, emotional development, infant
perception, motor development, parenting and development, play and
development, precursors to language and language development, and
socialisation.
ISSN: 1522 7227

European Journal of Social Psychology
Edited by FRITZ STRACK
Publishes innovative research in all areas of social psychology, and is
dedicated to fostering scientific communication within Europe and between
European and other social psychologists.
ISSN: 0046 2772